Taras Kuzio (Ed.)

RUSSIAN DISINFORMATION AND WESTERN SCHOLARSHIP

Bias and Prejudice in Journalistic, Expert, and Academic Analyses of East European, Russian and Eurasian Affairs

Bibliografische Information der Deutschen Nationalbibliothek

Die Deutsche Nationalbibliothek verzeichnet diese Publikation in der Deutschen Nationalbibliografie; detaillierte bibliografische Daten sind im Internet über http://dnb.d-nb.de abrufbar.

Bibliographic information published by the Deutsche Nationalbibliothek

Die Deutsche Nationalbibliothek lists this publication in the Deutsche Nationalbibliografie; detailed bibliographic data are available in the Internet at http://dnb.d-nb.de.

Cover image: ID 245244238 © Michal Bednarek | Dreamstime.com

ISBN-13: 978-3-8382-1685-0
© *ibidem*-Verlag, Stuttgart 2023
Alle Rechte vorbehalten

Das Werk einschließlich aller seiner Teile ist urheberrechtlich geschützt. Jede Verwertung außerhalb der engen Grenzen des Urheberrechtsgesetzes ist ohne Zustimmung des Verlages unzulässig und strafbar. Dies gilt insbesondere für Vervielfältigungen, Übersetzungen, Mikroverfilmungen und elektronische Speicherformen sowie die Einspeicherung und Verarbeitung in elektronischen Systemen.

All rights reserved. No part of this publication may be reproduced, stored in or introduced into a retrieval system, or transmitted, in any form, or by any means (electronic, mechanical, photocopying, recording or otherwise) without the prior written permission of the publisher. Any person who does any unauthorized act in relation to this publication may be liable to criminal prosecution and civil claims for damages.

Printed in the EU

Contents

Affiliations of the Contributors 7

Taras Kuzio
Introduction 9

Olga Bertelsen
Aspects of Russian Active Measures Targeting Western
Academia 17

Sergei I. Zhuk
"Academic Imperialism": Writing Soviet and Post-Soviet
History without Ukraine 61

Taras Kuzio
Russia's Full Spectrum Conflict and the Myth of Civil War in
Ukraine, 2014-2021 87

Paul D'Anieri
Conflict Studies and the War in Ukraine, 2014-2022 123

Sanshiro Hosaka
Japanese Scholars on the 'Ukraine Crisis' (2014–2015): Russia-
Centered Ontology, Aversion to Western Mainstream, and
Vulnerabilities to Disinformation 159

Veronika Krátka Špalková
Propaganda Targeting Foreign Audiences: A Comparative
Analysis of Soviet and Russian Propaganda in the
Czechoslovak Socialist Republic / Czech Republic 197

Andrei Znamenski
Collusion and Conspiracy Theories: US Domestic Politics and
Russian Active Measures 237

Andreas Heinemann-Grüder
German Self-Images and Russia's Influence 267

Martin Schulze Wessel
Empire, Sonderwege and Russia: The German Historical
Debate about Ukraine 287

Michal Wawrzonek
Poland and the Russian Question Prior to the 2014 Crisis:
Between Naïve Pragmatism and Accusations of
"Russophobia" 297

Petro Kuzyk
Western Russophilism, Russian Disinformation and the Myth
of Ukraine's Regional Divide 337

Andreas Umland
Russian Narratives, Ukraine, and US Right-Wing Punditry:
How Kremlin Propaganda Used a 2021 Washington Think-
Tank Debate 359

Affiliations of the Contributors

Olga Bertelsen — Tiffin University

Sergei Zhuk — Ball State University

Taras Kuzio — National University of Kyiv Mohyla Academy

Paul D'Anieri — University of California at Riverside

Sanshiro Hosaka — University of Tartu

Veronika Krátka Špalková — European Values Security Centre

Andrei Znamenski — University of Memphis

Andreas Heinemann-Grüder — University of Bonn

Martin Schulze Wessel — University of Munich

Michal Wawrzonek — Jesuit University in Cracow

Petro Kuzyk — Lviv National University

Andreas Umland — National University of Kyiv Mohyla Academy

Introduction

Taras Kuzio

This book brings together twelve chapters about the influence of Russia's information war on Western scholarship after the 2014 crisis and up to Russia's invasion of Ukraine on 24 February 2022. Western scholars, think tank experts, and journalists were unprepared to understand and write about Russia's military aggression and often followed the Kremlin's templates.

One major reason they were unprepared for a Russian-Ukrainian war in 2014, and especially in 2022, was that Western historiography of Russia since World War II uses a nineteenth-century Russian imperial nationalist framework that fits the Kremlin's imperial nationalist templates. Both Western historians of Russia and the Kremlin's propagandists portray Ukraine as an error of history, an appendage of Russia, that was born together with Russia and Belarus in Kyivan Rus'. Both credit Russia with being the main inheritor of Kyivan Rus' through Vladimir-Suzdal', Muscovy, the Russian Empire, the USSR, and the Russian Federation. Ukraine appears only occasionally in this imperial nationalist framework, leading to the abnormal outcome of the sudden appearance of an independent Ukrainian state run by Ukrainian squatters on 'Russian land.' Thus, the Western approach to 'Russian' history mirrors that propagated by the Kremlin (Putin 2021); firstly, portraying the eastern Slavs as a united group confusingly identified as 'Russians,' and secondly, interpreting Ukraine as an accident of history.

An outgrowth of this has been a long tendency among Western scholars and policymakers to tie Ukraine's fate to that of Russia's. This was especially the case through to the launching of the EU's Eastern Partnership in 2010. Prior to this the EU had viewed Ukraine as an appendage of Russia and believed it could not invite Ukraine into membership without Russia. It took the Euromaidan Revolution, 2014 crisis, and 2022 invasion for the EU to grudgingly change its attitudes and come round to viewing Ukraine as separate to Russia. NATO meanwhile always argued that inviting Ukraine into membership would antagonize Russia while south-eastern Ukrainians did not support membership. Both factors are no longer applicable after Russia's invasion which has increased support for NATO membership to high levels in Ukraine's south-east.

Closely tied to the use of a nineteenth-century imperial nationalist framework is a view about Crimea among Western historians of Russia that excuses Russia's 2014 illegal land grab. Many Western historians of Russia, and their fellow historians, see Crimea as having been 'unnaturally' included in Ukraine and therefore agreed with the Kremlin line that Crimea's return to Russia rectified an historical injustice.

This line is an anomaly in Western historical scholarship, and it is one that could open accusations of racism against Western historians of Russia. Beginning Crimea's history in 1783, when the Russian Empire annexed the peninsula, they ignore six centuries of life under the First Nation who were Tatars. Present-day Western historians of Canada, the US, and Australia would never deem it fit to begin their histories with Quebec, Jamestown, and the arrival of Captain Cook respectively as such an approach would ignore the First Nations who already lived there. In contrast, the approach taken by Western historians of Russia towards Crimea is an outgrowth of their adoption of outdated nineteenth-century imperial nationalist frameworks. No Western history of Russia is based on the Russian Federation nation-state; all are based on the Russian and Soviet empires. In continuing to pursue this approach Western historians serve to reinforce the weak Russian support for a (non-imperial) civic identity grounded in the Russian Federation. Meanwhile, Western scholars tend to write the histories of Ukraine and the other non-Russian former Soviet republics as histories of those nation-states that came into existence in 1991.

This should not be surprising. Western university departments and think tanks devoted to the former USSR are run by Russianists who overwhelmingly dominate the field of post-Soviet studies and Eurasian affairs. Russianists provide the bulk of the external reviewers to specialized journals and therefore act as gatekeepers (in reality, censors), determining what is and is not published. Since 2014 I have experienced this firsthand in my dealings with numerous Western journals devoted to the post-Soviet space.

If a scholar or expert is an expert on Brazil or China, they do not usually claim to be also expert on all of Latin America or Asia. The situation is different in the case of the former USSR where many Russianists believe they are experts and therefore have a right to comment, publish, and lead analysis not only on Russia but on the other fourteen former Soviet republics as well. Russianists have predominated among those experts invited to comment about the 2014 crisis and Russian invasion via TV, radio, webinars, and podcasts.

This is despite the fact Russianists have a poor understanding of Ukraine. They tend to view the country through Moscow's eyes, and to rely exclusively on sources from Russia in their commentary in Ukraine, using Ukrainian sources only very rarely. One of the first books to be published about the 2014 crisis by a British scholar, for example, extensively used Russian sources but only the *Kyiv Post* from Ukraine. There are of course some exceptions, such as Paul D'Anieri who has traced the origins of the 2014 crisis to Russia's long inability since the disintegration of the USSR in 1991 to accept an independent Ukrainian state.

A second factor is that Western journalists continue to cover the former USSR from Moscow—just as they did during the Soviet period. This reinforces the viewpoint commonly found in the West that Moscow-based journalists are also automatically 'experts' on the fourteen non-Russian republics. In fact, there is no reason why this should be the case; such journalists usually visit the other republics only very rarely, perhaps once in every few years to follow elections. There are of course exceptions, such as *The Guardian's* Luke Harding who has been based in Ukraine throughout the time since the Russian invasion.

Given the above, it is perhaps not surprising how much of the writing about Ukraine in 2014–2022 drew, wittingly or not, on the Kremlin's disinformation templates. A long-time favorite was the notion that Ukraine was a severely divided country and therefore more brittle than a 'normal' country. This Western media cliché was remarkably like the Kremlin line for the last two decades that Ukraine is a 'fake' artificial country that had been cobbled together.

According to the Western stereotype, Ukraine is supposedly composed of two different civilizations, one of which in the southeast has always been closely tied to Russia and is a natural part of the 'Russian World'. This is music to the ears of the Kremlin as it reflected the Russian view of Ukraine as an artificial construct whose south-eastern part comprised 'ancient Russian lands' wrongfully incorporated into Ukraine by Vladimir Lenin with the western territories taken from Poland, Hungary, and Romania.

Over the past three decades the greatest number of Western scholarly articles on Ukraine dealt with regional diversity in Ukraine and the alleged conflict between Russian and Ukrainian speakers. Numerous studies focused on the fate of Russian speakers in Ukraine and whether they were being subjected to Ukrainianization by a 'nationalizing state'. No Western studies ever condemned Russia's pursuit of Russification in occupied Crimea and the Donbas, or earlier in Russian official statements condemning Ukrainian language policies. Some scholars bizarrely portrayed the DNR (Donetsk People's Republic) and LNR (Luhansk People's Republic) as examples of 'multiculturalism', while claiming that Ukraine was run by 'nationalists' (effectively synonymous with 'Nazis' as per Russian disinformation) who had come to power violently in 2014.

With little or no grounding in theories of nationalism, when it came to Ukraine, Western Russianists used the Kremlin's definitions of terms such as 'nationalist.' This had nothing to do with the scholarly understanding of 'nationalism' and everything to do with anti-nationalist propaganda in the Soviet Union. In the USSR, and later in the Russian Federation, the label 'Ukrainian nationalist' was applied to anybody, irrespective of their position on the political spectrum, who did not support Ukraine's future in the USSR or the 'Russian World' and instead opposed Russification and Soviet nationality policies and backed greater sovereignty for the Ukrainian SSR within the Soviet Union or Ukrainian independence and European integration. A political science definition of nationalism would show Ukraine has the one of the lowest levels of electoral support in Europe for populist nationalists and the far right.

The above factors came together in the early days of the 2022 invasion when Western 'experts,' who influenced the views of policymakers, agreed with the Kremlin that the 'mighty' Russian army was certain to defeat Ukraine within two to three days. Again, there are some exceptions, such as Lawrence Freedman whose insightful analysis is a product of a long career in international security studies that took place outside the field of Russian and Eurasian studies.

Western 'experts' held rose-tinted views of the Russian military, believed the Putin regime's propaganda about its military reforms, and ignored deep levels of corruption in what has been described for over a decade as a 'mafia state'. As Russianists they had always been assumed—especially after the 2014 crisis—to be also 'experts' on Ukraine, which of course they never were. Their approach to Ukraine as an appendage of Russia made them unable to explain or analyze why Ukrainian society was so resilient and displayed such high levels of national integration, or why most of Ukraine's Russian speakers were Ukrainian patriots. Indeed, both Kremlin propagandists and Western Russianists find it difficult, perhaps impossible, to get over their view of Ukraine's Russian speakers as disloyal and 'pro-Russian.' Yet sustaining this view will become even more untenable in the wake of the invasion as opinion polls show there are no longer regional variations in attitudes to language policies, memory politics, and foreign policy orientations.

Ukrainian society is so much more resilient than Russia's because it has a deeply imbedded civil society that is a product of three popular revolutions (1990, 2004, 2013–2014) that have successfully demanded the country's rulers deal with them as citizens and have become involved in local politics after the decentralization of the state following the Euromaidan Revolution. Since the late 1980s, Ukraine has undergone de-Sovietization and de-Stalinization and, since 2015, de-communization. In contrast, Russia's last revolution was in 1917 and its people have stagnated even further into subjects with no rights during Vladimir Putin's re-Sovietization and the revival of the religious cult of the Great Patriotic War and Joseph Stalin. Ukraine's extensive volunteer movement and better performing armed forces are the product of a horizontally organized society of citizens with agency. Russia is a vertically organized society of subjects with no volunteer movement and is unable to function without the boss barking orders.

Being only able to view Ukrainians through Moscow's eyes, drawing as they do on the Kremlin's disinformation templates, Western Russianists find it very difficult to understand both Ukraine's fight back during the 2014 crisis and especially the successes of the Ukrainian armed forces since the 2022 invasion. Ignoring two decades of dehumanization of Ukrainians in the Russian media has made it impossible to analyze the roots of Russia's genocide in Ukraine. Barely any of the many studies of the Russian media focused on its obsession with dehumanizing Ukraine and Ukrainians. Meanwhile, downplaying and denying the existence of nationalism in Putin's Russia was all the vogue among western Russianists; indeed, two major book-length studies of Russian nationalism published in 2016 and 2020 ignored the dominant influence of White Russian émigré imperial nationalist perceptions of Ukraine and Ukrainians.

Taken together these developments produced the intellectual vacuum that formed the backdrop to the publication in July 2021 of Putin's long essay 'On the Historical Unity of Russians and Ukrainians.' Western Russianists had no intellectual resources or tools to explain the ideological drivers behind Russia's military aggression against Ukraine and the brutality of Russian soldiers against Ukrainian civilians. Putin's essay, published at the same time as the decision was made to invade Ukraine, did not appear from nowhere but was a product of the transformation of Russian imperial nationalism over the previous two decades that now culminated in an ideological treatise justifying Russian imperialist territorial claims towards Ukraine and denial of the existence of a Ukrainian nation.

The stagnation of Russian nationalism, which still relies heavily on the ideas prevailing among pre-war White Russian émigrés, has been accompanied by a loss of memory. For all their widespread and growing Soviet nostalgia, Russians have forgotten—or have chosen to ignore—the fact that Ukraine was not a peasant nation in the latter decades of the USSR but in fact an urbanized, industrialized, and modernized republic. The Soviet Ukrainian republic was a major industrial and intellectual center for the Soviet Union and the home of a large military-industrial complex. The first Encyclopedia of Cybernetics in the USSR was published in the 1960s in Soviet Ukraine. *Pivdenmash* (*Yuzhmash*), which employed fifty thousand people in the closed Ukrainian city of Dnipropetrovsk, was the biggest producer of nuclear missiles in the world. Studies published by the Rand Corporation think tank in the 1980s described Ukrainians as prized soldiers in the Soviet army who dominated the rank of sergeant and were disproportionately found among middle-ranking officers. Taking all this into account, it is striking how much Russians had been made to forget to be convinced liberating Ukraine would be a cakewalk; presumably they believed that Ukrainian peasants would only have pitchforks to hand!

Aspects of Russian Active Measures Targeting Western Academia

Olga Bertelsen

Numerous scholarly works have stressed the pervasive character of the ideological and psychological proxy war that the Russian Federation is waging against the West.[1] This war has its roots in the Cold War and is conducted by non-military hybrid measures known as 'active measures.' An important component of Soviet, and since 1991 Russian, active measures has been promoting cooperation between Russian and foreign scholars and think tank experts. Sergei I. Zhuk writes that, under the close supervision of the Soviet secret services, the Institute of Slavic Studies and Balkan Studies (*Institut slavianovedeniia*) was founded as part of the USSR Academy of Sciences in 1947. Its goal was to research and monitor Soviet international connections through Il'ia Solomonovich Miller (1918-78), a former officer of SMERSH (*Smert' shpionam*/Death to Spies) under the NKVD. Such scholars not only represented the Soviet secret services in academic institutions in Moscow and the non-Russian republics but were also responsible for ties to foreign institutions.[2] Soviet and Russian active measures have included disinformation, and the manipulation of the media, politics, and public opinion of so-called 'enemy' countries through forgeries, front organizations, and agents of influence targeting foreign politicians, journalists, and academics.[3]

---

1   An expanded version of this study entitled 'Russian Front Organizations and Western Academia' was published in *International Journal of Intelligence and Counterintelligence*, vol. 36, no. 2 (2023).
2   Sergei I. Zhuk, *'Use Your Enemy': The KGB, Russian Academic Imperialism, and Western Academia, 1958-2022* (London: Routledge, forthcoming).
3   On the history and the institutional structures that support active measures, see Jolanta Darczewska and Piotr Żochowski, *Active Measures: Russia's Key Export* (Warsaw: Ośrodek Studiów Wschodnich im. Marka Karpia/Centre for Eastern Studies, 2017), pp. 12-27.

Under the leadership of Yevgenii Primakov, Head of Russia's Foreign Intelligence Service (1991–96), Minister for Foreign Affairs (1996–98), and Prime Minister (1998–99), Russian foreign and security policy acquired a well-defined anti-American rhetoric. Primakov substituted Russia as part of the common European home, an idea promoted by Soviet leader Mikhail Gorbachev from the late 1980s and Foreign Minister Andrei Kozyrev in the early 1990s, with Russia as the center of Eurasia in opposition to the West. This trend has been strengthened under President Vladimir Putin, especially following his well-known speech to the February 2007 Munich Security Conference. Subsequently, Putin has on repeated occasions threatened the West in general and the U.S. in particular with 'symmetrical' and 'quick and tough' responses to the West's attempts to 'encroach' on Russia's security interests.[4]

The response to the West in the form of hybrid warfare seems more effective and less costly to the Russians than any type of conventional warfare. Jolanta Darczewska and Piotr Żochowski have aptly noted that Russia's hybrid war is a persistent effort designed to subvert the West—a process that has required systematic reconceptualization, the mobilization of its agents on all fronts, and training new generations of professionals who assist in various ways, wittingly or otherwise, to successfully carry out the Kremlin's foreign policy and implement its objectives.[5]

Information warfare in the domain of history has become especially important to the Russian political leadership. The Russian secret services systematically design (dis)information operations, promoting historical myths about Russia as a great power with a right to dominate Eurasia, denigrating Ukraine as a fake state, and claiming Ukrainians are one of three branches of the pan-Russian nation. This is done with careful attention to the cultural,

---

4   Andrew Higgins and Peter Baker, 'Russia Claims U.S. is Meddling Over Ukraine,' *New York Times*, February 6, 2014. Available at https://www.ny times.com/2014/02/07/world/europe/ukraine.html; Vladimir Isachenkov, 'Putin Vows a 'Quick and Tough' Russian Response for its Foes,' *ABC News*, April 21, 2021. Available at https://abcnews4.com/news/nation-world/in-an nual-address-putin-warns-russias-foes-will-be-sorry; and Darczewska and Żochowski, *Active Measures*, pp. 37–39.
5   Darczewska and Żochowski, *Active Measures*, pp. 14, 19.

ideological, historical, scientific, and philosophical complexities of the specific places where these operations are implemented.[6] Their objectives are to change the adversary's strategies and to shape public opinion and people's psyches. According to Dmitrii Rogozin, former Director of Russia's *Roskosmos* (May 2018–July 2022) and former Deputy Prime Minister of Russia for Defense and Space Industry (2011–2018), the major task of these operations is to achieve superiority in all spheres of human activity, to undermine political, economic and social systems of a target state, and to shape the views of military personnel and the political and intellectual elites.[7]

The formation and dissemination of historical myths has a special place among a wide range of Russian active measures. Reinforced domestically through Russian legislation and distributed abroad through active measures, state-sponsored historical narratives play a significant role in the Russian politics of memory.[8] Since 2002, the Russian state has used anti-extremist legislation as an instrument of censorship and state control, including as part of its ongoing campaign to 'counter the falsification of Russian history.'[9] The anti-extremist law helps the state silence dissent and ban and criminalize historical publications and narratives inconsistent with Soviet and state-sponsored discourse. The law has been 'improved'

---

6 Blagovest Tashev, Michael Purcell, and Brian McLaughlin, 'Russia's Information Warfare: Exploring the Cognitive Dimension,' *MCU Journal*, vol. 10, no. 2 (2019), p. 132 (pp. 129–47); and Timothy L. Thomas, 'Dialectical versus Empirical Thinking: Ten Key Elements of the Russian Understanding of Information Operations,' *Journal of Slavic Military Studies*, vol. 11, no. 1 (1998), pp. 40–62.

7 Dmitrii Rogozin *et al.*, 'Informatsionnnaia voina.' In: *Voina i mir v terminakh i opredeleniiakh: Voenno-tekhhnicheskii slovar'*, ed. D. O. Rogozin (Bucharest: Veche Publishing House, 2017).

8 Halya Coynash, 'Comparing Stalin to Hitler Could Soon Get You Prosecuted in Russia,' *Kharkiv Human Rights Protection Group*, May 7, 2021. Available at http://khpg.org/en/1608809059?fbclid=IwAR0_asj-NLMQfi_lXTMqBRvwR pmP8UnvI1kS79OfDQtqP2GSQVb_I9C1SU; and 'V Dumu vnesli zakonoproekt o zaprete publichno otozhdestvliat' roli SSSR i Germanii,' *TASS*, May 5, 2021. Available at https://tass.ru/obschestvo/11310865

9 See the full text of the Federal Law N114-FZ 'On Combating Extremist Activity,' *Sistema Garant*, July 5, 2002. Available at http://ivo.garant.ru/#/document/ 12127578/paragraph/11340:0

through subsequent legislative amendments (the 2016 'Yarovaia Package' and the 2017 expansion of the Criminal Code to include 'propaganda of terrorism') that employed a broad and all-inclusive definition of extremism that lacked clarity, inviting systematic misuse and arbitrary interpretations of the legislation.[10] By 2017, more than four thousand publications had been included in the Federal List of Extremist Materials, in existence since 2004. This legislation has been used to close the Ukrainian library in Moscow, ban Ukrainian organizations in Russia, and declare a wide range of Ukrainian books to be 'extremist.' These included various texts that challenged Soviet and Russian historical narratives. Storage and distribution of texts included in the list are illegal in the Russian Federation.[11]

More recently, on 5 May 2021, following Putin's instructions, the head of the State Duma Committee on Culture Yelena Yampol'skaia, the First Deputy Speaker of the Duma Aleksandr Zhukov, and senator Aleksei Pushkov registered a draft bill that prohibited any public statements that deny the 'decisive role of the Soviet people in the defeat of Nazi Germany and the humanitarian mission of the USSR in liberating the countries of Europe.' The obvious intent of the bill is to conceal the Soviets' active collaboration with Nazi Germany and to obscure the goal and the content of the 1939 Molotov–Ribbentrop Non-Aggression Pact.[12] The official spokesperson of Russia's Investigative Committee Svetlana Petrenko expressed the Committee's support for the legislation in a rather transparent statement:

---

10 See 'Russia's Overuse and Misuse of Anti-Extremism Laws,' *European Human Rights Advocacy Centre* (EHRAC), December 19, 2019, https://ehrac.org.uk/en_gb/blog/russias-overuse-and-misuse-of-anti-extremism-laws/; Maria Kravchenko, 'Inventing Extremists: The Impact of Russian Anti-Extremism Policies on Freedom of Religion or Belief,' *United States Commission on International Religious Freedom*/Washington D.C., January 2018. Available at https://www.uscirf.gov/sites/default/files/Inventing%20Extremists.pdf; on practical applications of the Anti-Extremist Law in Russia, see Olga Bertelsen, 'A Trial *in Absentia*: Purifying National Historical Narratives in Russia,' *Kyiv-Mohyla Humanities Journal*, no. 3 (2016), pp. 57–87.
11 Kravchenko, 'Inventing Extremists,' p. 4.
12 Coynash, 'Russian Legislators.'

attempts to rewrite history must receive a warranted response in the legal realm, just like any other actions which denigrate the symbols of military glory and insult the memory of the victorious nation. The proposed additions to the law should become another effective and timely way of protecting historical memory and the conclusions of the International Military Tribunal at Nuremberg [...] In conditions of a continuing information war, efforts have been seen to rehabilitate Nazism both within our country and abroad, false assessments of the role of our country in the victory over fascism.[13]

Russian propagandists are equally active abroad, reinforcing Soviet historical narratives in Western academia where, as the articles in this collection show, there already exist Russophile approaches to Russian–Ukrainian relations, the annexation of Ukraine's Crimea, and the 2014 revolution in Ukraine. A wide range of active measures are conducted to undermine Western scholars' critical perspectives and to sustain historical myths about the nature of Joseph Stalin's regime, the role of Russia in the Second World War, and contemporary Russia's methods of governing. The ultimate objective of these disinformation operations is to shape the domestic policy of leading democracies, to co-opt and subvert their intellectual elites, and to influence public opinion that would make it easier to achieve Russia's foreign policy goals. Importantly, Russia combines covert action and subversion with hard power and direct violence, a process that, in the view of the Russian political leadership, increases Russia's chances to succeed in pursuing its economic and geopolitical goals.[14] Russian information operations are pushing against an already open door with a large body of Western historians and political scientists being Russophiles, upholders of the view that 'Crimea was always Russian' (see Sergei I. Zhuk's article

---

13 'SK podderzhal proekt o zaprete otozhdestvleniia deistvii SSSR i Germanii vo Vtoroi mirovoi,' *Parlamentskaia gazeta*, May 6, 2021. Available at https://www.pnp.ru/politics/sk-podderzhal-proekt-o-zaprete-otozhdestvleniya-deystviy-sssr-i-germanii-vo-vtoroy-mirovoy.html

14 Andrew Radin, Alyssa Demus, and Krystyna Marcinek, 'Understanding Russian Subversion Patterns, Threats, and Responses,' *RAND Corporation*, February 2020. Available at https://www.rand.org/content/dam/rand/pubs/perspectives/PE300/PE331/RAND_PE331.pdf, p. 3.

in this collection), and portraying Ukraine as an appendage of Russia, rather than a country with independent agency.[15]

Over the last two decades, Moscow 'disinformers' and co-opted Russian academics have established and fostered relationships with Western educational centers and scholars who more frequently than not were unaware they were communicating with Russian agents of influence or supporters of Russian imperialism. The question of whether it was wise to cooperate with Russian academics only became a subject of debate after Russia's 2022 invasion of Ukraine, leaving open the question of why this had not become a critical matter in the preceding eight years following Ukraine's 2014 revolution and Russia's occupation and annexation of Ukrainian territory. Many Western and Ukrainian scholars continued to cooperate with Russian colleagues after 2014, uncritically distributing Russian official narratives, often being oblivious of their origin, falsities, and intent. Ultimately, they have become participants in Russian covert operations, contributing greatly to the popularity of pro-Kremlin narratives in the West.[16] Some, however, curtailed their collaborative work after Russia's invasion.

These dynamics will be evident from two examples. The greatest number of Western scholarly articles since 1991 on Ukraine have exaggerated its regional divisions,[17] an approach which in many ways resembled a lighter version of Russia's disinformation trope of an artificial and weak Ukraine. After 2014 this translated into upholding the Kremlin's view of a 'civil war' taking place in Ukraine between Russian and Ukrainian speakers.[18] In 2022 this lay behind the widespread Western view that Ukraine would be quickly defeated by an invading Russian force because eastern Ukraine would

---

15 Taras Kuzio, *Crisis in Russian Studies? Nationalism (Imperialism), Racism and War* (Bristol, England: E-International Relations Publishing, 2020), pp. 9–35. Available at https://www.e-ir.info/publication/crisis-in-russian-studies-nationalism-imperialism-racism-and-war/
16 Radin, Demus, and Marcinek, 'Understanding Russian Subversion Patterns,' p. 14.
17 Petro Kuzyk, 'Ukraine's National Integration Before and After 2014. Shifting 'East-West' Polarization Line and Strengthening Political Community,' *Eurasian Geography and Economics*, vol. 60, no. 6 (2019), pp. 709–35.
18 Kuzio, *Crisis in Russian Studies?*, pp. 106–32.

welcome them as liberators or at the very least remain passive towards them.[19]

A second example is the misuse of the term 'nationalist.' This term has been used in negative connotations and applied against one side, Ukrainians, but never against its Soviet or Russian opponents. This has been reinforced by Western scholars denying or downplaying the existence of nationalism in Putin's Russia.[20] Similar to various Western scholars, historian Georgiy Kasianov applies the label 'nationalist' to Ukrainian presidents whom he views through the lens of Russian propaganda.[21] Such an approach, in turn, reinforces the Kremlin line on 'nationalists' having come to power in the Orange and Euromaidan Revolutions and having subdued pro-Russian voices and Russian speakers. Kasianov's first foray into nationalism was far more objective in outlining theories of nationalism, nation-building, and nationhood, offering a historical survey of Ukrainian nationalism by using a wide range of Western literature.[22] As with some other Russophile scholars in Ukraine, Kasianov presumably became more critical of Ukrainian nationalism after the Orange Revolution. He defended memory politics under President Viktor Yanukovych, arguing then that the Ukrainian Institute of National Memory had the best perspective to become a 'serious academic and analytical centre.'[23] Kasianov's stand on this issue (his positive assessment of the activities of the Ukrainian Institute of National Remembrance under Yanukovych) places him in

---

19 Taras Kuzio, 'How Western Experts Got the Ukraine War So Wrong,' *Geopolitical Monitor*, November 14, 2022. Available at https://www.geopoliticalmonitor.com/how-western-experts-got-the-ukraine-war-so-wrong
20 Taras Kuzio, 'The Nationalism in Putin's Russia that Scholars Could Not Find But Which Invaded Ukraine,' *Ideology, Theory, Practice/Journal of Political Ideologies*, April 4, 2022. Available at https://www.ideology-theory-practice.org/blog/the-nationalism-in-putins-russia-that-scholars-could-not-find-but-which-invaded-ukraine
21 Georgiy Kasianov, 'The War Over Ukrainian Identity: Nationalism, Russian Imperialism, and the Quest to Define Ukraine's History,' *Foreign Affairs*, May 4, 2022. Available at https://www.foreignaffairs.com/articles/ukraine/2022-05-04/war-over-ukrainian-identity
22 Georgiy Kasianov, *Teorii natsii ta natsionalizmu* (Kyiv: Lybid, 1999).
23 Georgiy Kasianov, *Past Continuous: istorychna polityka 1980-kh-2000-kh: Ukraina ta susidy* (Kyiv: Laurus/Antropos-Lohos-Film), pp. 113, 142.

an unenviable minority among Ukrainian (and even Western) scholars. Kasianov's proposition that decommunization allegedly helped 'liquidate the Soviet symbolic space of memory and simultaneously fill the now-free space with nationalist symbols'[24] is not only an attempt to denigrate the efforts of Ukrainian patriots to shed the oppressive Soviet past, but, most importantly, was consistent with a pro-Kremlin narrative about Ukraine. According to this narrative, Ukraine, a US puppet state, has been ruled by a 'fascist junta' since 2014, which allegedly transformed the country into 'anti-Russia.'

Furthermore, Kasianov sought to rehabilitate the odious Dmytro Tabachnyk, a fugitive wanted by the Ukrainian secret services since 2014, writing that, as Minister of Education during Yanukovych's presidency, Tabachnyk only changed history writing in a 'cosmetic' manner while the fundamental basis of an 'ethnocentric narrative remained unchanged.'[25] This is simply not the case. In 2008, two years before Yanukovych's election as president, Communist Heorhiy Kriuchkov and Tabachnyk published a book in which they attacked Yushchenko's presidency as 'fascist.' This showed how the anti-Ukrainian camp had already begun echoing Russian propaganda and disinformation against Ukraine. Using 'nationalist' and 'fascist' in the above manner reveals a subjective and parochial understanding of the phenomenon and the realities in Ukraine, an approach consistent with the Kremlin's misuse of these terms in the Soviet and post-Soviet eras.[26] In Putin's Russia, anyone who is not in agreement with the Russian viewpoint has been identified as a Ukrainian 'nationalist' or a 'Nazi.' This is clearly seen in the 'de-nazification' policies implemented by Russian occupation forces who have kidnapped, tortured, and killed Ukrainian patriots of different political persuasions.

---

24   Georgiy Kasianov, 'The 'Hard Talk.' The Ukrainian-Polish Controversy over the Past, 1990s–2000s' (a conference paper presented at the 14–15 January 2019 conference 'Ukraine and its Neighbors: Cross-Cultural and Transnational Interactions' in Naples, Italy).
25   Kasianov, *Past Continuous*, p. 125.
26   Kuzio, *Crisis in Russian Studies?*, pp. 82–105.

In this context, it is important to remember that in contrast to propaganda where the message and its intent are typically transparent for targeted audiences, in covert action and disinformation operations, the intent of 'altering' reality is camouflaged: to be effective, these operations must be covert, and their target must remain oblivious to their intent.[27] Disinformation includes the spread of 'false, incomplete, or misleading data passed on to groups or individuals in a manner calculated to inspire full confidence in the message carried.'[28] Disinformation messages always contain elements of falsehood ('deceptive portions') that seem credible and believable to targeted audiences due to the efforts of specially trained disinformers who, by using certain techniques, are able to build a 'climate of trust' and confidence. Importantly, disinformation inflicts harm on the target whose action or inaction becomes self-destructive because the target's perceptions of reality have been distorted by false messages.[29]

The openness and relatively free discussions in Western academia make it susceptible to false narratives emanating from the Russian Federation that can often build on long established Russophile positions and the sloppy use of terms such as 'nationalism.' To sustain these false narratives, the Russians have been using a variety of techniques: educational exchange and cultural diplomacy; oral and written disinformation distributed among Western academics whose nostalgia for an earlier period in their careers in the USSR makes it easier to sustain it;[30] the use of mass and social media and agents of influence who persuade, co-opt, or recruit Western scholars, encouraging their Russophile views of Soviet and

---

27 Natalie Grant, *Disinformation: Soviet Political Warfare, 1917-1992* (Washington, D. C.: Leopolis Press, 2020), p. xxv. For an enlightening discussion about these tactics and Russian disinformation, see Michael Weiss, 'The Menace of Unreality: Combatting Russian Disinformation in the 21st Century' (talk), *YouTube*, November 3, 2014. Available at https://www.youtube.com/watch?v=KwZZFuiiQ2I. The 30 October 2014 panel discussion 'The Menace of Unreality' was hosted at the Legatum Institute in cooperation with the Atlantic Council and the US Department of State.
28 Grant, *Disinformation*, p. xxv.
29 *Ibid.*
30 See Zhuk's article here.

Russian history; and the establishment of international front organizations that assist the Russian secret services in subverting Western scholarly institutions.

Eugene Rumer, a realist scholar, has suggested that after 1991 Russia's aggressive political course and active measures illuminate Russia's attempt to restore a balance disrupted by the end of the Cold War in its relationship with the West, and to sustain a historical narrative 'written by the victors,' a narrative of the economic and military glory of the victorious nation, Russia, that won the Second World War.[31] Rumer has clearly noted that in an attempt to restore this balance, '[d]eception and active measures have long been and will remain a staple of Russian dealings with the outside world for the foreseeable future.'[32] Importantly, sustaining historical myths from the past helps Russia perpetuate more recent myths about wars in Georgia (2008) and Ukraine (from 2014) as responses to NATO's encroachment into Russia's spheres of interest, and Putin's military deployment in Syria (from 2015) as the restoration of 'Russia's traditional foothold in the Middle East.'[33] Since as far back as 1993, Russian leaders have been demanding the West recognize Eurasia as their exclusive sphere of influence from which NATO and the EU are prohibited, and UN peacekeepers cannot be deployed in its frozen conflicts. Kyiv has fought an uphill struggle for decades to obtain Western recognition of Ukraine as an independent and sovereign actor, as opposed to being viewed as an appendage of Russia with whom its fate has been forever tied.

Russia's annexation of Crimea, its invasion of the eastern Ukrainian region of the Donbas in 2014, and Russia's full-fledged war against Ukraine launched on 24 February 2022 fundamentally broke U.S.-Russian relations and escalated tensions between Russia and the West, prompting Russia to intensify its hybrid warfare

---

31 See the testimony of Eugene Rumer, Senior Fellow and Director, Russia and Eurasia Program, Carnegie Endowment for International Peace, at the Hearing before the Select Committee on Intelligence of the United States Senate, March 30, 2017. In: *Disinformation: A Primer in Russian Active Measures and Influence Campaigns* (panel I) (Washington, D.C.: U.S. Government Publishing Office, 2017), p. 21 (pp. 21–22).
32 *Ibid.*, p. 22.
33 *Ibid.*, p. 26.

activities. Russian intelligence has identified Western academia and think tanks as pivotal targets of active measures.[34] Moreover, because of their inability to cut ties to Russian scholars and experts after 2014, Western intellectual elites appear to be vulnerable and unprepared to deal with Russian ideological subversion. Russian front organizations, sponsored by the FSB and the Russian presidential administration, have been key players in Russian covert operations conducted in Western academia. As a result of their activities, Soviet and pro-Kremlin narratives have endured.

Penetrating Western Academia

Russian active measures targeting Western academia remain largely under-investigated by scholars and practitioners, which is a major reason for this collection of essays. Unpacking the objectives of the Russians in this domain seems necessary to better understand their strategies and tactics vis-à-vis the West and to conceptualize effective counterintelligence strategies to mitigate the consequences of Russian active measures targeting Western intellectuals. Through covert action, Moscow pursues several general objectives:

- undermining trust in democratic systems and their national governments;
- fomenting chaos and division within Western societies;
- promoting pro-Russian sentiment and popularizing Russian foreign policy goals in the West; and
- inciting confusion and misperception by muddling the lines between fact and disinformation, thereby ultimately

---

[34] 'Putin's Asymmetric Assault on Democracy in Russia and Europe: Implications for U.S. National Security' (a minority staff report prepared for the use of the Committee on Foreign Relations, U.S. Senate, 115 Congress, Second Session, 10), *Govinfo*, January 10, 2018. Available at https://www.govinfo.gov/cont ent/pkg/CPRT-115SPRT28110/html/CPRT-115SPRT28110.htm; 'Scholars or Spies: Foreign Plots Targeting America's Research and Development' (Joint Hearing before the Subcommittee on Oversight & Subcommittee on Research and Technology, Committee on Science, Space, and Technology, House of Representatives, 115 Congress, 2nd Session), *Govinfo*, April 11, 2018. Available at https://www.govinfo.gov/content/pkg/CHRG-115hhrg29781/html/CHRG-115hhrg29781.htm; see also Kuzio, *Crisis in Russian Studies?* and Bertelsen, 'Russian Front Organizations and Western Academia.'

changing the perceptions of reality among academics and broader audiences in the West.[35]

Back in the 1980s, in a study of Soviet active measures, the former Head of the Active Measures Working Group[36] Dennis Kux distinguished between:

- 'white' or overt operations that include diplomatic, trade, aid, and propaganda efforts;
- 'gray' clandestine disinformation activities that are conducted with the assistance of front organizations, ultra-left or ultra-right organizations, radio stations, and media outlets; and
- 'black' top-secret operations that use agents of influence who spread disinformation among foreign politicians, journalists, and scholars, forgeries and other doctored documents that help Russia deceive the 'enemy' and 'mask Moscow's hand in the operation.'[37]

Employing Kux's classification of Soviet active measures, contemporary Russian covert operations targeting Western academia typically fall within the category of 'black' operations. Work with foreign scholars requires clandestine activities conducted by an army of agents of influence and scholars who seek to collaborate with and to co-opt Western scholars by cultivating in them trust and faith in Russian cultural, scientific, and political agendas. Yet contemporary operations conducted by the Russian intelligence services constitute a mixture of 'white,' 'gray,' and 'black' activities.

---

35 See the testimony of Clint Watts (Robert A. Fox Fellow at the Foreign Policy Research Institute) at the Hearing before the Select Committee on Intelligence of the United States Senate, March 30, 2017. In: *Disinformation: A Primer in Russian Active Measures and Influence Campaigns* (panel I) (Washington, D.C.: U.S. Government Publishing Office, 2017), p. 30.

36 The Interagency Active Measures Working Group was established during the Reagan administration in 1981 and led by the U.S. Department of State and later by the U.S. Information Agency (USIA) to counter Russian disinformation.

37 Dennis Kux, 'Soviet Active Measures and Disinformation: Overview and Assessment,' *The U.S. Army War College Quarterly: Parameters*, vol. 15, no. 1 (1985), p. 19 (pp. 19–28); see also Steve Abrams, 'Beyond Propaganda: Soviet Active Measures in Putin's Russia,' *Connections: The Quarterly Journal*, vol. 15, no. 1 (2016), p. 12 (pp. 5–31).

Secrecy is especially relevant in cases of industrial and technological espionage and recruiting activities and, as Daniel Golden has demonstrated, cutting-edge research centers and universities are especially vulnerable,[38] with far less oversight by the Department of Justice (DOJ) of foreign donations to think tanks than to political consultants which has been monitored by the DOJ's FARA (Foreign Agent Registration Act). Foreign penetration of Pentagon-funded or government-funded research programs and initiatives severely damages American national security interests and defense systems.[39] The American intelligence community and Senator Mark Warner, vice chairman of the Senate Intelligence Committee, warned American institutions of higher learning about national security threats and attempts by foreign students and faculty to steal intellectual property, calling on universities to initiate a 'robust threat analysis and risk mitigation program to meet the challenge of the advanced persistent threat of academic espionage.'[40]

It is important to keep in mind that the threat posed by Russian scientific and academic espionage is not a new phenomenon; it has a long history, going back to the Stalin era.[41] This threat persisted throughout the Cold War period. According to the U.S. Senate Intelligence Committee, at the height of the Cold War in 1976, 25 percent of Soviet students, who were part of cultural and educational exchange and came to the United States between 1965 and 1975, were intelligence agents.[42] Ladislav Bittman, an intelligence officer specializing in disinformation for the Czechoslovak intelligence service who defected to the United States in 1968, wrote that

---

38 Taras Kuzio, 'Ukrainian Kleptocrats and America's Real-Life House of Cards: Corruption, Lobbyism and the Rule of Law,' *Communist and Post-Communist Studies*, vol. 50, no. 1 (2017), pp. 29–40.
39 Daniel Golden, *Spy Schools: How the CIA, FBI, and Foreign Intelligence Secretly Exploit America's Universities* (New York: Henry Holt and Co., 2017).
40 Suzanne Folsom and Robert Garretson, 'The Continuing Danger of Academic Espionage,' *Inside Higher Ed*, May 5, 2020. Available at https://www.inside highered.com/views/2020/05/05/threat-academic-espionage-should-not-be-overlooked-even-time-pandemic-opinion
41 Jerrold and Leona Schecter, *Sacred Secrets: How Soviet Intelligence Operations Changed American History* (Washington, D.C.: Brassey's Inc., 2002).
42 Ladislav Bittman, *The KGB and Soviet Disinformation: An Insider's View* (Washington, D.C.: Pergamon-Brassey's International Defense Publishers, 1985), p. 208.

the efforts of Soviet-bloc agents to penetrate U.S. scientific centers have intensified since the early 1970s, both in number and aggressiveness. Some 5,000 Soviet students, scientists, artists, and scholars, as well as commercial representatives, entered the United States, every year, and many of them came with specific secret assignments.[43]

As a result of these efforts, Soviet military achievements and scientific 'discoveries' during this time were tremendous, due to 'stolen Western technological secrets.'[44] These activities continued after the disintegration of the USSR in 1991. In his February 2012 interview in the FBI's Washington headquarters, Frank Figliuzzi, FBI assistant director for counterintelligence, noted that there had been ample evidence to suggest that American universities had been consistently targeted by foreign intelligence services, including Russia and China.[45]

Under Putin's leadership, Russian espionage operations designed to steal cutting-edge research conducted at American and European universities run parallel to active measures aimed at popularizing Russian narratives pertaining to Russian, European and world histories, and promoting pro-Kremlin talking points addressing Russian domestic and foreign policies.[46] These operations require patience and vigorous research activities to identify and

---

43 *Ibid.*
44 *Ibid.*, p. 209.
45 Daniel Golden, 'American Universities Infected by Foreign Spies Detected by FBI,' *Bloomberg*, April 8, 2012. Available at https://www.bloomberg.com/news/articles/2012-04-08/american-universities-infected-by-foreign-spies-detected-by-fbi; on Chinese espionage at American universities, see Emily Feng, 'FBI Urges Universities to Monitor Some Chinese Students and Scholars in the U.S.,' *National Public Radio*, June 28, 2021. Available at https://www.npr.org/2019/06/28/728659124/fbi-urges-universities-to-monitor-some-chinese-students-and-scholars-in-the-u-s; on the most recent case, see 'Charles Lieber: Harvard Professor Guilty of Hiding Ties to Chinese Programme,' *BBC News*, December 22, 2021. Available at https://www.bbc.com/news/world-us-canada-59723343
46 See for example: Jon Henley and Pjotr Sauer, 'Norway Arrests 'Brazilian Researcher' Accused of Spying for Russia,' *Guardian*, October 25, 2022. Available at https://www.theguardian.com/world/2022/oct/25/norway-arrests-brazilian-researcher-accused-of-spying-for-russia. See also 'Vladimir Putin's Historical Disinformation,' *U.S. Department of State*, May 6, 2022. Available at https://www.state.gov/disarming-disinformation/vladimir-putins-historical-disinformation/

cultivate relationships with Western scholars who have the potential to serve as speakers at international scholarly forums and conferences defending pro-Kremlin narratives. The Russian intelligence services seek opportunities to establish 'scholarly' contacts with these individuals and offer handsome financial support for their research in the form of grants and paid conference trips. These initial stages are necessary to further control and manipulate scholars who, through their publications, talks, and conference presentations, help solidify Russian historical myths, and, ultimately, shape cultural perceptions and policymaking. This became especially important after the 2014 Ukrainian revolution when the Russian political leadership realized that Ukraine was leaving Russia's sphere of influence.

Several approaches are instrumental to the success of these operations:

- sending Russian citizens (undercover agents) to be educated at and/or employed by American universities;
- using academic exchange programs for recruiting American students as agents of influence;
- co-opting American scholars through grants, awards, scholarships, and other incentives that boost the scholars' reputation and prestige;
- using front organizations to facilitate ideological subversion of scholars and broader audiences, a subtle and lengthy process that shapes the scholars' worldviews and inspires them to serve the Russian political leadership's goals, including building on long-established Russophilia through the promotion of Kremlin-approved historical narratives.

The overarching objective of these activities is three-fold: first, to build on existing nostalgia for the USSR and Russophilia; second, to legitimize the Putin regime's methods of governing and political behavior; and third, to undermine the arguments of Russia's opponents and portray them as Russophobes, tied to Western intelligence agencies and Nazi sympathizers.[47]

In addition, social media, including Facebook, play a significant role in spreading disinformation and cultivating group thinking which assists the Russian secret services in the manipulation of American academia. Beyond being a means of social communication, Facebook (like any other social media platform) serves academic audiences as a networking and academic news platform, and most Western scholars are oblivious to the fact that the Russian secret services effectively employ Facebook to distribute divisive messages and disinformation across Western academic and professional groups created within Facebook.[48] Indeed, Western governments only came to understand the power of information warfare in 2014 but took the step of banning Russian media outlets, such as RT (formerly *Russia Today*), only after the 2022 invasion.

The use of 'faceless sources' and 'faceless attributions' (expressions such as 'According to official sources,' 'According to unofficial sources,' 'According to well-informed sources,' and 'According to the best available information') serve to boost the credibility of the 'news' being disseminated in this way.[49] The goal is to reinforce narratives sponsored by the Russian state, and possibly to sow discord among Western academia.[50] 'Troll factories,' such as the infamous Internet Research Agency in St. Petersburg, were successfully used to buttress state-sponsored historical or ideological narratives

---

47 Geir Hågen Karlsen, 'Divide and Rule: Ten Lessons about Russian Political Influence Activities in Europe,' *Palgrave Communications*, vol. 5, no. 19 (2019), p. 10 (pp. 1–14).
48 Elizabeth Bodine-Baron, Todd C. Helmus, Andrew Radin, and Elina Treyger, 'Countering Russian Social Media Influence,' *RAND Corporation*, 2018. Available at https://www.rand.org/content/dam/rand/pubs/research_reports/R R2700/RR2740/RAND_RR2740.pdf; Sheera Frenkel and Cecilia Kang, *An Ugly Truth: Inside Facebook's Battle for Domination* (New York: Harper, 2021); Nina Jankowicz, *How to Lose the Information War: Russia, Fake News, and the Future of Conflict* (London: I. B. Tauris, 2020).
49 Karen S. Johnson-Cartee, *News Narratives and News Framing: Constructing Political Reality* (New York: Rowman & Littlefield Publishers, Inc., 2005), pp. 228–29; and Jankowicz, *How to Lose the Information War*.
50 'Report on Russian Active Measures,' *House Permanent Select Committee on Intelligence*, March 22, 2018. Available at https://docs.house.gov/meetings/IG/ IG00/20180322/108023/HRPT-115-1_1-p1-U3.pdf, p. 33.

concerning the West, Ukraine, and other neighboring states in Eurasia.[51]

In addition, the Russian Federation employs a large and technologically sophisticated media propaganda apparatus that helps shape Western public opinion in general, and historical master narratives that influence Western scholarly discourse in universities and think tanks. Among Russian state-sponsored agencies are *Rossiya Segodnya*, a state media company that serves as an umbrella for other propaganda outlets, such as *RT* and *Sputnik*. Funding to these outlets jumped sharply in the wake of the 2014 revolution in Ukraine. The Russian press reported that 'in September 2014, Moscow tripled *Rossiya Segodnya*'s budget to 6.4 billion rubles and increased *RT*'s 2015 budget by 41 percent to 15.38 billion rubles, which is equivalent to roughly $600 million.'[52] Through TV and newspapers, *RT* and *Sputnik*, as well as *Russia Beyond*, promote pro-Russian and anti-Western narratives, shaping public opinion in many European countries and the United States.[53]

The use of women by the Russian secret services has been a reliable tradition, and the niche of human intelligence (HUMINT) in American academia has included women spying for the SVR (Foreign Intelligence Service), FSB (Federal Security Service), and GRU (military intelligence). Among them have been Lidiia Gurieva (cover name Cynthia Murphy), who received two undergraduate degrees from New York Universities and an MBA from Columbia Business School; Natalia Pereverzeva (cover name Patricia Mills), who earned a BA in Business at the University of Washington Bothell; and Maria Butina, who received a Master's degree in

---

51 On 'troll factories,' see Abrams, 'Beyond Propaganda,' p. 20; Peter Tanchak, 'The Invisible Front: Russia, Trolls, and the Information War against Ukraine.' In: *Revolution and War in Contemporary Ukraine: The Challenge of Change*, ed. Olga Bertelsen (Stuttgart/New York: *ibidem*-Verlag/Columbia University Press, 2016), pp. 253–82.
52 'Report on Russian Active Measures,' March 22, 2018, p. 140.
53 *Ibid*. *Sputnik* is based in 28 countries and operates in 33 different languages. See also Marcel H. Van Herpen, 'The Many Faces of the New Information Warfare.' In: *Russian Active Measures: Yesterday, Today, Tomorrow*, ed. Olga Bertelsen (*ibidem*-Verlag/Columbia University Press, 2021), pp. 37–59.

International Relations from American University, Washington, D.C.⁵⁴ They all had similar tasks posed by their handlers—to infiltrate U.S. universities and establish contacts with students and professors who were well connected with American policymaking circles or also worked or used to work for government institutions and the U.S. secret services. Collecting intelligence and expanding networks in academic and political circles were also part of their agenda. Butina's ambitious goals seem to be the most interesting and elaborate scheme that included establishing close connections with the leadership of the National Rifle Association and gaining access to Republican presidential candidates Scott Walker and Donald Trump.⁵⁵ With governments more on alert following the

---

54 For more on Gurieva, Pereverzeva, and Butina, see 'Ten Russian Agents Plead Guilty and Are to Be Removed from the United States,' *Department of Justice/Office of Public Affairs*, July 8, 2010. Available at https://www.justice.gov/opa/pr/ten-russian-agents-plead-guilty-and-are-be-removed-united-states; 'Russian National Sentenced to 18 Months in Prison for Conspiring to Act As an Agent of the Russian Federation within the United States,' *Department of Justice/Office of Public Affairs*, April 26, 2019. Available at https://www.justice.gov/opa/pr/russian-national-sentenced-18-months-prison-conspiring-act-agent-russian-federation-within; 'Russian Spies Living in the Neighborhood,' *The International Massmedia Agency*, July 20, 2020. Available at https://intmassmedia.com/2017/07/20/russian-spies-living-in-the-neighborhood/; James Ross Gardner, 'The Russian Spies Who Fooled Seattle,' SeattleMet, October 30, 2017. Available at https://www.seattlemet.com/news-and-city-life/2017/10/the-russian-spies-who-fooled-seattle; 'Spies at the Museum,' *Institute of Modern Russia*, July 2, 2012. Available at https://imrussia.org/en/russia-and-the-world/257-spies-at-the-museum; Daniel Golden, 'Why Russian Spies Really Like American Universities,' *ProPublica*, July 23, 2018. Available at https://www.propublica.org/article/why-russian-spies-really-like-american-universities; and Joseph Fitsanakis, 'Russian Spies Arrested by the FBI in 2010 Had Targeted Hillary Clinton,' *Intelnews.org*, October 24, 2017. Available at https://intelnews.org/2017/10/24/01-2202/.

55 For more on Butina and Aleksandr Torshin, a high-ranking member of Vladimir Putin's United Russia Party, see Tim Mak, 'Exclusive: Documents Detail Meetings of Russians with Treasury, Federal Reserve,' *National Public Radio*, May 10, 2019. Available at https://www.npr.org/2019/05/10/721763041/exclusive-documents-detail-meetings-of-russians-with-treasury-federal-reserve; Yuri Felshtinsky, 'My name is Fedyashin, Anton Fedyashin,' *Gordon*, September 21, 2018. Available at https://english.gordonua.com/news/exclusiveenglish/my-name-is-fedyashin-anton-fedyashin-who-is-anton-fedyashin-and-what-was-he-teaching-maria-butina-investigation-by-yuri-felshtinsky-342703.html; and Kateryna Smagliy, *Hybrid Analytica: Pro-Kremlin Expert Propaganda in Moscow*,

invasion of Ukraine and with the deterioration of the West's relations with Russia, Sergei Cherkasov was exposed as a GRU agent after he attempted to infiltrate the International Criminal Court (ICC), using the alias Viktor Muller Ferreira and pretending to be Brazilian.[56] In Norway another Russian spy, José Assis Giammaria, was arrested after claiming to be a Brazilian 'researcher.'[57]

A close analysis of the most recent patterns of tactics and strategies employed by the Russian secret services suggests that, rather than recruiting an American citizen who works for the State Department, Pentagon, or an intelligence agency, the Russian secret services favor placing a student or a professor at an American or European university, individuals who would potentially be hired by a federal agency or able to befriend a colleague with access to sensitive information.[58] These information-gathering tactics, which have been further expanded under Putin, are also designed to build on and expand established pro-Russian and anti-Western narratives, which are endorsed and spread by some scholars in Russian and Eurasian studies.[59] Again, the openness of Western and

---

Europe, and the U.S.: A Case Study on Think Tanks and Universities (New York, NY: The Institute of Modern Russia: 2018), p. 42.

56 Gordon Corera, 'Russian GRU Spy Tried to Infiltrate International Criminal Court,' *BBC News*, June 16, 2022. Available at https://www.bbc.co.uk/news/world-europe-61831961.

57 Jon Henley and Pjotr Sauer, 'Norway Arrests 'Brazilian Researcher' Accused of Spying for Russia,' *The Guardian*, October 25, 2022. Available at https://www.theguardian.com/world/2022/oct/25/norway-arrests-brazilian-researcher-accused-of-spying-for-russia

58 Anthony Bishop, 'International Espionage on Campus,' *The Cipher Brief*, November 6, 2016. Available at https://www.thecipherbrief.com/column_article/international-espionage-on-campus; and 'Evidence Links Russian Spies Inside U.S. Universities as Students and Professors…,' *Newman & Shapiro*, April 12, 2019. Available at https://newmanshapiro.com/evidence-links-russian-spies-inside-u-s-universities-as-students-and-professors-using-free-academia-to-gather-sensitive-info-on-america/

59 Despite Russia's unprovoked invasion of Ukraine, in August 2022, Putin's policies were approved by 84% of Russian citizens and 79% of Russian citizens and dual nationals holding both Russian and U.S. passports: Statista Research Department, 'Vladimir Putin's Approval Rating in Russia Monthly 1999-2022,' *Statista*, November 3, 2022. Available at https://www.statista.com/statistics/896181/putin-approval-rating-russia. For those who would like to listen Western academics' presentations that are informed by pro-Kremlin narratives, attend any ASEEES Annual Convention.

American campuses and the absence of any procedures in place that would prevent Russian active measures at schools of higher learning indeed make them targets for Russian and other international spies, including Russian scholars co-opted by the regime. Academic discussions about whether to no longer invite Russian scholars to Western academic conferences only began in 2022, and these have shown how many are still reluctant to impose bans, despite the fact that most Russian scholars, at least publicly, support Russia's invasion of Ukraine and its goal of destroying the Ukrainian state.

Russian Front Organizations: The Izborskii Club

The Russian state has also pursued ideological subversion and the enactment of geopolitical change through front organizations (or NGOs). They have become key players capable of changing people's perceptions of reality that in turn are transforming geopolitics, conflicts, and operational environments on an unprecedented scale in the new millennium.[60] Over the last decade, Russian front organizations mushroomed in the West, and their agendas have become more conspicuous for intelligence analysts. These organizations try to conceal their ties with the Kremlin, as well as the sources of their financial support. Many of these propaganda associations and councils were established on Russian soil, albeit with truly extensive global reach and opportunities for coopting and recruiting Western scholars to advocate and popularize pro-Kremlin narratives. According to the Global Engagement Center (GEC) at the U.S. Department of State, Russia continues to be a 'leading threat' to U.S. national security, spreading disinformation and working through American academia to undermine the analytical strength of the intellectual and scholarly community.[61]

---

60 Jeffrey V. Dickey, *Russian Political Warfare: Origin, Evolution, and Application* (Master's Thesis) (Monterey, California: Naval Postgraduate School, 2015), p. 138. Available at *Calhoun/The Institutional Archive of the Naval Postgraduate School*, June 2015, https://core.ac.uk/download/pdf/36737948.pdf.

61 'GEC Special Report: Pillars of Russia's Disinformation and Propaganda Ecosystem,' *U.S. Department of State/Global Engagement Center*, August 2020. Available at

Today there are countless Russia-aligned outlets, organizations, and foundations in Europe, Canada, and the United States, as well as pro-Kremlin institutions created on Russian soil, that help the Russian political leadership cultivate 'witting and unwitting proliferators' of Russian propaganda narratives.[62] Analyzing the profiles of these front organizations, the GEC report has demonstrated that, beyond their contribution to the Russian disinformation campaign against the West, these institutions and individuals affiliated with them 'benefit greatly from an association with the Kremlin.' Others try to distance themselves from them, yet nevertheless promote pro-Kremlin narratives and Russian state-sponsored historical myths.[63]

Beyond the well-known *Rossotrudnichestvo* (Federal Agency for the Commonwealth of Independent States Affairs, Compatriots Living Abroad, and International Humanitarian Cooperation), working with Russian compatriots in the United States, the United Kingdom, India, and Mexico among other states,[64] and *Global Research* (a Canadian website that 'has become deeply enmeshed in Russia's broader disinformation and propaganda ecosystem'),[65] several organizations were registered in Moscow that served the same purpose—spreading disinformation and establishing scholarships. These include:

---

https://www.state.gov/wp-content/uploads/2020/08/Pillars-of-Russia%E2%80%99s-Disinformation-and-Propaganda-Ecosystem_08-04-20.pdf, p. 3.
62 *Ibid.*, p. 9.
63 *Ibid.*, p. 11.
64 According to its official site, *Rossotrudnichestvo* was established on September 6, 2008 in accordance with Presidential Decree no. 1315, operating under the jurisdiction of the Russian Ministry of Foreign Affairs. The mission of its foreign chapters is to implement the state policy of 'international humanitarian cooperation' and to promote the 'objective image of contemporary Russia.' Its chapters are in 80 states and represented by 97 offices. Among them are 67 Russian centers for science and culture located in 62 states. In addition, *Rossutrudnichestvo* is represented by 24 individuals working in Russian Embassies in 21 states.
See the official site of *Rossutrudnichestvo*. Available at https://rs.gov.ru/en/about, which was stripped of any information relevant to the organization sometime after 24 February 2022; see also Olga Bertelsen, 'Introduction.' In: *Russian Active Measures*, pp. 16–17; and Karlsen, 'Divide and Rule,' pp. 1–14.
65 'GEC Special Report,' p. 12.

- *The Strategic Culture Foundation* (https://strategic-culture.org/): an online English-language journal registered in Russia that is supervised by Russia's SVR and has close ties with the Russian Ministry of Foreign Affairs, publishing works by pro-Russian Western scholars and observers;
- *New Eastern Outlook* (https://journal-neo.org/): a 'pseudo-academic publication of the Russian Academy of Science's Institute of Oriental Studies that promotes disinformation and propaganda focused primarily on the Middle East, Asia, and Africa,' serving as a platform for spreading pro-Kremlin and anti-American views of Russian academics;[66]
- *NewsFront* (en.news-front.info): a Crimea-based disinformation and propaganda outlet publishing anti-Western and anti-American texts for Western audiences;[67]
- *SouthFront* (https://southfront.org/): an online disinformation site registered in Russia, publishing analytical and intelligence texts in different languages based on Kremlin talking points;
- *Katehon* (https://katehon.com/en): a 'Moscow-based quasi-think-tank' with close connections to the Russian secret services and other official Russian agencies that publishes anti-Western disinformation and propaganda texts in five languages;[68]
- *Geopolitica.ru* (https://www.geopolitika.ru/): Russian-language disinformation and propaganda site that publishes anti-Western texts and op-eds inspired by the Russian neo-imperialist Aleksandr Dugin whose goal is to destroy Western institutions and to 'exterminate the Ukrainians.'[69]

---

66 Ibid.
67 For more details on *NewsFront*, see Karin Kőváry Sólymos, Josef Slerka, Julia Dauksza, and Anna Gielewska, 'NewsFront: From Crimea with Hate,' *Vsquare*, October 8, 2022. Available at https://vsquare.org/newsfront-from-crimea-with-hate/
68 'GEC Special Report,' p. 13.
69 *Ibid.*, pp. 12–13. See Dugin's statements ('Ubivat', ubivat' i ubivat'!') on *YouTube*, July 17, 2014. Available at https://www.youtube.com/watch?v=dwgn3JGNrUo; on Dugin's ideology, see Anton Shekhovtsov and Andreas Umland, 'Is Aleksandr Dugin a Traditionalist? 'Neo-Eurasianism' and Perennial Philosophy,' *The Russian Review*, no. 68 (2009), pp. 662–78.

The role of these organizations in ideological subversion in Western academia is enormous. Ideological subversion, a pervasive process of brainwashing and co-optation of scholars, appears to be a quite effective tactic employed by the Russian secret services. Russian agents of influence, working for the secret services, collaborate with the members of these NGOs, and also attend reputable international scholarly conventions as keynote speakers, presenters, or guests, mingling with scholars of various ethnicities and citizenships.

Sometimes, through non-transparent channels and decision-making processes, the organizers of forums and conferences invite keynote speakers, Russian politicians and scholars with questionable political and scholarly reputations. For instance, Sergei Stepashin, who between 1993 and 1998 served as First Deputy Security Minister, Director of the Federal Counterintelligence Service (FSK), Director of the Federal Security Service (FSB), Head of the Administrative Department of the Russian Government Administration, Minister of Justice, and Minister of the Interior, was invited as a keynote speaker to the Ninth International Council for Central and East European Studies (ICCEES) World Congress held on 3–8 August 2015 in Makuhari, Japan, where he appeared in the company of two bodyguards.[70] The organizers might have overlooked that during the terrorist act in the Budenovsk hospital, Russia in June 1995, where 166 hostages were killed and 541 injured in the special forces' operation attack on the hospital, Stepashin, Director of the FSK at the time, played a key role in establishing priorities that served as a template for future special forces practices where the lives of civilian hostages became a secondary consideration.[71] According to many observers, Japanese academics, like many others

---

70 See the article by Sanshiro Hosaka in this collection.
71 In another terrorist attack in Beslan in 2004, for instance, the casualties were higher: 334 people, including 186 children, died because of the failed special forces operation and violence during an attempt to release the hostages. Katerina Kochkina, 'Dlia nyneshnei elity eto bylo unizitel'no,' *Nastoiashchee vremia*, June 19, 2020. Available at https://www.currenttime.tv/a/budyonnovsk-25-years-politics/30679871.html; and Vladimir Kara-Murza, 'Zagadki beslanskoi tragedii — 13 let spustia,' *Radio Svoboda*, September 1, 2017. Available at https://www.svoboda.org/a/28711454.html

among the international scholarly community, fell victim to Russia's memory politics aimed at the systematic erasing of collective memory about *siloviki* (security forces) and other federal forces operations in Budennovsk, the Moscow 'Nord-Ost' theater, and Beslan.[72] This operation was one of many that Putin's regime launched against Chechnya which amounted to genocide, and served as a template for Russian genocide in Syria from 2015 and renewed genocide in Ukraine from 2022.

In addition, the 2015 scholarly forum in Japan notoriously invited two 'scholars' from Donetsk who in 2014, supported by Russian *siloviki*, had taken over Donetsk State University. Kirill Cherkashin was one of them who, with automatic weapon in hand, later proclaimed himself Dean of the School of History; the other was Dmitrii Muza, professor of history at Donetsk State University and co-head of the *Novorossiia* branch of the Izborskii Club, established in the DNR in 2014 with the support of Russia's Izborskii Club.[73] Advocates of the projects of *Novorossiia* ('New Russia') and *Russkii Mir* (Russian World),[74] Cherkashin and Muza carried out

---

72 Semen Charnyi, 'Pravozashchitniki napomnili o posledstviiakh terakta,' *Kavkazskii uzel*, June 21, 2020. Available at https://www.kavkaz-uzel.eu/arti cles/351056/
73 'Boeviki zakhvatili Donetskii universitet,' *Zn.ua*, September 19, 2014. Available at https://zn.ua/UKRAINE/istoriki-doneckogo-universiteta-otkazalis-prisya gat-dnr-153678_.html; 'Cherkashin Kirill Vladimirovich,' *Donetskii natsional'nyi universitet/Kafedra politologii*. Available at http://donnu.ru/hist/plsc/cher kashin-kirill-valeryevich; 'Dmitrii Evgenievich Muza,' *Donetskii natsional'nyi universitet/Kafedra mirovoi i otechestvennoi kul'tury*. Available at http://donnu. ru/phil/wnc/muza-dmitriy-evgenyevich. In September 2016, Denis Pushilin, Head of the People's Council of the Donetsk People's Republic (DNR), congratulated Dean Cherkashin on the twenty-third anniversary of the Department of Political Science. See 'Predsedatel' Narodnogo Soveta DNR Denis Pushilin pozdravil politologov DonNU s prazdnikom,' *Donetskii natsional'nyi universitet* website, September 13, 2016. Available at http://news.donnu.ru/2016/09/ 13/predsedatel-narodnogo-soveta-dnr-denis-pushilin-pozdravil-politologov-donnu-s-prazdnikom/
74 On the Novorossiia concept, see Marlene Laruelle, 'The Three Colors of Novorossiya, or the Russian Nationalist Mythmaking of the Ukrainian Crisis,' *Post-Soviet Affairs*, vol. 32, no. 1 (2015), pp. 55–74. See further: Aleksandr Nekrot, 'Ukraine pridetsia priniat' Donbass russkim,' *Ritm Evrazii*, February 4, 2021. Available at https://www.ritmeurasia.org/news--2021-02-04--ukraine-pridets ja-prinjat-donbass-russkim.-ili-otkazatsja-ot-nego-53098; Dmitrii Pavlenko, 'Andrei Purgin: 'Spetsoperatsiiu' po osnovaniiu DNR fakticheski proveli tri

aggressive verbal attacks, bullying Ukrainian scholars at the 2015 Congress and labeling them and the current political leadership in Kyiv as 'fascists.'

The Izborskii Club was initially founded in Moscow in 2012 by red (pro-Soviet)-white (pro-Tsarist and Russian Orthodox fundamentalists)-brown (fascist) backers of the 1993 coup against President Boris Yeltsyn and supporters of Putin. Stalinist and national-Bolshevik Russian writer Aleksandr Prokhanov and editor-in-chief of Russia's neo-fascist newspaper *Tomorrow* (*Zavtra*) became the Izborskii Club Chair. Its goal was to offer the Russian political elite and Russian society analytical reports that would shape their 'civic position' and imperialistic nationalism. The organizers intended to create the Club's branches in all regions of the Russian Federation and beyond to promote the Club's red-white-brown agenda of destroying the Ukrainian state and to curtail the liberals' and Western attempts to destabilize Russian society 'ideologically and morally.'[75] Through mass media, the Club was to form a new agenda and new leaders, nationalists with an imperial consciousness who were able to resist the manipulations of Russian politics by Western centers and a 'fifth column' active within the Russian Federation. The Izborskii Club has gathered under its roof the most extreme individuals in Russia who consistently used inflammatory rhetoric and hate-speech against Ukraine and Ukrainians, Russian liberal oppositionists, and Western democracies. Nearly two decades of Russia's dehumanizing hate speech paved the way for the recurring

---

cheloveka,' *Tsargrad.tv*, April 7, 2018. Available at https://tsargrad.tv/artic les/purgin-specoperaciju-po-osnovaniju-dnr-fakticheski-proveli-tri-cheloveka _123774; 'V 'DNR' zaiavili o simpatiiakh Kieva fashizmu,' *Chas.ua*, October 15, 2021. Available at http://timeua.com/kyivnews/2/41217.html; Kirill Cherkashin, 'Ukraina iavliaetsia slabym...,' *Novoross.info*, April 2, 2014. Available at http://www.novoross.info/politiks/24663-kirill-cherkashin-razdvoennost-ya vlyaetsya-estestvennoy-chastyu-politiki-ukrainy.html; Tat'iana Zarovnaia, 'Istfak DonNU gotovil ubezhdennykh shovinistov i ideiinykh terroristov,' *Argument*, August 29, 2014. Available at http://argumentua.com/stati/istfak-donnu-gotovil-ubezhdennykh-shovinistov-i-ideinykh-terroristov; and Dmitrii Muza, 'DNR—zaslon protiv fashizma,' *Izborskii Klub*, May 13, 2021. Available at https://izborsk-club.ru/21045

75 For details, see the official site of the Izborskii Club. Available at https://izborsk-club.ru/about

genocide being committed by Russia's invading troops.[76] Through support and influential connections with the Kremlin, and through popularization of its views via international forums and publications, the Club was able to solidify its position and institutionalize its postulates. The national renaissance of Russia and the 'Russian doctrine' have been routinely discussed at various Izborskii Club gatherings attended by Patriarch Kirill, members of the nationalist movement *Rossiia molodaia* (Young Russia), and the Russian political elite.[77]

The DNR branch of the Izborskii Club was established to popularize similar ideas and, in particular, to promote the concepts of *Novorossiia* and the *Russkii Mir*. These ideas transcended the 'borders' of the DNR through Muza's and Cherkashin's publications and propaganda speeches at international conferences, including, again, the 2015 ICCEES World Congress in Makuhari, Japan,[78] where both speakers mimicked the agenda of their patrons in Moscow, Aleksandr Prokhanov, Vitalii Aver'ianov, and Aleksandr Nagornyi.[79]

Delivered in Russian, Cherkashin's passionate anti-Ukrainian and anti-Western propaganda speech at this academic forum had nothing to do with scholarship or scholarly analysis, but, sadly, was favorably received by several American and Japanese scholars. It is, alas, hardly surprising that scholars identifying as specialists in 'post-Soviet Eurasia' (a Russian propaganda term implying a common security zone and legitimizing a Russian sphere of

---

76 'When Words Kill—From Moscow to Mariupol,' *EUvsDisinfo*, June 17, 2022. Available at https://euvsdisinfo.eu/when-words-kill-from-moscow-to-mariupol/
77 The official site of the Izborskii Club. Available at https://izborsk-club.ru/; on the Izborskii Club's nature, structure, and membership, see Edwin Bacon, 'Policy Change and the Narratives of Russia's Think Tanks,' *Palgrave Communications*, vol. 4, no. 94 (2018). Available at https://doi.org/10.1057/s41599-018-0148-y
78 In 2015, the Izborskii Club of Novorossiia published a collection of essays entitled *The Ideology of the Fatherland* and initiated a research project *The Dictionary of the Fatherland's Patriot* with the aim of challenging the views of Russian liberals and intellectual elites 'who lost their ideological direction and patriotic core.'
79 For brief biographies of these individuals, see *Izborskii Klub*. Available at https://izborsk-club.ru/members

influence),[80] would draw their knowledge about identity politics and political dynamics in Russia and Ukraine from presentations by people like Muza and Cherkashin. What, however, comes as a surprise is that these same American professors receive prestigious prizes for their publications and Fulbright scholarships for their research. This raises a serious concern about the state of American academia and academic professional associations, and about the position of American governmental institutions.

Intriguingly, the final version of the Congress's program did not include Cherkashin as a participant or as a presenter. According to then Vice-President of ICCEES Kimitaka Matsuzato, Cherkashin's presentation was a late addition to the program, made at the final hour (long after the deadline for applications had passed).[81] It is even more intriguing that, at the time of Cherkashin's stay in Japan, he was wanted by Ukraine's Security Service (SBU) for treason, and his photos with a Kalashnikov gun while taking over Donetsk State University in 2014 were available on the internet. Moreover, according to the Ukrainian Consulate in Tokyo, the SBU monitored Cherkashin's and Muza's activities in Japan but could do little, as they apparently traveled to Japan as Russian citizens, carrying Russian passports. After the Congress, Matsuzato published an article under the rubric 'Special Cluster on ICCEES IX World Congress' entitled 'Slavic Eurasian Studies in the World after Makuhari' in which he announced his resignation from his position as Vice President of ICCEES 'because of some disagreement regarding organizational rules.'[82] It is unknown whether this 'bitter decision,' using Matsuzato's words, pertained to inviting people like Stepashin, Cherkashin, and Muza with deeply dubious reputations and biographies. Whatever the case might be, to the surprise of many serious scholars present who were aware of these

---

80 On Eurasianism, see Marlene Laruelle, *Eurasianism and the European Far Right: Reshaping the Europe-Russia Relationship* (New York: Lexington Books, 2015).
81 At Cherkashin's panel, my question about the reasons for adding Cherkashin to the program in May 2015 long after the submission deadline had passed was addressed to Dr Matsuzato in written form. Dr Matsuzato's written response, which is quite vague, is in my possession.
82 Kimitaka Matsuzato, 'Slavic Eurasian Studies in the World after Makuhari,' *Japanese Slavic and East European Studies*, no. 36 (2015), p. 9 (pp. 3–11).

individuals' activities in Donetsk and beyond, most of the Congress participants never challenged the organizers or asked them inconvenient questions about either the keynote speaker or other Russian propagandists, participants of the Congress, whom they invited.

Like other Russian 'subverters,' Cherkashin and Muza freely spread pro-Russian and anti-Western historical narratives at other scholarly conferences, reenforcing the Soviet and Russian emphases on Russian victimhood, the perfidious nature of the West, and a 'civil war' brought about by Ukrainian 'nationalists' (fascists) coming to power in a 'putsch' in the Euromaidan Revolution and launching a war against Russian-language speakers. Blaming Euromaidan nationalists rather than Russia for causing a 'civil war' in Ukraine in 2014, a narrative emanating from the Kremlin, was also part of Serhiy Kudelia's argument,[83] and of an array of Russophile scholars.[84] The vitality and the longevity of this historical myth circulated at various conferences confirms observations and analyses by Western analytical think tanks and national security agencies,

---

[83] Serhiy Kudelia, 'Domestic Sources of the Donbas Insurgency,' *PONARS Policy Memos* 351, September 29, 2014. Available at http://www.ponarseurasia.org/memo/domestic-sources-donbas-insurgency; Serhiy Kudelia, 'The Donbas Rift,' *Russian Social Science Review*, vol. 58, no. 1 (2017), pp. 212-34; and Serhiy Kudelia and Johanna van Zyl, 'In My Name: The Impact of Regional Identity on Civilian Attitudes in the Armed Conflict in Donbas,' *Nationalities Papers*, vol. 47, no. 5 (2019), pp. 801-21. See Andreas Umland's response to Kudelia, 'In Defense of Conspirology: A Rejoinder to Sergiy Kudelia's Anti-Political Analysis of the Hybrid War in Eastern Ukraine,' *PONARS Eurasia*, September 30, 2014. Available at https://www.ponarseurasia.org/in-defense-of-conspirology-a-rejoinder-to-serhiy-kudelia-s-anti-political-analysis-of-the-hybrid-war-in-eastern-ukraine/; and Yuriy Matsiyevsky, 'The Limits of Kudelia's Argument: On the Sources of the Donbas 'Insurgency',' *PONARS Eurasia*, October 31, 2014. Available at https://www.ponarseurasia.org/the-limits-of-kudelia-s-argument-on-the-sources-of-the-donbas-insurgency/. See also Kudelia's responses: 'Reply to Andreas Umland: The Donbas Insurgency Began at Home,' *PONARS Eurasia*, October 8, 2014. Available at https://www.ponarseurasia.org/reply-to-andreas-umland-the-donbas-insurgency-began-at-home/; and 'Getting to the Bottom on the Sources of the Donbas Insurgency,' *PONARS Eurasia*, November 6, 2014. Available at https://www.ponarseurasia.org/getting-to-the-bottom-on-the-sources-of-the-donbas-insurgency/

[84] See the article by Taras Kuzio in this volume.

arguing that history matters in the 'invisible' information war between Russia and the West.[85]

Similarly, Kasianov has argued that the best way to understand the war in Ukraine is through a clash of historical myths promoted by Ukrainian 'nationalists' and those with a Soviet or Russophile outlook (the latter are never defined by him as nationalists).[86] His approach ignores the central driver of the war which is the stagnation of Russian nationalism from a Soviet recognition of Ukraine (albeit within the USSR) to a White Russian emigre denial of the existence of Ukraine.[87] By not applying the term 'nationalist' to Putin's Russia, Kasianov has implicitly included himself in the group of Western Russophile scholars who have downplayed and denied the fact that the Putin's regime is nationalist.[88] It is difficult to define this approach as objective on Russian-Ukrainian relations; nor is such a framework capable of fully embracing Putin's obsession with Ukraine and the brutality of his invading forces committing genocide against Ukrainians.[89]

The Russian state, its interlocutors, and scholars who have adopted its official narratives, skillfully manipulate facts, writing revisionist history and shaping an imperial-minded discourse. This discourse promotes Russian geopolitical goals, undermines

---

85   Duncan Allan *et al.*, 'Myths and Misconceptions in the Debate on Russia: How They Affect Western Policy, and What Can Be Done,' *Chatham House*, May 2021. Available at https://www.chathamhouse.org/sites/default/files/2021-05/20 21-05-13-myths-misconceptions-debate-russia-nixey-et-al.pdf, p. 12. Chatham House is the Royal Institute of International Affairs, a world-leading policy institute based in London.
86   Kasianov, 'The War over Ukrainian Identity.'
87   Taras Kuzio, *Russian Nationalism and the Russian-Ukrainian War: Autocracy-Orthodoxy-Nationality* (London: Routledge, 2022).
88   Kuzio, 'The Nationalism in Putin's Russia.'
89   Taras Kuzio in collaboration with Stefan Jajecznyk-Kelman, *Fascism and Genocide: Russa's War Against Ukrainians* (Stuttgart/New York: *ibidem*-Verlag/Columbia University Press, 2023); and Kristina Hook, 'Why Russia's War in Ukraine Is a Genocide,' *Foreign Affairs*, July 28, 2022. Available at https://www.foreignaffairs.com/ukraine/why-russias-war-ukraine-genocide; see also 'An Independent Legal Analysis of the Russian Federation's Breaches of the Genocide Convention in Ukraine and the Duty to Prevent,' *New Lines Institute for Strategy and Policy and Raoul Wallenberg Centre for Human Rights*, May 2022. Available at https://newlinesinstitute.org/wp-content/uploads/English-Report-1.pdf

Ukrainian statehood, and discredits the West.[90] Russia's long-standing grand strategic aims under its last two presidents have included uncontested control of a Eurasian sphere of influence, US recognition of Russia as a great power, and promotion of a view on the war in Ukraine as Russia's struggle against a US-led unipolar world and US global hegemony. The promotion of a sanitized historical record plays a major role in enabling Russia's propaganda and hybrid warfare against the West, which have dramatically expanded since the mid-2000s as Putin's Russia evolved into an extreme nationalist regime. Russia's need for sanitizing historical records was further augmented by the 2020 changes in the constitution that made Russia a totalitarian dictatorship with Putin as president for life, and by the 2022 invasion and atrocities committed in Ukraine.

The Council on Foreign and Defense Policy (SVOP)

According to Sergei I. Zhuk, in the 1990s, the successor structures of the former Soviet secret service sought to influence the appointment of the heads of the Russian and Ukrainian offices of international organizations, such as the Carnegie Endowment and Soros Foundations, with the aim of ensuring that only 'KGB-checked, reliable and loyal scholars' were accepted. Zhuk cites Leonid Leshchenko, a former Soviet Ukrainian Americanist, who noted:

> the KGB and its successor organizations (FSB and SBU) always promoted the careers of so-called reliable scholars, especially in international organizations which funded research in humanities and social studies. During the Cold War, these were IREX and Fulbright, and during the late 1980s and 1990s it became the Soros Foundation in both Russia and Ukraine.[91]

Zhuk writes that historians Vladislav Zubok, Alexey Miller, and Kasianov became the first exchange scholars during perestroika. Zubok's close encounters with the KGB during perestroika led to

---

90 Jeffrey J. Czerewko, 'Joint Staff Preface,' *Russian Strategic Intentions: A Strategic Multilayer Assessment (SMA) White Paper, Department of Defense/Politico.com*, May 2019. Available at https://www.politico.com/f/?id=0000016b-a5a1-d241-adff-fdf908e00001, p. ii.
91 Zhuk, *'Use Your Enemy.'*

his first experiences of travel to the West.[92] Later, in 2008, he became a recipient of funding from the 'Russkiy Mir' Foundation. In 1995-97 and 2010-2011, Miller received grants from Soros's Open Society Institute (Moscow).[93] Miller, as well as Dmitri Trenin, former GRU colonel and director of the Carnegie Moscow Center office from 2008 until early 2022, were also regular participants in Putin's Valdai Discussion Club, an annual gathering that brought together Russophile Western and Russian scholars and think tank experts.[94] Zhuk analyzes how after the disintegration of the USSR, close personal connections between Russian and Ukrainian heads of international organizations became a common ground for collaborative projects of which the most popular was the Soros Foundation's Higher Education Support Program. From 2009, through its summer schools, Kasianov, who became director of the education program of the International Renaissance Foundation in Kyiv, closely cooperated with Miller and Zubok.

It is important to keep this pre-history in mind, if we want to better understand the objectives and collaborative patterns of another Russian front organization, known as the Council on Foreign and Defense Policy (*Sovet po Vneshnei i Oboronnoi Politike*, SVOP). This Moscow-based organization was established in February 1992 by a group of Russian politicians, oligarchs, military, scientific, and intellectual elites, *siloviki*, and Russian mass media tycoons with the explicit goal to study and shape public opinion favorable to Russia among academics and broader audiences.[95] While it is officially an NGO, its members have close ties with the Kremlin, and they actively engage in collaboration with the Russian secret services. One

---

92   Sergei I. Zhuk, *Soviet Americana: The Cultural History of Russian and Ukrainian Americanists* (New York: I. B. Tauris, 2018), p. 234.
93   Zhuk, '*Use Your Enemy.*'
94   Trenin was also affiliated with the Carnegie Endowment for International Peace in Washington, D.C. until early 2022. See Zhuk, '*Use Your Enemy*'; and Alexander J. Motyl, 'The Two Dmitris: A Lesson for the West,' *The Hill*, January 4, 2023. Available at https://thehill.com/opinion/international/3789029-the-two-dmitris-a-lesson-for-the-west/
95   See the official website of the Council on Foreign and Defense Policy at http://svop.ru/about/; and Victoria A. Malko, 'Russian (Dis)Information Warfare vis-à-vis the Holodomor-Genocide.' In: *Russian Active Measures*, pp. 246-47 (pp. 215-62).

of its founding members, Sergei Karaganov, who has been a spokesperson for Russian hard-line foreign policy towards the West and Ukraine, has been a regular invitee to Western conferences and for interviews with Western media outlets. Karaganov has denigrated Ukraine for over a decade and called for its subjugation and defeat in the war.[96] Karaganov has supported Russia's war in Ukraine and unashamedly argued that Russia is at war with the West in Ukraine.[97] This argument is shared by Trenin, a regular participant in Western conferences, who camouflaged his support for Putin's aggressive foreign policies until the invasion when he came out in support of the war.[98]

Another Carnegie affiliate Fyodor Lukyanov is the chairman of the presidium of the SVOP and research director of the Valdai International Discussion Club. He was also hired as editor-in-chief of a state-sponsored outlet, the *Russia in Global Affairs* magazine. Lukyanov had gained valuable experience prior to these appointments in the US-based Sawyer Miller Group.[99] The Sawyer Miller Group's staff have been identified as 'spin doctors to the world: the Sawyer Miller Group uses the tricks of political campaigns to change the way you think about foreign governments, big business and any client in need of an image lift.'[100] Many of SVOP's board members are sons and daughters of former KGB associates, who served as

---

96 Kuzio, *Russian Nationalism and the Russian-Ukrainian War*, pp. 130, 133, 167.
97 See Bruno Macaes, "Russia Cannot Afford to Lose, So We Need a Kind of a Victory': Sergey Karaganov on What Putin Wants,' *New Statesman*, April 2, 2022. Available at https://www.newstatesman.com/world/europe/ukraine/2022/04/russia-cannot-afford-to-lose-so-we-need-a-kind-of-a-victory-sergey-karaganov-on-what-putin-wants; and Federico di Fubini, 'Sergey Karaganov: 'We Are at War with the West. The European Security Order Is Illegitimate',' *Corriere della Sera*, April 8, 2022. Available at https://www.corriere.it/econom ia/aziende/22_aprile_08/we-are-at-war-with-the-west-the-european-security -order-is-illegitimate-c6b9fa5a-b6b7-11ec-b39d-8a197cc9b19a.shtml
98 Dmitri Trenin, 'Politika i obstoiatel'stva. Sposobny li my sokhranit' stranu i razvivat' ee dal'she,' *Rossiia v global'noi politike*, May 20, 2022. Available at https://globalaffairs.ru/articles/politika-i-obstoyatelstva/
99 See Lukyanov's profile: The *Russian International Affairs Council* website. Available at https://russiancouncil.ru/en/fedor-lukyanov/
100 Barry Siegel, 'Spin Doctors to the World,' *Los Angeles Times*, November 24, 1991. Available at https://www.latimes.com/archives/la-xpm-1991-11-24-tm-417-story.html

heads and presidents of major Soviet cultural and educational institutions or were part of the Soviet intelligence community.[101] According to SVOP's charter, the organization can establish chapters in the Russian Federation and abroad, and Russian and foreign citizens can be members of the organization, if they so desire. Its major objectives are consistent with those of Russian foreign policy, which includes the conduct of Russian active measures targeting the West and the organization's close cooperation with Russia's Presidential Administration.[102] One of SVOP's routine practices is organizing scholarly conferences and webinars. The participants and presenters are awarded honoraria, and their proposals and research projects are financed from SVOP's budget.[103]

On 14 May 2020, six years after the 2014 Russian annexation of Crimea and invasion of the Donbas, SVOP sponsored a webinar entitled 'Memory Wars: Truce in the Time of the Quarantine?'[104] It is no coincidence that, among other scholars, the organizers invited Miller, a historian from the European University in St. Petersburg, Russia and a SVOP board member, and Kasianov, head of the Department of Modern History and Politics in the Institute of History of the National Academy of Sciences in Ukraine. Miller and Kasianov co-authored several texts and organized panels at international forums, expressing views about Ukrainian memory politics and recent events in Ukraine that often promoted Soviet and Russian historical narratives. They denigrated Ukrainian narratives by labeling them 'ethnocentric' and 'nationalistic.'[105] Both scholars

---

101 See SVOP membership list at https://svop.ru/члены-совета-а/.
102 'Ustav SVOP,' *SVOP*, July 24, 1997. Available at http://svop.ru/wp-content/uploads/2018/07/UsSVOP.pdf.pdf
103 *Ibid.*
104 'Voiny pamiati' (webinar), *SVOP*, May 23, 2020. Available at http://svop.ru/meeting/33123/; also available at https://www.youtube.com/watch?v=8gY-VV-aXvI. For other SVOP videos, see https://www.youtube.com/@svopevents/videos.
105 See Georgiy Kasianov, 'Manipulirovaniie istoricheskoi politikoi,' *YouTube*, August 26, 2019. Available at https://www.youtube.com/watch?v=NEHEDcT_r34; on Kasianov's denial of the genocidal nature of the Holodomor, see his interview by Leonid Shvets, 'Istorik Kasianov o Golodomore,' *Fokus.ua*, January 14, 2010. Available at https://focus.ua/politics/92637; on Miller's inaccurate claims about Johannes Remy's book *Brothers or Enemies: The Ukrainian National*

regularly used the terms 'ethnocentric' and 'state-sponsored' narratives, arguing, among other things, that such policies dominated contemporary Ukraine, but not, it would seem, Putin's Russia. Obviously, such an approach, implying that Russia, a country that denies the existence of Ukraine and Ukrainians, did not pursue nationalistic memory politics while Ukraine, a country that has never denied the existence of Russia and Russians, did pursue 'nationalistic' memory politics, could not be understood as balanced.[106] Moreover, Miller took this illogical argument to the extreme by claiming, with all the evidence pointing in the opposite direction, that in the Russian Federation, there is freedom of expression, and historians 'are practically free,' writing whatever they want.[107] Importantly, both rejected the accusations of scholars who pointed to how Miller's and Kasianov's narratives were consistent with Russian narratives emanating from the Kremlin. The following passage from one of Miller's interviews is telling, and warrants quoting at some length:

> [in] Eastern Europe, [...] [i]f you need to undermine your domestic Communist rivals, as well as the Russian minorities' claims for citizenship and cultural rights, you present them as agents of Moscow. There was a range of motives, and as a result, Eastern European countries came up with their own vision of 20th-century history centered on the concept of totalitarianism. For,

---

Movement and Russia from the 1840s to the 1870s, see Miller's review in *Scando-Slavica*, vol. 63, no. 2 (2018), pp. 231–34, and Johannes Remy's response to Miller's claims: 'But That Is Not What I Wrote: Response to Alexey Miller's Review of My Brothers or Enemies,' *Scando*-Slavica, vol. 64, no. 1 (2018), pp. 112–16; see also Roman Szporluk's criticism of Miller's *The Ukrainian Question: The Russian Empire and Nationalism in the Nineteenth Century*, trans. Olga Poato (Budapest/New York: Central European University Press, 2003), a book in which Miller's explanation of the Russian failure to make Ukrainians Russian is at the very least questionable: *The Russian Review*, vol. 64, no. 1 (2005), pp. 136–38; for Kasianov's and Miller's co-authored publications, see Georgiy Kasianov and Aleksei Miller, *Rossiia-Ukraina: Kak pishetsia istoriia* (Moscow: RGGU, 2011); and Wolfram Dornik, Georgiy Kasianov, Hannes Leidinger, Peter Lieb, Aleksei Miller, and Bogdan Musial, *Die Ukraine: zwischen Selbstbestimmung und Fremdherrschaft 1917–22* (Leykam, 2011).
106 Kasianov, 'Manipulirovaniie istoricheskoi politikoi.'
107 Alexey Miller (interview by Maria Lipman), 'Clashing Memory 'Cultures' in Russia and Europe,' *PONARS Eurasia*, June 19, 2018. Available at https://www.ponarseurasiaorg/clashing-memory-cultures-in-russia-and-europe-an-interview-with-alexey-miller/.

if the main issue, if the main tragedy is the Holocaust, then the Red Army that put an end to the Holocaust and liberated Auschwitz can't be equated with the Nazis. But in a system centered on totalitarianism, 'red terror' is no different from 'brown terror.'[108]

Miller goes on to emphasize the freedom that historians enjoy in Putin's Russia:

> It should be understood — and this is especially important for foreign readers — that the current Russian 'politics of memory' is radically different from the one that existed in the Soviet Union. Back then, politics drew on a dogma and the single true doctrine. Unlike that period, today, professional historians are practically free — one can write whatever one wants. Very diverse views can be expressed in the media. What the state is concerned about is not that everyone thinks alike. The Kremlin's concern is that Russian people at-large receive messages that follow roughly the same line. And this goal has been successfully achieved. The state does not seek to correct historians' minds. What it seeks instead is that those historians who share the state's vision — whether voluntarily or for the money — be granted broader opportunity in order to influence the mindset of the Russian people.[109]

The logic of these statements can be challenged on several levels but what is important here is that these ideas are consistent with claims vocalized by Russian disinformation. Where Miller is correct is regarding the willingness of the current Russian political leadership to offer handsome rewards and 'broader opportunity' to those historians whose publications follow the Kremlin's talking points and its official version of history. Unsurprisingly, back in February 2015, Miller ruminated about two types of Ukrainian identity that began to change after the 'most recent events' in Ukraine yet failed to name the key reasons behind this phenomenon — Russia's annexation of Crimea and part of Ukraine's Donbas. He observed that 'many of those residents of the country, who oppose the Maidan, are ceasing to identify as Ukrainians. This can be seen in the example of the Donetsk and Luhansk *opolchentsy* [volunteer militia]' — in other words, the Donbas in flames was the result of local residents' irredentism (a view, as we have seen earlier, argued by Western scholars such as Kudelia), rather than a Russian–Ukrainian war or

---

108 *Ibid.*
109 *Ibid.*

Russia's occupation of the Donbas,[110] suggestions that are entirely consistent with *RT* and leading Russian propagandists such as the odious Russian TV presenter Vladimir Solov'ev who has repeatedly called for the destruction of Ukraine and genocide against Ukrainians.[111]

The aforementioned 2020 SVOP webinar served Kasianov as a platform where he, faithful to his previous practices, ridiculed the efforts of Ukrainian historians to construct 'ethnocentric' historical narratives (narratives that in fact differed from Soviet truncated discourse),[112] reinforcing his portrayal of memory politics under Yanukovych as the most 'civic' and best of those conducted by Ukrainian presidents.[113] Kasianov could have been more balanced if, instead of making general observations in defense of Soviet and pro-Kremlin narratives, he were to include works published by Ukrainian and Western scholars of Ukrainian history, those who challenge Soviet narratives, contributing greatly to a nuanced understanding of Soviet and Ukrainian histories, including the history of Ukrainian–Russian and Ukrainian–Polish relations. Kasianov never cites HURI (Harvard Ukrainian Research Institute) or CIUS (Canadian Institute of Ukrainian Studies) publications, including works by Paul R. Magocsi and Serhii Plokhy. Magocsi,[114] the most prolific historian of Ukraine in the West, has been completely ignored and is never cited in Kasianov's *Past Continuous*. Orest Subtelny's *Ukraine. A History*[115] is dismissed as a 'standard

---

110 Alexey Miller (interview by Andrei Mozzhukhin), 'Ukrainskaia identichnost' sformirovalas'' v XX veke,' *Lenta.ru*, February 12, 2015. Available at https://lenta.ru/articles/2015/02/12/ukrid/
111 Julia Davis regularly places clips from Solov'ev's shows and other Russian television programs on Twitter @JuliaDavisNews. See her analysis at: https://www.thedailybeast.com/author/julia-davis
112 See the video of the webinar at *SVOP*, May 23, 2020. Available at http://svop.ru/meeting/33123/
113 Kasianov, *Past Continuous*, pp. 113, 142.
114 Paul R. Magocsi, *A History of Ukraine* was published by the University of Toronto Press in two editions in 1996 and 2010 with the second edition renamed *A History of Ukraine. The Land and Its Peoples*.
115 Orest Subtelny's *Ukraine. A History* was published by the University of Toronto Press in four editions in 1988, 1994, 2000, and 2009.

ethnonationalist narrative.'[116] Kasianov has a similar dismissive view of the doyen of Ukrainian history, Mykhaylo Hrushevsky, whose work he describes as 'archaic, antiquarian.'[117] Kasianov's claims pertaining to Ukraine's political leadership and Ukrainian historians who have allegedly embraced 'ethnocentric' views and narratives about the exceptional status of the Ukrainian nation as victim lack evidence and analytical focus, and have been refuted by the meticulous analysis of Oleksandr Hrytsenko.[118]

Furthermore, Kasianov's attitudes toward Volodymyr Viatrovych, a historian and former Director of the Ukrainian Institute of National Remembrance in Kyiv, are consistent with that of some Western scholars, such as Tarik Cyril Amar,[119] who are also obsessed with fighting Ukrainian nationalism. Perhaps not surprisingly, Amar combined his scholarly pursuits with working for Putin's *RT* propaganda television channel that has been a major outlet for hate speech and genocidal rhetoric against Ukraine and Ukrainians.[120] At the January 2019 international conference 'Ukraine and its Neighbors: Cross-Cultural and Transnational Interactions,' organized by the Italian Association of Ukrainian Studies (AISU) at Naples University, Kasianov, in response to critical comments about his paper and his aggressive position toward Viatrovych's arguments, shouted in anger: 'He is a Banderite!'[121] Needless to say, this statement had little to do with scholarly discourse as it amounted to dismissing his work as not of a scholarly nature.

---

116 Kasianov, *Past Continuous*, p. 23.
117 *Ibid.*, p. 205.
118 Oleksandr Hrytsenko, *Prezydenty i pam'iat': Polityka pam'iati prezydentiv Ukrainy (1994–2014): pidgruntia, poslannia, realizatsiia, rezul'taty* (Kyiv: 'K.I.S.,' 2017), esp. p. 670.
119 Taras Kuzio, 'Ideological Zealots Fighting a Non-Existent Ukrainian Nationalist Enemy: A Reply to Tarik Amar's Review of *Red Famine*,' *Kyiv-Mohyla Humanities Journal*, no. 6 (2019), pp. 209–16. Available at http://ekmair.ukma.edu.ua/handle/123456789/16882?locale-attribute=en
120 'Kolyshnii doslidnyk istorii Lvova...,' *Istorychna pravda*, December 20, 2021. Available at https://www.istpravda.com.ua/short/2021/12/20/160671/
121 This happened in the presence of scholars, including George Grabowicz, Simone Attilio Bellezza, Giovanna Brogi, and many other participants from nearly 15 countries. 'Banderites' (followers of nationalist leader Stepan Bandera) is a derogatory term used by the Soviet secret police officers who, in using this term, typically referred to any Ukrainian suspected of nationalism.

In fact, Viatrovych's approach to the Ukrainian-Polish conflict in the 1940s has always blamed both sides for killing civilians, in the same manner as Magocsi and Timothy Snyder.[122] On this question Viatrovych is in fact far more objective than Kasianov, who only blames Ukrainian nationalists. While the UPA (Ukrainian Insurgent Army) is routinely condemned for massacring Polish civilians, there is barely any condemnation by scholars (including Kasianov) of the Armia Krajowa (the Home Army consisting mostly of Polish partisans and underground forces) for killing Ukrainian civilians. More generally, Russophile scholars are seemingly much more reluctant to condemn the Polish Institute for National Memory for publishing books glorifying Polish nationalists who killed Ukrainian civilians.[123]

As mentioned earlier, Kasianov's criticisms of Ukrainian memory politics did not change in response to Russia's invasion of Ukraine in 2014, but hardened in response to the passage of four decommunization laws. Similar to various Western scholars, he sought to discredit attempts to de-Sovietize Ukraine's space through the four decommunization laws. A month after they were adopted an open letter organized by David Marples was signed on Facebook by an astounding seventy scholars. In the only in-depth analysis of the laws, Anna Oliynyk and Kuzio have shown how the criticisms written by Marples, and backed by those who had signed the open letter, were factually wrong on every point they raised.[124] Unfortunately, myths about the grave danger of Ukrainian

---

122 See Taras Kuzio, 'The Polish-Ukrainian War: A Historical and Political Context.' In: Volodymyr Viatrovych, *The Gordian Knot: The Second Polish-Ukrainian War 1942–1947* (Toronto, CA: Horner Press, 2020), pp. 7–33.
123 See the book about the Polish extreme nationalist 'Wołyniak' at: https://ipn.gov.pl/pl/publikacje/ksiazki/12485,Wolyniak-legenda-prawdziwa.html. Wołyniak's forces massacred hundreds of Ukrainian civilians in the current border region; one of the eyewitness survivors lives in Canada. See the article by the son of the survivor Andrew Fesiak, 'Personal Memoir: My Family in the Polish-Ukrainian Borderlands Killing Zone,' *Euromaidan Press*, January 3, 2019. Available at https://euromaidanpress.com/2019/01/03/my-family-in-the-polish-ukrainian-borderlands-killing-zone/
124 Anna Oliynyk and Taras Kuzio, 'The Euromaidan Revolution of Dignity, Reforms and De-Communisation in Ukraine,' *Europe-Asia Studies*, vol. 73, no. 5 (2021), pp. 807–36.

nationalism and Ukraine's 'nationalistic' laws, which have absolutely nothing to do with reality, continue to be promoted by Kasianov and other scholars, as seen by the publication of Kasianov's book *Past Continuous* in 2018 and his attempts to publish it in languages other than Ukrainian.

Interestingly, Kasianov only saw fit to change his position in the wake of Russia's full-scale invasion of Ukraine on 24 February 2022 (and not after 2014). Now residing in Poland, he has finally awakened to the existence of nationalism in Putin's Russia, using the term 'twisted' to describe Putin's historical narrative about Ukraine and Ukrainians and even occasionally placing 'Ukrainian nationalists' in quotation marks.[125] Nevertheless, Kasianov continues to describe the roots of the war as a domestic struggle over Ukrainian identity[126] rather than a fundamental change in Russian nationalism from Soviet acceptance of Ukraine and Ukrainians (albeit within the USSR) to White Russian émigré denial of Ukraine and Ukrainians.[127] His views continue to shape those of Western journalists and scholars who cling to the misguided notion that only Ukrainians are nationalists, but not those upholding Soviet and Russophile views.[128]

In other respects, the invasion has not led to Kasianov undertaking a perestroika of his earlier stances. He remains of the opinion that 'Ukrainian right-wingers' had 'tried to impose the history of their political party on the whole of Ukraine.'[129] He appears to be unaware of current opinion polls which show that the views he disparages were not imposed by a minority group but are an outgrowth of Russian imperialism and genocide against the Ukrainian

---

125 Georgiy Kasianov, 'From Historical Fallacy to Tragic, Criminal Loss: Putin's Case for Invading Ukraine,' *Ukrains'ka Pravda*, April 20, 2022. Available at https://www.pravda.com.ua/eng/news/2022/04/20/7340865
126 Kasianov, 'The War over Ukrainian Identity.'
127 Kuzio, *Russian Nationalism and the Russian-Ukrainian War*.
128 Maria Lipman, 'Memory Crash: The Politics of History in and Around Ukraine, 1980s-2010s,' *Foreign Affairs*, vol. 101, no. 3 (May–June 2022), pp. 205–06; and Patrick Wintour, 'The Revenge of History in Ukraine: Year of War Has Shaken Up World Order,' *The Guardian*, December 26, 2022. Available at https://www.theguardian.com/world/2022/dec/26/ukraine-war-revenge-of-history-how-geopolitics-shaping-conflict
129 Kasianov, 'The War over Ukrainian Identity.'

state and Ukrainian people undertaken since 2014. Kasianov is in fact on an uphill struggle to catch up with the radical and rapid changes in Ukrainian identity that have destroyed support for Soviet nostalgia and pro-Kremlin narratives and have led to de-Russification from the ground up.[130] He may find it difficult to come to terms with the fact that 93 percent of Ukrainians believe the 1933 *Holodomor* was a genocide;[131] 81 percent positively view Ukrainian nationalist groups UPA and OUN (Organization of Ukrainian Nationalists); 74 percent hold positive views on Stepan Bandera, one of the OUN leaders;[132] only three percent hold a positive view of Russia;[133] and 89 percent believe Russia's invading army is committing genocide against Ukrainians.[134] Kasianov's book *Past Continuous* was published a year before Volodymyr Zelenskyy was elected president. In the light of these dramatic changes in Ukrainian identity one must ponder whether Kasianov would also describe Zelenskyy as a 'nationalist' in the context of the banning of twelve pro-Russian political parties and five pro-Russian TV channels and threats to ban the Russian Orthodox Church under his presidency.

Cooperation and cross-fertilization among the outlets and organizations that influence public opinion in the Russian Federation and beyond are implemented through forums like the May 2020 SVOP webinar, presentations by scholars like Miller and Kasianov,

---

130 See Kuzio in collaboration with Jajecznyk-Kelman, *Genocide and Fascism*, pp. 207–34; and Taras Kuzio, 'Review: Russia's Invasion Has United Ukraine,' *Atlantic Council*, December 22, 2022. Available at https://www.atlanticcouncil.org/blogs/ukrainealert/2022-review-russias-invasion-has-united-ukraine/
131 'Some 93% of Ukrainians Consider 1932-1933 Holodomor as Genocide of Ukrainian People—Poll,' *Interfax-Ukraine*, November 25, 2022. Available at https://en.interfax.com.ua/news/general/874602.html; see also 'The Dynamics of Attitude towards the 1932–33 Holodomor (November 2022),' *Rating Group*. Available at https://ratinggroup.ua/en/research/ukraine/dinam_ka_stavlennya_do_golodomoru1932-33_rr_listopad_2022.html
132 'The Tenth National Survey: Ideological Markers of the War (April 27, 2022),' *Rating Group*. Available at https://ratinggroup.ua/en/research/ukraine/desyatyy_obschenacionalnyy_opros_ideologicheskie_markery_voyny_27_aprelya_2022.html
133 'Seventeen National Survey: Identity. Patriotism. Values (August 17–18, 2022),' *Rating Group*. Available at https://ratinggroup.ua/en/research/ukraine/s_mnadcyate_zagalnonac_onalne_opituvannya_dentichn_st_patr_otizm_c_nnost_17-18_serpnya_2022.html
134 'The Tenth National Survey.'

pseudo-academic publications, and state financial support. One does not have to be a rocket scientist to notice that research topics such as critiques of the 'nationalistic' nature of Ukrainian memory politics attract Russian state funding. Scholars engaging in this research are invited to international conferences and paid honoraria for participating in scholarly and political forums. Some indeed believe in their research findings; others are more cynical, and material incentives in the form of free trips abroad and monetary rewards is the factor that motivates them to continue. Many even enjoy the status and title of a 'critical voice' they were given by the international scholarly community for criticizing Ukrainian 'ethnocentric' narratives, and their arguments, consistent with Russian propaganda, routinely go unchallenged.

Conclusion

This analysis of selected aspects of Russian influence on Western academia is but a sample of the wide range of firmly established Russian practices fundamentally entrenched in Soviet and Russian intelligence traditions. Russia's foreign policy has been historically informed and shaped by covert action that included techniques and strategies to ideologically subvert the West and to sustain the power of Russia's political leadership and its national security establishment.[135]

This critical discussion about the views of scholars, however, should not be interpreted as a suggestion that they should not be allowed to say or to publish what they say or publish. Open debate is a fundamental feature of democracy. At the same time, the Western academic community should be aware, especially since the invasion, of manipulations employed by the Russian secret services that promote fallacious discourses, narratives, propositions, and pure disinformation that often inform Western analyses and shape Western decision-making. As an example, on the eve of the invasion Western 'experts' were on the same page with the Kremlin, arguing that Ukraine would be defeated in a few days.

---

135 Rumer's testimony in *Disinformation: A Primer in Russian Active Measures*, p. 27.

Russian ideological subversion of Western academia manifests itself in firmly embedded and long-standing Russophile preconceptions about Russia in the minds of some scholars, preconceptions that have little to do with realities but are rather based on carefully built and argued constructs. According to the suggestion of the contributors to a Chatham House report, it is crucial that Western academic institutions should build expertise and develop pools of experts in Russian history, culture, and politics 'to ensure trustworthy analysis of Russia's actions.'[136]

Kuzio's article in this collection shows that some scholars in Russian and Eurasian studies found it difficult to understand the events of 2014 in Ukraine, let alone the 2022 invasion. In addition, Kuzio's analysis demonstrates how it is analytically misguided to differentiate between bad 'nationalist' and good 'non-nationalist' Ukrainian presidents, because there is greater continuity than discontinuity between them. The Ukrainian Institute of National Remembrance's approach to controversial aspects of Ukrainian history, such as Polish–Ukrainian questions, has barely changed between Viatrovych and his successor Anton Drobovych. Furthermore, there are far more similarities than dissimilarities between Poroshenko and Zelenskyy over their approaches to memory politics. In fact, of Ukraine's six presidents the exception on memory politics has been Yanukovych, a rogue president charged with treason whose memory politics seem more prudent to Kasianov.

In this context, raising the questions of how to ensure balanced and informed historical analyses in Russian and Eurasian studies and how to mitigate Russian covert action targeting American universities seems appropriate and timely. The most effective countermeasures include an insightful analysis of Russian covert action, its exposure, and further research on its influence on Western academics. To facilitate these processes and to alleviate the threat of Russian disinformation and ideological subversion among Western intellectuals, effective strategic interinstitutional communications are indispensable, a suggestion offered by a number of scholars, counterintelligence analysts, and specialists on Russian hybrid warfare

---

136 Allan *et al.*, 'Myths and Misconceptions in the Debate on Russia,' p. 103.

and disinformation, including Fletcher Schoen and Christopher J. Lamb.[137] Interagency collaboration and analytical contributions by various experts are crucial to preventing the spread of Russian state-sponsored historical narratives and disinformation and, most importantly, limiting their effects on Western academics and new generations of students. Inspired by Russian agents of influence to embrace hostile and false narratives about either Ukraine, the United States, or other Western countries and to adopt a critical stance toward their own governments that sometimes borders on the treasonous, they can produce little of intellectual value, and can only harm the causes of democratic state and nation-building.

---

137 Fletcher Schoen and Christopher J. Lamb, 'Deception, Disinformation, and Strategic Communications: How One Interagency Group Made a Major Difference,' *Strategic Perspectives* 11 (June 2012) (Washington, D.C.: Center for Strategic Research/Institute for National Strategic Studies/National Defense University). Available at https://ndupress.ndu.edu/Portals/68/Documents/stratperspective/inss/Strategic-Perspectives-11.pdf, p. 120.

"Academic Imperialism"
Writing Soviet and Post-Soviet History without Ukraine

Sergei I. Zhuk

The international humanities and social sciences community experienced real epistemological shock and overall cultural division after the Euromaidan Revolution in 2013–2014. Not only experts in Slavic Studies (especially former Western Sovietologists), but also specialists in American and European Studies (especially Americanists) became divided on the issue of what attitude to take towards the Ukrainian war of independence against Russian aggression, especially after President Vladimir Putin's Russia annexed Crimea and invaded Ukraine's Donbas. Paradoxically, an influential part of this international community demonstrated an obvious "Russo-centrism" (or Russophilia) and outrageous Ukrainophobia, trying to justify Putin's politics in Ukraine and criticizing Ukraine and Ukrainians. To this day, many Western and Russian scholars still do not want to face the "inconvenient truth" about direct Russian military aggression and interference in the domestic politics of independent Ukraine, long before Russia's full-scale invasion of Ukraine on 24 February 2022.[1] Why did this happen? What were the reasons for this rise in pro-Russian and anti-Ukrainian sentiments among so many Western and post-Soviet academics? Were these Russophile feelings connected to the very important

---

1   I have already tried to discuss some issues of this divide in both English and Russian: Sergei I. Zhuk, 'Ukrainian Maidan as the Last Anti-Soviet Revolution, or the Methodological Dangers of Soviet Nostalgia (Notes of an American Ukrainian Historian from Inside the Field of Russian Studies in the USA),' *Ab Imperio*, no. 3 (2014), pp. 195–208; and *idem*, "Ukrainskii Maidan i epistemologicheskie opasnosti sovetskoi nostal'gii," *Historians.in.ua* website, 6 April 2015. Available at http://www.historians.in.ua/index.php/en/dyskusiya/1482-sergej-zhuk-ukrainskij-majdan-i-epistemologicheskie-opasnosti-sovetskoj-nostalgii.

epistemological and geo-political changes affecting the humanities? This article is an attempt to answer these questions.

As a former Soviet Ukrainian historian who moved from post-Soviet Ukraine to the United States in 1997, I had problematic relations with my cultural, professional, and ethnic identity. Despite an annual obligatory summer visit to Ukraine with my family and travels between my hometown of Dnipropetrovsk and Moscow, I felt more and more distanced from the real practical issues of everyday life in both Ukraine and Russia, identifying with my American colleagues and professional historians, sharing common professional interests and cultural practices with Americans, and gradually adjusting to American college life and values. Moreover, as a former Soviet historian-Americanist, who became a historian of imperial Russia and the Soviet Union in the US, I experienced an identity crisis, attempting to unite in my professional life skills and practices from both historical fields. Since the disintegration of the Soviet Union in 1991, like many of my Soviet co-citizens, I had lived through another crisis of identity. All this had exacerbated my cultural distancing from my Americanist colleagues in Moscow, for whom I was just another "annoying provincial Ukrainian scholar."

Despite my native Russian-language skills (I spoke Russian at home), my Moscow colleagues always demonstrated a very condescending attitude to people like myself, who they viewed as (I paraphrase what Dr Boris Shpotov from the Institute of World History said about Ukrainian scholars in 1999) "narrow-minded stupid provincials, claiming that they know something in history..."[2] Therefore, I began distancing myself from my Moscow colleagues, shaping my own intellectual identity vis-à-vis Muscovites. This mental distancing from Moscow gradually increased during the 1990s when I began traveling abroad using Western research grants. I felt more Ukrainian and less Soviet than my former Moscow colleagues whom I left behind. What was shocking for me that while I was

---

2   I quote Boris Shpotov, speaking during the International Conference in Connection with the Bicentennial of the Russian-American Company, 1799–1999: Institute of World History, Russian Academy of Sciences, Moscow, September 7, 1999.

"ACADEMIC IMPERIALISM" 63

losing ties with my Soviet past during those years, all my Moscow colleagues, whom I was visiting almost every summer, expressed stronger and stronger feelings of "Soviet nostalgia" and blamed the West, and especially America, for the dissolution of the USSR and deterioration of their lives in post-Soviet Russia. Moreover, many of my Moscow friends also began blaming Ukrainians (including Russian speakers like myself), for betraying East Slavic unity, destroying the Soviet Union, and voting in 1991 for the independence of Ukraine (which for them is still a "historical part of sacred Orthodox Christian Russia ... with Kiev—a center of Holy Russia").[3]

Paradoxically, this kind of "Soviet nostalgia" and underlying accusations of Ukrainian "betrayal" became evident also in the writing and professional practices of my American colleagues—"Russianists" and "Sovietologists"—experts in Russian, Soviet, and post-Soviet studies. When I began my new academic and teaching career as an American "Russian" historian in 2002 in the US I encountered (surprisingly) a certain negative reaction to my Ukrainian identity and my research topics, which were related to my research work, based on material from my native Ukraine. Thus, when I finished my first American book, a cultural history of Ukrainian peasant evangelicals in the southern Ukrainian provinces of the late Russian Empire, and offered it for publication under the title *Ukraine's Lost Reformation*, all my American reviewers immediately suggested it be replaced with a new title, *Russia's Lost Reformation*, arguing that nobody would be attracted to a book title containing a name of the new "unknown" nation of Ukraine.[4] As the late Richard Stites joked in November 2008:

> Sergei, you will be surprised to see how Russian-centered and Moscow-focused are all your American friends, historians of the Russian Empire and Soviet Union. Your new Ukrainian nation with your provincial interests just

---

3   I quote Dr Sviatoslav Dmitriev, Associate Professor of Ancient History at Ball State University, my Russian colleague (originally from Moscow), who took a very pro-Putin, anti-Ukrainian, Russian chauvinistic position in our discussion of the Ukrainian-Russian crisis, on January 30, 2014, in Muncie, Indiana.

4   I refer to Sergei I. Zhuk, *Russia's Lost Reformation: Peasants, Millennialism and Radical Sects in Southern Russia and Ukraine, 1830-1917* (Baltimore, MD: the Johns Hopkins University Press & Washington, D.C.: Woodrow Wilson Center Press, 2004).

does not fit such an historical "imperial" imagination. Many of these American historians still prefer the traditional perception of all multi-national history of the entire post-Soviet space from a Moscow and *Velikorusskaia* (Great Russian) point of view. They still live in their own historical nostalgic space in the Leonid Brezhnev era in Moscow or Leningrad, when they were young scholars, recalling meetings and adventures with their (mainly) Russian friends and colleagues, who are still communicating with them, strengthening their nostalgia for the Soviet past.[5]

To some extent, my second American book became another challenge to the so-called "Muscovite paradigm" in both post-Soviet Russian and Western historiography, which dominated mainstream history writing in American studies of the Soviet Union. This book was a history of Soviet cultural consumption and identity formation—not in Moscow, or in Soviet Russia, but rather in one industrial city in Soviet Ukraine, my "provincial" hometown of Dnipropetrovsk. Portraying the cultural situation in this multinational Soviet Ukrainian city during the Brezhnev era, I traced the gradual formation of local Ukrainian identity vis-à-vis the Soviet identity imposed by Moscow, even before the collapse of the Soviet Union.[6] But despite my idealization of Ukrainian identity in this book, I still had some ambiguous feelings about Ukraine, especially after 2010, observing rule by the most corrupt (in the entire Ukrainian history) regime of President Viktor Yanukovych. I did not like Putin's Russian militocracy, but I also disliked the high levels of corruption in Ukraine.

My ambivalence towards Ukraine changed dramatically after November 2013. By the end of February of 2014 following revolutionary events on television and via the internet, and communicating with my relatives and friends in Ukraine, I had begun feeling a tremendous respect for the Ukrainian people who challenged the

---

5   I quote my interview with Richard Stites, Philadelphia, at the 40th National Convention of the American Association for Advanced Slavic Studies, November 21, 2008. Compare with various case studies in Samuel H. Baron and Cathy A. Frierson (eds), *Adventures in Russian Historical Research: Reminiscences of American Scholars from the Cold War to the Present* (Armonk, NY: M.E. Sharpe, 2003).
6   I refer to Sergei I. Zhuk, *Rock and Roll in the Rocket City: The West, Identity, and Ideology in Soviet Dniepropetrovsk, 1960-1985* (Baltimore, MD: Johns Hopkins University Press & Washington, D.C.: Woodrow Wilson Center Press, 2010).

corrupt regime and overthrew Yanukovych and the Donetsk criminal clan. Moreover, I felt a certain pride that my hometown of Dnipropetrovsk, led by a group of talented and patriotic Jewish-Ukrainian and Russian-speaking oligarchs such as Igor Kolomoiskyy, Gennadii Korban, and Boris Filatov, could suppress pro-Russian separatists and transform my city into a bastion of democracy, cultural and linguistic toleration, and Ukrainian patriotism in the eastern, mainly Russian-speaking, region of post-Soviet Ukraine. My entire family (with our Russian, Jewish, Ukrainian, and Greek roots) in the United States became not only new patriots of post-Maidan anti-Soviet Ukraine, but also loyal followers of our Dnipropetrovsk leaders with their different ethnic and religious backgrounds, such as Jewish businessman Korban, Russian Orthodox Filatov and Dmytro Yarosh, Ukrainian nationalist and head of *Pravyy Sektor* (Right Sector). The Euromaidan Revolution and subsequent political and social upheaval in our hometown dealt a final blow to Soviet identity. Moreover, watching Russian television and communicating with our Moscow relatives after November 2013 became a real cultural shock for our family as well. For us the Euromaidan was a revolution of dignity, a revolt against the corrupt post-Soviet oligarchy, and we expected that ordinary Russians, who suffered from a similar oligarchic regime, would support such a revolution and express solidarity with it.

But alas, the Russian media and my Moscow relatives and colleagues adopted a very anti-Ukrainian position. And the Russian leadership began open military aggression against Ukraine when it annexed Crimea in March 2014. The long campaign of demonizing the Euromaidan Revolution, which had begun in Putin's controlled Russian media in November 2013, kept portraying the brutality and violence of "fascist" Stepan Bandera followers who participated in an "American conspiracy" against Russia, claiming that they were killing and torturing innocent Russians and Jews in Ukraine. As a result of this massive and professionally organized anti-Ukrainian propaganda, not only ordinary Russian consumers of TV information, but also Russian intellectual leaders and prominent representatives of the Russian cultural establishment, such as famous film director Nikita Mikhalkov and orchestra conductor Valery

Gergiev, supported Putin's aggression against Ukraine in the name of the liberation of "all Russians in Ukraine, who are threatened by [Stepan] Bandera fascists."[7]

Even the famous skeptic of Putin's politics, the last Soviet President Mikhail Gorbachev, applauded Putin's annexation of Crimea as the restoration of "historical justice" by collecting "Russian" territories.[8] Meanwhile, in response to Western sanctions, a popular presenter on Russian state television, Dmitrii Kiselev explained to his viewers that Russia is the only country capable of turning the United States into "radioactive ashes."[9] He then went on to use animated maps to show exactly how Russia would automatically respond with nuclear missiles if its command and control were attacked or disabled by a U.S. attack. Many Russian and Western scholars and experts, such as Stephen F. Cohen and Henry Kissinger still talk of the "justified historical role" of Russia in protecting her geopolitical interests, even if this meant the dismembering of Ukraine. Some of them justified their support for Putin through claims about Russia's "historical rights" to territories in Ukraine.[10]

Putin's imperial claims to Ukraine, his imperialist project of *Novorossiia* (the very word is derived from late imperial Russian vocabulary!) in eastern-southern Ukraine, and the sending of Russian military troops to the Donbas (Donetsk and Luhansk *oblasts*) was infused with Soviet nostalgic rhetoric and symbols. Pro-Russian proxies in the Donbas always referred to Soviet symbolism and used Soviet cultural practices. The ongoing war against Ukraine is presented as a kind of sequel to the Great Patriotic War when Soviet

---

7   I quote Dr Dmitriev.
8   See: "To Ukrainians, Gorbachev Remained an 'Imperialist'," *Voice of America*, August 31, 2022. Available at https://www.voanews.com/a/to-ukrainians-gorbachev-remains-an-imperialist-/6724612.html.
9   See: Robert Mackey, 'Russia Could Still Turn U.S. 'Into Radioactive Dust,' News Anchor in Moscow Reminds Viewers,' *New York Times*, March 16, 2014. Available at https://archive.nytimes.com/thelede.blogs.nytimes.com/2014/03/16/russia-could-still-turn-the-u-s-into-radioactive-dust-news-anchor-in-moscow-reminds-viewers/.
10 Not everybody in Russia supports Putin's policy. Such Russian historians like Andrei Zubov and rock musicians like Andrei Makarevich (and many other Russian intellectuals like Boris Akunin, Vladimir Sorokin, and Liudmila Ulitskaia) criticized publicly Putin's aggression against Ukraine.

Donbas fought the Nazis in 1941–45. Russian instructors and volunteers, like Igor Girkin, who became leaders of pro-Russian proxies in Donbas in Spring 2014, even used the discursive practices of the Great Patriotic War (including Stalin's orders in 1941 to execute criminals on occupied territories) when they controlled the city of Slovyansk in Donetsk *oblast*. For many Muscovites and residents of the Donbas, the best (and idealized) period of their life was the Leonid Brezhnev era in the 1970s and first half of the 1980s. They deny the historical existence of independent Ukraine.

Surprisingly for me, a similar rejection of Ukraine's rights to protect its territorial integrity in both Crimea and the Donbas was found among some of my American colleagues, historians of Russia and the Soviet Union. In spring 2014, this was also evident when I attempted to disseminate information about the Euromaidan, Crimea, and Putin's military aggression at the Midwest Russian History Workshop and other venues of American Slavic and East European Studies. These American Slavists criticized my pro-Ukrainian position as "nationalistic," repeating Russian mass media clichés about the supposed "fascist, anti-Jewish and anti-Russian" goals of the Euromaidan, defending and justifying repression by the Yanukovych regime and security forces against protestors and activists. A year after the Euromaidan I witnessed during academic events in Barcelona, Berlin, and Rome some of my American and European colleagues justifying Putin's anti-Ukrainian politics as the "anti-imperialist and anti-American reaction of the Russian people."[11]

One of the frequent visitors to the United States, Russian historian Vyacheslav Nikonov, who served as Executive Director of

---

11 Many Western historians had already described the rise and danger of Russian nationalism and Soviet (post-Soviet) imperialism. See Ben Fowkes, 'The National Question in the Soviet Union under Leonid Brezhnev: Policy and Response' In: Edwin Bacon and Mark Sandle (eds), *Brezhnev Reconsidered* (New York: Palgrave Macmillan, 2002), pp. 68–89; Gerhard Simon, *Nationalism and Policy toward the Nationalities in the Soviet Union: From Totalitarian Dictatorship to Post-Stalinist Society*, translated by Karen Forster and Oswald Forster (Boulder: Westview Press, 1991); and Yitzhak M. Brudny, *Reinventing Russia: Russian Nationalism and the Soviet State, 1953–1991* (Cambridge, MA: Harvard University Press, 1998).

the *Russkii Mir* (Russian World) Foundation from 2007 to 2012, was explicitly anti-Ukrainian and anti-American, criticizing the Orange Revolution and Euromaidan Revolution as "American conspiracies against Russia." In his 2015 textbook, whose publication was funded by *Russkii Mir* Foundation, Nikonov presented the United States as the major geo-political enemy of Russia. He interpreted events in Georgia, Moldova, and Ukraine since the disintegration of the Soviet Union as a product of "US expansionism." According to Nikonov, the US major goal is to "weaken" and "punish" Russia using recent developments in Ukraine. Moreover, Nikonov supports Russian expansionism, Russia's annexation of Crimea, and Russian military aggression against eastern Ukraine. He justifies Russian aggressive policies in Ukraine as the "historical mission" of the Russian state to "defend" its state and national interests against "American imperialism" in Eastern Europe and in post-Soviet geopolitical space.[12] Unfortunately, many young Russian Americanists also follow Nikonov in their criticism of US "public diplomacy," accusing the US of being behind "Ukrainian revolutions." Thus, in her recent research, Natalia Tsvetkova, a representative of the "Leningrad school of American Studies of Aleksander Fursenko" accuses US politicians of seeking to "take out" Ukraine from the Russian sphere of influence since 2003–2004. According to her study, US "public diplomacy" focused its efforts on pro-Western Ukrainian youth, trying to organize the so-called "Orange" and other anti-Russian revolutions in Ukraine. Like Nikonov, Tsvetkova repeats old concepts about "America's anti-Russian conspiracy." She emphasized that since 2003 "the USA was able to create [in Ukraine] a solid human potential, oriented to the West."[13]

Putin has attempted to reproduce the "Russian state-builder" approach towards the US, which was always supported by Soviet

---

12 V. A. Nikonov, *Sovremennyi mir i ego istoki* (Moscow: Izd-vo Moskovskogo universiteta, 2015), esp. pp. 302–04.
13 N. A. Tsvetkova, 'Publichnaia diplomatiia SShA: ot kholodnoi voiny k novoi kholodnoi voine' In: Vladimir V. Noskov (ed.), *Rossiia i SShA: poznavaia drug druga. Sbornik pamiati akademika Aleksandra Aleksandrovicha Fursenko* (Saint-Petersburg: Nestor-Istoriia, 2015), pp. 82–97, citations are from p. 92 and p. 93.

Americanists, such as Nikolai Sivachev and Aleksandr Fursenko. Their former students, like Vyacheslav Nikonov, became the most influential experts in US history and politics in post-Soviet Russia. The imperial ideal of Tsarist Russia mixed with Soviet political and cultural stereotypes shapes not only political, but also academic discourse in the post-Soviet space.[14]

As a historian of cultural consumption and knowledge production, I find one of the most important and interesting among the many different reasons for these pro-Russian and anti-Ukrainian feelings of American experts in Slavic Studies to be what I call the methodological paradigm of "historiographic Soviet nostalgia." In my opinion, this is related to a serious paradigmatic shift in historical analysis during the late Soviet period and the rise of "revisionist" American studies of Soviet and Russian history and culture, especially during the 1990s. Earlier generations of American experts in Soviet studies concentrated on contradictions and problems in late socialist USSR, including corruption, the black market, nationalism, religiosity, and political dissent. After the disintegration of the USSR, scholars began emphasizing their research on everyday life and consumption, dismissing or avoiding serious internal problems and conflicts in late Soviet society. This approach was manifested in a lack of attention to Russian and Soviet imperialist policies against Ukraine.[15]

During the Cold War, especially before the 1980s, Soviet society was presented as a one-dimensional, monolithic, and predictable entity on both sides of the ideological divide in both Soviet studies in the West and in histories of the USSR and Communist Party

---

14 For a more optimistic vision of American studies in post-Soviet Russia, see Ivan Kurilla, 'Reflections from Russia' In: Nicolas Barreyere a.o. (eds), *Historians across Borders: Writing American History in a Golden Age* (Oakland: University of California Press, 2014), pp. 174-180. Compare with an earlier position of another Russian Americanist, a talented historian and anthropologist, Valery Tishkov, who had supported openly the idea of the *Russkii mir* and diplomacy of Putin in post-Soviet space as early as May of 2007. See further Michael Moser, *Language Policy and the Discourse on Languages in Ukraine under President Viktor Yanukovych (25 February 2010 – 28 October 2012)* (Stuttgart: *ibidem* Press, 2014), p. 142.

15 Of course, many colleagues of mine still addressed these issues. See, e.g., Yitzhak M. Brudny, *Reinventing Russia: Russian Nationalism and the Soviet State, 1953-1991* (Cambridge, MA: Harvard University Press, 1998).

in the Soviet Union. Despite the prevailing different theoretical models of interpretation—a totalitarian and modernization model in the West and Orthodox Marxism-Leninism in the USSR—Soviet studies in both the capitalist West and socialist East explained major developments in similar ways, emphasizing mostly political, economic, and ideological aspects against the backdrop of a never-changing stable Soviet civilization.

During the 1970s and the 1980s, the sudden rise of the "revisionist" school in Western historiography, especially studies by Sheila Fitzpatrick, Stephen F. Cohen, Leopold Haimson, and other Western scholars, revealed new data from the Soviet and Russian archives and introduced fresh ideas, social theories, and cultural history. A new generation of Western scholars, including Richard Stites, Vera Dunham, Laura Engelstein, Jeffrey Brooks, and Denise Youngblood replaced the traditional one-dimensional interpretation of Soviet society with an approach that took into account different cultural practices which they had "discovered" in the everyday life of Soviet peoples. This approach changed the development of Soviet studies, and eventually contributed to the popularity of cultural studies among both Western and post-Soviet historians.[16]

The rise of the Western "revisionist" school was further stimulated by *perestroika* and then by the disintegration of the Soviet Union in 1991. During this period new archival collections were opened in the Soviet Union and post-Soviet states. Many former Soviet scholars could travel abroad and use funding and resources

---

16   On revisionism in American Soviet studies, see David C. Engerman, *Know Your Enemy: The Rise and Fall of America's Soviet Experts* (New York: Oxford University Press, 2009), pp. 9, 286, 294, 305–08. On the new popularity of cultural studies and on mutual influences between western and former Soviet scholars, see: Laura Engelstein, 'Culture, Culture Everywhere: Interpretations of Modern Russia, Across the 1991 Divide,' *Kritika*, no. 2 (Spring 2001), pp. 363–93. Soviet historians also were influenced by the charismatic medievalist Aron Gurevich who popularized the ideas of the French *Annales* among the Soviet reading audience; see Roger D. Markwick, 'Cultural History under Khrushchev and Brezhnev: From Social Psychology to *Mentalités*,' *The Russian Review*, vol. 65, no.2 (April 2006), pp. 283–301. See also Catriona Kelly, Hilary Pilkington, David Shepherd, and Vadim Volkov, 'Introduction: Why Cultural Studies' In: Catriona Kelly and David Shepherd (eds), *Russian Cultural Studies: An Introduction* (New York: Oxford University Press, 1998), pp. 1–17.

"ACADEMIC IMPERIALISM"   71

from Western research centers. Scholarly dialogue and collaboration between Western and former Soviet scholars were established. Many talented Soviet intellectuals with different professional backgrounds, such as Serhii Plokhy (trained as a historian of early modern Ukraine), Yuri Slezkine (originally a linguist specializing in Portuguese), Irina Paperno (trained as an expert in Russian literature and associated with the Tartu school), Dmitry Shlapentokh (a historian of France and Russia), Alexei Yurchak (a radio engineer and producer for famous Leningrad rock bands), Andrei Znamenski (a historian of American Native Peoples), Vladislav Zubok (trained as an expert in US politics), and myself (a historian of colonial British America), left their post-Soviet countries and joined Western academia where they taught Soviet, Russian, and Ukrainian studies in US universities. This experience contributed to expanding and changing the field of Soviet and post-Soviet studies. At the same time, Sovietology in the West was losing its traditional anti-Soviet critical focus and began to stress conformist features in Soviet historiography.[17]

The first serious theoretical justification for the new paradigmatic shift in the direction of the conformist, non-confrontational, non-conflict approaches for American studies of Soviet society during the Cold War was the work of a Soviet émigré from Leningrad, anthropologist Alexei Yurchak. He attempted to explore ideological aspects of everyday life, theories, and practices in the latter part of the USSR, and discursive practices and identity formation in post-Stalin Soviet society. Yurchak investigated "internal shifts that were emerging within the Soviet system during late socialism at the level of discourse, ideology, and knowledge but that became apparent for what they were only much later, when the system collapsed."[18] According to Yurchak, after Khrushchev's de-Stalinization, communist ideology in Soviet society underwent a so-called *performative shift*, when Stalin's authoritative discourse lost its importance, becoming mere rituals for many Soviet people, who tried

---

17   See Engelstein, 'Culture, Culture Everywhere,' pp. 389ff.
18   Alexei Yurchak, *Everything Was Forever, Until It Was No More: The Last Soviet Generation* (Princeton, NJ: Princeton University Press, 2005), 32.

to exist outside this communist ideological discourse. He primarily used material from his hometown of Leningrad to show how different forms of cultural production and consumption in the late Soviet period, especially rock music and Western fashions, influenced Soviet youth, including *Komsomol* activists and officials. According to Alexei Yurchak, "rock and roll culture" became a part of "nonofficial discourses and practices in late socialism." In contrast to authors such as Thomas Cushman, who insisted on the countercultural character of rock music in the Soviet Union, Yurchak argued that non-official practices (such as listening and playing rock music) involved:

> not so much countering, resisting, or opposing state power as simply *avoiding* it and carving out symbolically meaningful spaces and identities away from it. This avoidance included passive conformity to state power, the pretence of supporting it, obliviousness to its ideological messages, and simultaneous involvement in completely incongruent practices and meanings behind its back.[19]

The entire theoretical framework of Yurchak's study was directly influenced by French thinkers such as Michel Foucault and Michel de Certeau. According to de Certeau, in modern European society, "imposed knowledge and symbolisms become objects manipulated by practitioners who have not produced them." In de Certeau's interpretation, such practitioners usually subverted practices and representations that were imposed on them from within, not by rejecting them or transforming them (though that occurred as well), but in many other ways. Practitioners of knowledge production "metaphorised the dominant order: they made it function in another register. They remained within the system which they assimilated and which assimilated them externally. They diverted it

---

19 *Ibid.*, 36–76. This thesis had already been criticized and analyzed: Sheila Fitzpatrick in *London Review of Books* vol. 28, no. 10 (25 May 2006), pp. 18–20; Kevin Platt and Benjamin Nathans in *Novoe literaturnoe obozrenie* no. 101 (2010), pp. 167–84 (in Russian); and Kevin Platt and Benjamin Nathans, 'Socialist in Form, Indererminate in Content: The Ins and Outs of Late Soviet Culture,' *Ab Imperio* 2 (2011), pp. 301–23 (in English).

without leaving it."[20] These ideas, combined with Mikhail Bakhtin's concept of authoritative discourse, became the foundation of Yurchak's theoretical framework.[21]

As Yurchak argued, the obsession with Western cultural products became the most important feature of cultural consumption in the closed socialist society of the post-Stalin era. Yurchak focused in particular on the cultural and discursive phenomenon known among social scientists as the "Imaginary West."[22] According to Yurchak, the "Imaginary West" is a:

> local cultural construct and imaginary that was based on the forms of knowledge and aesthetics associated with the "West," but does not necessarily refer to any "real" West, which also contributed to "deterritorializing" the world of everyday socialism from within.[23]

Yurchak rejected previous readings that emphasized the confrontational and countercultural character of the "imaginary West" in Soviet cultural consumption. He instead offered a consensual and conformist interpretation of this metaphor. Using the ideas of the Russian cultural critic Tatyana Cherednichenko, Yurchak attempted to show how Western music (as a part of the "Imaginary

---

20   Michel de Certeau, *The Practice of Everyday Life*, trans. Steven Rendall (Berkeley: University of California Press, 1989 [1st pr.: 1984]), p. 31.
21   As he explained, "for Bakhtin, authoritative discourse coheres around a strict external idea or dogma... and occupies a particular position within the discursive regime of a period," while "all other types of discourse are organized around it"; Yurchak, *Everything Was Forever*, p. 14. See especially an American edition of Bakhtin's work with insightful comments: Mikhail Bakhtin, *The Dialogical Imagination: Four Essays by Mikhail Bakhtin*, ed. Michael Holquist (Austin: University of Texas Press, 1994), pp. 342–43. Compare with Slava Gerovitch, *From Newspeak to Cyberspeak: A History of Soviet Cybernetics* (Cambridge, Mass.: The MIT Press, 2004); Stephen Lovell, *The Russian Reading Revolution: Print Culture in the Soviet and Post-Soviet Eras* (New York: St. Martin's, 2000); and Juliane Fürst, *Stalin's Last Generation: Soviet Post-War Youth and the Emergence of Mature Socialism* (New York: Oxford University Press, 2010).
22   See how various scholars used this metaphor before Yurchak: Gordon K. Lewis, *The Growth of the Modern West Indies* (New York: Monthly Review Press, 1968), pp. 57ff.; and Robert D. English, *Russia and the Idea of the West: Gorbachev, Intellectuals, and the End of the Cold Wa*r (New York: Columbia University Press, 2000), p. 22.
23   Yurchak, *Everything Was Forever*, pp. 34–35, 161–62.

West") contributed to the "production of a whole generational identity" for the last Soviet generation.[24]

At the same time, he ignored problems of regional, national, and religious identities which were shaped by the consumption of Western cultural products in various parts of the Soviet Union. Yurchak disregarded the importance of the idea of the West for political dissent in the USSR. Yurchak's interpretation exaggerated the role of discursive practices and in his interpretation visual elements, especially Western films, lost their role of influencing both ideological discourse and local identity among Soviet consumers.[25]

As a result, Yurchak interprets Soviet society during late socialism as a society void of any serious social problems or conflicts. Prevalent problems during this period such as the involvement of Soviet officials in the activities of the black market, Russification, street gang culture, popular religiosity, nationalism, and anti-Semitism are ignored in Yurchak's study. Yurchak also underestimated the importance of the KGB and police interference in cultural consumption, which especially affected provincial cities where the majority of the Soviet youth lived.[26]

Yurchak's study attracted many American and post-Soviet scholars who were tired of the traditional emphasis on political dissidents and who wanted the "more positive and friendly

---

24   See in Tatyana Cherednichenko, *Tipologiia sovetskoi massovoi kul'tury. Mezhdu Brezhnevym i Pugachevoi* (Moscow: RIK Kul'tura, 1994).
25   Most of Yurchak's material and interviews are from the Leningrad area. Moreover, the majority of his material and information came from the educated elite of this city, the loyal representatives of the Soviet middle and upper classes, and conformist Soviet intellectuals from Leningrad. He entirely ignores the working-class youth, the major consumers of heavy metal and adventure films in the Soviet society. Another problem with Yurchak's study is his uncritical attitude to interviews. Many of Yurchak's interviewees tended to idealize or exaggerate their "socialist experience" as a time without conflicts in contrast to the brutal reality of "bandit capitalism" during the Yeltsin era. In many cases, using his "speech acts" approaches, Yurchak took his interviewees' information at face value, uncritically, without checking archival sources. On his methods, see Yurchak, *Everything Was Forever*, pp. 29-33.
26   Even the list of forbidden rock bands, which Yurchak published in his book, came from the Ukrainian provincial town of Nikolaev. With only a few exceptions, all Yurchak's information derived from his hometown, Leningrad/St. Petersburg; see Yurchak, *Everything Was Forever*, pp. 214-15.

approaches towards defeated and humiliated (by the West) post-Soviet Russians, who lost their Soviet Empire at the end of the Cold War."[27] Yurchak's ideas influenced new studies about post-war Soviet history, especially the history of Soviet youth. One of the best studies of post-war Soviet youth, *Stalin's Last Generation*, drew on Yurchak's ideas and approaches. According to Juliane Fürst (who follows Yurchak verbatim), the result of this imagination was the creation of a socialist "modernist" culture during late Stalinism as a "complicated conglomerate of performative practices, collective habits, individual mechanisms of survival, strategies of self-improvement, and segregated spaces for action, all of which were linked and interacted with each other in the person of the Soviet subject and citizen."[28]

In contrast to Yurchak, Fürst used not only material from the Soviet Russian cities, such as Leningrad and Moscow; she also introduced archival documents from Russian and Ukrainian regional archives and used these to create a lively picture of cultural consumption among Soviet young people during the late 1940s and early 1950s. She enriched the historiographical terrain of late Stalinism, based on classical studies by Soviet and Russian historian Elena Zubkova while adding new concepts from Western cultural studies, including Yurchak's ideas.[29]

Citing Yurchak's work has become practically obligatory in recent Soviet and post-Soviet studies in the West, especially in the US. Even good oral history studies by Donald Raleigh, drawing on Yurchak, continue to stress the non-conflict "positive" side of Soviet history. To my knowledge, Raleigh's research about the last Soviet generation was the first Soviet oral history study by a Western scholar to be based exclusively on personal oral interviews, using only primary sources and oral history methodology in presenting

---

27 Author's interview with Richard Stites, Philadelphia, 21 November 2008. For an example of a defense of Yurchak against my criticism, see a review essay by a young Russian scholar: A. V. Golubev, "V poiskakh vnenakhodimosti," *Istoricheskaia ekspertiza* no. 1 (2015), esp. pp. 20-21.
28 Fürst, *Stalin's Last Generation*, p. 26.
29 *Ibid.*, pp. 25, 100, 103, 297, 301, 362. Compare with Elena Zubkova, *Russia after the War: Hopes, Illusions, and Disappointments, 1945-1957*, trans. and ed. Hugh Ragdale (Armonk, New York: M. E. Sharpe, 1998).

and explaining these interviews.[30] For his second book, published in 2012, Raleigh interviewed sixty 1967 graduates of two Soviet magnet schools with intensive instruction in English, one in Moscow and one in the provincial city of Saratov. This project began as an extension of his previous book, which contained only interviews conducted in Saratov among former graduates from Saratov's school No. 42.[31] Some of the major characters from the first book and their interviews played an important role in his later book as well.

What is more original in the 2012 book is the addition of interviews with Muscovites which created an important social and cultural dimension to the historical comparison of two different, but elitist cohorts of Soviet students from elite schools specializing in English—one from the "closed" Soviet provincial city of Saratov, and another from the centre of Soviet civilization, a capital city of Moscow. Unfortunately, serious social and political problems, including the growth of Russian nationalism and the exclusive position of Muscovites in the Soviet cultural hierarchy, which are the psychological foundations for Soviet Russian imperialism, completely disappeared from view in Raleigh's oral history of "Soviet baby boomers." At the same time, both Fürst and Raleigh adopted a principled anti-Putin and pro-Ukrainian position. Moreover, during the summer of 2017, Raleigh visited the city of Dnipro where he presented his new research project on a biography of Brezhnev for his Ukrainian colleagues and expressed his solidarity and sympathy with Ukrainian patriots.[32]

Unfortunately, many of Fürst's and Raleigh's colleagues did not share these pro-Ukrainian sympathies. Some of their colleagues continue to prefer an image of Soviet society without social conflicts coupled with an obvious nostalgia for and idealization of the Soviet

---

30   Donald J. Raleigh, *Soviet Baby Boomers: An Oral History of Russia's Cold War Generation* (New York: Oxford University Press, 2012).
31   Donald J. Raleigh (ed.), *Russia's Sputnik Generation: Soviet Baby Boomers Talk about Their Lives* (Bloomington, IN: Indiana University Press, 2006).
32   See information about Professor Raleigh's presentation to the Dniprovsky Historical Club in the city of Dnipro, July 16, 2017. Available at http://tkuma.dp.ua/en/outreach-activities/dniprovsky-historical-club/1602-zanyattya-dniprovskogo-istorichnogo-klubu-z-prof-donaldom-rejli.

past, and rejection of Western influences on Soviet developments, even during the Brezhnev era.[33] A majority of the recent Anglo-American studies on Soviet national politics still represent a "Moscow-centric" point of view by openly ignoring the non-Russian republics.[34]

For many American experts in Soviet studies, the non-confrontational, conformist, and "emotionally positive" approaches to an analysis of Soviet and post-Soviet society and culture offered by Yurchak became the most popular theoretical model, leading to very dangerous epistemological and methodological consequences. This "conformist" model led to the ignoring of the "brewing" problems of Soviet Russian imperialism and Russian nationalism. Confronted with the "unexpected" Euromaidan Revolution in Ukraine, American Sovietologists and historians of Russia and the Soviet Union were not ready to discard their historiographical concepts. Therefore, they distanced themselves from "controversial" Ukrainian developments by denying their historical validity and focusing instead on more familiar and predictable developments in post-Soviet Russia. For the historical "nostalgic" imagination of the experts in Soviet and post-Soviet studies, the phenomenon of the Euromaidan rejected and destroyed the traditionally accepted Moscow-centred and Russian-focused approaches to political, social, cultural, and economic developments in the post-Soviet space. Eventually, epistemological Soviet nostalgia led scholars, like Richard Sakwa and Nikolai Petro, to open support and justification of Putin's foreign and security policies in Eurasia and Eastern Europe.[35] Many American Sovietologists still dismiss problems of

---

33 See especially: Alexey Golubev and Olga Smolyak, 'Making Selves Through Making Things: Soviet Do-It-Yourself Culture and Practices of Late Soviet Subjectivation,' *Cahiers du monde russe* vol. 54, no. 3–4 (July–December 2013), pp. 517–41.
34 See, e. g., Jeremy Smith, *Red Nations: The Nationalities Experience in and after the USSR* (New York: Cambridge University Press, 2013), and its criticism for obvious pro-Russian bias by Audrey L. Altstadt in *American Historical Review* vol. 120, no. 1 (February 2015) pp. 358–359.
35 See especially Richard Sakwa, *Frontline Ukraine: Crisis in the Borderlands* (London: I.B. Tauris, 2016) and Nikolai Petro, 'Understanding the Other Ukraine: Identity and Allegiance in Russophone Ukraine' In: Agnieszka Pikulicka-

Russian/Soviet imperialist politics, which led to a genocide of the Ukrainian nation. One of them, Stephen Kotkin, professor of history at Princeton University, who wrote a trilogy about Stalin's life, completely ignores the Ukrainian Holodomor, a famine artificially created by the Stalinist regime, which killed at least 5 million Ukrainians in 1932–33. Kotkin's students, such as Tarik Cyril Amar, not only openly support Putin's regime and its war against independent Ukraine, but also work for the Russian propagandist television station RT (Russia Today), promoting Russian imperialist and genocidal ideas.[36]

In 2005, Nikolai Bolkhovitinov, a Russian Soviet historian-Americanist and author of path-breaking studies about the beginnings of Russian–American relations, joked about Russian historians in the US:

> Nothing has changed in the Russian intellectual mindset of our specialists in American history since the times of Nicholas I. These people still dream about the restoration of the strong imperial Russian state, despising their Slavic brothers in Ukraine and Belarus' and hating "imperialist" America, which in their imagination served the image of a Russian enemy, at least since 1917. They developed a so-called "imperial complex," which affected all Russian academia, especially the humanities, including Russian *Amerikanistika* (American Studies).[37]

During the mid-1970s, as he later recalled, Ukrainian Americanist historian Arnold Shlepakov encountered manifestations of Russian nationalism among his Moscow and Leningrad colleagues.

> For many years, during my visits to Moscow, I was used to a more relaxed, liberal, and even cosmopolitan atmosphere in Moscow, especially during unofficial meetings with Russian intellectuals. I still recalled how open-

---

Wilczewska & Richard Sakwa (eds.), *Ukraine and Russia: People, Politics, Propaganda and Perspectives* (Bristol: E-International Relations, 2015), pp. 19–35.

36 See Tarik Cyril Amar, 'Politics, Starvation, and Memory: A Critique of Red Famine,' *Kritika*, vol. 20, no. 1 (Winter 2019), p. 145 and examples such as the following: Tarik Cyril Amar, 'Russia is Right: The West Promised Not to Enlarge NATO and These Promises were Broken,' *RT*, January 15, 2022. Available at https://www.rt.com/russia/546074-russia-nato-relations-lie/; and 'The Origins of Ukraine's Fascists and Why It Matters, with Historian Tarik Cyril Amar,' *BreakThrough News*, April 6, 2022. Available at https://www.youtube.com/watch?v=5C7DE2KFJHs.

37 Author's interview with Nikolai Bolkhovitinov, Moscow, July 10, 2005,.

minded and sympathetic toward us were the guests from Kyiv, our colleagues, namely [Georgii] Arbatov, [Nikolai] Inozemtsev, [Nikolai] Bolkhovitinov, [Grigorii] Sevost'ianov and [Valerii] Tishkov. But at the same time, I noticed a rise in strange anti-Ukrainian and anti-Semitic Russian nationalism among a few of my colleagues who were Americanists. Certain phrases or observations made in my presence by Nikolai Sivachev from Moscow and Aleksandr Fursenko from Leningrad, regarding the "humiliation of Great Russia and Russian culture" in Soviet domestic politics and about the omnipresence of *"khokhly"* [a Russian derogatory slur for Ukrainians] — ranging from Brezhnev to the leadership of the Soviet Academy of Sciences — put me on immediate guard. Moreover, they constantly criticized the "total domination of Soviet American Studies by the *evreiskaia shaika* [Jewish gang] from ISKAN [the Institute for US and Canadian Studies in Moscow]," led by "the big Jew" Arbatov. I even complained about this to the first [KGB] department of our Institute in Kyiv. But in 1975, nobody paid attention to my complaints about the expressions of Great Russian chauvinism among my Moscow colleagues.[38]

As another Ukrainian historian-Americanist Leonid Leshchenko has noted, during the 1980s, Shlepakov never forgot "Sivachev's Great Russian chauvinism," and over time he became more careful in his communication with "Muscovites." He tried to distance himself from Sivachev's Moscow State University students who began playing an important role in the studies of the US political system and international relations.[39]

At the same time, Leonid Leshchenko began distancing himself from his Moscow colleagues as well. On occasion he even felt offended by the open expression of condescension and contempt demonstrated by Americanists from MGU, ISKAN, and other Moscow centers devoted to American Studies. As Leshchenko recalled in October 1991, "instead of a word of advice, which we could have used in Kyiv from our Russian colleagues in Moscow, we Ukrainian scholars often received unsubstantiated and condescending criticism of our proposals when Moscow experts simply disregarded our archival findings in Canada or the United States." During his visits to Moscow, Leshchenko witnessed overt public expression of Russian nationalism and anti-Semitism when, for example, during one such visit he overheard Sivachev complaining to his MGU

---

38 Author's interview with Arnold M. Shlepakov, Kyiv, April 4, 1991.
39 Author's interview with Leonid Leshchenko, Kyiv, June 25, 2013.

colleagues that "those Jews and Ukrainians came here and overcrowded Moscow, controlling ISKAN and the Institute of World History." Eventually, he realized that Sivachev was complaining about Arbatov's leadership of ISKAN and the frequent visits to Moscow by Semion Appatov from Odesa (both Arbatov and Appatov were Jewish–Ukrainians). Paradoxically, Sivachev and his MGU colleagues, although anti-Semites, tried to be "very polite and civilized with American visiting scholars (such as Eric Foner), who were of Jewish origin," while at the same time they "openly despised the Ukrainian and Russian Jews from Soviet Ukraine." According to Leshchenko, he could still recall when he felt "unfriendly attitudes toward Ukrainian scholars from Kyiv" which were demonstrated by two Russian historians who were the organizers of American Studies in the Soviet Union. One of these historians was Aleksandr Fursenko from Leningrad while the other historian was Nikolai Sivachev from Moscow. As Leshchenko revealed in 1991, he:

> could remember only four Muscovites who were respectful towards their Ukrainian colleagues, who always tried to assist Ukrainian visitors and invited Ukrainian Americanists to participate in the compilation of Moscow publications devoted to American Studies. These were Arbatov from ISKAN, Inozemtsev from IMEMO, Bolkhovitinov from the Institute of World History and Tishkov from the Institute of Ethnography. In striking contrast to them, Fursenko (from Leningrad), Sivachev, Dementiev and Krasnov (from Moscow), who travelled to the US with Ukrainian colleagues, had always distanced themselves from Soviet Ukrainians and showed only condescension and disrespect to us... Of course, I knew about Shlepakov's official complaint regarding Fursenko's and Sivachev's Great Russian chauvinism and their anti-Semitism. He filed this complaint with our KGB supervisors (from the international department) as early as 1975. But I did not follow Shlepakov's example. I did not complain officially, I simply tried to distance myself from my Moscow colleagues and concentrate on my own research in Kyiv.[40]

It is noteworthy that American colleagues in their official reports also noted expressions of "Russian nationalism," authoritarian "Stalinist" mentality, and an "exclusive" cultural mission among

---

40 I quote my interviews with Leonid Leshchenko, Berlin, Kennedy Institute, Free University Berlin, November 1–3, 1991.

Soviet visitors to the US. One of Fursenko's American hosts described this manifestation of Fursenko's Russian nationalist "Stalinist" identity in the following way:

> ... I found him [Fursenko] occasionally too Russian, almost Stalinist, sometimes too abrupt in his manners, too harsh in his judgments, too convinced of his mission and importance, too inconsiderate and inflexible, even arrogant when his work was at stake, impatient, yet trying very hard to be thoughtful ...[41]

Russian historian Sivachev became the official representative of Soviet Americanists in all the exchange programs during the era of détente. Sivachev was a serious historian-researcher and a very good psychologist who understood what his American partners expected from Soviet guests. In contrast to his image of a "pedantic boring university professor" and "orthodox communist ideologist," used for "domestic consumption" to his Soviet students and colleagues, Sivachev projected a very different image of himself to his American colleagues. For Americans, he always looked optimistic, smiling, open-minded, humorous, and ready for discussions, trying to avoid any ideological debates and distancing himself from explicit communist propagandist clichés.[42] At the same time, his American colleagues noticed demonstrations of "Stalinist Russian anti-Semitic nationalism" in private conversations with Sivachev who behaved like "a stout Russian nationalist (although ethnically he is a Mordovian) ..."[43]

By the 1980s, some former liberal scholars, such as Vladimir Lukin who were protected by Arbatov in ISKAN from KGB persecution, also expressed Slavophile views, similar to what Sivachev considered "normal Russian patriotism." Later these Slavophile-

---

41   Library of Congress. IREX Papers (Hereafter—LC. IREX), RC 21, F 109, letter by Theodore Von Laue, May 15, 1973, pp. 1–2. And he finished his letter with the phrase, "Poor man: his visit in the U.S. was so hectic, too much to be observed and digested! I wonder how he feels now, back in Leningrad, with all his presents and his memories..."
42   Various people, like his former MGU students Vladislav Zubok and Marina Vlasova, and his American colleague Donald Raleigh, noted this.
43   LC. IREX. RC 21, F 17, Vladimir Petrov's letter of 3 February 1975, p. 2.

Americanists became known as "Russian *derzhavniki* (state-builders)."⁴⁴

But overall, during Khrushchev's thaw, through Brezhnev's détente and Gorbachev's *perestroika*, Westernizing concepts of American history became the prevailing trend in Soviet academia. This process was interrupted by humiliation during Boris Yeltsin's presidency and Putin's authoritarianism. The post-Soviet Russian state, with a Russian nationalist and state ideology, pushed Americanist-Westernizers to the margins of post-Soviet academia. Their place was taken by Slavophile *pochvenniki* (those who advocated a return to the "native soil") and *derzhavniki* interpretations of the American past that came to dominate historical perceptions of the US in Putin's Russia. Moreover, the traditional Soviet legacy of confrontational discourse in American studies and a tendency to view Western allies, including Americans, as unreliable, replaced the discourse of cultural dialogue and mutual understanding. In his final notes, written in April 2005, Nikolai Bolkhovitinov again complained about the strong role of the post-Soviet Russian authoritarian state which had destroyed the creativity and autonomy of post-Soviet scholars and restored the "traditional Soviet state business" in the field of American studies:

> [Here in Russia] the same authoritarian regime survived without any significant changes. Our rich country remains an object of looting [by politicians]. There is no hope for progress in the social sciences and humanities. In the field of history we have the same old leaders such as A. Fursenko and worse G. N. Sevost'ianov, who is 89 years old and still rules historical scholarship [in Russia] ... Now we no longer have communist party committees but the political situation in our country has not changed much [compared to Soviet times]. Putin's United Russia party is becoming more like the former monolithic CPSU [Communist Party of the Soviet Union] ...⁴⁵

Many talented post-Soviet Americanists actively engaged in the development of university-level American Studies programs, keeping

---

44 Russian historian Robert Ivanov mentioned this in 1991. See also Robert English, *Russia and the Idea of the West: Gorbachev, Intellectuals, and the End of the Cold War* (New York: Columbia University Press, 2000), pp. 236–237.

45 Nikolai N. Bolkhovitinov, *Vospominaniia* (Moscow, 2005) [unpublished, typewritten manuscript of 62 pages, which begins with the crossed-out title 'Schastlivaia pora detstva,' pp. 60, 61, 62.

alive Russian–American scholarly dialogue and fighting popular anti-Americanism by making frank statements to the mass media. Unfortunately, they face manifold challenges due to the current crisis in Russian–American relations. On the one hand, the demand for professional knowledge about the United States in Russia is fast diminishing and American Studies programs in Russia are being closed down. The post-Soviet authorities no longer need their consultations and expert opinions, unlike during the Soviet period. On the other hand, mass anti-American xenophobia is on the rise, and the Russian authorities have made it one of the cornerstones of the country's national identity. This anti-Americanism is promoted by political journalists without professional training who pretend to be experts in everything related to the US. Far from supporting this campaign, professional Russian Americanists oppose it and fight it through the mass media.[46]

Nevertheless, "state business" is a prominent trend among post-Soviet scholars. Some post-Soviet Americanists in contemporary Russia, such as Andranik Migranian, have revived the "confrontational" position towards the US, blaming Americans for "creating" domestic and international problems for the Russian state. Some of them not only became official advisors to Yeltsin's and Putin's administrations, but they also play an active role as "state-builders" in Putin's nationalistic Russia.[47]

As in the nineteenth century the state (currently it is Putin's nationalist autocracy) dominates Russian interpretations of US history and politics. Meanwhile, post-Soviet Americanists, such as Nikonov, continue to call on Russian politicians to "resist by all available means" the "American threat."[48]

---

46 See *ibid.*, p. 62.
47 Among numerous publications of former Soviet Americanists in Russia see: E. Ia. Batalov, M. G. Noskov, *Amerika, Evropa, Rossiia v transatelnticheskom prostranstve* (Moscow: In-t Evropy: Rus. souvenir, 2009); and Andranik Migranian, 'Putin Triumphs in Ukraine,' *The National Interest*, 6 March 2014. On the role of Andranik Migranian as an advisor to both Presidents Yeltsin and Putin, see Eugeniusz Górski, *Civil Society, Pluralism and Universalism (Polish Philosophical Studies, VIII)* (Washington, DC: The Council for Research in Values and Philosophy, 2007), pp. 57, 58, 61.
48 V. A. Nikonov, *Sovremennyi mir*, pp. 371–80, 427–46.

Conclusion

Paradoxically, Ukrainophobia in both Western and post-Soviet Russian academia was and remains rooted in the old "imperialist epistemological complex" of Russian and Soviet history which has influenced the humanities and social sciences in Russia and the West. Moreover, this epistemological complex was reinforced by both a significant influx of immigrant scholars from the Soviet geopolitical space into Western academia and by the rise of Soviet nostalgia among Western and post-Soviet academics who could not imagine the existence of an independent Ukraine because it would destroy their "Russian and Soviet imperialist complex" as well as challenging their nostalgic feelings for the Soviet past.

As a result, "inconvenient" facts about Ukrainian history have largely gone ignored by Western historians of the Soviet Union today, even at a time of open Russian war against independent Ukraine. Moreover, this anti-Ukrainian approach was rooted in the old KGB traditions to present the Ukrainian independence movement as "fascist," "anti-Soviet" operations run by Western (mainly American) intelligence services and funded by the Ukrainian "fascist" diaspora. Overall, through the entire Cold War, and even today, Soviet/Russian intelligence has attempted to persuade Western audiences that the Ukrainian diaspora and the entire Ukrainian movement for independence were organized by the followers of Stepan Bandera and by the "fascist" Ukrainian collaborators with the Nazis during World War II, who fled to America and who were used by the American intelligence agencies in various American "imperialist wars" against the Soviet Union and now against the Russian Federation.[49] Through the various KGB (and now Russian intelligence) operations in the West, Soviet/Russian intelligence agents and their "useful assets" in Western academia and media, spread this disinformation about Ukraine, trying to discredit its

---

49 See about this in detail in: Sergei I. Zhuk, *KGB Operations against the USA and Canada in Soviet Ukraine, 1953–1991* (London and New York: Routledge, 2022). Compare with the best description of Russia's war against Ukraine in Luke Harding, *Invasion: The Inside Story of Russia's Bloody War and Ukraine's Fight for Survival* (New York: Vintage Books, 2022).

history and culture, and justify the Russian aggression among the Western public. And the peak of this blatant rejection of the independent Ukrainian history, separate from Russia, was presented in July 2021 in a historiographic essay "On the Historical Unity of Russians and Ukrainians", written by the former KGB operative Vladimir Putin, who as President of the Russian Federation, on 24 February 2022, started a bloody war, trying to implement in practice his "historiographic imperialism."[50]

---

50 Vladimir Putin's essay is 'On the Historical Unity of Russians and Ukrainians,' published on the official Kremlin site on July 12, 2021. Available at http://en.kremlin.ru/events/president/news/66181. See also about this in Harding, *Invasion*, pp. 23–26.

Russia's Full Spectrum Conflict and the Myth of Civil War in Ukraine, 2014-2021

Taras Kuzio

This chapter analyzes how Russian disinformation about the 2014 crisis, invasion and annexation of Crimea and conflict in the Donbas have been portrayed in Western scholarship. The chapter is divided into two parts. The first part engages with scholars who depict the Donbas conflict as a civil war and argues that evidence for this is predetermined by narrowly focusing on one year (2014) and one aspect (Russian military intervention). Scholars who support a civil war framework exaggerate regional divisions and nationalism in Ukraine while downplaying Russian military involvement. Sergei Kudelia incredulously writes 'Without question Russia exploited these events, but it did not define them.'[1] The chapter argues in favor of broadening existing scholarly discussions from that of only focusing on the military aspect in 2014 to full spectrum conflict that includes a wide variety of Russian policies. Full spectrum conflict points to a longer-term Russian interference in Ukrainian affairs which is dealt with in the second part of the chapter that analyzes different aspects of full spectrum conflict, such as Russian infiltration of Ukrainian security forces, information warfare, cyber-attacks and Russian nationalist policies towards Ukraine.

Western Scholars and the 2014 Crisis

Three decades ago, Sovietologists, most of who were Russia experts and Kremlinologists, largely ignored the nationality question and did not therefore predict how it would lead to the disintegration of the Soviet Union.[2] In 2014 and since, Western Russianists experienced, and continue to experience, a crisis in their ability to

---

1 Sergei Kudelia, 'The Donbas Rift.' *Russian Social Science Review*, 58, 1 (2017): 214.
2 See Orest Subtelny, 'American Sovietology's great blunder: The marginalization of the nationality issue,' *Nationalities Papers*, 22, 1 (1994): 141–155.

objectively assess Russia's occupation of Crimea and on-going military aggression against Ukraine.[3] In both 1991 and 2014, some Western Russianists have seen Ukraine through Russian eyes and have been therefore unable to understand or analyze Ukrainian politics, national identity and security policies. In the 2014 crisis and since the number of self-proclaimed 'Ukraine experts' dramatically increased.[4] Most of them were uniformed about Ukraine, did not know the Ukrainian language, have never travelled to Ukraine and the Donbas war zone. This lack of knowledge about Ukraine led to mistakes in scholarly work about the Ukraine crisis. They ignore Ukrainian primary sources, in what I have defined as 'academic orientalism';[5] indeed, many of the books published on the Ukraine crisis do not cite Ukrainian source and heavily quote from Russian sources. The only Ukrainian source used by Richard Sakwa[6] is the English-language *Kyiv Post*; if this approach was to be used by an MA or PhD student he or she would be graded with an F (Failed). Boris Kagarlitsky, Radhika Desai and Alan Freeman, whose collection of articles stems from a conference held in Crimea after it had been illegally annexed by Russia, do not include any Ukrainian authors in their edited collection and all the nine chapters do not cite a single Ukrainian source![7] Anna Arutunyan uses barely any Ukrainian sources and her hastily written last chapter on the Russian invasion of Ukraine has not a single Ukrainian reference.[8]

Scholarly discussion can sidestep Ukrainian public opinion which has never believed the Donbas conflict is a civil war; a 2018

---

3 Taras Kuzio, *Crisis in Russian Studies? Nationalism (Imperialism), Racism, and War* (Bristol: E-International Relations, 2020). https://www.e-ir.info/publication/crisis-in-russian-studies-nationalism-imperialism-racism-and-war/
4 T. Kuzio, *Putin's War Against Ukraine. Revolution, Nationalism, and Crime* (Toronto: Chair of Ukrainian Studies, 2017), 363-399.
5 Kuzio, *Crisis in Russian Studies?* 66-81.
6 Richard Sakwa, *Frontline Ukraine. Crisis in the Borderlands* (London: I. B. Tauris, 2015).
7 Boris Kagarlitsky, Radhika Desai and Alan Freeman (eds.,), *Russia, Ukraine and contemporary imperialism* (London: Routledge, 2019).
8 Anna Arutunyan, *Hybrid Warriors, Proxies, Freelancers, and Moscow's Struggle for Ukraine* (London: Hurst, 2022).

survey found only 13.4 percent of Ukrainians believed this.[9] Meanwhile, nearly three quarters of Ukrainians believe their country is at war with Russia.[10]

Biased and uniformed scholarship has been made worse by equally poor external reviewing by publishing houses and academic journals. Although there are many examples, three will suffice. Manchester University Press published what can only be described as Kremlin propaganda about Russia's shooting down of MH17 in July 2014 by a Dutch scholar.[11] The creeping integration of Russian conspiracy theories and disinformation into scholarship is seen in discussions about the shooting down of MH17. Anna Matveeva surprisingly devotes only half a page to the shooting down of MH17 by Russian troops while devoting an entire page to Russian disinformation denying its involvement.[12]

Another prestigious publishing house, Routledge published a book from a conference held in Yalta in Russian occupied Crimea in June 2014 that could be hardly viewed as objective or even academic. Little wonder the editors supported Russia's annexation of Crimea, stating nonchalantly that the peninsula 'transferred its allegiance to Russia.'[13] *Nationalities Papers*, a leading journal in the field of nationalism and the communist world, published an

---

9 'Viyna na Donbasi: Realii i Perspektyvy Vregulyuvannya,' *Natsionalna Bezpeka i Oborona* (Kyiv: Razumkov Centre, 1-2, 2019). https://razumkov.org.ua/uploads/journal/ukr/NSD177-178_2019_ukr.pdf

10 'Poshuky Shlyakhiv Vidnovlennya Suverenitetu Ukrayiny Nad Okupovanym Donbasom: Stan Hromadskoyii Dumky Naperedodni Prezydentskykh Vyboriv' (Kyiv: Democratic Initiatives Foundation 2019). https://dif.org.ua/article/poshuki-shlyakhiv-vidnovlennya-suverenitetu-ukraini-nad-okupovanim-donbasom-stan-gromadskoi-dumki-naperedodni-prezidentskikh-viboriv and 'Yak zminylosya dumka ukrayintsiv pro rosysko-ukrayinsku viynu za dva roky prezydentsva Zelenskoho' (Kyiv: Democratic Initiatives Foundation, 2021). https://dif.org.ua/article/yak-zminilasya-dumka-ukraintsiv-pro-rosiysko-ukrainsku-viynu-za-dva-roki-prezidenstva-zelenskogo.

11 See my review of Gordon M. Hahn, *Ukraine Over the Edge. Russia, the West and the new 'Cold War,'* (Jefferson, NC: McFarland and Company, 2018) and Van der Pijl, *Flight MH17, Ukraine and the New Cold War. Prism of Disaster*, Manchester: Manchester University Press, 2018) in *Europe-Asia Studies*, 71, 6 (2019), 1245-1248.

12 Anna Matveeva, *Through times of trouble: Conflict in Southeastern Ukraine explained from within* (Lanham: MD: Lexington Books, 2017).

13 Kagarlitsky, Desai, and Freeman, *Russia, Ukraine and contemporary imperialism*, 1.

unfounded and hyperbolic claim of 'President Poroshenko's undisputable war crime' that was worse than that committed by 'cruel Japanese militarism.'[14]

Interestingly, Kimitaka Matsuzato did not similarly accuse Russian President Vladimir Putin of committing war crimes during the 2014-2021 Donbas conflict. Anatol Lieven and Sakwa downplayed and obfuscated Russian war crimes after the 2022 invasion. Lieven admitted extra judicial killings and looting had taken place in the Kyiv region but brushed aside the widespread raping of children and women as 'some individual rapes' and denied there had been an organized campaign of the mass raping of Ukrainian women.[15] The UN, as well as other human rights bodies have documented hundreds of cases of rape from the ages of children from the age of four years old to women to the age of 82.[16] Lieven claimed he had heard nothing of 'massacres' of Ukrainians by Russian troops. The Ukrainian authorities documented nearly five hundred executions of non-combatants. Sakwa questioned whether Russian forces had committed war crimes in the Kyiv region, blamed the presence of the Azov Regiment for the destruction of the port city of Mariupol and claimed that the women had been evacuated prior to the maternity hospital in Mariupol being bombed by Russia.[17]

Western scholars who have written on Crimea and the Russian-Ukrainian war can be divided into three groups. The first are ideological zealots who focus their attention on combatting the evils of Ukrainian nationalism.[18] The second are Western scholars

---

14 Kimitaka Matsuzato, 'The Donbas War and politics in cities on the front: Mariupol and Kramatorsk,' *Nationalities Papers*, 46, 6 (2018), 1013.
15 https://responsiblestatecraft.org/2023/05/05/applebaum-goldberg-truth-attended-by-a-bodyguard-of-lies/
16 https://press.un.org/en/2022/sc14926.doc.htm#:~:text=As%20of%203%20Ju ne%2C%20the,to%20watch%20an%20act%20of
17 Interview with Sakwa at https://thegrayzone.com/2022/04/25/us-weapons-european-supplicants-block-peace-in-ukraine/ and https://www.youtube.co m/watch?v=4PBVa4XJEFE
18 T. Kuzio, 'Ni obyektyvnyy, ni liberalnyy,' *Zbruch*, 20 May 2020. https://zbr uc.eu/node/97770 and 'Ideological Zealots Fighting a Non-Existent Ukrainian Nationalist Enemy: A Reply to Tarik Amar's Review of Red Famine,' *Kyiv Mohyla Humanities Journal*, 6 (2019): 209–216. http://kmhj.ukma.edu.ua/article/ view/189122

who continue in the tradition of Sovietology and Kremlinology of analyzing Ukraine from a pro-Russian perspective.[19] A third group are *Putinversteher* (Putin-Understanders) who re-circulate Russian disinformation.[20] Academics can be members of more than one of the three groups; for example, Tarik Amar combines his scholarly obsession with the evils of Ukrainian nationalism as a journalist at the Kremlin's propaganda television channel RT.[21]

Ideologically driven, Russophile and *Putinversteher* scholars have written about the crisis drawing on four themes commonly found in Russian disinformation about Ukraine. First, they downplay or ignore Russian nationalism and exaggerate the influence of Ukrainian nationalism.[22] Second, they blame the West for the crisis and portray Russia as a victim.[23] Third, they justify and support

---

19 S. Kudelia, 'Domestic Sources of the Donbas Insurgency.' *Ponars Eurasia Policy Memo* 351, 2014. http://www.ponarseurasia.org/memo/domestic-sources-donbas-insurgency; 'Reply to Andreas Umland. The Donbass Insurgency Began at Home,' *PONARS Eurasia*. https://www.ponarseurasia.org/reply-to-andreas-umland-the-donbas-insurgency-began-at-home/; 'Getting to the Bottom on the Sources of the Donbas Insurgency,'. https://www.ponarseurasia.org/getting-to-the-bottom-on-the-sources-of-the-donbas-insurgency/; 'The Donbas Rift;' Lance Davies, 'Russia's 'Governance' Approach: Intervention and the Conflict in the Donbas,' *Europe-Asia Studies*, 68, 4 (2016): 726-749; Matsuzato, 'The Donbas War and politics in cities on the front;' Hahn, *Ukraine Over the Edge*; Paul Robinson, 'Russia's Role in the War in the Donbas, and the Threat to European Security,' *European Politics and Society*, 17,4 (2016): 506-521; Chris K. De Ploeg, *Ukraine in the Crossfire* (Atlanta, GA: Clarity Press, 2017); Stylianos A. Sotiriou, 'The irreversibility of history: the case of the Ukraine crisis (2013-2015)' In: Tracy German and Emmanuel Karagiannis (eds.), *The Ukrainian Crisis. The Role of, and Implications for, Sub-State and Non-State Actors* (Abingdon and New York: Routledge, 2018), 51-70.

20 Sakwa, *Frontline Ukraine*; Andrei Tsygankov, 'Vladimir Putin's last stand: the sources of Russia's Ukraine policy, *Post-Soviet Affairs*, 31, 4 (2015), 297-303; Davies, 'Russia's 'Governance' Approach;' Pijl, *Flight MH17*; Matveeva, *Through times of trouble;* A. Matveeva, 'No Moscow stooges: Identity polarization and guerrilla movement in Donbass' and Ivan D. Loshkariov and Andrey A. Sushentsov, 'Radicalization of Russians in Ukraine: From "accidental" diaspora to rebel movement' In: German and Karagiannis, (eds.,) *The Ukrainian Crisis,* 25-49 and 71-90; and Stephen F. Cohen, *War with Russia?: From Putin & Ukraine to Trump and Russiagate* (New York: Skyhorse Publishing, 2019).

21 https://www.istpravda.com.ua/short/2021/12/20/160671/

22 Anton Shekhovtsov denied Putin was a Russian nationalist. See his 23 December 2021 interview on the Kremlinfiles podcast, https://kremlinfile.com/

23 T. Kuzio, 'Russia-Ukraine Crisis: The Blame Game, Geopolitics and National Identity.' *Europe-Asia Studies,* 70, 3 (2018): 462-473.

Russia's annexation of Crimea.[24] Fourth, they downplay Russia's military involvement and portray the conflict as a civil war between Russian and Ukrainian speakers.[25]

Ideologically driven, Russophile and *Putinversteher* scholars exaggerate the 'fragility' of Ukraine echoing the Kremlin's most popular disinformation about Ukraine as an 'artificial' and 'failed state.'[26] The Economist's analysis of Putin's 'useful idiots' found they claimed Ukraine is an artificial construct on historically Russian land, a statement straight out of the Kremlin's disinformation.[27] Scholars who uphold a civil war view of the Donbas conflict view Ukraine as 'torn apart by internal contradictions which have deep roots in the country's history and societal structure' adding that these scholars invariably describe Russia as a restrained international actor and reacting to provocative policies by NATO and the EU.[28]

This chapter focuses on how Russia's misinformative portrayal of the Donbas a civil war is entering Western scholarship and journalism. This chapter makes two arguments. The first is that if we define Russian intervention as full spectrum conflict,[29] rather than narrowly focusing on military intervention, it has been taking place throughout the decade prior to the 2013-2014 Euromaidan Revolution and especially after Putin was re-elected president in 2012.[30] Russia heavily intervened throughout Viktor Yanukovych's

---

24 Kuzio, *Crisis in Russian Studies?* 36-65.
25 Kuzio, *Crisis in Russian Studies?* 106-132.
26 Petro Kuzyk, 'Ukraine's national integration before and after 2014. Shifting 'East-West' polarization line and strengthening political community,' *Eurasian Geography and Economics*, 60, 6 (2019): 709-735 and Peter Dickinson, 'Debunking the myth of a divided Ukraine,' *Atlantic Council of the US*, 29 December 2021. https://www.atlanticcouncil.org/blogs/ukrainealert/debunking-the-myth-of-a-divided-ukraine/
27 'Vladimir Putin's useful idiots,' *The Economist*, 3 July 2023.
28 Jakob Hauter, (ed.,) *Civil War? Interstate War? Hybrid War? Dimensions and Interpretations of the Donbas Conflict in 2014-2020* (Stuttgart: Ibidem, 2021), 13-14.
29 Oscar Jonsson and Robert Seely, 'Russian Full-Spectrum Conflict: An Appraisal After Ukraine, *The Journal of Slavic Military Studies*, 28, 1 (2015): 1-22.
30 Andrew Wilson, 'The Donbas in 2014: Explaining Civil Conflict Perhaps, but not Civil War,' *Europe-Asia Studies*, 68, 4 (2016): 631-652 and T. Kuzio, *Russian Nationalism and the Russian-Ukrainian War: Autocracy-Orthodoxy-Nationality.* London: Routledge, 2022), 156-176.

2010-2014 presidency and was *de facto* permitted to infiltrate Ukraine's security forces ahead of the invasion of Crimea and intervention by its *siloviki* (here understood as encompassing armed forces, FSB, and GRU) into Ukraine.[31] The second is that discussions of Russian military involvement and civil war have narrowly focused on only military aspects of the conflict[32] without considering many other aspects of full spectrum conflict which have been used by Russia against Ukraine in the decade before the 2014 crisis.[33]

Yuriy Matsiyevsky analyzes pro-Russian proxies in the Donbas and finds it to be unusual they took up arms.[34] Ukrainian opinion polls have never showed Ukrainians as experiencing language discrimination, there was no discrimination against a linguistic group in the Donbas and support for separatism never had majority support. He concludes that without Russia's intervention anti-Maidan protestors would not have become armed militants. Scholars describing the conflict as a civil war also need to explain why factors that transformed anti-maidan protestors into armed pro-Russian proxies was not repeated in six of the other Russian-speaking *oblasts* of south-eastern Ukraine.[35] Andrew Wilson believes that without Russian intervention the conflict in the Donbas would have melted away in the same manner as failed attempts to establish people's republics in Kharkiv and Odesa.

Even if we limit our discussion to only the *siloviki* the evidence points to Russian intervention long before the 2014 crisis and direct and covert involvement from February 2014 onwards (see Table 1). Nikolay Mitrokhin writes about the Russian Ministry of Defense establishing 'little green men' units for special operations in

---

[31] T. Kuzio, 'Russianization of Ukrainian National Security Policy under Viktor Yanukovych.' *Journal of Slavic Military Studies*, 25, 4 (2012): 558-581.
[32] Hauter (ed.,), *Civil War? Interstate War? Hybrid War?*
[33] Jonsson and Seely, 'Russian Full-Spectrum Conflict' and Wilson, 'The Donbas in 2014.'
[34] Yuriy Matsiyevsky, 'Internal Conflict or Hidden Aggression: Competing Accounts and Expert Assessments of the War in Ukraine' In: Hauter (ed.,) *Civil War? Interstate War? Hybrid War?* 170-171.
[35] Matsiyevsky, 'Internal Conflict or Hidden Aggression,' 180.

neighboring states a year before Crimea was invaded and annexed.[36] The bulk of the fighting causing the highest Ukrainian casualties was undertaken by Russian security forces and therefore Sanshiro Hosaka defines the Donbas as an 'inter-state war.'[37] Hosaka describes the DNR (Donetsk Peoples Republic) and LNR (Luhansk Peoples Republic) as Russian 'state-run entities' whose creators 'sit back in armchairs in the capital of the neighboring state giving determined instructions to the hired "separatist leaders".'[38] Until August 2014, the majority of the leaders of the DNR and LNR were Russian citizens.[39]

The Myth of a Civil War in Ukraine

Although Matveeva[40] presents Yanukovych and the Party of Regions as unwilling to cooperate with pro-Russian groups in fact Russian intelligence and pro-Kremlin political forces and civil society groups trained Donbas and Crimean pro-Russian groups throughout the decade between the Orange and Euromaidan Revolutions.[41] In Summer 2009, Russian diplomats were expelled for supporting extremist pro-Russian and separatist groups, the first occasion this had ever taken place and leading to President Dmitri Medvedev's vitriolic open letter outlining Russian demands to President Viktor Yushchenko.[42]

---

36 Nikolay Mitrokhin, 'Infiltration, Instruction, Invasion: Russia's War in the Donbas' In: Hauter, *Civil War? Interstate War? Hybrid War*, 113-146.
37 Sanshiro Hosaka, 'Enough with Donbas "Civil War" narratives? Identifying the main combatants leading the bulk of the fighting' In: Hauter (ed.,) *Civil War? Interstate War? Hybrid War?* 107.
38 Hosaka, 'Enough with Donbas "Civil War" narratives.'
39 Halyna Coynash, 'New United Russia party MP confirms that the fighting in Donbas is by "Russian forces"' *Kharkiv Human Rights Protection Group*, 29 October 2021. https://khpg.org/en/1608809673 https://khpg.org/en/1608809673
40 Matveeva, *Through times of trouble,* 57.
41 See A. Shekhovtsov, 'How Alexander Dugin's Neo-Eurasianists geared up for the Russian-Ukrainian war in 2005-2013.' *Anton Shekhovtsov's blog*, 26 January 2016. https://anton-shekhovtsov.blogspot.com/2016/01/how-alexander-dugins-neo-eurasianists.html
42 Dmitri Medvedev, 'V Otnosheniyakh Rossii i Ukrayiny dolzhnyj nastupyt novyj vremena,' 11 August 2009. http://blog.da-medvedev.ru/post/30 translated in T. Kuzio, *Ukraine: Democratization, Corruption and the New Russian Imperialism* (Santa Barbara, CA: Praeger, 2015), 438-439.

Russian intelligence officer Igor Girkin participated in the invasion of Crimea and intervened into mainland Ukraine weeks before Ukraine launched its Anti-Terrorist Operation (ATO). Girkin did not lead a 'local volunteer militia.'[43] While Georgia is accused of 'invading' South Ossetia, Kees van der Pijl criticizes use of the term 'invasion' to describe Russia's military aggression against Georgia and Ukraine.[44]

Matveeva writes that in 2014 Putin 'was elusive, zigzagging and non-committal' and 'military supplies switched on and off.'[45] Sakwa[46] writes that Russia sought to extricate itself from the Donbas. In fact, the Kremlin transformed anti-Maidan protestors into violent insurgents and built up a huge Donbas proxy army and military arsenal controlled by Russian military and intelligence officers. Sakwa's[47] denial of Russian military support to Donbas proxies is alongside his refusal to accept Russia's involvement in hybrid warfare activities against the West, such as interference in the 2016 US elections and the chemical weapons attack in the UK against Russian GRU defector Sergei Skripal.

Evidence of Russian military intervention is available from an array of official sources, think tanks and academic studies, including within Ukraine.[48] The DNR 1st Corps and LNR (Luhansk People's Republic) 2nd Corps had a combined 35,000-strong army which was larger than half of NATO's 30 members' and could only have been created with Russia's active military assistance.

Sakwa, Matveeva, Arutunyan and Arel and Driscoll describe the Donbas conflict as a civil war and a leaderless, bottom-up revolt with local roots.[49] Ignoring Russia's full spectrum conflict, Renfrey

---

43 Pijl, *Flight MH17*, 102.
44 Pijl, *Flight MH17*, 8, 26.
45 Matveeva, *Through times of trouble*, 112, 117.
46 R. Sakwa, *Russia against the rest: The post-cold war crisis of world order* (Cambridge University Press, 2017).
47 Sakwa, *Russia against the rest* and *Deception. Russiagate and the New Cold War* (Lanham, MD: Lexington Books, 2022).
48 See Jonathan Ferguson and N. R. Jenzen-Jones, *Raising Red Flags: An Examination of Arms & Munitions in the Ongoing Conflict in Ukraine*, Research Report no. 3 (Perth: Armament Research Services, 2014).
49 Matveeva, 'No Moscow stooges,' 2, 9; Arutunyan, *Hybrid Warriors, Proxies, Freelancers, and Moscow's Struggle for Ukraine* and Dominique Arel and Jesse

Clarke describes the violent proxies as a 'spontaneous, defensive response' to 'neo-liberal austerity' and 'hard-right nationalist' government.[50] Arel and Driscoll's claim of a civil war taking place in Ukraine from 2014 onwards was overtaken by the 2022 invasion and the title had to be quickly adapted. There is a disconnect between the theoretical and empirical sections of the book and the two scholars undertook no field research which, as I found during my own field work, would have easily disproved the conflict was a civil war. Arel and Driscoll deny the role of Russian agents anywhere outside the Donbas city of Slovyansk which suggests they undertook superficial research into the empirical section of their book. This is all rather odd as the authors took eight years to write the book during which a large amount of evidence has appeared which points to the fallacy of describing the 2014-2021 conflict as a civil war. In ignoring this widespread evidence, the two scholars will be unable to explain the causes of the 2022 full-scale Russian invasion.

As is common with all scholars who subscribe to this view, they also believe three inter-related stereotypes commonly found in Russian disinformation. Firstly, they deny or downplay Russian military involvement to portray the conflict as a civil war. Russia has always denied its security forces are involved in eastern Ukraine and has portrayed the conflict as Russian speakers defending themselves against west Ukrainian 'fascists' who came to power in the 2014 Euromaidan 'putsch.' The Kremlin's line did not waver after the election of Volodymyr Zelenskyy, who is Jewish-Ukrainian and from eastern Ukraine, in April 2019. Exaggerating the influence of Ukrainian nationalism in Ukraine, despite electoral evidence to the contrary, is undertaken by using a Soviet and Russian

---

Driscoll, *Ukraine's Unnamed War. Before the Russian Invasion of 2022* (Cambridge: Cambridge University Press, 2023). For an alternative Ukrainian viewpoint see *Evidence of Russian military aggression against Ukraine as vaccine against Russian disinformation and manipulation* (Lviv: Instytut Prosvity, 2020). https://iprosvita.com/evidences-of-russian-military-aggression-against-ukraine-as-vacine-against-russian-disinformation-and-manipulation/?fbclid=IwAR0jlGXNwFckGOwcr5NG6NglYvWiuOYL2_SfUqwrxaaSYsr4GZKO3qiyNss

50 Renfrey Clarke, 'The Donbass in 2014: Ultra-Right Threats, Working-Class Revolt, and Russian Policy Responses,' *International Critical Thought*, 6, 4 (2016), 535.

non-scientific definition of 'nationalism' to apply to everybody who supports a Ukrainian future outside the Soviet Union and Russian World.

Misuse of the term 'nationalism' is evident in its application to Ukrainian politics since 2014. Andrei Tsygankov and Sakwa repeat Russian disinformation of Zelenskyy as continuing the nationalist policies of his predecessor and being too weak to stand up to the 'Nazis' who seemingly run Ukraine.[51] Tsygankov and Dmitri Trenin, who resigned as head of the Moscow Carnegie office in 2022, use the Kremlin's discourse justifying its invasion of describing Ukrainian politics since as creating an 'anti-Russia' in Ukraine.[52]

Secondly, they allege Russian speakers in Ukraine are oppressed or threatened by Ukrainianization—while *never* referencing opinion polls that back up such claims. Referring to Yushchenko's presidency, Matveeva writes about the 'banning' of Russian language media in Ukraine.[53] If scholars were to investigate any media kiosk in Ukraine they would find a greater number of Russian-language than Ukrainian-language newspapers and magazines. Freedom House found no 'national intolerance' in Ukraine's media environment and has recorded improvement in media freedoms since 2014.

Matveeva wrongly claims Yushchenko closed Russian language television broadcasts 'with no Russian permitted until the 2012 language law was passed.'[54] Throughout Yushchenko's presidency Inter Channel broadcast mainly in Russian. The most radical steps taken against pro-Russian television channels has been by President Zelenskyy, who was a Russian speaker when he was elected. In February and December 2021, NewsOne, 112, ZiK and *Pershyy Nezalezhnyy* (First Independent) television channels owned by Opposition Platform-For Life party leader Viktor Medvedchuk,

---

51 Andrei Tsygankov, 'Between War and Peace: Russian Visions of Future Relations with Ukraine and the West,' *Russian Politics*, 8 (2): 230-246 and https://thegrayzone.com/2022/04/25/us-weapons-european-supplicants-block-peace-in-ukraine/
52 Tsygankov, 'Between War and Peace.'
53 Matveeva, 'No Moscow stooges.'
54 Matveeva, 'No Moscow stooges,' 53.

Putin's *de facto* political representative in Ukraine, were sanctioned.[55] Ukrainian civil society supported the sanctions.[56]

Ukrainians have traditionally ascribed a low level of importance to language issues and grievances over alleged discrimination against Russian speakers has always been low. In Donetsk and Luhansk, 9.4 and 12.7 percent respectfully were anxious at the imposition of one language while 59 percent in Donetsk and 80 percent in south-eastern Ukraine did not believe there is discrimination against Russian speakers in Ukraine.[57] As low as five percent of Ukrainians aged 18-29 had witnessed discrimination by language.[58] Ukraine has no common Russian-language community and therefore Ukrainians, 'failed to respond to attempts to politicize cultural and ethnolinguistic issues.' This translated into low levels of support for Putin's 2014 New Russia project to dismember Ukraine.[59]

Most Ukraine's Russian speakers supported Kyiv in and since the 2014 crisis. Upwards of two thirds of Ukrainian troops are Russian speakers and the highest proportion of casualties of Ukrainian security forces are from Russian-speaking south-eastern Ukraine (with Dnipropetrovsk by far the highest in 2014-2021). The Kremlin's information warfare and Western scholars who subscribe to

---

55 https://www.president.gov.ua/documents/642021-36753; https://www.president.gov.ua/documents/662021-36761; and https://www.president.gov.ua/documents/6842021-41065
56 https://detector.media/community/article/184599/2021-02-04-zakryttya-ka naliv-medvedchuka-ie-pytannyam-bezpeky-a-ne-svobody-slova-zayava-med iynykh-organizatsiy/ and https://detector.media/community/article/184603 /2021-02-05-statement-by-media-organizations-it-is-our-responsibility-to-def end-ourselves/
57 Elise Giuliano, 'Who supported separatism in Donbas? Ethnicity and popular opinion at the start of the Ukrainian crisis.' *Post-Soviet Affairs*, 34, 2-3 (2018): 158-178 and Volodymyr Kulyk, 'Shedding Russianness, recasting Ukrainianness: the post Euromaidan dynamics of ethnonational identifications in Ukraine.' *Post-Soviet Affairs*, 34, 2-3 (2018): 119-138.
58 Dariya Hayday, Kateryna Zarembo, Leonid Litra, Olha Lymar and Serhiy Solodkyy (ed.), *Ukrayinske Pokolinnya Z: tsinnosti ta orientyry* (Kyiv: New Europe Center, 2017), 19. http://neweurope.org.ua/analytics/ukrayinske-pokolinnya -z-tsinnosti-ta-oriyentyry/
59 Guiliano, 'Who supported separatism in Donbas,' 170 and T. Kuzio, 'Russian Stereotypes and Myths of Ukraine and Ukrainians and Why Novorossiya Failed,' *Communist and Post-Communist Studies*, 52, 4 (2019): 297-309.

these three tenets of Russian disinformation are unable to understand the concept of Russian speaking patriotic Ukrainians. Accepting Russian speakers are mainly patriots of Ukraine, and not the Russian World, would remove the basis for their stereotypes and myths about a regionally divided Ukraine and discrimination against Russian speakers.[60]

These myths are buttressed by another staple of Russian disinformation with roots in Soviet anti-nationalist propaganda; namely, denigration of Western Ukrainians. Matveeva[61] makes the unsubstantiated allegation — without citing any reference — that all Ukrainian ministers of culture since 1991 have been from western Ukraine who imposed a regional culture grounded in 'pastoral roots' on the national level to legitimise Ukrainian nationhood. In fact, of Ukraine's 17 ministers of culture only seven (41 percent) were from western Ukraine, another seven were from central Ukraine and three were from south-eastern Ukraine.[62]

Thirdly, exaggeration of regional divisions has been a staple since Ukraine's 1994 presidential elections which allegedly reflect deep fault lines and the artificiality of the country. This is surprising because Ukraine has held six presidential elections with three reflecting east: west divisions (1994, 2004, 2010) and three which did not (1999, 2014, 2019). More than a decade before Putin made the same claims, Lieven wrote that only 40 percent of Ukraine is historically Ukrainian while the remainder was settled jointly by Ukrainians and Russians.[63] Not surprisingly Lieven is an upholder of the Donbas conflict as a civil war and opposed to Western countries providing military assistance to Ukraine. Nicolai N. Petro[64] agrees

---

60 On Dnipropetrovsk and the war prior to the invasion see T. Kuzio, Sergei Zhuk and Paul D'Anieri (eds.,), *Ukraine's Outpost. Dnipropetrovsk and the Russian-Ukrainian War* (Bristol: E-IR Publishing, 2022). https://www.e-ir.info/publication/ukraines-outpost-dnipropetrovsk-and-the-russian-ukrainian-war/
61 Matveeva, 'No Moscow stooges.' 28.
62 Kuzio, *Russian Nationalism and the Russian-Ukrainian War*, 8.
63 Anatol Lieven, *Ukraine and Russia: A fraternal Rivalry* (Washington DC: US Institute of Peace, 1999).
64 Nicolai N. Petro, 'Understanding the Other Ukraine: Identity and Allegiance in Russophone Ukraine' In: Anna Pikulicka-Wilczewska and R. Sakwa (eds.,), *Ukraine, and Russia: People, Politics, Propaganda and Perspectives* (Bristol: E-IR

that south-eastern Ukraine was gifted by Russia.[65] Matveeva[66] claims south-eastern Ukraine has a 'weak association with new (Ukrainian) statehood.' Stylianos A. Sotiriou[67] repeats standard Russian disinformation of Ukraine as a 'land of irreconcilable differences' which is 'on the verge of disintegration into different parts' because it has a 'fragmented and porous national identity framework.' Such comments have been proven to be wrong since 2022 by the strong resilience and resistance of Ukrainians in the face of Russia's invasion, terror, and war crimes.

Table 1. Russian 'Full Spectrum Conflict,' February-April 2014

Date	Event
22 February	Yanukovych fled from Kyiv.
23 February	Large Russian military exercises by 150, 000 troops (38 percent of Russian ground forces) are held on the Ukrainian border.
27 February	Russia invades Crimea.
28 February	State Duma Chairman Sergei Naryshkin threatens that Russia would intervene to 'defend' Russians and Russian speakers in a telephone call with acting Ukrainian head of state Oleksandr Turchynov during an emergency meeting of Ukraine's National Security and Defence Council (RNBO).
1 March	Putin is given the green light by the Federation Council to militarily intervene in Ukraine until 'normalisation of the socio-political situation takes place' to 'protect the interests of Russian citizens and compatriots.' On the same day, from exile in Russia, Yanukovych calls for Russian troops to intervene in Ukraine. Pro-Russian rallies are launched in 11 *oblast* centers in south-eastern Ukraine.
1-4 March	Donetsk Republic's 'People's Militia of Donbas' stormed the *oblast* council building in Donetsk and

---

Publishing, 2015), 19, 35. https://www.e-ir.info/publication/ukraine-and-russia-people-politics-propaganda-and-perspectives/
65 Lieven, *Ukraine and Russia* and Vladimir Putin, 'On the Historical Unity of Russians and Ukrainians,' 12 July 2021. http://en.kremlin.ru/events/president/news/66181
66 Matveeva, 'No Moscow Stooges,' 31.
67 S. A. Sotiriou, 'The irreversibility of history,' 51.

	replaced the Ukrainian with a Russian flag. Pavel Gubarev is proclaimed 'People's Governor.'
9, 13, 14 March	Violence was unleashed against pro-Ukrainian rallies in Donetsk and Luhansk and an attack was launched on the Ukrainian nationalist HQ in Kharkiv which led to the deaths of two Russian nationalists.
7-9 April	Pro-Russian forces occupy state administration buildings in Donetsk, Luhansk and Kharkiv. The DNR is proclaimed. In Kharkiv, Russian citizens and pro-Russian activists are forcibly removed by Ministry of Interior 'Jaguar' *spetsnaz* who made 64 arrests.
12 April	GRU officer Igor ('Strelkov') Girkin and 50 Russian *spetsnaz* intervened into mainland Ukraine from Crimea and travel to Donetsk to lead pro-Russian forces.
16 April	Ukraine launches the Anti-Terrorist Operation (ATO).
17 April	Putin first talks of south-eastern Ukraine as 'New Russia' openly questioning Ukraine's territorial integrity.
27 April	Luhansk People's Republic (LNR) is proclaimed.
12 May	DNR and LNR hold referendum's and declare independence from Ukraine.

Source: Compiled by the author.

Russian Full Spectrum Conflict Against Ukraine, 2005-2014

Jonsson and Seely[68] define full spectrum conflict as combining military, informational, economic, energy and political components. Russian military aggression against Ukraine has included 'a mixture of strategic 21st century tactics, *maskirovka* [Russian military deception], and hybrid warfare.'[69]

Full spectrum conflict has integrated military (kinetic violence) and non-military components. Scholars who describe the Donbas conflict as a civil war prefer therefore to restrict discussion to Russian *siloviki* because a broader discussion of full spectrum

---

68   Jonsson and Seely, 'Russian Full-Spectrum Conflict.'
69   Julius Bodie, 'Modern Imperialism in Crimea and Donbas,' *Loyola of Los Angeles International and Comparative Law Review*, 40, 267 (2017): 267-306.

conflict undermines the main premise. David Lane[70] blames Ukraine's ATO (Anti-Terrorist Operation) for leading to a civil war, arguing 'there is no firm evidence of the involvement of the Russian army (though there certainly are volunteers) in east Ukraine.'

Non-military aspects of Russia's full spectrum conflict are ignored by some scholars. All the chapters in Hauter's[71] extensive edited volume on how to define the Donbas conflict focus exclusively on the military aspect. Leaks of Kremlin spin doctor Vladyslav Surkov's emails,[72] and Sergei Glazyev's telephone conversations provide abundant evidence of Russian full spectrum conflict during the Euromaidan Revolution and in Spring 2014.[73] Russia's full spectrum conflict converted 'a marginal movement into a mass phenomenon.'[74]

Russia undertook full spectrum conflict against Ukraine between the Orange and Euromaidan Revolutions that included Russia's extensive interference in the 2004 presidential elections in support of Yanukovych's candidacy and an attempted assassination of his main opponent, Yushchenko.[75] In 2005, Russia brokered an alliance between the Party of Regions and Crimean Russian nationalists who were installed into power by Russian invading forces in Spring 2014. President Yanukovych facilitated Russian infiltration of Ukrainian security forces which led to defections, treason, and leakage of intelligence in 2014 during the early stages of the Russian-Ukrainian war. From 2005, Russia provided financial support

---

70 David Lane, 'The International Context: Russia, Ukraine and the Drift to East-West Confrontation,' *International Critical Thought*, 6, 4 (2016), 641.
71 Hauter, *Civil War? Interstate War? Hybrid War?*
72 Alya Shandra and Robert Seely, *The Surkov Leaks. The Inner Workings of Russia's Hybrid War in Ukraine* (London: Royal United Services Institute, 2019). https://rusi.org/publication/occasional-papers/surkov-leaks-inner-workings-russias-hybrid-war-ukraine
73 Andreas Umland, *The Glazyev Tapes: Getting to the root of the conflict in Ukraine* (London: European Council on Foreign Relations, 2016). https://www.ecfr.eu/article/commentary_the_glazyev_tapes_getting_to_the_root_of_the_conflict_in_7165
74 Wilson, 'The Donbas in 2014,' 645.
75 T. Kuzio, 'Russian Policy to Ukraine During Elections.' *Demokratizatsiya*, 13, 4 (2005): 491-517.

to and paramilitary training of pro-Russian forces who took power in the Donetsk Peoples Republic (DNR) in 2014.

Putin's 'Gathering of Russian Lands,' 2012-2014

During the three years after Putin was re-elected and before the Ukraine crisis, he set about halting Ukraine's European integration and 'gathering Russian lands' which is synonymous with a pan-Russian nation of three eastern Slavs.[76] Towards these twin objectives, the Kremlin exerted heavy pressure on Yanukovych to not sign an Association Agreement with the EU, which he reneged on in November 2014, sparking the Euromaidan Revolution. Nevertheless, some scholars echo Russian disinformation in blaming the EU, not Russia, for undertaking a 'reckless provocation' in 'a divided country to choose between Russia and the West.'[77] The EU was allegedly at fault for pushing its Association Agreement, not Russia pressuring Ukraine to join the CIS Customs Union, which split Ukraine whose East has a 'shared civilization' with Russia.[78] Western 'political aggression' allegedly undermined 'centuries of intimate relations between large segments of Ukrainian society and Russia, including family ties.'[79] In fact, it was Russian military aggression which turned Ukrainians away from Russia. Paul D'Anieri provides a more balanced critique of EU and Russian policies towards Ukraine in the run up to the 2014 crisis by pointing out 'Ukraine's policy of picking which component of an agreement to adhere to would no longer be accepted.'[80]

Ultimately, the crisis was brought about by the Kremlin coming to view the presence of the EU in the same negative manner as how it had always viewed NATO—even though both organisations

---

76 Paul D'Anieri, *Ukraine and Russia. From Civilized Divorce to Uncivil War* (Cambridge: Cambridge University Press, 2019), 264; Nicholas Sambanis, Stergios Skaperdas and William C. Wohlforth, 'External Intervention, Identity, and Civil War,' *SSRN Research Library*, 17 August 2017. https://papers.ssrn.com/sol3/papers.cfm?abstract_id=3019206; and Kuzio, *Russian Nationalism and the Russian-Ukrainian War*.
77 Cohen, *War with Russia?* 17.
78 Cohen, *War with Russia?* 17.
79 Cohen, *War with Russia?* 83.
80 D'Anieri, *Ukraine and Russia*, 192.

have never offered membership to Ukraine. The EU Association Agreement offers integration but not membership. This was irrelevant to the Kremlin because both Russian presidents have viewed Eurasia as Russia's exclusive sphere of influence. As seen in Putin's November 2021 ultimatum to the West to provide 'written security guarantees,' 'Russia seeks an order based on the dominance of great powers that was widely accepted in the era prior to World War I.'[81] Added to this, Russian nationalism under Putin had stagnated into viewing Ukraine as a Little Russian branch of the pan-Russian nation.[82] D'Anieri writes: 'Putin saw the Association Agreement as threatening the permanent loss of Ukraine, which it had, since 1991, seen as artificial and temporary.'[83] Putin cannot imagine a Russian World without Ukraine.

Medvedchuk, Putin's *de facto* representative in Ukraine, was his vehicle to assist in the 'gathering of Russian lands.' Putin is the Godfather of Medvedchuk's daughter Darina. Writing about Medvedchuk, Neil Buckley and Roman Olearchyk write,'Many suspect him of being Mr Putin's agent.'[84] Mikhail Zygar[85] believes Medvedchuk has long been the 'main source of information about what was happening in Ukraine.' Medvedchuk is the only person Putin has fully trusted in Ukraine and he is 'effectively Putin's special representative in Ukraine.'[86] Tapes made illicitly in President Kuchma's office by security guard Mykola Melnychenko overheard a conversation about Medvedchuk having been a KGB informer. In the USSR, Medvedchuk had been a Soviet appointed 'defence attorney' for Ukrainian dissidents Yuriy Litvin and Vasyl Stus in 1979-1980 but nevertheless had supported their courts convictions. Lytvyn and Stus died in the Gulag in 1984 and 1985 respectively.

---

81 D'Anieri, *Ukraine and Russia*, 276.
82 Kuzio, *Russian Nationalism and the Russian-Ukrainian War*, 1-34.
83 D'Anieri, *Ukraine and Russia*, 251.
84 Neil Buckley and Roman Olearchyk 'Putin's friend emerges from shadows in Ukraine,' *Financial Times*, 24 April 2017. https://www.ft.com/content/097 2792c-1e96-11e7-a454-ab04428977f9
85 Mikhail Zygar, *All the Kremlin's Men. Inside the Court of Vladimir Putin* (New York: Public Affairs, 2016), 123.
86 Zygar, *All the Kremlin's Men*, 167.

Not surprisingly, Medvedchuk 'shared some of the 'Ukrainophobia' of Moscow officialdom.'[87]

Medvedchuk and Glazyev implemented Putin's goal of the 'gathering of Russian lands' through bringing Ukraine into the Russian World which would be the core of the CIS Customs Union (from 2015 Eurasian Economic Union). In Spring 2012, at the same time Putin was re-elected, Medvedchuk launched the Ukrainian Choice political party which resembled more a 'front for the Kremlin than independent organization.'[88] According to the Kremlin and some Western scholars, Ukraine could only maintain its identity at the centre of Eurasia rather than on the edge of Europe.[89] Since 2014, Ukraine's declining trade with Russia and growing trade with the EU shows this argument to have little merit.

In 2012-2013, Russia's full spectrum conflict targeted ideological, political, economic and information spheres in Ukraine. In summer 2013, Medvedchuk and Glazyev devised a trade war and a range of other policies to pressure President Yanukovych to turn away from the EU Association Agreement and join the CIS Customs Union.[90] Putin and Medvedchuk's allies worked with the Russian nationalist wing of the Party of Regions led by Igor Markov, Oleg Tsarev and Vadym Kolesnichenko who supported Russia's annexation of Crimea and New Russia project. Kolesnichenko was one of the organisers of the failed Ukrainian Front in Kharkiv.[91] In summer 2013, Ukraine was subjected to a trade boycott and demands for payment of its debts to *Gazprom*, pressure which were combined with a 'massive diplomatic offensive against Ukraine.'[92]

---

87 Zygar *All the Kremlin's Men*, 84.
88 S. Hosaka, 'The Kremlin's Active Measures Failed in 2013: That's Why Russia Remembered its Last Resort—Crimea,' *Demokratizatsiya: The Journal of Post-Soviet Democratization*, 26, 3 (2018): 341.
89 See Mikhail Molchanov, 'Choosing Europe over Russia: what has Ukraine gained?' *European Politics and Society*, 17, 4 (2016): 522-537.
90 'O komplekse mer po vovlecheniyu Ukrainy v evraziiskii integratsionyi protsess,' *Zerkalo Nedeli*, 18 August 2013. https://zn.ua/internal/o-komplekse-mer-po-vovlecheniyu-ukrainy-v-evraziyskiy-integracionnyy-process-_.html
91 Orysia Kulick, 'Dnipropetrovsk Oligarchs: Lynchpins of Sovereignty or Sources of Instability?' *The Soviet and Post-Soviet Review*, 46, 3 (2019): 359.
92 Karel Svoboda, 'On the Road to Maidan: Russia's Economic Statecraft Towards Ukraine in 2013,' *Europe-Asia Studies*, 71, 10 (2019): 1694.

Putin and Yanukovych held numerous one-on-one meetings prior to and during the Euromaidan which 'underlined the importance of the issue for Russia and the seriousness of the situation.'[93] In the year before the outbreak of military conflict, Russia 'combined diplomacy, propaganda, economic pressure and even the threat of military action.'[94]

Included in Medvedchuk-Glazyev's strategy was 'Operation Armageddon' launched on 26 June 2013 just three weeks after Azarov agreed Ukraine would become an Observer in the CIS Customs Union. 'Operation Armageddon' was a 'Russian state-sponsored cyber espionage campaign' designed to give Russia military advantage in any future conflict with Ukraine and towards this end it targeted Ukrainian government, military and law enforcement to obtain an insight into Ukrainian intentions and plans.[95] 'Operation Armageddon's' most important period of activity was from 1 December 2013, when the Euromaidan began to mobilise large numbers of protestors, to 28 February 2014, a day after Russia invaded Crimea. In other words, we need to understand cyber warfare as a component of full spectrum conflict. Russia's cyber-warfare intervention in Ukraine began six months before the Euromaidan Revolution and therefore much longer before the period scholars debate as to whether Ukraine was in the throes of a civil war in 2014.

'Operation Armageddon' was complimented by 'Operation Infektion' launched in February 2014 which continues to the present day.[96] In December 2021, the SBU issued a report on the FSB's seven year 'Operation Armageddon' against Ukraine.[97] Since 2014,

---

93 Svoboda, 'On the Road to Maidan,'1695.
94 Svoboda, 'On the Road to Maidan,'1700.
95 'Operation Armageddon. Cyber Espionage as a Strategic Component of Russian Modern Warfare,' *Lookingglass Cyber Threat Intelligence Group*, CTIG-20150428-01, 2015. https://lookingglasscyber.com/blog/threat-intelligence-in sights/operation-armageddon-cyber-espionage-as-a-strategic-component-of-russian-modern-warfare/
96 Francois Nimmo, Ronzaud Eib, Hernon Ferreira, and Tim Kostelancik, *Exposing Secondary Infektion. Forgeries, interference, and attacks on Kremlin critics across six years and 300 sites and platforms* (Washington DC: Graphika, 2020). https://sec ondaryinfektion.org/downloads/secondary-infektion-report.pdf
97 https://ssu.gov.ua/uploads/files/DKIB/Технічний%20звіт%20діяльності%20Армагедон.pdf

the FSB has launched over 5,000 cyber-attacks against Ukraine; a number which surely makes Ukraine the biggest global victim of such attacks.[98]

An important component of the Medvedchuk-Glazyev strategy was an invitation to Putin and Russian Orthodox Church Patriarch Kirill to speak at the July 2013 Kyiv conference to promote Orthodox-Slavic values and Ukraine's civilization choice as part of the Russian World.[99] Since 2009, Kirill has strongly identified with the Russian World, believed (like Putin) Ukrainians are a branch of the pan-Russian nation and the Donbas conflict is an 'internecine war.'[100]

Putin and Kirill used the celebrations of the anniversary of the 1025th anniversary of the Christianisation of Kyiv Rus to rebuild eastern Slavic unity within the Russian World. Putin said at Medvedchuk's conference: 'The baptism of Rus was a great event that defined Russia's and Ukraine's spiritual and cultural development for the centuries to come. We must remember this brotherhood and preserve our ancestor's land.'[101] In a clear reference to himself as the 'gatherer of Russian lands,' Putin described 'Russians' as the most divided people in the world.

Putin's Signalling to the Red (Soviet)-White (Orthodox)-Brown (Fascist) Coalition

Erin K. Jenne[102] writes that external lobbying and external patrons are key factors in determining mobilisation of minorities because they signal an intention to intervene which radicalises their

---

98 https://ssu.gov.ua/novyny/sbu-vstanovyla-khakeriv-fsb-yaki-zdiisnyly-pon ad-5-tys-kiberatak-na-derzhavni-orhany-ukrainy
99 D'Anieri, *Ukraine and Russia*,193; Sophia Kishkovsky, 'Putin in Ukraine to Celebrate a Christian Anniversary,' *New York Times*, 27 July 2013. https://www.nytimes.com/2013/07/28/world/europe/putin-in-ukraine-to-celebrate-a-christian-anniversary.html; and Zygar, *All the Kremlin's Men*, 258.
100 Serhiy Plokhy, *Lost Kingdom. A History of Russian Nationalism from Ivan the Great to Vladimir Putin* (London: Penguin Books, 2017), 331 and Kuzio, *Russian Nationalism and the Russian-Ukrainian War*, 204-227.
101 D'Anieri, *Ukraine and Russia*, 193-194.
102 Erin K. Jenne, *Ethnic Bargaining: The Paradox of Minority Empowerment* (Ithaca: NY: Cornell University Press, 2007).

demands towards the central government. This certainly is applicable to Putin's vocal support for Crimea's incorporation into Russia and questioning of Ukrainian sovereignty over New Russia (south-eastern Ukraine). Actual or expected intervention shapes bargaining calculations.[103]

Pro-Russian forces and the Red (Soviet)-White (Orthodox)-Brown (Fascist) coalition understood Putin's signalling as Russia's intention to either annex New Russia in the same way as it had Crimea or detach the region and create a semi-independent state aligned with Russia in the Eurasian Economic Union.[104] Putin's rhetoric emboldened Russian nationalists to believe the Russian authorities were no longer abiding by treaties they had signed with Ukraine and they thereby viewed Ukraine as a target for dismemberment or re-configuration into a loose confederation aligned with Russia in the Eurasian Economic Union.[105]

Russia's annexation of Crimea and destabilisation of south-eastern Ukraine should be treated together, Melnyk believes.[106] Sambanis[107] writes: 'expected intervention has a robustly positive and highly significant association with civil war.' Russia's invasion of Crimea 'radically transformed expectations of intervention in other Ukrainian regions, notably Donbas' and strongly influenced perceptions of Russian policies towards mainland Ukraine by Ukrainian policymakers.[108] Limited Ukrainian resistance in Crimea, brought about by years of Russian infiltration of Ukrainian security

---

103 Sambanis, Skaperdas and Wohlforth, 'External Intervention, Identity, and Civil War,' 27.
104 See Marlene Laruelle, 'The three colors of Novorossiya, or the Russian nationalist mythmaking of the Ukrainian crisis.' *Post-Soviet Affairs*, 32, 1 (2016): 55-74.
105 Oleksandr Melnyk, '"From the "Russian Spring" to the Armed Insurrection: Russia, Ukraine and Political Communities in the Donbas and Southern Ukraine,' *The Soviet and Post-Soviet Review*, 47, 1 (2020): 28-29.
106 Melnyk, 'From the "Russian Spring" to the Armed Insurrection,' 18.
107 N. Sambanis, 'A Review of Recent Advances and Future Directions in the Quantitative Literature on Civil War,' *Defence and Peace Economics*, 13, 3 (2002): 235.
108 Sambanis, Skaperdas and Wohlforth, 'External Intervention, Identity, and Civil War,' 27.

forces,[109] 'incentivized the Kremlin to press for continuing gains.'[110] Russia's annexation of Crimea led to a belief 'the Kremlin would unleash in the Donbas a similar operation to that in Crimea' which influenced the decisions and expectations of both Ukrainian and Russian policy makers.[111]

Russian Intelligence Forces

In 2009, Russian diplomats in Odesa and Crimea were expelled for supporting pro-Russian separatists in those two locations, further deteriorating Russian-Ukrainian relations. Russian intelligence forces were present in Ukraine throughout the Euromaidan Revolution, invasion and annexation of Crimea, transformation of anti-Maidan protestors into violent Russian proxies and the New Russia project. Wilson believes Russian resources were key to 'converting a marginal movement into a mass phenomenon.'[112] Sergei Aksyonov's Russian Unity Party received only four percent in the 2010 Crimean Supreme Soviet elections while the Donetsk Republic was a marginal and illegal political force in the Donbas for much of the decade prior to the 2014 crisis. Russian intelligence coordinated the intervention into Ukraine of *spetsnaz* forces, nationalist mercenaries, and Chechen paramilitaries. These forces assisted in the looting of Ukrainian arms or supplied them from Russian stocks. From May 2014, Russia increasingly supplied sophisticated military equipment to its assets and proxies in Ukraine.

Russian intelligence had financed and provided paramilitary training to pro-Russian groups and during the Euromaidan Revolution transformed Anti-Maidan protestors into violent proxy

---

109 Kuzio, 'Russianization of Ukrainian National Security Policy under Viktor Yanukovych.'
110 Andrew S. Bowen, 'Coercive diplomacy and the Donbas: Explaining Russian strategy in Eastern Ukraine,' *Journal of Strategic Studies*, 42, 3-4 (2019): 334.
111 Christopher Gilley, 'Review of Anna Matveeva, Through Times of Trouble. Conflict in Southeastern Ukraine Explained from Within,' *Europe-Asia Studies*, 71, 2 (2019): 323.
112 Wilson, 'The Donbas in 2014,' 644.

forces.[113] Intercepted telephone conversations of FSB intelligence officer Colonel Igor Egorov ('Elbrus'), who was first deputy commander of the 'New Russia' army, is evidence of him coordinating the so-called DNR Ministry of Defence.[114] Egorov[115] was a senior officer from the FSB elite *spetsnaz* unit, a successor to the KGB's V Department's elite *Vympel spetsnaz* unit. Bellingcat research and captured documents released by the SBU showed close ties between Surkov, the Moscow headquarters of Russian military intelligence (GRU), the FSB and Russian intelligence on the ground in Ukraine who coordinated and supplied military equipment to Russian proxies in the Donbas.[116]

On 12 April 2014, Russian intelligence officer Girkin and 50 Russian *spetsnaz* forces soldiers intervened from Crimea into mainland Ukraine. Ukraine launched its ATO on the 14th of April in response to Russian full spectrum conflict—not the other way around. Ignoring Girkin and other aspects of Russia's full spectrum conflict, Kagarlitsky blames Ukraine for the conflict, writing 'Kyiv had gone to war on its own people.'[117] Meanwhile, Clarke declared 'it was unrelenting bloody-mindedness on the part of Kyiv authorities that turned the struggle into a civil war.'[118]

A day after his intervention into mainland Ukraine, the SBU published intercepted telephone calls between Girkin and his handlers in Moscow. Girkin's intervention was a 'key escalatory move'

---

113 James Jones, 'The Battle for Ukraine,' *PBS Frontline*, 26 May 2014. https://www.pbs.org/video/frontline-battle-ukraine/ and https://www.pbs.org/wgbh/frontline/documentary/battle-for-ukraine/transcript/
114 'Identifying FSB's Elusive "Elbrus": From MH17 to Assassinations in Europe.' *Bellingcat*, 24 April 2020. https://www.bellingcat.com/news/uk-and-europe/2020/04/24/identifying-fsbs-elusive-elbrus-from-mh17-to-assassinations-in-europe/
115 Igor Egorov, 'SBU maye audio pro te, yak verbuvalnyk Shaytanova keruvav boyovykamy na Donbasi,' *Ukrayinska Pravda*, 9 July 2020. https://www.pravda.com.ua/news/2020/07/9/7258728/
116 '"K" for Kurator or Catch Me If You Can,' *Bellingcat*, 9 July 2020. https://www.bellingcat.com/news/uk-and-europe/2020/07/09/k-for-kurator-or-catch-me-if-you-can/ and https://www.bellingcat.com/app/uploads/2020/07/transcript.pdf
117 B. Kagarlitsky, 'Ukraine and Russia: Two States, One Crisis' In: Kagarlitsky, Desai, and Freeman (eds.,) *Russia, Ukraine and contemporary imperialism*, 35.
118 Clarke, 'The Donbass in 2014,' 538.

in Russia's full spectrum conflict against Ukraine.[119] Girkin undoubtedly 'coordinated his actions with Moscow, above all with Glazyev.'[120] Girkin's *spetsnaz* were augmented the following month by Chechen paramilitaries loyal to President Ramzan Kadyrov who fought in the Donbas between May-July 2014.[121] This was all testimony to Russia's broad-based intervention—not a civil war.

'Political tourists' were bussed into Kharkiv and other Ukrainian cities from Russia or into Odesa from the Russian-occupied Transdniestr region of Moldova to act as fake Ukrainian protestors. It is not a coincidence that rallies simultaneously began on 1 March 2014 in eleven south-eastern Ukrainian cities on the same day Putin received authorisation from the Federation Council to militarily intervene in Ukraine. Kudelia's argument the violent seizure of official buildings 'happened sporadically and in a decentralized manner' ignores the huge evidence of Russia's full spectrum conflict and is therefore unbelievable.[122] Rallies, beatings and seizures of state buildings were 'secretly organized, financially backed, and ideologically underpinned by the Russian leadership.'[123] The Glazyev tapes 'vividly illustrate Moscow's covert support for the still unarmed anti-government protests in Ukraine several weeks before the actual war started.'[124] Russia intervened to organise, support and enlarge pro-Russian rallies 'immediately after the victory of the Maidan revolution in early 2014' and 'actively fanned the flames of pre-existing ethnic, cultural and political tensions in the region.'[125] Viktor Nikolaenko, the former head of the Political Department in Donetsk city council, said 'I don't believe that in one

---

119 Sambanis, Skaperdas and Wohlforth, 'External Intervention, Identity, and Civil War,' 32.
120 Zygar, *All the President's Men*, 285.
121 Mairbek Vatchagaev (2015) 'Two Chechen Battalions Are Fighting in Ukraine on Kyiv's Side.' *Eurasia Daily Monitor*, 12, 153 (13 August 2015). https://jamestown.org/program/two-chechen-battalions-are-fighting-in-ukraine-on-kyivs-side/#.VdLmEfmqpBd
122 Kudelia, 'Domestic Sources of the Donbas Insurgency.'
123 Ivan Gomza, and Johann Zajaczkowski, 'Black Sun Rising: Political Opportunity Structure Perceptions and Institutionalization of the Azov Movement in Post-Euromaidan Ukraine,' *Nationalities Papers*, 47, 5 (2019): 774-800.
124 Umland, *The Glazyev Tapes*.
125 Umland, *The Glazyev Tapes*.

day across the entire east and south of Ukraine, the same protest breaks out' and 'Then all of a sudden, an armed resistance rises. I've been in politics too long to believe in such a coincidence.'[126] 'The synchronization is obvious,' Nikolaenko added.[127]

The pro-Russian rallies and violent attempts to seize buildings were actions imported from outside and unpopular among the population of south-eastern Ukraine. 11.7 percent of Ukrainians in south-eastern Ukraine supported the seizure of buildings while a very high 76.8 percent opposed this action. In Donetsk and Luhansk, where there was the highest support in the eight *oblasts* of south-eastern Ukraine, only 18.1 percent and 24.4 percent respectively supported the seizure of buildings while a much higher 53.2 percent and 58.3 percent were opposed.[128] Russia was importing violent strategies into south-eastern Ukraine and weaponizing extremist pro-Russian minority groups. Russia's full spectrum conflict emboldened 'insurgents in eastern Ukraine to ramp up demands and take armed actions.'[129] The transformation of anti-Maidan protestors into violent Russian proxies would have been impossible without 'increased expectations of intervention' with expectations of Russian military intervention into New Russia, like that in Crimea, influencing both sides to fight it out.[130]

Before storming the State Administration in Kharkiv pro-Russian activists admitted 'he and his colleagues met with Russian intelligence agents who were working in the east' who were from 'the Russian military and intelligence agencies.'[131] In Kharkiv '20 to 40 buses' from the nearby Russian city of Belgorod arrived in the

---

126 Julia J. Ioffe, 'Will Russia Invade Ukraine?' *The New Republic*, 9 April 2014. https://newrepublic.com/article/117314/will-russia-invade-ukraine
127 J. J. Ioffe, 'Will Russia Invade Ukraine?'
128 'The Views and Opinions of South-Eastern Regions Residents of Ukraine,' Kyiv International Institute of Sociology, 20 April 2014. https://www.kiis.com.ua/?lang=ukr&cat=reports&id=302&y=2014&m=4&page=1
129 Sambanis, Skaperdas and Wohlforth, 'External Intervention, Identity, and Civil War,' 32.
130 Sambanis, Skaperdas and Wohlforth, 'External Intervention, Identity, and Civil War,' 31.
131 Jones, 'The Battle for Ukraine.'

centre.'[132] Kharkiv journalist Andriy Borodavka estimated 'around 200' Russian citizens had been bused from Russia into Kharkiv. 'They delivered hardcore Kremlin activists, he said, some dressed in military-style fatigues. They waved Russian flags and cried: 'Russia, Russia.'[133] 'Together with local thugs, the 'tourists' stormed the main administrative building, at the opposite end of the square, and evicted the Ukrainian nationalists who had been occupying it, brutally beating several of them.' Moscow student blogger Arkady Khudyakov replaced the Ukrainian flag on the roof of the Kharkiv State Administration building with a Russian one, posting video and photos of his exploits on the social network site *LiveJournal*. It is not a coincidence a Russian flag was also raised by Russian citizen Mikhail Chuprikov on Donetsk city hall on the same day as in Kharkiv.[134]

The Kremlin aimed to transform anti-Maidan protests into pro-Russian uprisings which would take control of *oblast* and city councils and state administrations, declare they did not recognise the 'Kyiv junta' (i.e., Euromaidan Revolutionary authorities) and establish alternative power centres. These so-called 'people's republic's' would invite Russian forces to intervene to 'protect' ethnic Russians and Russian speakers from the 'fascist junta.' Russia's strategy was to create a fig leaf of 'Ukrainians' supporting the Kremlin's goals to provide Russia with justification for military intervention in 'a convincing picture of genuine local and even internal support for Russian ideas in Ukraine.' These full spectrum conflict activities were 'micromanaged by Kremlin officials.'[135] The low number of participants in pro-Russian rallies in New Russia and weak support for pro-Russian goals (as reflected in opinion polls) points to pro-Russian 'uprisings' being artificially imported from

---

132 Luke Harding, *A Very Expensive Poison. The Definitive Story of the Murder of Litvinenko and Russia's War with the West* (London: Guardian Books, 2016).
133 L. Harding 'Kiev's protesters: Ukraine uprising was no neo-Nazi power-grab,' *The Guardian*, 13 March 2014. https://www.theguardian.com/world/2014/mar/13/ukraine-uprising-fascist-coup-grassroots-movement
134 Andrew Roth, 'From Russia, 'Tourists' Stir the Protests,' *New York Times*, 3 March 2014. https://www.nytimes.com/2014/03/04/world/europe/russias-hand-can-be-seen-in-the-protests.html
135 Shandra and Seely, *The Surkov Leaks*, 38.

abroad, showing what was taking place in south-eastern Ukraine was not a civil war but Russia's full spectrum conflict.

Training and Support for Pro-Russian Proxies

In November 2004, Russia supported a separatist congress in Severodonetsk organised by Yanukovych in protest at the Orange Revolution denying him his fraudulent election victory. In February 2014, a similar congress of the Ukrainian Front in Kharkiv was planned after Yanukovych fled from Kyiv, but it failed to go ahead after regional leaders from south-eastern Ukraine failed to turn up.

Yanukovych's plans in 2004 and 2014 drew on pro-Russian so-called 'Internationalist Movements' established by the Soviet secret services in the late 1980s in Moldova, where it took power in the Transniestr with the assistance of Russian military intervention; Ukraine; and the three Baltic States. The Donetsk Republic, established after the Orange Revolution and which was brought to power in the DNR by Russia's full spectrum conflict, is a successor to the Inter-Movement of the Donbas founded in 1989 by Andrei Purgin, Dmitri Kornilov and Sergei Baryshnikov. Its allies were the Movement for the Rebirth of the Donbas and Civic Congress (which changed its name to the Party of Slavic Unity).[136]

The Donetsk Republic was launched in 2005 with support from Russian intelligence.[137] The Donetsk Republic and similar pro-Russian extremist groups in Ukraine were provided with paramilitary training in summer camps organised by neo-fascist and Eurasianist Aleksandr Dugin.[138] Donetsk Republic was banned by the Ukrainian authorities in 2007 but continued to operate 'underground' with the connivance of the Party of Regions who monopolised power in the Donbas. In 2014, the Donetsk Republic organisation became one of two ruling parties after 'winning' 68.3 percent of the vote in the DNR 2014 'election.'

---

136 Kuzio, *Putin's War Against Ukraine*, 88-89.
137 'Na terrritorii Donetskoy oblasty deystvovaly voyennye lagerya DNR s polnym vooruzheniyem s 2009 goda,' *Novosti Donbassa*, 20 July 2014. http://novosti. dn.ua/details/230206/
138 Shekhovtsov, 'How Alexander Dugin's Neo-Eurasianists geared up for the Russian-Ukrainian war in 2005-2013.'

Baryshnikov, Dean of Donetsk University in the DNR, and other leaders of the Donetsk Republic have always been extreme Russian chauvinists and Ukrainophobes.[139] Baryshnikov believes, 'Ukraine should not exist' because it is an 'artificial state.' He admits 'I have always been against Ukraine, politically and ideologically' showing the long ideological continuity between the Soviet Inter-Movement and Donetsk Republic.[140] Baryshnikov unequivocally states Ukrainians 'are Russians who refuse to admit their Russia-ness,' viewing Ukrainians as a branch of the pan-Russian nation. In a similar manner to Kremlin officials, Baryshnikov supports the destruction of Ukrainian national identity 'by war and repression' because it 'can be compared to a difficult disease, like cancer.'[141]

Russian Infiltration of Ukrainian Security Forces

Jonnson and Seely place Russia's full spectrum conflict within a long-term context of Russian subversion to weaken their opponent's security forces and increase their ties with Russia. This would be undertaken through pro-Russian political forces, Russian-language media, think tanks and NGO's.[142]

The Kremlin's intelligence services extensively infiltrated Ukrainian security forces during Yanukovych's presidency, especially the Security Service of Ukraine (SBU) and military intelligence.[143] Mass defections of Ukrainian security forces in Crimea, including 80 percent of SBU officers,[144] paved the way for limited resistance to Russian invading forces. In the Donbas war, early military operations in 2014 by Ukrainian security forces were thwarted

---

139 Kuzio, *Russian Nationalism and the Russian-Ukrainian War*, 248-252.
140 Kuzio, *Russian Nationalism and the Russian-Ukrainian War*, 248-252.
141 Tim Judah, *In Wartime. Stories from Ukraine* (New York: Tim Duggan Books, 2015), XVI, 11, 150, 152-153.
142 Mykhailo Gonchar, Volodymyr Horbach and Anatolii Pinchuk, *Russian Octopus in Action. Case Ukraine* (Kyiv: Centre for Global Studies (Strategy XXI) and Institute for Euro-Atlantic Cooperation, 2020), 41-51. https://geostrategy.org.ua/en/analysis/research/rosiyskiy-sprut-u-diyi-keys-ukrayina
143 Kuzio, 'Russianization of Ukrainian National Security Policy under Viktor Yanukovych.'
144 See Table 5.1 in Kuzio, *Crisis in Russian Studies?* 113.

by Russian infiltration and espionage, giving time for the Kremlin to transform protestors into armed proxies and establish the DNR and Luhansk Peoples Republics.

The extent of Russia's deep infiltration of Ukraine's security forces in the decade prior to 2014 continues to be evident to the present day with senior military and SBU officers detained and charged with treason.[145] In April 2020, the SBU detained FSB spy Valerii Shaitanov with the high rank of SBU General-Major.[146]

Russian Information Warfare

One important aspect of full spectrum conflict which is traditionally overlooked in discussions of the Donbas conflict is Russia's information warfare. This is surprising as Russian information warfare and disinformation is a central component of Russian full spectrum conflict towards Ukraine. Russian information warfare mobilised violent conflict and placed Ukraine 'on a war footing since the spring of 2014.'[147] Hysteria, hatred, aggressiveness and xenophobia have 'reached alarmingly high levels' and political murders and violence have 'become unremarkable.'[148] Russia's information warfare spewed the 'language of hate'[149] creating an aggressive, anti-Ukrainian climate in support of military and political operations in Crimea and the Donbas.[150] Russian information warfare assisted in the process of transforming anti-Maidan protestors into violent Russian proxies.[151]

Matveeva writes Russia had 'few soft power instruments at its disposal.'[152] Until the 2014 crisis, Moscow supported pro-Russian

---

145 Gonchar, Horbach and Pinchuk, *Russian Octopus in Action*, 3-22.
146 https://www.facebook.com/SecurSerUkraine/posts/2667396766823645
147 Julia Fedor, 'Introduction: Russia Media and the War in Ukraine,' *Journal of Soviet and Post-Soviet Politics and Society*, 1, 1 (2015): 1-12.
148 Fedor, 'Introduction,' 1, 5.
149 Tatiana Bonch-Osmolovskaya, 'Combatting the Russian State Propaganda Machine: Strategy of Information Resistance,' *Journal of Soviet and Post-Soviet Politics and Society*, 1, 1 (2015): 182.
150 Jurij Hajduk and Tomasz Stepniewski, 'Russia's Hybrid War with Ukraine: Determinants, Instruments, Accomplishments and Challenges,' *Studia Europejskie*, 2 (2016): 46-47.
151 Wilson, 'The Donbas in 2014.'
152 Matveeva, *'Through Times of Trouble,'* 273.

NGO's and civil society groups, and promoted its political influence through the Russian media, books, and social media. *VKontakte*, a major Russian social media site, had more Ukrainian members than Facebook up to 2014. Ukrainians used *Yandex* more than Google and .ru more than Gmail. It is therefore not the case Russia had 'few soft power instruments at its disposal' prior to and in 2014.[153]

Putin's deep obsession with Ukraine is evident in Russian information warfare. The EU's centre to counter disinformation wrote:

> 'Since Russia's illegal annexation of Crimea in 2014 and its support to separatists in Donbas, Ukraine has remained one of the main targets of pro-Kremlin disinformation attacks. Out of 13,000 examples of pro-Kremlin disinformation recorded in the EUvsDisinfo database, nearly 5,000 target Ukraine. Nearly eight years after Russia's invasion of Crimea, the Kremlin continues to be obsessed with using disinformation against Ukraine, its leadership and society. It is by far the most targeted country in the pro-Kremlin media globally.'[154]

Russian information warfare denigrated Ukraine in a brutal and chauvinistic manner daily. Russian media portray Ukraine as run by West Ukrainian fascists who came to power in the Euromaidan Revolution who are repressing and discriminating against Russian speakers who desire to be part of the Russian World. This stereotype is not only unable to comprehend Russian speaking Ukrainian patriotism but ignores 'fascist Ukraine' as having elected a Jewish president.

Ukraine is depicted as an artificial country and failed state and Ukrainians as a branch of the pan-Russian nation. The Ukrainian language is an artificial construct. The Ukrainian nation was created as an Austrian conspiracy in the late nineteenth century to divide the pan-Russian nation. Artificial Ukraine is a US puppet state where its 'fascist' rulers pursue Washington's Russophobic

---

153 Matveeva, '*Through Times of Trouble,*' 273.
154 'The Kremlin's Main Target of Disinformation,' *EUvsDisinfo*, 16 December 2021. https://euvsdisinfo.eu/the-kremlins-main-target-of-disinformation/

policies. Kyiv's European aspirations are mocked, Europe is disinterested, and Ukraine will eventually return to the Russian World.[155]

Military Invasion

Beginning in late June 2014, Russia launched hundreds of artillery attacks against Ukrainian targets in what 'can only therefore be considered acts of war of the Russian Federation against Ukraine.'[156] Russia launched the attacks along the entire Donetsk and Luhansk border in response to Ukrainian forces moving towards the border. The aim of the artillery attacks was to thwart Ukraine regaining control of the border which would have prevented Russia from supplying its own forces and Russian proxies in the Donbas.

The military aspects of full spectrum conflict only function when there is popular support among the local population which did not exist in six of the eight *oblasts* of south-eastern Ukraine; even in the Donbas the population was divided. In a detailed study of Russian control over the parts of Donbas it has occupied, Donald N. Jensen brushes aside the violent insurgency as an outcome resulting from civil war or popular uprising and believes the conflict was manufactured by Russia to prevent Ukraine's integration into the West.[157] Jensen documents how Russia's Donbas proxies were controlled by the Kremlin from their inception with all their major military decisions made in Moscow. The DNR and LNR were led from their birth to August 2014 by Russian citizens. Russia supplied training, leadership, fuel, ammunition, military technology, and intelligence to veterans of past Russian military and intelligence, operations in frozen conflicts in Eurasia and former Yugoslavia. In addition to veterans, Russia also used members of organised crime

---

155 Kuzio, *Crisis in Russian Studies?* 97-104 and *Russian Nationalism and the Russian-Ukrainian War*, 156.
156 Sean Case, *Putin's Undeclared War: Summer 2014 – Russian Artillery Strikes against Ukraine*, Bellingcat, 21 December 2016. https://www.bellingcat.com/news/uk-and-europe/2016/12/21/russian-artillery-strikes-against-ukraine/
157 Donald N. Jensen, 'Moscow in the Donbas: Command, Control, Crime and the Minsk Peace Process,' *NDC Research Report* 1 (Rome: NATO Defence College, 2017). http://www.ndc.nato.int/news/news.php?icode=1029

and nationalist and fascist extremists, such as members of the Russian National Unity (RNE) Party.[158]

Nationalist Aleksandr Borodai admitted on Russian television that Russian citizens had controlled the DNR and LNR between April-May-August 2014; that is for the first 4-5 months of their existence. Borodai said 'I am from Moscow. My first deputy was from Moscow. The power ministries [i.e., *siloviki*] were controlled by Muscovites, and defense minister Igor Strelkov (Igor Girkin) was also from Moscow. It was a little too blatant from a propaganda perspective.'[159] Borodai added that in the Donbas 'there were Russian forces, and the armed forces of the Russian Federation who were also Russian forces. Both the first and the second [Corps] are Russian forces. Yes, one lot are called DNR corps, the other LNR people's militia, and the other Russian army corps. What's the difference [between them]?'[160] The continued presence of Russian military forces in the Donbas was confirmed in December 2021 by a court in the Russian city of Rostov-on-the-Don which passed a sentence on corruption by a person involved in supplying food to the Russian armed forces. The court documents inadvertently wrote about foodstuffs being sent 'to the military units of the Armed Forces of the Russian Federation deployed on the territory of the DNR and LNR.'[161]

'Russia's supporting hand was evident from the beginning' with 'Russian troops, intelligence officers, and political advisers [who] were alleged to be either supporting or directly controlling the separatists.'[162] Luke Harding describes the war as a

---

158 A. Shekhovtsov, 'Neo-Nazi Russian National Unity in Eastern Ukraine,' *Anton Shekhovtsov's blog*, 14 August 2014. https://anton-shekhovtsov.blogspot.com/2014/08/neo-nazi-russian-national-unity-in.html and Kuzio, *Crisis in Russian Studies?* 84-85.
159 Coynash, 'New United Russia party MP confirms that the fighting in Donbas is by "Russian forces".'
160 Coynash, 'New United Russia party MP confirms that the fighting in Donbas is by "Russian forces".'
161 Todd Prince, 'Russian Court Verdict Indicates Russian Troop Presence in Ukraine, Contradicting Kremlin Narrative,' *RFERL*, 17 December 2021. https://www.rferl.org/a/russia-court-troops-eastern-ukraine-/31613343.html
162 Bowen, 'Coercive diplomacy and the Donbas,' 325, 331.

'Frankenstein-like conflict' artificially created by the Russian government.[163] Control has been exercised through Kremlin 'curators,' such as Suslov who oversaw the DNR and LNR in 2014-2020 on behalf of the Kremlin. Military advisers and Russian intelligence coordinate their policies through the Centre for the Management of Reconstruction while the Inter-Ministerial Commission for the Provision of Humanitarian Aid for the Affected Areas in the South-east of the Regions of Donetsk and Luhansk acts as Russia's shadow government.

From May 2014, Russia was providing surface to air missiles to Russian proxies and its *spetsnaz* forces. These shot down five Ukrainian helicopters, 2 fighter jets, an AN-30 surveillance plane and Ilyushin IL-76 over the course of the next two months. Because of a high number of casualties among Donbas Russian proxies and Russian *siloviki* from Ukrainian air power, Russia sought to change the military balance on the battlefield by suppling the sophisticated surface to air BUK missile system. Unfortunately, a Russian manned BUK shot down MH17 killing 298 innocent civilians and crew, including 88 children.

Prelude to Russia's Invasion of Ukraine

This chapter analyzes Western scholarly writing on the 2014 crisis and the following eight years of Crimea's occupation and Russian hybrid warfare in the Donbas. As a prelude to the conclusion, it is interesting to analyze how scholars who adopted the Kremlin's talking points on the 2014 crisis reinvented themselves after Russia's invasion.

Scholars who *prior* to the invasion claimed south-eastern Ukraine has weak links to the Ukrainian state call for ceasefires and peace talks *since* the invasion. In the first instance they accepted Putin's historical revisionism denying Kyiv legitimacy over south-eastern Ukraine while in the second, calls for a ceasefire would freeze the frontline and leave occupied south-eastern Ukraine in

---

163 Harding, *A Very Expensive Poison*, 304-305.

Russian hands.[164] Sakwa attended rallies calling for peace in Ukraine with far-left former leader of the Labour Party Jeremy Corbyn whose anti-Americanism always made him pro-Russian.

Prior to the 2022 Russian invasion, scholars such as Lieven supported the Russian interpretation of the 2014-205 Minsk accords that would have created a weak, federalized, neutral Ukraine as a de facto Russian satellite state. Since the invasion they have called for an end to the war by Ukraine agreeing to a ceasefire that would benefit Russian military aggression.[165] Unable to openly support Russia's illegal military aggression against Ukraine, that includes horrific war crimes, *Putinversteher* scholars are forced to camoflage their Russophilism by pretending to be impartial peaceniks.

Lieven is particularly incensed at Ukraine's goal of returning Crimea to Ukrainian sovereignty. Like Sakwa, Lieven wrongly believes the peninsula 'was always Russian.'[166] Crimea's history did not begin in 1783 anymore than US and Canadian history began in the first decade of the seventeenth century.

Conclusions

Russia's full spectrum conflict against Ukraine took place throughout the decade from the Orange to the Euromaidan Revolutions and was placed on steroids after Putin was re-elected in 2012. In the decade prior to the 2014 crisis, pro-Russian extremists were given paramilitary training and Russian intelligence infiltrated Ukraine's security forces, especially in Crimea. With a high level of infiltration of Ukrainian security forces, it is not surprising the early operations of the ATO sometimes failed. Russian intelligence was active on the ground in Ukraine in 2013-2014 during the Euromaidan Revolution and in Spring 2014. Russian intelligence *spetsnaz*, nationalist mercenaries, 'political tourists' (trained by Russian intelligence and bused

---

164 A. Lieven, 'Ending the Threat of War in Ukraine: A Negotiated Solution to the Donbas Conflict and the Crimean Dispute,' *Quincy Paper* (Washington DC: Quincy Institute for Responsible Statecraft, 4 January 2022). https://quincyinst.org/report/ending-the-threat-of-war-in-ukraine/
165 https://quincyinst.org/author/alieven/
166 A. Lieven, 'Applebaum & Goldberg: Truth attended by a bodyguard of lies' (Washington DC: Quincy Institute for Responsible Statecraft, 5 May 2023). https://responsiblestatecraft.org/2023/05/05/applebaum-goldberg-truth-attended-by-a-bodyguard-of-lies/

into Ukraine from Belgorod to Kharkiv and Moldova's Transniestr region to Odesa) transformed anti-Maidan protestors into violent Russian proxies. Pro-Russian 'Kadyrov' Chechen forces arrived in Ukraine in May 2014. Throughout most of 2014, Russian forces assisted local pro-Russian groups in looting Ukrainian military stories, directly supplied military equipment through 'humanitarian convoys', transformed anti-Maidan protestors into violent and loyal proxies and installed extreme nationalist politicians in Crimea and the DNR who had minority public support.

Russian information warfare was on a war footing from 2012-2013 onwards and has continued to denigrate Ukraine and Ukrainians to the present-day reflecting Putin's personal obsession with Ukraine.[167] Russia launched 'Operation Armageddon' months before the Euromaidan Revolution which undertook over 5,000 cyberattacks in the following eight years.

Taken together, these different aspects of full spectrum conflict provide evidence of Russian's intervention throughout the 2014 crisis which cannot be therefore defined as a civil war. Western scholars should place greater trust in the Ukrainian public who have never believed a civil war has been taking place in their country since the 2014 crisis.[168]

---

167 Putin, 'On the Historical Unity of Russians and Ukrainians.'
168 'Poshuky Shlyakhiv Vidnovlennya Suverenitetu Ukrayiny Nad Okupovanym Donbasom' and 'Yak zminylosya dumka ukrayintsiv pro rosiysko-ukrayinsku viynu za dva roky prezydentsva Zelenskoho.'

Conflict Studies and the War in Ukraine, 2014-2022

Paul D'Anieri

Prior to Russia's full-scale invasion of Ukraine in February 2022, Ukraine and Russia had been at war in Eastern Ukraine since 2014, and that conflict spurred a significant literature. Among the major themes in research and in policy analysis were the causes of the conflict that began in 2014, the barriers to a solution, the impact on combatants and non-combatants, the impact on Ukrainian national identity, and the policies that various actors should adopt to bring the conflict to an acceptable end. There was immense disagreement on what constituted an acceptable outcome to the Minsk process, and various actors strived to shape discourse on the nature of the conflict, who was to blame for it, and what solutions should be considered acceptable and unacceptable. In the West, the conflict drew the attention of some of the most well-known academic scholars of international relations, who previously wrote little about this region (i.e., John Mearsheimer and Stephen Walt) as well as some of the most prominent scholars of Russia (such as Richard Sakwa), who had previously written little about international politics or Ukraine.[1]

Despite the range of scholars who applied themselves to war in Donbas, the massive literatures on international conflict, civil war, and conflict resolution were rarely applied to the conflict. At most, concepts from them were applied in an ad-hoc way.[2] Only a

---

1   John J. Mearsheimer, "Why the Ukraine Crisis Is the West's Fault: The Liberal Delusions That Provoked Putin" *Foreign Affairs*, September/October (2014), pp.1-12; Stephen M. Walt, "What Would a Realist World Have Looked Like." *ForeignPolicy.com*, 8 January 2016. https://foreignpolicy.com/2016/01/08/what-would-a-realist-world-have-looked-like-iraq-syria-iran-obama-bush-clinton/; Richard Sakwa, *Frontline Ukraine: Crisis in the Borderlands* (London: I.B. Tauris, 2016).
2   Samuel Charap and Timothy J. Colton, *Everyone Loses: The Ukraine Crisis and the Ruinous Contest for Post-Soviet Eurasia* (London: International Institute of Strategic Studies, 2017); Sakwa, *Frontline Crisis*.

few studies, including work by D'Anieri and Arel and Driscoll explicitly applied literature from conflict studies to the war in Donbas.

The result is that scholars have underutilized the theories, concepts, and findings that have been found most valid across a wide range of conflicts beyond this one. We are missing not only important opportunities to understand the conflict of 2014–22 and insight on why Russia escalated so dramatically in 2022 but also the opportunity to push back against the politicization of research on the topic.

How can the literatures on international conflict, civil war, and conflict resolution inform our understanding of this conflict? This article seeks to identify a series of questions, concepts, and findings that can be applied to better understand limited war in Eastern Ukraine from 2014 to 2022. While the focus is on that period, the implications for the current war are equally important. The goal here is to formulate a partial agenda and to provide a sense of what we are missing.

In applying this literature, we focus on *durable peace* as an outcome. Much of the literature on the period from 2014 to 2022 advocated ways of stopping the fighting but did not consider the durability of the proposed arrangements. In contrast, much of the literature on international and civil conflict examines the durability of different kinds of solutions or outcomes, for the obvious reason that a "solution" is not really a solution if it breaks down in a few years' time, which occurs in many cases. Many international conflicts are accounted for by the same rivals fighting repeatedly.[3] Will Ukraine and Russia come to fit that category, or will the current war lead to an enduring settlement? The fact that many regarded the Minsk process as potentially leading to stable peace demonstrates the problem. "Thus 'durable solutions' is not a redundancy but rather a quality to be enhanced, and outcomes need to be evaluated for

---

3   Suzanne Werner, "The Precarious Nature of Peace: Resolving the Issues, Enforcing the Settlement, and Renegotiating the Terms," *American Journal of Political Science* vol.43, no.3 (1999), p. 913.

durability."[4] Were this not an issue, the 1994 Budapest Memorandum or 1997 Russia–Ukraine Friendship Treaty would have definitively ruled out the use of force between the two countries. Virginia P. Fortna provides a sense of the danger: of the 48 cases in her dataset, 21 experienced a renewal of conflict.[5]

The discussion begins with a review of rationalist theories of conflict. Rationalist explanations of conflict underpin much of the related discussion of conflict resolution, both in civil and international wars. The rationalist focus on commitment problems points to a barrier to peace that received insufficient attention in the Donbas case and has important implications for long-term peace.[6] That discussion is followed by an overview of conflict resolution and specifically mediation. In what kind of circumstances does mediation tend to succeed, and what sorts of actors are best suited to mediation? Specifically, when does stalemate make a conflict "ripe" for successful mediation? This literature does not reach consensus but shows why we should have been skeptical about the likelihood that the Minsk process would lead to enduring peace. Because the mediation literature addresses both international and civil wars, it forces us to address the controversial question of the domestic and international dimensions of the conflict that begin in 2014. Leaving aside the empirical problems with classifying this as a civil war, the point stressed here is that the literature increasingly recognizes that many conflicts have both domestic and international roots and is therefore putting less emphasis on a clear distinction between the two. Therefore, one does not need to agree that the conflict was a civil war to ask what the literature on power sharing and regional autonomy tells us about the likelihood that power-sharing or regional autonomy, a central element of contention in the Minsk agreements, could lead to lasting peace in Donbas or in the larger

---

4 I. William Zartman, "Putting Humpty-Dumpty Together Again," in David A. Lake and Donald Rothchild eds., *The International Spread of Ethnic Conflict: Fear, Diffusion, and Escalation* (Princeton: Princeton University Press, 1998), p.317.
5 Virginia Page Fortna, "Scraps of Paper? Agreements and the Durability of Peace," *International Organization* vol.57, no.2 (2003), pp.337–72.
6 Paul D'Anieri, "Commitment Problems and the Failure of the Minsk Process: The Second-Order Commitment Challenge," *Post-Soviet Affairs* (2022), pp. 1-16.

war. The discussion then addresses another question raised in discussions of "ripeness," namely the extent to which public opinion, especially in Ukraine, may come to support a peace agreement as the cost of war in terms of increased casualties. Literature heavily based on US cases indicates a negative relationship between casualties and support for war, but we do not yet see much evidence of this in Ukraine or Russia. Therefore, we broaden the discussion of domestic factors to include the literature on two-level games, which shows how domestic constituencies can narrow the range of solutions that state leaders can reach. The conclusion then considers how these different literatures taken together can improve our understanding of the conflict that began in 2014 and the much larger one beginning in 2022.

Rationalist Theories of Conflict

Much of the contemporary literature on international and domestic conflict is informed by rationalist theories of conflict.[7] These theories begin with a simple observation: given the high cost of war, it is an expensive way to arrive at whatever the end result is. Put differently, if one knew ahead of time how a war would end, it would be much cheaper (and therefore preferable to both sides) to arrive at that result without the immense costs of war. War, therefore, is from the rational choice perspective, irrational. Why do actors nonetheless engage in it? The rationalist answers have shaped much subsequent literature and turn out to be highly relevant, both for the conflict in Donbas from 2014 to 2022 and the current war.

James D. Fearon and other scholars generally identify three obstacles to the problem of avoiding costly war.[8] The first is the information problem. While both sides prefer to avoid war, they also want to avoid making concessions. Therefore, they have powerful incentives to bluff, exaggerating their demands and their level of commitment to achieving what they want. This helps them strike a

---

7 For an influential statement of this approach, see James D. Fearon, "Rationalist Explanations for War," *International Organization* vol.49, no.3 (1995), pp.379–414.
8 Fearon, "Rationalist Explanations for War."

better bargain. But because both sides misrepresent their true positions and know that the other side is doing the same, a bargained solution that is preferable to war may not be apparent. War reveals more information about costs and commitments, and in the rationalist perspective, a primary function of war is to reduce gaps in information.[9] For example, had the parties in World War I known in 1914 what they knew in 1918 about their adversaries' ability and will to sustain casualties, they would have made more substantial concessions in order to avoid the conflict.

The information problem in the Ukraine–Russia conflict was vividly illustrated in late 2021 when Russia deployed forces that could support a massive invasion of Ukraine while Vladimir Putin issued both threats and demands concerning Ukraine's relations with Russia and the West. Western states responded by rejecting most of the Russian demands, but considerable uncertainty remained. Would Russia really endure the costs of a significant new invasion of Ukraine, or was Putin bluffing to get the West to make concessions (or to urge Ukraine to make concessions)? And what would the costs to Russia be? Would the US move to cut Russia's access to the SWIFT financial system? Would it supply Ukraine with the weapons to raise Russia's costs? Or were threats to do so merely bluffs, intended to induce Russia to settle for the status quo? Had the various actors known in early February 2022 what they knew a few months later, they might have made greater efforts to secure peace, but the only way to gain that information was to go to war.

A second rationalist obstacle to peace is that of indivisible goods. While in theory a bargaining solution always exists, that is not true if some important good is indivisible. If this good (perhaps a piece of territory) must go entirely to one side or the other, then it may not be possible to find a bargain that both sides prefer to war. The term "territorial integrity" captures the belief that territory should not be infinitely divisible. In theory, rationalists argue, the

---

9   Branislav Slantchev, "The Principle of Convergence in Wartime Negotiations," *American Political Science Review* vol.97, no.4 (2003), pp.621–32.

problem of indivisibility is manageable.[10] One reason is that territory, over which many wars are fought, is always divisible in any number of ways. The redrawing of borders was a common outcome of peace treaties, at least until the post-World War II era,[11] and since February 2022, a range of territorial divisions that might accompany a peace agreement has been discussed. A second reason is that even when a good is indivisible, a "side payment" can compensate the side that does not receive it. In such a case, the bargaining is simply over the size of the side payment, and there is always some division that is preferable to war. Perhaps, for example, Russia and the West could compensate Ukraine for losing territory by allowing it to join NATO.

A final problem, on which much rationalist theory focuses, is the commitment problem.[12] Nearly every deal to end a conflict depends on the actors' making commitments about what they will and will not do in the future: this may refer to holding elections, respecting the rights of minorities, not violating another state's sovereignty, and so on. The problem is that while these future commitments are essential to any peace agreement, it is extremely difficult to guarantee that they will be honored, making it less rational to agree to a peace deal based on them. The commitment problem is distinct from the bargaining problem: even when the terms of a deal can be reached, if the two sides do not have confidence that they will be honored, they cannot complete the deal. Thus, agreeing on the terms of a deal is a necessary, but not sufficient, condition for ending conflict. Mechanisms to enforce commitments are also necessary.

What does all this mean for the conflict in Eastern Ukraine prior to February 2022? Regarding the information problem, rationalist theories point to a paradoxical reason why the conflict appeared stalemated: the level of casualties between 2014 and 2022 was relatively modest. If war begins because actors have

---

10 Robert Powell, "War as a Commitment Problem," *International Organization* vol.60, no.1 (2006), p. 170.
11 Mark W. Zacher, "The Territorial Integrity Norm: International Boundaries and the Use of Force," *International Organization* vol.55, no.2 (2001), pp.215-50.
12 Powell, "War as a Commitment Problem."

incomplete information about each other's will and capabilities, then it ends when the war clarifies just how high the costs are, and who will have to bear how much of them. In this view, one of the main functions of war is to reduce uncertainty over who would win. Once expectations about capabilities, costs, and will converge, the two sides can reach a bargained solution.[13] To be clear, the cost of arriving at this convergence can be quite high, and there is no guarantee that the solution will be just. The titles of two widely cited articles, "Give War a Chance" and "The Case for Rebel Victory" capture the argument.[14] In this view, good news in the short term (the low level of killing between 2014 and 2022) was bad news in the long term. Because the war was limited, the vital exchange of information about capabilities, costs, and will did not take place, and the conditions that lead to war in the first place (incomplete information) persisted.

From the rationalist perspective, the escalation of 2022 was necessary to further narrow disagreements about capabilities, costs, and will. It was widely assumed that Russia would prevail in such an escalation. After the Minsk II agreement in February 2015, an important question was why Russia did not escalate, given expectations that it could break the stalemate and prevail. One plausible explanation was that it was satisfied with its *de facto* control over a portion of Donetsk and Luhansk *oblasts*. Another was that it believed that it could get what it wanted more cheaply by being patient and applying other kinds of pressure. A third was that it believed that it would become easier to win militarily in the future. The decision to wage all-out war in 2022 indicates that Russia no longer believed that the Minsk stalemate served its interests or that biding its time would lead to increasing pressure on Ukraine to capitulate or to an evaporation of the West's resolve to support Ukraine. While many analyses have posited Putin's delusions as a cause of the war, from the rationalist perspective, Russia's decision

---

13 Slantchev, "The Principle of Convergence."
14 Edward N. Luttwak, "Give War a Chance," *Foreign Affairs* vol.78, no.4 (1999), p.36–44; Monica Duffy Toft, "Ending Civil Wars: A Case for Rebel Victory?" *International Security* vol.34, no.4 (2010), pp.7–36.

to attack stemmed from the end of the delusion that the Minsk process would achieve Russia's aims.

To the extent that Russia could extract a better resolution by escalating the conflict, why did Ukraine not settle the conflict before the terms of a resolution deteriorated? Would not the autonomy that Russia sought for Donetsk and Luhansk have been better than the likely results of the current war? One answer is that because Russia did not appear willing to incur the costs of all-out invasion, Ukraine had an incentive to hold out for a better outcome. With conflict at a relatively low level after Minsk 2, the cost to Ukraine of waiting for something better was relatively low. Ukraine may have held out hope that eventually something would change for the better: Perhaps political change in Moscow would lead to a change in policy. Perhaps the West would bring greater pressure to bear on Russia or provide Ukraine with the weaponry to negotiate a better deal. Perhaps the post-2014 status quo, with the most pro-Russian voters in Ukraine no longer part of the electorate, was sufficiently tolerable that Ukrainian leaders were disinclined to endure significant risks or costs to try to change it.

In sum, it seems that both Russia and Ukraine believed that time was on their side until early 2022. Russia then came to believe that time was not on its side (perhaps due to gradual NATO training of Ukraine's military). Overall, however, the lesson from the rationalist approach is sobering: the likelihood of ending a war increases as the costs of fighting it increases.[15] A significant empirical literature covering both civil and international wars finds that decisive victories are more likely to lead to peace than compromise.[16] This has important implications for the West's ongoing policy. Support sufficient to keep Ukraine in the war, but insufficient to help it actually defeat Russia, is likely to prolong the war but not to end it.

---

15 Daniel S. Morey, "When War Brings Peace: A Dynamic Model of the Rivalry Process," *American Journal of Political Science* vol.55, no.2 (2011), pp.263-75.

16 Zeev Maoz, "Peace by Empire? Conflict Outcomes and International Stability, 1816-1976," *Journal of Peace Research* vol.21, no.3 (1984), pp.227-41; Paul R. Hensel, "One Thing Leads to Another: Recurrent Militarized Disputes in Latin America, 1816-1986," *Journal of Peace Research* vol.31, no.3 (1994), pp.281-98; Roy Licklider, "The Consequences of Negotiated Settlements in Civil Wars, 1945-1993," *American Political Science Review* vol.89, no.3 (1995), pp.681-90.

As long as the war is stalemated, the information problem (the difficulty of predicting who will actually win) remains, and no bargaining solution can be found.

The indivisibility problem also hampered a resolution in Ukraine and continues to do so. In theory, the territory in dispute can be divided in any number of ways (the shift from Minsk I to Minsk II represented a revision of the boundary between the occupied territories and the rest of Ukraine). In practice, however, territory is harder to divide in some places than in others. Both sides, for example, sought control of the city of Donetsk, but a city split in two is not really a city in the same way. Thus, even when pro-Russian forces controlled Donetsk at the beginning of 2015, they felt that they had to control the airport as well, and renewed fighting to achieve that goal. It is hard to imagine dividing Crimea, and it is difficult to sustain Crimea without controlling its water supply in Kherson region.

Even if the territory can be divided, however, certain principles cannot. Is Ukraine going to be a unitary or federal state? Are some territories going to have autonomy within the state? Will Russia be allowed a treaty-guaranteed veto on its neighbors' alliance choices? Is the principle that borders are not to be changed by force to endure or not? On issues such as these, splitting the difference is not easy. A significant literature finds that solving territorial disputes is much more difficult than the rationalist literature implies.[17]

While much of the literature on the conflict from 2014 to 2022 focused on the substantive disagreements between the sides, the commitment problem was at least as significant a barrier to peace.[18] Ukraine was expected to amend its constitution to allow for regional autonomy in Donetsk and Luhansk, while Russia's proxies were expected to return control of the border to Ukraine and to hold elections freely and under Ukrainian law. Neither side wanted to take the steps required of it unless it was assured that the other side

---

17   Ron E. Hassner, "To Halve and to Hold: Conflicts over Sacred Space and the Problem of Indivisibility," *Security Studies* 12, 3 (2003), pp.1–33; Monica Duffy Toft, "Issue Indivisibility and Time Horizons as Rationalist Explanations for War," *Security Studies* vol.15, no.1 (2006), pp.34–69.
18   D'Anieri, "Commitment Problems and the Failure of the Minsk Process."

would meet its commitments. The problem was that once one side implemented a concession, the incentives for the other side to not meet its commitments would increase, because its position would have improved. The literature on the commitment problem shows that this is a generic problem.[19]

While the rationalist literature shows that, over time, war will tend to solve the bargaining problem by increasing information about costs, capabilities, and will, it has no such impact on the commitment problem. Thus, the commitment problem is likely to persist even if differences on the terms of a deal narrow. Any such bargain involves commitments about the future. Ukraine was expected to commit not only to granting autonomy, but to not reversing it later. Russia would have had to agree not only to leave Ukraine, but not to invade again later, not to encourage further separatism beyond Donbas, and to not encourage Donetsk and Luhansk to pursue secession if they were granted autonomy. If Russia got its way, NATO would have committed to never integrating Ukraine and to permanently constraining the rights of post-1997 members.

How could such commitments be made credible, especially given the history of the 1994 Budapest Memorandum, the 1997 Russia–Ukraine Friendship Treaty, and the Russian perception that various commitments have been violated by the West? The answer in the rationalist literature, which shows up as well in literature on conflict resolution, is for some external actor to guarantee either that violations will be prevented (met with high cost) or that the potential victims will be protected.

This need for an external guarantor helps us understand why it was so hard to solve the conflict that began in 2014 and why it will be even harder to solve the larger war. One potential external guarantor, Russia, is a party to the conflict. Others, including the US, EU, and NATO are deeply involved. Moreover, Russia considers the idea of a NATO guarantee for Ukraine's security itself a cause for war, while several NATO members remain highly resistant to such a commitment.

---

19   Powell, "War as a Commitment Problem."

Overall, the rationalist literature points to a sobering conclusion: if the commitment problem cannot be solved, then the bargaining problem will have to be solved much more thoroughly. In essence, this means the war must escalate to the point where the costs become so high that one or both sides prefer an agreement that cannot be guaranteed to continued fighting. Put differently, it requires one side to be decisively defeated on the battlefield. In this way, the rationalist approach helps explain why a stalemate might persist and why that is unlikely by itself to end the war.

Mediation and Conflict Resolution

Almost from the beginning, external actors sought to mediate an end to the Donbas conflict. As the literature on the commitment problem shows, external actors play an important role in bringing many conflicts to an end. Looking at civil wars, Barbara F. Walter finds that external guarantees are an essential component of successful conflict resolution.[20] A broader literature on mediation addresses the circumstances in which external mediation is likely to be effective, and the kinds of mediation that are likely to be effective.

The key defining factor of mediation is the involvement of a third party to help two conflicting parties bridge their differences. Peter Wallensteen and Isak Svensson, in a survey of research on international mediation, argue that research to date "provides credible evidence of its effectiveness, although the particular conditions under which mediation is effective are still debated."[21] Under what conditions does mediation succeed? The literature focuses on at least four broad categories to explain the success or failure of mediation: the characteristics of the conflict, the relationship between the warring parties, the identity of the mediators and the provisions of the agreement. This helps us think about why mediation did not

---

20 Barbara F. Walter, "The Critical Barrier to Civil War Settlement," *International Organization* vol.51, no.3 (1997), pp.335–64.
21 Peter Wallensteen and Isak Svensson, "Talking Peace: International Mediation in Armed Conflicts," *Journal of Peace Research* vol.51, no.2 (2014), pp.315–27.

resolve the conflict prior to escalation in 2022, and what the prospects might be in the future.

A substantial line of research on the characteristics of the conflict focuses on "ripeness."[22] As conflicts drag on, the argument goes, they become "riper" for settlement, as participants become wearier and costs mount. Mediation should be most successful when it is applied at moments that are ripe for settlement. The concept of ripeness meshes neatly with the rationalist notion that conflict narrows information asymmetries over time. As those asymmetries narrow, ripeness should increase. How close the situation in Eastern Ukraine is to ripeness and what might bring it closer are crucial questions from this perspective. In contrast to the rationalist literature, which sees most clarity in one side prevailing, the focus on ripeness implies that stalemate might be a source of peace.

While some found signs of ripeness in the Donbas conflict prior to 2022,[23] there is no ready measure. On one hand, the conflict endured for eight years and the prospects for any of the sides to dramatically improve their position at an acceptable cost always seemed limited. In some research, duration of conflict by itself increases ripeness. On the other hand, because the rate of casualties was brought to relatively low levels after early 2015, one might argue that the sides felt little pressure to end the conflict. Zartman focuses on the narrower concept of "hurting stalemate," in which actors perceive a potential impending disaster if a settlement is not reached.[24] As pointed out earlier, there is an unwelcome connection between the cost of war and the likelihood of resolving it.

---

22 Marieke Kleiboer, "Ripeness of Conflict: A Fruitful Notion?" *Journal of Peace Research* vol.31, no.1 (1994), pp.109–16; I. William Zartman, "Ripeness: The Hurting Stalemate and Beyond," in Paul C. Stern and Daniel Druckman eds., *International Conflict Resolution after the Cold War* (Washington, DC: National Academy Press, 2000), pp.225–50.

23 Jesse Driscoll, "Ukraine's Civil War: Would Accepting This Terminology Help Resolve the Conflict?" *PONARS Eurasia Policy Memo* 572, 6 February 2019. https://www.ponarseurasia.org/ukraine-s-civil-war-would-accepting-this-terminology-help-resolve-the-conflict/

24 Zartman, "Ripeness: The Hurting Stalemate."

An important distinction can be made between the intensity of a conflict and its duration.[25] Some research indicates that while duration correlates with successful mediation, intensity (the casualty rate) does not. If that is correct, the conflict in Eastern Ukraine might have been gaining ripeness, and *contra* the rationalist perspective, an increase in costs (casualties) would not have made peace more likely. If casualties do not by themselves lead to ripeness, and eight years of war in the Donbas did not lead to sufficient ripeness to settle the conflict, then the broader war now underway may have quite some way to run, even though casualties are much higher. The impact of the level of violence and casualties on the likelihood of settlement remains in dispute in the empirical literature, and that should be taken into account in the assumptions we make about the Russia–Ukraine war.

One important finding in the literature is that mediation is more likely to be accepted in international conflicts than in civil wars, presumably because governments involved in civil wars do not want to legitimize rebel groups by engaging in mediation with them.[26] That was an important barrier in Ukraine between 2014 and 2022, though the participation of DNR and LNR (Luhansk People's Republic) in mediated negotiations indicates that it was not insurmountable. The current war is unambiguously a Russian war (and Russia's annexation of Donetsk and Luhansk means that the DNR and LNR no longer formally exist), so that one small barrier to settlement has been removed.

Alternatively, ripeness might arise because of internal change in one or more of the combatants. Clearly Russia hoped for that after Ukraine's 2019 presidential elections and continued to promote pro-Russian forces in Ukraine. Many in the West appear to hope that Russia will fundamentally change its position, either because the Russian people will force a change in leadership or when Vladimir Putin passes from the scene.

---

25 Kleiboer, "Ripeness of Conflict," p. 364.
26 Molly M. Melin and Isak Svensson, "Incentives for Talking: Accepting Mediation in International and Civil Wars," *International Interactions* vol.35, no.3 (2009), pp.249–71.

These questions of who accepts mediation and when complicate efforts to evaluate the effectiveness of mediation. To the extent that actors choose mediation when it is most likely to succeed, we are likely to overestimate the effectiveness of mediation due to selection bias. To the extent mediation is applied to especially challenging cases, we are likely to underestimate its impact.

The identity of the mediators is also the subject of a great deal of research. Some research finds that mediation succeeds most when mediators are seen as being fair and impartial. That points to a factor that hampered efforts to bring the conflict in Eastern Ukraine to an end. The obvious problem was that Russia insisted on playing the role of mediator despite being a combatant. Less obvious was the perception by Russia and the Donbas separatists that other external actors, such as France, Germany, and the EU, were not fair and impartial either. Looking forward, one wonders what actor (international organization, NGO, or state) might be seen as fair and impartial by all the combatants.

Others question the importance of impartiality, finding some circumstances in which bias may increase the influence of mediators. As stressed in the rationalist perspective, the question is whether information asymmetries can be reduced and commitment problems addressed. Mediators, even (or especially) biased ones, can help reduce information asymmetries. For example, if a mediator that is especially trusted by one side can convince that actor that its demands are unlikely to be met, it might be easier to persuade that side to modify its demands.[27] In contrast, mediators concerned mostly with peace lack credibility because they are suspected of "lying to hasten the end of the war...making the message uninformative and hence unbelievable."[28] In the case of Ukraine between 2014 and 2022, the West could have sought to persuade Ukraine of the limits of what was possible, or Russia might have persuaded the separatists (for example, that secession was not an

---

27 Andrew Kydd, "Which Side Are You On? Bias, Credibility, and Mediation," *American Journal of Political Science* vol.47, no.4 (2003), pp.597–611.
28 Alastair Smith and Allan Stam,) "Mediation and Peacekeeping in a Random Walk Model of War," *International Studies Perspectives* vol.5, no.4 (2003), p.127.

option). Throughout 2022, many have argued that the West should persuade Ukraine to make territorial concessions or forswear NATO membership in order to secure peace. The problem of who might convince Russia to moderate its demands remains especially challenging.

The literature distinguishes between pure mediation and "mediation with muscle," in which external mediators coerce warring parties to make the concessions needed to end a conflict. Some find that mediators who can punish "spoilers" are more likely to succeed. Christopher Gelpi finds that great powers are particularly well-suited to being mediators.[29] If Ukraine were merely experiencing a civil war from 2014 to 2022, Russia might have played a positive role as a mediator. The reality, of course, was quite different. While mediation with muscle might help push actors toward agreement, it can only go so far before it runs into another finding in the literature; that is, to the extent that settlements are imposed externally rather than agreed to voluntarily, they are unlikely to last. An actor who has a settlement forced on it is likely not only to be resentful, but to take the first opportunity to revise the situation. France after the Franco–Prussian war and Germany after World War I are classic examples, and Azerbaijan in the Second Karabakh War with Armenia is a more recent one.

Even in this brief review, several tensions become clear. The literature indicates that the powers closest geographically to a conflict are most likely to serve as mediators. However, those closest are probably least likely to be entirely disinterested in the results of a conflict, either because they back one of the sides or because they are concerned primarily with limiting the fallout of the conflict. Similarly, "mediation with muscle" conflicts with the need for impartiality, as the more coercion is applied, the less likely a participant is to see the coercing mediator as impartial.[30] Trying to

---

29 Christopher Gelpi, "Alliances as Instruments of Intra-allied Control," In Helga Haftendorn, Robert O. Keohane, and Celeste A. Wallander, eds., *Imperfect Unions: Security Institutions over Time and Space*. Oxford: Oxford University Press, 1999), pp.107–39.
30 Laurie Nathan, "When Push Comes to Shove: The Failure of International Mediation in African Civil Wars," *Track Two* vol.8, no.2 (1999), pp.1–23.

combine trustworthiness and power in a single mediator or team of mediators is likely to be very challenging. While external mediation will likely be part of any eventual solution in Ukraine, the case is clearly not an easy one for mediation to apply successfully.

This finding that imposed settlements tend to fail is in tension with that concerning the effects of victory. Two distinct arguments are made, and the durability of peace is crucial. One argument concerns whether two sides will reach an agreement. The victory of one side is likely to lead to an imposed peace. The second concerns the durability of peace, and for this, the future distribution of power becomes crucial. An imposed settlement will endure only if the aggrieved party remains too weak to contest it, and only if the victorious power does not later gain the ability to seize even more. While realists have suggested that due to Russian power, the West should accede to its demands towards Ukraine, imposing a settlement on Ukraine is a solution only if the distribution of power remains such that Ukraine cannot seek revision and Russia cannot seek to seize more territory.

Research on what provisions of agreements are most likely to lead to an enduring peace provides potentially significant insight about the failure of the Minsk II agreement. Fortna breaks down the characteristics of agreements that are more likely to lead to durable peace:[31]

1. Strong agreements appear to support the duration of peace. Strong agreements are those which include specific mechanisms intended to reduce incentives to attack (troop withdrawals, creation of buffer zones, arms control agreements, external guarantees), reduce uncertainties about intentions (clear and specific cease-fire lines and rules of engagement, verification arrangements), and prevent accidental violations (troop withdrawals and buffer zones).
2. External mediation does not by itself improve the duration of peace and correlates with an increased risk of renewed

---

31 Virginia Page Fortna, "Scraps of Paper? Agreements and the Durability of Peace," *International Organization* vol.57, no.2 (2003), pp.337-72.

war. Commissions made up of representatives of the combatants have a better record.
3. External mediation that results in explicit guarantees by outside powers does increase the durability of peace.
4. The introduction of peacekeepers tends to increase the duration of peace, but is far from fool-proof, especially when confronted by powerful armies (Fortna cites the example of the Turkish intervention in Cypress in 1974, despite the presence of UN peacekeepers).[32]
5. Political agreement on the underlying issues over which the war was fought is a powerful predictor of durability but is rare.

Keeping in mind that findings such as these continue to be contested within the literature, it is interesting to compare the Minsk II agreement with this set of criteria. On the positive side, the Minsk II agreement specified the need to withdraw heavy weapons, though the sides were never able and willing to do so. The introduction of peacekeepers would likely have helped, but was impossible because their placement was widely seen as prejudicing the outcome of negotiations.

On the negative side, without explicit commitments by external powers, mediation appears to do as much harm as good. Therefore, the combination of the West's refusal to guarantee an agreement and Russia's insistence that Ukraine did not receive security guarantees must be seen as predicting that peace based on the Minsk process would not last. Similarly, the absence of even basic agreement on the underlying political issues removed one of the strongest predictors of the success of negotiated agreements. Any settlement that does not resolve the underlying issues contains within it the permissive conditions for a return to war. [33]

Settlement or cease-fire may not be the only bar by which mediation efforts are measured.[34] To the extent that the alternative to

---

32 Fortna, "Scraps of Paper?" p.349.
33 Werner, "The Precarious Nature of Peace," p.914.
34 Marieke Kleiboer, "Understanding Success and Failure of International Mediation," *Journal of Conflict Resolution* vol.40, no.2 (1996), pp.360–89.

Minsk was the massive escalation we saw in 2022, the Minsk process might be seen as a success. But to the extent to which Minsk simply led to this escalation, it was a failure. There is nothing in the broader literature on conflict to suggest that the Minsk agreement had the characteristics likely to lead to enduring peace. That may explain why, while the sides accepted it as a baseline, they were unwilling to fully implement it. As negotiators seek a solution to the current war, they will need to weigh the benefits of ending the war sooner against the costs of an agreement that cannot last. Overall, previous research does not lead us to optimism about mediation: if success is defined as a cease-fire or more comprehensive settlement, mediation succeeds less than half the time, and has been less successful since the Cold War ended.[35]

International or Civil War?

Applying the mediation literature to the conflict that began in 2014 raises the question of whether the war in Donbas was a civil (intrastate) or international (inter-state) war. For most of the purposes of this article, and for most discussions of what might lead to peace, the civil versus international distinction contributes little analytical leverage. Distinctions in the literature are made primarily for analytical convenience in the construction of data sets, not to assert any clear distinction between the two.

The question of whether the conflict in Donbas a civil or international war is has been immensely controversial for at least three reasons.[36] First, viewing the conflict as a civil war bolstered the notion that Russia was not an aggressor in the conflict, with implications for assigning blame, for how the conflict could be solved, and

---

35 Paul F. Diehl, and J. Michael Greig, *International Mediation*. (Cambridge: Polity 2012).
36 Arel and Driscoll, *Ukraine's Unnamed War*; Ivan Gomza, "Quenching Fire with Gasoline: Why Flawed Terminology Will Not Help to Resolve the Ukraine Crisis," *PONARS Eurasia*, February 2019. https://ponarseurasia.org/quenching-fire-with-gasoline-why-flawed-terminology-will-not-help-to-resolve-the-ukraine-crisis/; Kristian Åtland, "Destined for Deadlock? Russia, Ukraine, and the Unfulfilled Minsk Agreements," *Post-Soviet Affairs* vol.36, no.2 (2020), pp.122–39.

for whether Russia could serve as a mediator. Second, international law has very different implications for civil versus international war. Third, recommendations about solutions seem to correlate with assessments of whether the war is international or civil. Those who saw it as a civil war tended to discuss autonomy for the Donbas and to ascribe some degree of legitimacy to Donbas separatists, while those who saw it as international conflict tended to discuss restoring Ukraine's territorial integrity and pushing back against Russian military aggression, seeing separatists primarily as proxies of Russia. Russia's propaganda presenting the conflict as an internal Ukrainian affair muddied the waters and increased the temperature of discussions.

From the perspective of the literature on conflict, the question is important in some respects and irrelevant in others. While much of the literature on conflict and conflict resolution addresses either international or civil war, many of the same concepts concerning causes and solutions are posited for both categories. Moreover, few in the field would try to extend the conceptual distinction between civil and international war (intra- and inter-state conflict) to the messiness of the real world. Increasingly, literature on conflict moves beyond the distinction between civil and international conflict, combining all large conflicts into the same data sets.[37]

The literature recognizes that purely international or civil wars are actually rather rare, leading to the concept of "internationalized civil wars." If the debate about the Donbas conflict were serious (see Kuzio's article in this special issue), the category of "civil war" would quickly have been dismissed, because of Russia's involvement. Instead, we would be debating whether the conflict is simply an international war or an "internationalized civil war." Using the definitions of the Uppsala Conflict Data Program, a case can be made either way. The Uppsala Conflict Data Program definition of "interstate conflict" states: "The primary warring parties, who

---

37 David E. Cunningham and Douglas Lemke, "Combining Civil and Interstate Wars," *International Organization* vol.67, no.3 (2013), pp. 609–27; Gleditsch, Nils Petter, Steven Pinker, Bradley A. Thayer, Jack S. Levy, and William R. Thompson, "The Decline of War," *International Studies Review* vol.15, no.3 (2013), pp.396–419.

first stated the incompatibility, must be government parties for a conflict to be classified as interstate."[38] This raises the question of who first "stated the incompatibility" at stake in the Donbas. Some might locate this first such statement in the Donbas in 2014, while the long history of territorial claims against Ukraine by Russian politicians points to the first incompatibility being between Ukraine and Russia. Viewing the conflict as beginning in the Donbas means regarding it as entirely separate from the Russian seizure of Crimea which immediately preceded it and was carried out by some of the same people.[39]

If one must define the conflict as either an international war or civil war, the literature shows why it should be seen as an international conflict.[40] Several prominent works agree that grievances that might lead to civil war exist in nearly every country, and hence cannot explain variation in the outbreak of civil wars. Instead, civil war (or its absence) is explained largely by variation in conditions that allow these movements to grow into insurgencies.[41] James D. Fearon and David D. Laitin focus, for example, on topography, state strength, and population, while Paul Collier, Anke Hoeffler and Nicholas Sambanis focus on the rent-seeking prospects of rebels.[42]

Thus, the question is not only whether ethnic separatism existed in Donbas, or who organized the seizure of buildings, but why the Ukrainian state could not manage the challenge in 2014 after 23

---

38   Uppsala Conflict Data Program, "Conflict, Interstate," https://www.pcr.uu.se /research/ucdp/definitions/#tocjump_26785261831571205_10.
39   Andrew Wilson, *Ukraine Crisis: What It Means for the West* (New Haven: Yale University Press, 2014), 129-130.
40   For an expansion of this argument, see Taras Kuzio and Paul D'Anieri, *The Sources of Russia's Great Power Politics: Ukraine and the Challenge to the European Order* (Bristol, UK: E-International Relations Publishing), pp.86-92.
41   Ted Robert Gurr, *Minorities at Risk*, (Washington, DC: US Institute of Peace, 1993), p.136; Ted Robert Gurr, *Peoples Versus States: Minorities at Risk in the New Century* (Washington DC: US Institute of Peace, 2000); James D. Fearon, and David D. Laitin, "Ethnicity, Insurgency, and Civil War," *American Political Science Review* vol.97, no.1 (2003), pp.75-90; Paul Collier, Anke Hoeffler and Nicholas Sambanis, *The Collier-Hoeffler Model of Civil War Onset and the Case Study Project Research Design* (Washington, DC: World Bank, 2005).
42   Fearon, and Laitin, "Ethnicity, Insurgency, and Civil War;" Collier, Hoeffler and Sambanis, *The Collier-Hoeffler Model*.

years of doing so successfully. Russian intervention is the only plausible answer.[43] Those who see the conflict as a civil war point to evidence of local support for, and participation in, seizing buildings.[44] At the same time there is strong evidence of Russian support and organization almost from the beginning.[45] The seizure of buildings was quickly suppressed in most cities, and by the summer of 2014 the Donbas and Luhansk insurgencies were on the verge of defeat by Ukrainian armed forces and pro-government militias. Only massive intervention by the Russian army allowed the insurgency to continue, and only the threat of deeper intervention—which local forces could not have carried out—compelled Ukraine to negotiate the first Minsk agreement. If the conflict in Ukraine had been a purely domestic affair, it would have ended in the summer of 2014. The overtness of Russian aggression in 2022 might make this debate moot, but it remains possible that claims that Ukrainian territory should be transferred to Russia will be justified by arguments about indigenous secessionist movements in Ukraine in 2014.

Power Sharing and Regional Autonomy as a Possible Solution

From the outset of the conflict in 2014, regional autonomy for Donetsk and Luhansk was a central point of contention. Russia and its proxies placed regional autonomy for Donetsk and Luhansk *oblasts* at the center of both rounds of the Minsk negotiations. Ukraine, against its will, agreed to the formula in which its constitution would be amended to provide for regional autonomy. While some argued that regional autonomy would be a necessary part of a peace deal, and many others regard such a step as fundamentally

---

43 Andrew Wilson, "The Donbas in 2014: Explaining Civil Conflict Perhaps, But Not Civil War," *Europe-Asia Studies* vol.68, no.4 (2016), pp.631–52.
44 Kimitaka Matsuzato, "The Donbass War: Outbreak and Deadlock," *Demokratizatsiya: The Journal of Post-Soviet Democratization* vol.25, no.2 (2017), pp.175–200; Arel and Driscoll, *Ukraine's Unnamed War*.
45 Wilson, *Ukraine Crisis*, 129-30; Jakob Hauter, *Civil War? Interstate War? Hybrid War? Dimensions and Interpretations of the Donbas Conflict in 2014–2020* (Stuttgart: ibidem, 2021).

wrong, there was little analysis of whether it would help resolve the conflict. Does regional autonomy help resolve conflict? In what circumstances? The broader literature can help address these questions.

A great deal of research, beginning with literature on "consociational democracy" in ethnically plural societies, found that federalism and regional autonomy were viable long-term solutions to the problems of divided societies.[46] Regional autonomy, in this view, allows concentrated minorities a say in their own affairs and gives their elites a stake in the existing arrangements. Power sharing also signals the government's and broader society's benevolent aims toward the minority group.

More recent literature, based partly on the breakups of the Soviet Union and Yugoslavia, is more skeptical, finding that decentralization is as likely to increase conflict as to decrease it.[47] The reason is simple: decentralization gives separatist politicians more resources with which to pursue separation. Jack Snyder states that regional autonomy has a "terrible track record" of preventing violence.[48] One fear in Ukraine was that granting regional autonomy would not end conflict in Donbas, but rather create a more tangible platform for regional elites, assisted by Russia, to pursue secession. Crimean autonomy under the Ukrainian constitution did not prevent Russia from annexing it under the argument that its people were being mistreated. An additional fear was that granting Donetsk and Luhansk autonomy would lead to other regions demanding it as well.

---

46   Arend Lijphart, "Consociational Democracy," *World Politics* vol.21, no.2 (1969), p.207-25.
47   Philip G. Roeder, "Soviet Federalism and Ethnic Mobilization," *World Politics* vol.43, no.2 (1991), pp.196-232; Will Kymlicka, "Is Federalism a Viable Alternative to Secessionism?" In: Percy B. Lehning ed., *Theories of Secessionism* (New York: Routledge, 1998), pp.111-50; Carol Skalnik Leff, "Democratization and Disintegration in Multi-National States: The Breakup of the Communist Federations," *World Politics* vol.51, no.2 (1999), p.205-35. An earlier statement is Eric Nordlinger, *Conflict Regulation in Divided Societies* (Cambridge, MA.: Harvard University Center for International Affairs 1972).
48   Jack Snyder, *From Voting to Violence: Democratization and Nationalist Conflict* (New York: W. W. Norton, 2000), p.327.

Given this disagreement about whether regional autonomy helps or hurts, research has focused on trying to identify the conditions under which regional autonomy has different impacts. David A. Lake and Donald Rothchild find that regional autonomy increases the chances of peace under conditions of stable democracy, moderate leadership, and mixed settlement.[49] Lars-Erik Cederman *et al.* argue that power sharing can help prevent conflict from beginning, but that after violence has broken out, "regional autonomy is likely to be 'too little, too late.'"[50] Moreover, they find that power-sharing within central government institutions, rather than regional autonomy, is the practice most effective in preventing secessionist conflict.

While power sharing agreements are intended in part to ameliorate commitment problems, the conditions in which they do so are limited. Scott Gates *et al.* posit three types of power sharing, and find that only one — limiting the coercive capacity of the authorities through mechanisms such as independent courts and strong civil liberties guarantees — reduces separatism, because this is the only mechanism that effectively addresses the commitment problem. Dispersive arrangements, such as regional autonomy, fail to curb conflict for two reasons. First, while they give power to regional elites, they do little to protect most individuals. Second, over time, the incentives for regional elites to turn to violence can increase.[51] Such institutions are especially unlikely to be effective in post-conflict societies, which is how they were being recommended in Ukraine before 2022.

---

49 David A. Lake, and Donald Rothchild, "Territorial Decentralization and Civil War Settlements" In: Philip G. Roeder and Donald Rothchild eds., *Sustainable Peace: Power and Democracy After Civil Wars* (Ithaca, NY: Cornell University Press, 2005), pp.109–32.

50 Lars-Erik Cederman, Simon Hug, Andreas Schädel and Julian Wucherpfennig, "Territorial Autonomy in the Shadow of Conflict: Too Little, Too Late?" *American Political Science Review* vol.109, no.2 (2015), p. 368.

51 Scott Gates, Benjamin A.T. Graham, Yonatan Lupu, Håvard Strand and Kaare W. Strom "Power Sharing, Protection, and Peace," *Journal of Politics* vol.78, no.2 (2016), pp.512–26.

In cases where regional parties perform well, decentralization appears to make future conflict more likely, not less.[52] That description fits the Donbas conflict well. The Party of Regions dominated voting in Donetsk and Luhansk, and its successors, the Opposition Bloc and Opposition Platform-For Life also performed extremely well in those regions, but not in the rest of Ukraine. Therefore, Ukraine was probably not a promising case for regional autonomy to lead to enduring peace.

The focus on power-sharing in central government institutions might help explain why conflict broke out in the Donbas in the first place. Eastern Ukraine, and the Donbas in particular, consistently had powerful representation centrally, especially after 1994.[53] Even after the 2004 Orange Revolution, a major reversal for the Donetsk-based Party of Regions, the East had powerful representation in Kyiv through the Party of Regions parliamentary faction and later when Viktor Yanukovych became prime minister. Similarly, Yanukovych's abdication in 2014 did not necessarily represent a major loss of representation, though it did represent the loss of dominance, and some argued that worse was to come. Ironically, it was the separation of many voters in the Donbas (and Crimea) from the electorate after 2014 that minimized the weight of Donbas-based forces in parliament and their ability to vie for the presidency[54].

Moreover, Ukraine also fits broader patterns of a state that is especially likely to resist regional autonomy. As Walter shows, "Refusing to negotiate with the very first challenger and incurring the costs of an immediate war, even though seemingly irrational in the short term, becomes part of a very rational strategy to eliminate the

---

52 Dawn Brancati, "Decentralization: Fueling the Fire or Dampening the Flames of Ethnic Conflict and Secessionism?" *International Organization* vol.60, no.3 (2006), pp.653-53.
53 Paul D'Anieri, "Ethnic Tensions and State Strategies: Understanding the Survival of the Ukrainian State," *Journal of Communist Studies and Transition Politics* vol.23, no.1 (2007), p.4-29.
54 Paul D'Anieri, "Gerrymandering Ukraine? Electoral Consequences of Occupation," *East European Politics and Societies* vol.33, no.1 (2019): 89-108; D'Anieri, "Ukraine's 2019 Elections: Pro-Russian Parties and The Impact of Occupation," *Europe-Asia Studies* vol.74, no.2 (2022), pp.1915-36.

higher long-term costs of multiple future wars."[55] Similarly, Philip G. Roeder argues that once a group gains regional autonomy, other elites are likely to pursue the same advantages.[56] Put simply, the more likely are future internal or external challenges to territorial integrity, the greater the cost the state is willing to bear to beat back a present challenge. This was especially salient in Ukraine, where secessionist uprisings were foiled in several cities beyond Donetsk and Luhansk in 2014, and where Russian leaders openly and repeatedly discussed their desire to take over a larger swath of Ukrainian territory.[57] In sum, the literature on power-sharing shows both why Ukraine has resisted regional autonomy and why it would likely fail to produce long-term peace even if Ukraine had agreed to it.

Some scholars are so skeptical of the prospects for regional autonomy that they find total separation to be a more viable path to peace.[58] Essentially the argument is that since regional autonomy is likely to lead to further conflict, it is better to skip that step and go straight to separation. Once separatist conflict has occurred, its future onset becomes more likely. A compatible argument is made by Monica D. Toft, who argues that long-term peace is more likely to result from a rebel victory than from a government victory, because separation is less likely to lead to further contestation than keeping a rebellious territory and people within a state.[59] At least in one respect, the case of Ukraine is counterevidence, because even 25 years after Ukraine separated from the Soviet Union, Russia remained willing to go to war to regain at least part of it.

---

55 Barbara F. Walter, "Explaining the Intractability of Territorial Conflict," *International Studies Review* vol.5, no.4 (2003), p.138.
56 Philip G. Roeder, "Power Dividing as an Alternative to Ethnic Power Sharing," In: Philip G. Roeder and Donald Rothchild eds., *Sustainable Peace: Power and Democracy After Civil Wars* (Ithaca, NY: Cornell University Press, 2005), pp.51-82.
57 Taras Kuzio, "Russian Stereotypes and Myths of Ukraine and Ukrainians and Why Novorossiya Failed," *Communist and Post-Communist Studies* vol.52, no.4 (2019), pp.297-309.
58 Chaim Kaufmann, "Possible and Impossible Solutions to Ethnic Civil Wars," *International Security* vol.20, no.4 (1996), pp.136-75.
59 Toft, "Ending Civil Wars."

To summarize, the literature on power sharing and regional autonomy does not reveal clear predictions regarding exactly which arrangements increase and decrease the likelihood of reaching peace and maintaining it. The record is sufficiently mixed that it should have tempered the widely-expressed confidence that granting regional autonomy to Donetsk and Luhansk would lead to peace. Moreover, several factors identified in the literature as causing power-sharing or autonomy to fail appeared to exist in this case. Further still, the discussion of autonomy rested on the questionable assumption that conflict between the Donbas elites and the government in Kyiv, rather than conflict between Moscow and Kyiv, was the central cause of the conflict.

With all-out war between Russia and Ukraine, the question of regional autonomy that was a focus of the Minsk agreements might be moot. It remains possible, however, that Russia will try to insist on some kind of autonomy arrangements for regions formerly under its occupation. A desire to stop fighting might make it tempting to accede to such demands, but the evidence suggests that such arrangements would undermine rather than strengthen the durability of peace.

Public Opinion and Casualties

Above, we noted the widespread view that as casualties (costs) increase, peace becomes more likely. From the rationalist perspective, the reason is that the size of the bargaining range (the range of solutions that both sides find preferable to war) is a function of the costs of the war. In less formal terms, the assumption is that as more people are killed, a society's willingness to fight will decrease, and the concessions it will endure to gain peace will increase. That is the logic behind the "ripeness" hypothesis.

However, another line of research focuses on the hostility that is engendered by war and by the action-reaction cycles that sometimes lead violence to beget further violence. Valerie Sticher argues that "while fighting reveals information, it also fuels or entrenches mutual hatred."[60] Several related mechanisms are thought to be involved. First, violence goes from being unthinkable to being an accepted tactic of contestation. Second, killing can lead to a desire for revenge.[61] Third, violence can lead to hatred, lowering the future bar for the resort to violence.[62]

An immense amount of research has been carried out on casualties and public support for war.[63] The general finding is that increased casualties tend to reduce public support for war, though there is considerable disagreement on whether the aggregate number of casualties or the rate of accumulation is more important. This literature, however, is limited by the fact that almost all of it is based on research conducted on the US. One question, therefore, is whether the relationships identified are unique to the US or hold globally. A second question is at what rate or aggregate number of casualties politically relevant opposition might emerge. The numbers involved in the two largest cases that drive research in the US (roughly 37,000 killed in Korea and 58,000 in Vietnam) were reached in the early months of World War I and after Russia's 2022 invasion without engendering much opposition. Even if there is a relationship between casualties and support for conflict, it would appear to be highly contextualized.

The issue is relevant to Ukraine because both the combatants' strategies to prevail and outsiders' strategies to end the conflict are constrained by beliefs about what kinds of costs are, or are not, tolerable. All we knew prior to February 2022 was that the level of deaths reached by then (roughly 15,000, unequally spread among Ukrainian government forces, separatist forces, Russian forces, and

---

60 Valerie Sticher, "Negotiating Peace with Your Enemy: The Problem of Costly Concessions," *Journal of Global Security Studies* vol.6, no.4 (2021), pp.1–20.
61 Stathis N. Kalyvas, *The Logic of Violence in Civil War* (New York: Cambridge University Press, 2006).
62 Roger D. Petersen, *Understanding Ethnic Violence: Fear, Hatred, and Resentment in Twentieth Century Eastern Europe* (Cambridge: Cambridge University Press, 2022); Daniel Bar-Tal, *Intractable Conflicts: Socio-Psychological Foundations and Dynamics* (Cambridge: Cambridge University Press, 2013).
63 A recent treatment is Scott S. Gartner and Gary M. Segura, *Costly Calculations: A Theory of War, Casualties, and Politics* (Cambridge: Cambridge University Press 2021).

non-combatants), was insufficient to elicit meaningful concessions. At the same time, the relatively low rate of casualties after 2015 implied that neither side was willing to endure higher casualties in order to try to win the war. That clearly changed in 2022, and by October, deaths approaching 100,000 on both sides had seemed to steel resolve, rather than undermining it.

Is the impact of increased casualties on support for the war positive or negative? It seems possible, based on other conflicts, that it will be positive up to a point, and then turn negative. If that is true, where that inflection point might be is a crucial question about which we know very little. How this happens in Ukraine and Russia will likely determine how long the conflict lasts and who makes the most significant concessions to end it. Without regularly measured public opinion across a substantial set of conflicts, we cannot answer these questions in general, and without good polling in Ukraine and Russia, we cannot place this conflict within general patterns. To return to the rationalist problem of incomplete information, this uncertainty over the various sides' sensitivity to costs is precisely the kind of information problem that obstructs a bargained solution.

Two-Level Games

For public opinion to shape bargaining outcomes, the public opinion must constrain the policies of leaders. In this respect, any negotiation to end the Russia–Ukraine war, like others, is a "two-level game" as elaborated in Robert Putnam's widely cited article.[64] The literature on casualties and war posits that public opinion constrains leaders only in the direction of seeking peace. The two-level games approach is more agnostic, finding that public opinion and other domestic constituencies can obstruct as well as promote agreement. To the extent that concessions are unpopular or can be exploited by one's political rivals, negotiators might resist a deal that they would otherwise find acceptable.[65]

---

64 Robert D. Putnam, "Diplomacy and Domestic Politics: The Logic of Two-Level Games," *International Organization* vol.42, no.3 (1988), pp.427–60.
65 Sticher, "Negotiating Peace with Your Enemy."

This appeared to be the case after Ukraine's election in 2019, when President Volodymyr Zelenskyy appeared to voice his acceptance of the "Steinmeier formula" for ordering the steps envisioned in Minsk II. Violent protests broke out in Kyiv, and a new group against "capitulation" was formed. Zelenskyy quickly walked back from his earlier statement. "Granting the self-proclaimed 'republics' special status and amnestying pro-Russian militants — without a sustainable ceasefire, Russia's withdrawal of its fighters and equipment, and regaining control of the Russia–Ukraine border — would amount to a political suicide not only for Zelensky's administration, but likely for his successors as well."[66]

More generally, it appeared that Zelenskyy was more likely to face electoral danger from the national-democratic side (in the form of former President Petro Poroshenko) than from the pro-Russian side. This dynamic has only strengthened since February 2022. Any talk of ending the war without regaining all of Ukraine's territory, including Crimea, is seen as unacceptable among much of the Ukrainian population and elites.[67] Similarly, in Russia, Vladimir Putin appears to be under much more pressure from hawks demanding more aggressive prosecution of the war than from anyone advocating peace.[68]

It may be the case that for leaders in Ukraine and Russia, a belligerent position is of net benefit politically. This fits with the hypothesis of diversionary war, which posits that political leaders will sometimes welcome international conflict to bolster their

---

66 Olena Lennon, and Olena Sotnyk, "Ukraine's Strategic Choices vis-à-vis Occupied Donbas: Striking a Balance between the Possible and the Desirable," *Krytyka*, May 2020. https://krytyka.com/en/articles/ukraines-strategic-choices-vis-vis-occupied.
67 Ilko Kucheriv Democratic Initiatives Foundation "How the War Changed the Way Ukrainians Think About Friends, Enemies, and the Country's Strategic Goals," 30 May 2022. https://dif.org.ua/en/article/how-the-war-changed-the-way-ukrainians-think-about-friends-enemies-and-the-countrys-strategic-goals.
68 Amy MacKinnon, "Putin Hasn't Gone Far Enough for Russia's Hawks," *Foreign Policy*, 27 May 2022. https://foreignpolicy.com/2022/05/27/putin-russia-dissent-ukraine-war-hawks/.

standing.⁶⁹ President Putin seems to have benefited from annexing Crimea and conflict with Ukraine, as his popularity, which had fallen to its lowest point in early 2014, increased later that year. Speculation that Putin might escalate the conflict to boost his flagging popularity supported that view, and some argued that the escalation was driven primarily by Russian domestic politics.⁷⁰

There is less reason to believe that Putin is tightly constrained from making concessions (his ability to control media, opposition groups, and elections is well-developed), but his documented concern about public opinion might nonetheless shape his attitudes toward the conflict. In sum, the question concerning public opinion is not only whether it will constrain the various actors from prosecuting the war, but whether it might positively motivate them to do so and punish them for making concessions to end it.

Not only public opinion, but various elites may also benefit from war. Most obvious is the ability of well-placed firms and individuals to earn outsized profits selling war material to the combatant powers. As well, politicians may benefit from being seen publicly as patriotic supporters of the war effort. There has been essentially no organized opposition to the war in Russia either before or after February 2022. In Ukraine, the pro-Russian Opposition Platform-For Life party was clearly opposed to the war in Donbas after 2014, but its leader, Viktor Medvedchuk, was arrested in 2021 and four TV channels affiliated with it were closed due to their apparent funding from Russia. Nowhere, therefore, is there viable elite opposition to the conflict, while there appears plenty of elite support.

These generalizations, to the extent that they hold, lead us to question a fundamental assumption of the rationalist model— namely, that war is costly.⁷¹ It is this assumption that makes war a

---

69 Jack Levy, S. "The Diversionary Theory of War: A Critique" In: Manus I. Midlarsky ed. *Handbook of War Studies*. Boston: Unwin Hyman 1989), pp.259–88.
70 Leon Aron, "Could Putin Launch Another Invasion?" Politico. March 15, 2021, https://www.politico.com/news/magazine/2021/03/15/russia-putin-invasion-ukraine-baltics-nato-475527; Robert Person, and Michael McFaul, "What Putin Fears Most," *Journal of Democracy*, vol.33, no.2 (2022), pp.18-27.
71 Giacomo Chiozza and H.E. Goemans, "International Conflict and the Tenure of Leaders: Is War Still Ex Post Inefficient?" *American Journal of Political Science* vol.48, no.3 (2004), pp.604–19.

sub-optimal outcome, the motivating puzzle of the rationalist approach. If, on the other hand, war has positive utility for the key actors involved, the paradox disappears. To the extent that war provides benefits to leaders, either because the elites they benefit from it or because war is popular among citizens, we need neither information problems nor the commitment problem to explain it. "For Kiev [sic], behind the principled consensus on territorial integrity, the conflict helps consolidate unity and a Ukrainian identity in the rest of the country, boosts patriotism, keeps Ukraine on the international agenda (which attracts attention and assistance from Western countries), justifies the sanctions against Russia and, occasionally, explains the slowness or failure of some reforms."[72]

The discussion of costs and of domestic constraints on concessions highlights an important question. Is the Ukrainian public more concerned with the costs of fighting or with the costs of concessions? Related to this, is the Ukrainian leadership more constrained from enduring (or increasing) the cost of the conflict or making the concessions necessary to end it? As Darren Filson and Suzanne Werner show, various combinations of cost- and concession-sensitivity options are possible in democracies.[73] It has long been noted that democracies have a better record of prevailing in wars than do non-democracies.[74] Viewed in that context, Ukrainians' opposition to concessions appears less anomalous.

Conclusion

Applying the literature on conflict to the 2014–2022 war over Donbas or to the larger post-2022 war runs into two challenges. First, the literature on conflict reaches no consensus on many of the issues that are of most interest to us. Rather, in the absence of simple

---

72 Emmanuel Dreyfus and Jean-Baptiste Jeangène Vilmer, "A People-Oriented Peace Formula for the Donbass," *The Washington Quarterly* vol.42, no.2 (2019), p.118.
73 Darren Filson and Suzanne Werner, "Sensitivity to Costs of Fighting versus Sensitivity to Losing the Conflict: Implications for War Onset, Duration, and Outcomes," *Journal of Conflict Resolution* vol.51, no.5 (2007), pp.691–714.
74 David A. Lake, "Powerful Pacifists: Democratic States and War," *American Political Science Review* vol.86, no.1 (1992), pp.24–37.

overall patterns, researchers in recent years have been pursuing more contingent hypotheses about what kinds of factors might make war less likely to start or more likely to end in different kinds of circumstances. While the literature on conflict provides few neat solutions, it points to three conclusions that have so far been underemphasized in the work on the Ukraine conflict.

First, commitment problems need to be addressed for any negotiated solution to work in the long term. The Minsk process provided few reliable mechanisms to ensure that actors would not renege on important commitments. The primary danger was that Russia would violate its commitments to Ukraine. The possibility that Ukraine would violate commitments made to separatists (perhaps, for example, by granting autonomy and then reversing this step sometime in the future) was also a concern. While Russia could have played a credible role in guaranteeing commitments made to the separatists, the question of who would guarantee commitments made to Ukraine remained unanswered. Only the West could make credible guarantees, but it refused to do so, and Russia opposed this as well. Ukraine, having seen the commitments made in the Budapest Memorandum turn out to be irrelevant, was disinclined to make the same mistake again.

Second, the Minsk process envisioned granting regional autonomy to Donetsk and Luhansk *oblasts*. This struck some as a reasonable compromise, and the fact that it was a central demand of Russia, and the separatists made it seem like granting it would lead to enduring peace. While many opposed this demand on principle, relatively little attention was given to the question of whether it would lead to lasting peace. However, the literature on power sharing and regional autonomy shows that regional autonomy often fails to lead to enduring peace and that the conditions under which it succeeds do not resemble the situation in Ukraine under the Minsk agreements.

Third, the Minsk process proceeded as though domestic politics were irrelevant. Most notably, Ukrainian negotiators, pushed by Russia and the West, agreed to amend the Ukrainian constitution, which they had no constitutional right to do and could not deliver on. Any Ukrainian government that tried to deliver on

Ukrainian commitments under Minsk would likely have lost power at the next election or been forcibly ejected through protests. While the literature on conflict is more developed on domestic opposition to war than on opposition to peace, the literature on two-level games stresses the limits that domestic politics place on international negotiations.

While the conflict literature shows how some of the proposals to resolve the Donbas conflict were never likely to work, it did not offer easily implementable strategies for peace. Even decisive victory by Russia, which superficially would appear to provide for stability going forward, does not fit the conditions in which decisive victory is posited to produce stability. Rather, to the extent that Russia manages to dominate Ukraine, one would likely find that Ukrainians would again seek independence, as they have repeatedly throughout history. If neither the atrocities perpetrated on Ukraine during the *Holodomor* of the 1930s nor the repressions that accompanied the seizure of Western Ukraine in 1939 were sufficient to eradicate Ukrainian national sentiment, it seems unlikely that losing the Donbas would have done so. The same is likely true for a larger Russian victory in the current war. In this respect, we must question the realism of the self-identified "realists" who advocate that the West accept Russian hegemony in Ukraine. While the West can do great harm to Ukraine's cause by cutting support for it, it is naïve to think that Ukrainian opposition to rule from Moscow depends on the West's support (it did not in 1939 or 1991). Thus, a Russian victory would be unlikely to bring peace to Ukraine.

This is one place where the international/domestic war distinction breaks down. Prior to 1991, Ukraine's push for independence (including post-World War II guerrilla warfare) would be classified as civil conflict within the Soviet Union. With Ukraine having gained independence, the current conflict is an international war between Russia and Ukraine. That international conflict would end if Russia conquered Ukraine, but it would almost certainly be replaced by a bitter insurgency.

Is stalemate or the defeat of one side more likely to lead to peace? It may well be that stalemate is likely to lead to a "thin" peace, meaning an unstable reduction in the level of violence, while the imposition of a settlement by a winner over a loser may be more conducive to a lasting peace, in part because an imposed settlement may be less vulnerable to the commitment problem. As noted however, this case does not fit the findings in the literature for lasting peace based on victory.

This summary of the literature essentially identifies two paths to peace. The first is resolution of the issues (perhaps induced by stalemate), the second is imposition of a settlement by a victorious power. Either of these solutions might be strengthened by guarantees by powerful third parties. If the underlying dispute is resolved the commitment problem no longer exists, while victory by one side bolstered by third-party guarantees would mitigate it.

Which of these solutions seem most likely in the Ukraine conflict? The prospects for a resolution of the issues appear very small and have shrunk since Russian atrocities and intent to destroy Ukrainian national identity have become apparent. It is possible that Russian public opinion or leadership change in Moscow will allow a dramatic narrowing in positions to emerge. It is also possible that opinion in Ukraine will shift to become more tolerant of concessions to end the war. But all the evidence so far points in the opposite direction. Support for Russian claims towards Ukraine is shared across the Russian political spectrum, while conflict has led to the consolidation of anti-Russian opinion in Ukraine among those who were formerly ambivalent. Since the escalation, Ukrainian resolve has only strengthened.[75] Similarly, while in the early months of Russia's escalation many speculated that Russia's war effort would be constrained by domestic opposition, that had yet to occur by fall 2022. A central question for both combatants and theorists is when and under what conditions resolve—conceptualized as domestic opposition to concessions—might peak and begin to weaken. Such inflections have taken place in many wars

---

75 Volodymyr Kulyk, "National Identity in Ukraine: Impact of Euromaidan and the War," *Europe-Asia* Studies vol.68, no.4 (2016), pp.588–608; Ilko Kucheriv Democratic Initiatives Foundation "How the War Changed the Way Ukrainians Think."

throughout history, but while the causes seem apparent in retrospect, when an inflection will occur in any particular war is hard to predict.

Looking at the Ukraine case can enrich this broader literature in at least two ways. First, it can help us deepen our understanding of the relationship between public opinion, support for war, and peace negotiations. The literature on public opinion and conflict focuses primarily on casualties and is derived heavily from the US case. Rationalist theories of war point out that any eventual outcome could have been achieved at lower cost if the trauma of war were avoided, and surely that will be true, in some abstract sense, when this one ends. At the same time, many appear to believe that to arrive at defeat in war *without* having paid an immensely high price is unacceptable.

Second, this conflict is providing important new evidence about the role of commitment problems and the difficulties of overcoming them. The Minsk process failed in part because it relied on commitments that were not credible. Recommendations for how to end the current war have focused more on solving the bargaining problem (especially concerning the territorial terms of a settlement) and much less on the commitment problem. Unless Ukraine can be credibly assured that territorial concessions, which are extremely unpopular, will guarantee the country's long-term security rather than undermining it by demonstrating the viability of Russian efforts to conquer new territory and then solidify gains through a new peace treaty, Ukraine will have little reason to stop fighting.

Japanese Scholars on the 'Ukraine Crisis' (2014–2015) Russia-Centered Ontology, Aversion to Western Mainstream, and Vulnerabilities to Disinformation

Sanshiro Hosaka

The so-called 'Ukraine crisis' generated a massive flow of contested narratives on Ukraine.[1] The Kremlin termed the pro-European and anti-Viktor Yanukovych regime protests in Kyiv a 'coup d'état' by 'fascists' supported by the West, defending the rationale for the annexation of Crimea by portraying Russia as a victim forced to react to NATO enlargement. In the same vein, Moscow has camouflaged and denied its armed aggression against Ukraine, framing the ensuing conflict as a 'civil war.' There has been a rich body of research on Russian narratives on the Ukraine crisis.[2] However, an important question remains open: who delivers the Kremlin's narratives to its target audiences outside Russia?; and how and why Russian narratives are communicated to the domestic audience of western democracies?

Drawing on discourse analysis of narratives of scholars on the Ukraine crisis, this article sets out to contribute to the current state

---

1 'The Ukraine crisis' – the term used most often in media and academia – obfuscates the identity of the aggressor who caused the crisis. Volodymyr Kulyk, 'Western Scholarship on the "Donbas Conflict": Naming, Framing, and Implications', *PONARS Eurasia*, 16 December 2019, https://www.ponarseurasia.org/western-scholarship-on-the-donbas-conflict-naming-framing-and-implications/. With this nuance in mind, however, I use this term to refer to the series of controversial events in, around, and over Ukraine that started in late 2013.
2 For example, see Katri Pynnöniemi and András Rácz, *Fog of Falsehood: Russian Strategy of Deception and the Conflict in Ukraine* (Helsinki: The Finnish Institute of International Affairs, 2016); Yevhen Fedchenko, 'Kremlin Propaganda: Soviet Active Measures by Other Means', *Sõjateadlane (Estonian Journal of Military Studies* 2 (2016): 140–69; Artem Babak et al., *Words and Wars. Ukraine Facing Kremlin Propaganda* (Kyiv: Internews Ukraine, 2017).

of knowledge on strategic narratives, i.e., on how states instrumentalize narratives to shape the behavior of domestic and international audiences.[3] It seeks to address a gap in the relevant literature, which has to date devoted little attention to how strategic narratives are delivered to external national audiences. Although mass media editors are traditionally regarded as gatekeepers deciding what events, including those occurring beyond national borders, are newsworthy and important for their domestic audiences,[4] at moments of international crisis, much of this role is delegated to Area Studies scholars who, as specialists on particular countries or regions, select, translate, interpret, promote, reproduce or critique narratives of foreign states to domestic audiences. While scholars are aware of positionality and potential research bias relating to race, gender, culture, ethnicity, and disability,[5] less attention has been paid to consequences associated with scholars' academic identities and affiliations that may also affect all phases of the research process and knowledge production.

As the 'Ukraine crisis' demonstrates, reducing this problem to a matter of a given scholar's political-ideological standpoint on the left-right spectrum obscures rather than clarifies. Although the primary supporters of Soviet narratives were leftists rather than rightists during the Cold War, such a view barely explains the contemporary phenomenon; in multiple European countries, both the far-left and far-right supported Putin's narratives on Ukraine.[6] Equally

---

3 Alister Miskimmon, Ben O'Loughlin, and Laura Roselle, *Forging the World: Strategic Narratives and International Relations*, First paperback (Ann Arbor: University of Michigan Press, 2017).
4 Alister Miskimmon, Ben O'Loughlin, and Laura Roselle, *Strategic Narratives: Communication Power and the New World Order* (New York: Routledge, 2013), p.185.
5 David Coghlan and Mary Brydon-Miller, eds., *The SAGE Encyclopedia of Action Research* (Sage: SAGE, 2014), p.465.
6 Peter Pomerantsev and Michael Weiss, *The Menace of Unreality: How the Kremlin Weaponizes Information, Culture and Money* (New York: Institute of Modern Russia, 2014), pp.26-28; Anna Veronika Wendland, 'Levyi neoimperializm i sostoianie "rossiiskikh" issledovanii: participant observation nemetskogo diskursa ob ukrainskom krizise" [Left-wing neo-imperialism and the state of 'Russian' research: participant observation of German discourse on the Ukrainian crisis', *Ab Imperio*, no.3 (2014),pp.183-94; Veronika Golianová and Aliaksei Kazharski, 'The Unsolid': Pro-Kremlin Narratives in Slovak Cultural and Educational Nstitutions', *The RUSI Journal*, vol.165, no.4 (2020): 10-21, https://doi.org/

inadequate is the simple hypodermic needle model of influence whereby people's perception is directly shaped by received (dis)information, such that foreign scholars are reduced to 'useful idiots' that automatically disseminate the Kremlin's messages without fully comprehending the propagandistic intentions behind them. Thus, the issue requires detailed empirical elaboration in terms of ontological, epistemological, and methodological foundations unique to scholars.

The literature on the Western academic narratives on the Ukraine crisis, though not abundant to date, has revealed several important aspects. First, Russia's ontological denial of Ukrainian state sovereignty has permeated the attitude of many scholars of Russia who reject the need for examining Ukraine as a separate subject of their academic inquiry.[7] Such an ontology can be seen among two, to some extent overlapping, groups of scholars. One is characterized by adherence to the 'Russian imperial historical framework' that subsumes Ukraine and Ukrainians within Russian history[8]; 'historiographic Soviet nostalgia' held by many former Sovietologists[9]; or a new 'orientalism' that places the Russian state in a

---

10.1080/03071847.2020.1796521; Massimiliano Di Pasquale and Luigi Sergio Germani, 'Russian Influence on Italian Culture, Academia, and Think Tanks', in *Russian Active Measures: Yesterday, Today, Tomorrow*, ed. Olga Bertelsen, Soviet and Post-Soviet Politics and Society (Stuttgart: Ibidem Verlag, 2021).

7   Already in the early 1990s, manifestations of Russia's denial of Ukraine's sovereignty were seen in the discourse of a broad spectrum of Russian political elites (Gretskiy 2020) and in the Russian intelligence operations and military policy in the 'near abroad.' James Sherr, 'The New Russian Intelligence Empire', *Problems of Post-Communism* vol.42, no. 6 (1995), pp.11–17. Likewise, in Russian academia, Ukrainian Studies was 'not an entirely legitimate scholarly field.' Yaroslav Hrytsak, 'Ignorance Is Power', *Ab Imperio*, no. 3 (2014), p.219, https://doi.org/10.1353/imp.2014.0074; see also Sergei Zhuk, 'Ukrainian Maidan as the Last Anti-Soviet Revolution, or the Methodological Dangers of Soviet Nostalgia (Notes of an American Ukrainian Historian from Inside the Field of Russian Studies in the United States)', *Ab Imperio*, no. 3 (2014), p.196.

8   Taras Kuzio, 'Western Historians of Russia and the Crimea: Why Do They Continue to Use Imperialist and Racist Frameworks?', *Cicero Foundation Great Debate Paper* 18, no. 2 (2018), pp.5–6; J.S. Reshetar, 'Rozuminnya y Neporozuminnya Pry Studiyakh Nad Istorieyu Ukrainy v SSHA [Understanding and Misunderstanding at the Studios over the History of Ukraine in the USA]', *Suchasnist*, 1983, p.72.

9   Zhuk, 'Ukrainian Maidan', p.201.

hierarchically superior position, denying the dignity of Ukrainians and other smaller peoples of Eastern Europe.[10] The other group comprises would-be 'realists,' such as John Mearsheimer and Richard Sakwa, whose academic narrative portrays Ukraine as a mere geopolitical battleground of the great powers, blames NATO enlargement, and rationalizes Putin's actions as an understandable response to this threat.[11] One puzzle that remains, however, is that even many Ukrainian studies researchers, that is, scholars who we might expect to be critical of a Russia-centered ontology, are nevertheless in the thrall of Russian narratives about a 'civil war' in the Donbas, for example.

An important epistemological feature of the worldview of many Western scholars of post-Soviet space has been pointed out

---

10 Fabio Belafatti, 'Orientalism Reanimated: Colonial Thinking in Western Analysts' Comments on Ukraine', *EuromaidanPress*, 2014, https://euromaidanpress.com/2014/10/27/western-commentators-should-rid-themselves-of-old-prejudices-dating-back-from-the-age-of-colonialism-before-commenting-on-eastern-european-affairs/; Taras Kuzio, *Crisis in Russian Studies? Nationalism (Imperialism), Racism and War* (Bristol: E-International Relations Publishing, 2020). For an earlier work on post-Soviet Russian imperialism in western academia, see Ewa Thompson, *Imperial Knowledge: Russian Literature and Colonialism* (Westport: Greenwood Press, 2000). Although Thompson's work has been criticized for its methodological shortcomings, it is useful in its attempt to demonstrate how Russian authors used their superior positions as 'spokesperson[s] for the growing empire' to impose Russia-centered narratives on the domestic and foreign readership of Russian literature, obscuring discourses of the colonized nationalities.

11 For critiques of the 'realist' discourse on the Ukraine crisis, see Taras Kuzio and Paul D'Anieri, *The Sources of Russia's Great Power Politics: Ukraine and the Challenge to the European Order* (Bristol: E-International Relations, 2018), pp.8-9; Igor Gretskiy, 'Lukyanov Doctrine: Conceptual Origins of Russia's Hybrid Foreign Policy—The Case of Ukraine', *Saint Louis University Law Journal*, vol.64, no.1 (2020), pp.4-5. I will not delve into the problem of 'realists' in this article, but Martin Wight makes an important and relevant observation on a key tenet of realists—the balance of power. According to Wight, Machiavelli did not advocate policies of the balance of power but just observed the phenomenon of equilibrium. However, the conception later transformed itself from description into prescription, from analysis into policy. Similarly, contemporary 'realist' discourse which explains Russia's annexation of Crimea in terms of the balance of power while blaming NATO expansion and its failure to comprehend this 'realist' worldview seems rather prescriptive and political than descriptive and analytical. Martin Wight, 'The Three Traditions of International Theory', in *International Theory: The Three Traditions*, ed. Martin Wight, Gabriele Wight, and Brian Porter (London: Leicester University Press, 1991), pp.7-24.

by Sergei Zhuk.[12] Zhuk elaborates on the 'nonconfrontational, conformist, and 'emotionally positive' approaches' of Western scholars of Russia that ignored the problems of Soviet-Russian imperialism and Russian nationalism. Zhuk explains the appearance of these approaches in the post-Soviet era by the 'performative shift' of scholars, exemplified by Alexei Yurchak, which emphasizes the power of discursive practices. Indeed, Yurchak's study on Soviet youth culture attracted many Western scholars, who were tired of dissidents' negative discourse about the USSR and sought 'more positive and friendly approaches toward defeated and humiliated (by the West) post-Soviet Russians,' thereby underestimating the problems and contradictions (corruption, the black market, political dissent, etc.) in the late Soviet society. Such a conformist and nonconfrontational approach is, however, observed among a broader range of researchers beyond the performative scholars.[13]

Another key to understanding the problem can be found in the critical work by Andrey Makarychev and Viatcheslav Morozov. They criticize the epistemological relativism of the national school of 'Russian IR' that puts forward anti-colonial resistance to Western hegemony and the doctrine of a 'multipolar world.' These pro-regime narratives disguised as academic ones often assert Russia's civilizational uniqueness, which, in the rhetoric of this school, cannot be understood by 'Western' science.[14] This epistemology seems to have permeated the thinking of many Western scholars of Russia too, who employ precisely the same logic: that Russians are inherently 'different,' and hence different criteria must be applied. Sometimes this goes as far as the 'psychologization' of Russian motives, i.e., justification of Russia's actions with historical, cultural, and psychological explanations, often with the formula 'Moscow

---

12 Zhuk, 'Ukrainian Maidan'.
13 Richard Stites cited in Zhuk, p.205; Alexei Yurchak, *Everything Was Forever, Until It Was No More: The Last Soviet Generation* (Princeton: Princeton University Press, 2005).
14 Andrey Makarychev and Viatcheslav Morozov, 'Is "Non-Western Theory" Possible? The Idea of Multipolarity and the Trap of Epistemological Relativism in Russian IR', *International Studies Review*, vol.15, no. 3 (2013), pp.328–50, https://doi.org/10.1111/misr.12067.

perceives' or 'Russia believes.'[15] These academics censure the West for failing to understand Russian motives, nearly echoing Putin's assertion: Russia 'has its own national interests that need to be taken into account and respected.'[16]

In terms of methodology, Kuzio points out the preference of international experts for Russian sources over Ukrainian: 'for Western Russianists, the default is always to use sources from Russia'.[17] In this connection, Kuzio argues for the importance of fieldwork research in Ukraine, decreasing reliance on secondary sources, and commends Anna Matveeva for her fieldwork in the occupied Donbas and interviews with the leaders of the 'Russian spring,' although she has not conducted similar fieldwork in the Ukraine-government controlled area.[18] Kuzio further points out that a lack of a rigorous external review process has produced numerous factual errors in the writing about Ukraine. However, as Kuzio is aware, external review is less effective if the entire scholarship of the field

---

15 Nadiia Koval, 'Fukidid u kolhospi tvaryn: hrets'kyy pidkhid do ukrayins'ko-rosiys'koho konfliktu'[Thucydides in the Animal Collective Farm: The Greek Approach to the Ukrainian-Russian Conflict]', in *Interpretatsiyi rosiys'ko-ukrayins'koho konfliktu v zakhidnykh naukovykh i ekspertno-analitychnykh pratsyakh [Interpretation of the Russian-Ukrainian Conflict in Western Scientific and Expert-Analytical Works]*, ed. Volodymyr Kulyk (Kyiv: IPiEND im. I. F. Kurasa, 2020), pp.216–19.

16 Vladimir Putin, 'Address by President of the Russian Federation', President of Russia, 18 March 2014, http://en.kremlin.ru/events/president/transcripts/statements/20603.

17 Taras Kuzio, 'Euromaidan Revolution, Crimea and Russia–Ukraine War: Why It Is Time for a Review of Ukrainian-Russian Studies', *Eurasian Geography and Economics*. vol.59, no.3–4 (2018), pp.530–31, https://doi.org/10.1080/15387216.2019.1571428; see also Kuzio, *Crisis in Russian Studies?*, p.66; Volodymyr Kulyk, 'Analizuyuchy Analityku: Pro Zasady Doslidzhennya Zakhidnykh Naukovykh Ta Ekspertno-Analitychnykh Publikatsiy Na Temu Rosiys'ko-Ukrayins'koho Konfliktu' [Analyzing the Analysis: On the Principles of Research of Western Scientific and Expert-Analytical Publications on the Topic of the Russian-Ukrainian Conflict]', in *Interpretatsiyi Rosiys'ko-Ukrayins'koho Konfliktu v Zakhidnykh Naukovykh i Ekspertno-Analitychnykh Pratsyakh [Interpretation of the Russian-Ukrainian Conflict in Western Scientific and Expert-Analytical Works]*, ed. Volodymyr Kulyk, Kulyk. (Kyiv: IPiEND im. I. F. Kurasa NAN Ukrayiny, 2020), pp.5–6.

18 Kuzio, 'Euromaidan Revolution, Crimea and Russia–Ukraine War', p.530; Anna Matveeva, *Through Times of Trouble. Conflict in Southeastern Ukraine Explained from Within* (Lanham: Lexington Books, 2018).

is 'ideologically driven,' i.e., sharing the common ontological and epistemological axioms.[19]

This article attempts to synthesize these mutually complementary discussions into a coherent scheme by highlighting the phenomenon in three separate but intertwined layers of entrapment (see Figure 1). The first trap is ontological — one that denigrates the significance of Ukraine as an object of academic inquiry. The second trap is an epistemological aversion to the Western mainstream discourse. The flipside of this epistemology is scholars' preoccupation with 'alternative' explanations of Russian autocracy and aggressive foreign policies denounced by what they mentally reduce to the 'Russophobic' or 'anti-Russian' West.[20] The third trap is methodological. Scholars' empirical and theoretical passions may entail strong bias at the methodological level if they are captured by either or both of the ontological and epistemological pitfalls, and, no less importantly, if they are ill-equipped to correct the bias incurred by Russian political technology and information manipulation.[21]

---

19 Kuzio, *Crisis in Russian Studies?*, pp.76–77.
20 I distinguish my argument from Sergei Zhuk's work in that the underpinning motive for a 'conformist approach' is not in the 'performative shift' but the epistemological aversion to the Western mainstream discourse and a search for alternative explanations. This pattern of thought is widely observed among Slavists and partially manifested in this statement by Alexei Yurchak: 'much of the academic and journalistic writing about Soviet socialism and post-Soviet transformation is built on assumptions that socialism was 'bad,' 'immoral,' and 'imposed,' and/or was experienced as such by Soviet people, and that the collapse of the Soviet system was predicated on that.' Alexei Yurchak, 'Soviet Hegemony of Form: Everything Was Forever, Until It Was No More', *Comparative Studies in Society and History*, vol.45, no.3 (2003), p.483.
21 See e.g., Sanshiro Hosaka, 'The Kremlin's Active Measures Failed in 2013: That's When Russia Remembered Its Last Resort — Crimea', *Demokratizatsiya: The Journal of Post-Soviet Democratization*, vol.26, no.3 (2018), pp.326–27; Sanshiro Hosaka, 'Welcome to Surkov's Theater: Russian Political Technology in the Donbas War', *Nationalities Papers*, vol.47, no.5 (2019), p.764, https://doi.org/10.1017/nps.2019.70.

Figure 1. Three Traps for Scholars Studying Ukraine.

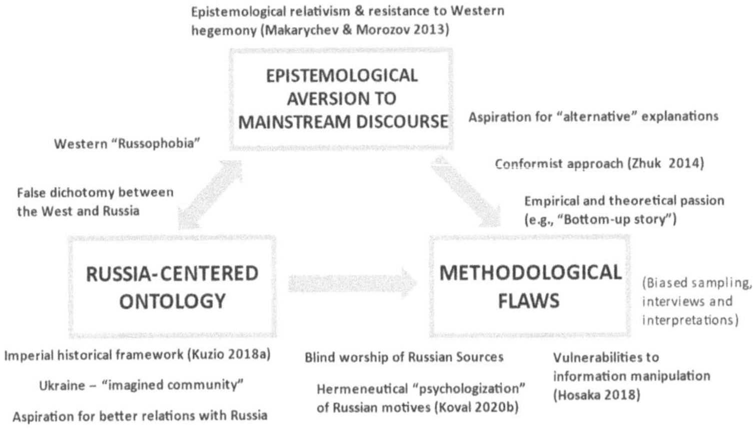

Epistemological relativism & resistance to Western hegemony (Makarychev & Morozov 2013)

EPISTEMOLOGICAL AVERSION TO MAINSTREAM DISCOURSE

Western "Russophobia"

Aspiration for "alternative" explanations

Conformist approach (Zhuk 2014)

False dichotomy between the West and Russia

Empirical and theoretical passion (e.g., "Bottom-up story")

RUSSIA-CENTERED ONTOLOGY

METHODOLOGICAL FLAWS (Biased sampling, interviews and interpretations)

Imperial historical framework (Kuzio 2018a)

Ukraine – "imagined community"

Aspiration for better relations with Russia

Blind worship of Russian Sources

Hermeneutical "psychologization" of Russian motives (Koval 2020b)

Vulnerabilities to information manipulation (Hosaka 2018)

More specifically, scholars caught by the ontological trap most likely go to Moscow for direct interviews and data collection, paying little attention to sources in Kyiv even if their topic concerns Ukraine.[22] Researchers who evade this first trap may venture on fieldwork in Ukraine, but the second trap—their antipathy towards mainstream and craving for alternative explanations—may affect not only the choice of topics but also the research methodology, including the selection of interviewees and collection and interpretation of data. For example, the work of Anna Matveeva seems to have overcome the first ontological trap by conducting fieldwork in part of Ukraine. Nevertheless, what she calls the 'bottom-up story of the rebellion' ends up describing the war in Donbas as a 'civil war,' heavily relying on interviews from a 'Russian volunteer leader' and the first 'DPR prime minister' Aleksandr Borodai. Borodai is mentioned 96 times while the person who remotely supervised the political process in Donbas, Putin's senior adviser on

---

22 For typical problems and caveats for scholars conducting field research in contemporary Russia, a hybrid regime, see J. Paul Goode, 'Redefining Russia: Hybrid Regimes, Fieldwork, and Russian Politics', *Perspectives on Politics*, vol.8, no.4 (2010), pp.1055-75, https://doi.org/10.1017/S153759271000318X.

Ukraine issues, Vladislav Surkov,[23] is not mentioned once in her 337-page monologue.[24] Matveeva's epistemological aversion to mainstream discourse (the second trap) is clear from the introductory chapter titled 'Talking Donbas, Not Putin' that says: 'Every recent book about Ukraine or Russia is a book about Putin. This one will be different.'[25]

To illustrate these traps empirically, this article examines Japanese scholars' narratives on Ukraine and Russia in 2014–2015. There are two merits in choosing Japan for this study. First, Japan is the sole Asian country that joined Western-led economic sanctions on Russia when the latter illegally annexed Ukraine's Crimean Peninsula in 2014. At the same time, Tokyo aspired to improve bilateral relations with Russia, which was a priority of its diplomacy under Prime Minister Shinzo Abe (2012–2020).[26] Thus, Tokyo's 'delicate balancing act' (Maria Shagina) triggered diverse, sometimes highly emotional, narratives on the Ukraine crisis in the academic and intellectual milieu.[27] Second, the Japanese case demonstrates not only scholars' narratives resonating with Russian propaganda points but also the interaction of the three traps set out above. Specifically, the ontological trap is well articulated in the narratives of Japanese members of the Kremlin-supported epistemic community — the Valdai Discussion Club. The epistemological trap with its methodological consequences is evident in a symposium on the Ukraine crisis during the 2015 Japan-hosted congress of the International Council for Central and East European Studies (ICCEES), where the representatives of the 'Donetsk

---

23 Listen to the phone conversation between Surkov and Borodai in July 2014. Politie, 'Witness Appeal June 2019: Chain of Responsibility in the Russian Federation 4 (8)', 18 June 2019, https://www.youtube.com/watch?v=hPGmFJH2ZO8.
24 Matveeva, *Through Times of Trouble*.
25 Matveeva's earlier work titled 'No Moscow Stooges' also speaks for itself. Anna Matveeva, 'No Moscow Stooges: Identity Polarization and Guerrilla Movements in Donbass', *Southeast European and Black Sea Studies*, vol.16, no.1 (2016), pp.25–50.
26 Sanshiro Hosaka, 'China-Russia "Alliance": Lessons from Japan's Failed "Detachment" Strategy' (Tallinn: International Centre for Defence and Security / Estonian Foreign Policy Institute, 2021).
27 Maria Shagina, 'Japan's Dilemma with Sanctions Policy Towards Russia: A Delicate Balancing Act', *Focus Asia Perspective & Analysis*, 2018.

People's Republic' and 'Crimea parliament' were invited by a Japanese scholar to provide 'alternative views.'

The next section provides a brief overview of the asymmetry between Russian studies and Ukrainian studies in Japan and local political conditions that affected the narratives of scholars on the Ukraine crisis. It is followed by discourse analysis of the publications authored by Japanese members of the Valdai Discussion Club, and other influential Russianists–agenda-setters in Japanese academia. Most of these publications were examined with a view to identifying the patterns observed in a quantitative content analysis of more than 400 texts on the Ukraine crisis.[28] A primary focus of discourse analysis is how scholars' knowledge is produced by way of intertextual references, i.e., what kind of narratives and sources they use to construct and substantiate their arguments. To supplement this, where possible, I also conducted open-source intelligence (OSINT) investigations and cited fact-checking materials to reveal Russian political technology and disinformation operations. The concluding section summarizes the findings and discusses implications for further research into disinformation targeting academia.

Japanese Russianists on the Eve of the Ukraine Crisis

In Japan, after the disintegration of the USSR, various Area Studies associations and programs automatically replaced 'the Soviet Union' with 'Russia' in their names (but without adding in the labels 'post-Soviet' or 'Eurasia'), thus giving a false sense that it would be no longer necessary to study the former Soviet republics other than Russia. Tomohiko Uyama, a Japanese scholar of Central Asia,

---

28 This paper is part of my PhD dissertation which comprises a content and discourse analysis of 479 writings of Japanese scholars and intellectuals on the Ukraine crisis published in 2014–2019. The ad hoc corpus includes not only peer-reviewed articles (15 pieces; 3% of the total), but also pieces in university bulletins and thinktank reports (146 pieces; 30%), and essays in popular magazines (183 pieces; 38%). The findings of the content analysis will be published separately. Data for this research were collected within the framework of the project 'Individual Project-Based Collaborative Research' of the Slavic-Eurasian Research Center, Hokkaido University, Japan.

noticed this tendency, especially in the academic discourse of Russian studies that, while universalizing Russian issues, paid little attention to the countries and regions adjacent to Russia.[29] Twenty-two years later, Sergii Geraskov, a Ukrainian scholar who undertook interviews with Japanese experts and students, noted that a critical lack of knowledge about Ukraine has led many Japanese to view Ukraine merely as the battleground of a proxy war between the US and Russia, and that the construction of Ukraine's image is still often subordinated to 'the Russian factor.'[30]

The preponderance of Russian studies over Ukrainian studies is evident in figures. According to the list of Slavic-Eurasia researchers issued by the Japanese Slavic-Eurasian Research Center in 2012, of 1467 scholars registered, only 15 explicitly linked their field of interest with Ukraine. The ratio between Japanese Russianists and Japanese Ukrainianists is roughly 80:1. Multiple academic associations for Soviet and Slavic studies were established in the 1960s–1980s, while a separate association for Ukrainian studies was founded only in 1994, with a far smaller membership.[31] Due to the limited demand and interest in the Japanese university setting, studying 'small countries' sometimes makes it difficult for

---

29 Tomohiko Uyama, 'Nihon no Roshia kenkyu wa doko e iku no ka? — Todai shinpojiumu bochoki" [Where is Japan's Russian studies going? A Note on the University of Tokyo Symposium', Slavic Research Center News, October 1996, http://src-h.slav.hokudai.ac.jp/jp/news/67/uyama.html.In 2014, Uyama was among the first to debunk Russia's false claims on Crimea and 'Novorossiia.' Tomohiko Uyama, 'Henshitsu suru Roshia ga yurashia ni hirogeru fuan: Shinka suru ken'i shugi, meiso suru "teikoku"' [Changing Russia spreads anxiety to Eurasia: evolving authoritarianism, a stray "empire"', *Gendai shiso,* vol.42, no.10 (2014), pp.129-43.
30 Sergii Geraskov, 'Ukraine's Image in Japan: Forming Factors', *Kobe Gakuin Economic Papers,* vol.50, no.3 (2018), p.118.
31 According to the Japanese Association for Ukrainian Studies, its initial membership was around 20 researchers in 1994, and is currently around 60. For comparison, the Japan Association for Russian [Soviet] and East European Studies (1971-) has 400 members; the Japanese Society for the Study of Russian History (1956-): 246 members; the Japan Association for the Study of Russian Language and Literature (1950-): 445 members; Japan Association for Comparative [Socialist] Economic Studies (1963-): 216 members; the Japan Society for the Study of Slavic Languages and Literatures (1984-): 82 members (figures cited from the website of the Japanese scholarly society directory, Gakkai Meikan: https://gakkai.jst.go.jp/gakkai/).

researchers to make ends meet; partly for this reason, some scholars cover both Eastern European countries and Russia as their academic targets.[32] When public interest in Ukraine increased in 2014–2015 against the backdrop of the crisis, due to the deficit of specialists in Ukrainian studies, the media often invited well-known Russianists to comment on the Ukraine crisis. Narrating the Ukraine crisis thus became a part-time job for many scholars of Russian studies, and it was done not without shortcomings due to their lack of knowledge of Ukrainian issues.[33]

For the Japanese government, the Ukraine crisis unfolded amid its effort toward revitalizing the relationship with Russia to solve the problem of the 'Northern Territories,' which has been a major legacy issue between the two countries since the end of World War II. Thus, Prime Minister Abe declared relations with Russia a priority of Japan's diplomacy in 2012, and by the end of his tenure in 2020 he held bilateral talks with Vladimir Putin 27 times. On 19 March 2014, the day following Putin's speech on the annexation of Crimea, Tokyo hosted the Japan–Russia investment forum with a thousand participants from both countries, including Igor Sechin, Putin's close ally and *Rosneft* CEO. Nevertheless, as a G7 member, Japan became the only country in Asia that joined the economic sanctions on Russia, though Tokyo's unpublished sanctions were regarded as somewhat symbolic).[34] Tokyo condemned Russia's annexation of Crimea as 'an attempt to change the status quo with force' — the phrase conventionally used to refer to China's actions in the East China and South China seas. This discursive technique served not only to substantiate Japan's claim about Chinese assertiveness but also to switch the focus and avoid placing excessive blame on Russia.[35]

---

32 Akihiro Iwashita et al., 'Zadan-kai: Chiiki to chiiki no aida o yomitoku tame ni [To understand between regions]', *Chiiki kenkyu*, vol.16, no.1 (2015), p.34.
33 Toshihiko Ueno, 'Ukuraina kiki ni yosete [Ukrainian crisis and our stance]', *Roshia Touou kenkyu*, vol.43 (2014), p.1.
34 Shagina, 'Japan's Dilemma with Sanctions Policy Towards Russia: A Delicate Balancing Act'.
35 Hosaka, 'China-Russia "Alliance": Lessons from Japan's Failed "Detachment" Strategy'.

None of the political parties in the Japanese parliament endorsed Russia's unlawful annexation of Crimea. Meanwhile, an outright supporter of Russia's cause was *Issuikai,* a fringe neo-right organization affiliated with Vladimir Zhirinovsky's LDPR and Jean-Marie Le Pen's French National Front. The leader of *Issuikai* has been a regular visitor to the illegally occupied territories of Georgia and Ukraine and a participant in 'international election observer missions' organized by Moscow.[36] The news that ex-prime minister Yukio Hatoyama joined the neo-right leader on his tour to Crimea in 2015 embarrassed the Japanese government.[37]

Russia-Centered Ontology: The Valdai Discussion Club

The best-known venue for the Kremlin's influence activities involving international academia is the annual Valdai Discussion Club, an international conference hosted by Russia since 2004. This club is a sort of 'epistemic community,' whose members share normative and principled beliefs, causal beliefs, notions of validity, and a joint policy enterprise.[38] Many foreign participants are imbued with a shared hermeneutical approach that makes out 'the year-to-year changes in the official rhetoric' of Putin, Lavrov, or other dignitaries and 'what is said during the coffee breaks'.[39] Thus, a unique opportunity to meet the Russian president and 'authoritative' experts has attracted leading Western experts[40]; more than 1000 representatives

---

36 Issuikai, 'Katsudou houkoku [Activity reports]', Issuikai, n.d., http://www.iss uikai.jp/katudou_index.html.
37 Robin Harding, 'Japan's Ex-Prime Minister, Yukio Hatoyama, Answers His Critics', *Financial Times*, 20 July 2016.
38 Peter M. Haas, 'Introduction: Epistemic Communities and International Policy Coordination', *International Organization,* vol.46, no.1 (1992), pp.1–35, https:// doi.org/10.1017/S0020818300001442; Olga Löblová, 'When Epistemic Communities Fail: Exploring the Mechanism of Policy Influence: When Epistemic Communities Fail', *Policy Studies Journal,* vol.46, no.1 (2018), pp.160–89, https:// doi.org/10.1111/psj.12213.
39 Daniel W. Drezner, 'Is There Value in Valdai?', *The Washington Post*, 26 October 2016, https://www.washingtonpost.com/posteverything/wp/2016/10/26/is -there-value-in-valdai/.
40 C. Vendil Pallin and S. Oxenstierna, 'Russian Think Tanks and Soft Power' (Stockholm: Swedish Defence Research Agency, 2017), p.26.

of the international scholarly community from 85 countries have participated in this event.[41]

The Japanese old-timer in the Valdai Discussion Club is Nobuo Shimotomai, an influential scholar of Russian politics and history, who has held his membership since 2007. He served in important academic and public positions as chair of the Japanese Research Association of International Relations in 2002–2004; member of the Russian–Japanese Emeritus Club in 2004–2006; and co-chair of the organizing committee of the 9th ICCEES World Congress in 2015. The other regular Japanese participant is Taisuke Abiru, a senior expert of the Tokyo Foundation who has taken part in the Valdai Club since 2010.

Both were highly visible in public discourse on the Ukraine crisis. In 2014, Shimotomai published at least two books and ten articles in various magazines, including one co-authored with former Prime Minister Yukio Hatoyama and neo-right writers who openly supported Putin's annexation of Crimea.[42] Abiru also published around ten articles and columns. They also gave lectures to the country's energy and business elites and journalist community. Despite having published few peer-reviewed academic works on Ukraine, they were invited to conferences and TV programs to comment on the Ukraine crisis as 'experts' on the topic. Shimotomai also exerted influence as an agenda-setter in the Japanese Association for Russian and East European Studies and related policy discussions among academics.[43] In this section, I will examine

---

41 'Valdai Club Foundation', Valdai Club, accessed 8 April 2022, https://vald aiclub.com/about/valdai/.
42 Yukio Hatoyama et al., *Ukuraina kiki no jisso to nichiro kankei [The reality of the Ukraine crisis and Japan-Russia relations]* (Kadensha, 2015).
43 In Autumn 2017, at the annual conference of Japanese Association of Russian and Eastern European Studies, Shimotomai publicly remarked that the next conference should address a topic that was raised at the Valdai Discussion Club he took part in a few days earlier. Shimotomai also co-chaired a symposium co-sponsored by the ICCEES Organizing Committee and Japan-Russia Association on the Ukraine crisis and Japan-Russia Relations in June 2014. Read his introductory remarks that reflect Russia's perspectives on the events, such as the 'violent takeover of power' and Ukraine's 'civil war' between east and west. 'Ukuraina josei to nichiro kankei [The situation in Ukraine and Japan-Russia relations]', *Ajia jiho*, vol.45, no.9 (2014), pp.96–98.

narratives illustrative of the ontological and epistemological foundations of their views and commentary.

False Dichotomy Between the West and Russia — No Subjectivity for Ukraine

What Sergei Zhuk described as the Soviet nostalgia of Western former Sovietologists is expressed in Shimotomai's narrative. During his lecture to the country's energy sector elite, the Japanese professor argued that in the West, Ukrainian issues had been discussed from the perspective of a group of Ukrainians who collaborated with Nazis and moved to the United States and the United Kingdom after World War II:

> Moreover, after the collapse of the USSR, the American intelligence community and educational institutions started to train 'Sinologists' (experts on China). At the same time, they hardly prepared 'Russianists' (Sovietologists) familiar with Russian issues. Neither did Japan. As a result, no one has a balanced view of what is happening in Ukraine. There is little information from Ukraine.[44]

Further, Shimotomai maintained that the information the Japanese audience receives about Ukraine is 'quite biased.' The Japanese scholar, introducing himself as a former Sovietologist, reduced the Ukraine crisis to 'two perspectives' — a dichotomy between the East (Russia) and the West (the US). It follows from his logic that only Russianists, legitimate successors to Sovietologists who cover voices from the little-represented 'East,' can provide a trustworthy picture of Ukraine.[45] However, Shimotomai's 'balanced view' depicted the events in Ukraine, using the typical Russian monikers such as 'coup,' 'civil war,' 'fraternal states,' and 'Chocolate king Poroshenko.' The Japanese scholar went as far as to assert:

---

44 Nobuo Shimotomai, *Nyuenerugi koen: Ukuraina mondai to sekai seiji no henyo* [*New energy lecture: The Ukraine problem and transformation of world politics*] (Tokyo: Toshi enerugi kyokai, 2014), pp.32-33.
45 Shimotomai, pp.32-33.

In fact, during this time, Western Ukrainian nationalists hired snipers to shoot both the people and the government security forces. Yanukovych escaped because of this horror. This is the truth that the media failed to tell.[46]

This conspiracy theory that Ukrainian nationalists shot Euromaidan protestors in a false flag operation has been debunked by journalists and the 3-D model 'Euromaidan Event Reconstruction.'[47]

Elsewhere, Shimotomai complained to the Japanese journalist community that coverage and editorials on the Ukraine crisis were 'one-sided.' He even speculated that some journalists had not known there were Russian troops stationed initially in Crimea. In his opinion, the mainstream media blamed Moscow 'without checking the doubtful legitimacy of the [Ukrainian] interim government.' Shimotomai thus called for a better understanding of the bias of the US media during the 'information war.'[48]

In introducing international scholarly discussions on the Ukraine crisis, the Japanese scholar criticised Timothy Snyder for his attempt to 'defend the Ukraine policy of the West, especially the United States' by dividing Ukraine and Russia. He supported Stephen F. Cohen, who 'warned of the danger of ['Neocons' such as Victoria Nuland] who initiated the Ukrainian conflict'; and praised Henry Kissinger, John Mearsheimer, Aleksei Arbatov, and Dmitri Trenin for presenting the 'realist' view that reduces the cause of the Ukraine crisis to NATO enlargement. Shimotomai actively promoted his perspective, like Samuel Huntington's 'Clash of Civilizations,' that Ukraine is 'torn between the Eastern Orthodox Church and European Christianity.'[49]

---

46 Shimotomai, p.33.
47 Kuzio, *Crisis in Russian Studies?*, pp.79–80.
48 Nobuo Shimotomai, 'Kiki no haikei ni aru tozai no nijusei: Rekishi to shukyo no shiten kara [Duality of east and west behind the crisis: from historical and religious viewpoints]', *Shinbunkenkyu*, no. 755 (2014), pp.42.This narrative is widespread among leading Japanese Russianists. See subsection 'A Mission to Counter "Russophobia."'
49 Nobuo Shimotomai, 'Futatsu no kirisutokyo sekai: Ukuraina kiki no bunkaron teki kigen [Two Divergent Christian Worlds: Cultural Origins of the Ukraine Crisis]', *Asteion*, no. 81 (2014), pp.149–53.

According to the other regular Valdai participant Abiru, experts on Russia are those who understand the country in a positive light: 'Originally I'm a Russia expert, so I'm a person who treats Russia with understanding.'[50] This mode of thinking risks turning the object of their inquiry into an object of affection. Thus, in his piece titled 'Foreshadowing of the US-Russia 'Ukraine Crisis'' published in April 2014, the Japanese expert told the story of the geopolitical struggle between Washington and Moscow over Ukraine. As is the case with Shimotomai, his attempt to juxtapose the US and Russian perspectives led to a bizarre repetition of the Kremlin's most egregious propaganda points on Ukraine. Abiru argued, for example, that 'the pro-Russian Yanukovych administration was overthrown by the opposition coalition with the active support of the West;' that one of the drivers of these events was US hardliners' desire to take revenge on Russia to offset US diplomatic defeat in the Syrian chemical weapons deal; and that the intercepted phone conversation with US State Department official Victoria Nuland was evidence of Washington's active involvement in the crisis.[51] In his lecture organized by the Japan Press Research Institute for Japanese media representatives in May 2014, Abiru asserted, 'the interim government of Ukraine was created through an illegal process, with extreme, radical right-wing and neo-Nazis occupying the main posts of the government.'[52]

Blind Worship of Russian Sources

One distinctive epistemological feature of foreign participants of the Valdai Club is that they highly value their exclusive membership in this community, making claims based on privileged

---

50 Taisuke Abiru, 'Ukuraina kiki o kaibo: Ro ni tobu shinko no senryaku-teki rieki nai: "Renritsu seiken koso" o kowashita yato Amerika seiken to neokon, zantei seiken ni Neonachi [Anatomy of the Ukrainian Crisis: No strategic benefits for Russia to invade the east: the "coalition" plan was undermined by the opposition and the US Administration and Neocon, Neo-Nazis in the interim government]', *Media Tenbo* (July 2014), p.15.
51 Taisuke Abiru, 'Bei ro "Ukuraina kiki" no fukusen [Foreshadowing of the US-Russia "Ukraine Crisis"]', *Facta* 9, no. 4 (2014), pp.14–15.
52 Abiru, 'Ukuraina kiki o kaibo', p.13.

information sources and appealing to authority, such as high-ranking Russian officials or internationally well-known experts. A prominent scholar even said that 'he *knew* Russia had no aggressive designs on any other neighbors—because he had been told so by Putin and Lavrov while seated as a guest of honor in the front row at Valdai' [italics original.[53] In off-the-record conversations during the conference, gullible participants seek to discover the key to Russia's thinking behind 'some very sensitive foreign policy questions.'[54]

Shimotomai is fond of referring to his membership in the Valdai Discussion Club. In a 2012 report on the prospects of a third term for Putin and its implications for Japan–Russia bilateral relations, his statement indicates how much this scholar, as the sole Valdai participant from Japan, values exclusive access to Putin, and the information he receives through this channel:

> There is currently only one Japanese in the international Valdai Club that meets President Putin. Recently, regional organizations [of the Valdai Club] were launched in Asia as well as in the United States. This Asia-Valdai conference had been initially held only with China before it was joined by members from South Korea, Singapore and Japan in July.[55]

Japanese Valdai participants cherish their proximity to direct utterances of Russian political actors and quasi-experts. Shimotomai, who describes the Valdai Club as 'an international advisory council surrounding Putin,' stated:

> At the 10th anniversary meeting last October, I heard Putin saying that the expectations for Eurasian integration are not incompatible with improving relations with the EU.[56]

---

53   Keir Giles, *Moscow Rules: What Drives Russia to Confront the West* (Washington, D.C: Brookings Institution Press, 2019), p.33.
54   Drezner, 'Is There Value in Valdai?'
55   Nobuo Shimotomai, 'Daitoryo senkyo-go no Roshia josei to nichiro kankei [The situation in Russia after the presidential election and Japan-Russia relations]' (Northern Territories Issue Association, 2012), p.6, https://www.hoppou.go.jp/assets/docs/research/H24_rep_shimotomai.pdf.
56   Shimotomai, 'Futatsu no kirisutokyo sekai', p.146.

Shimotomai continued that the protests for European integration in Kyiv were perceived by Putin calmly, but 'the violent overthrow of the government by pro-western, illegitimate forces' pushed Moscow to annex Crimea.[57] In the Valdai Club, the voice of the Russian president is divine, bringing important perspectives to the attention of Valdai participants. Thus, on one occasion, Putin opened the eyes of the Japanese scholar to Russia's frustration with the shale gas revolution in the United States: Shimotomai stated, 'I am not an expert on this issue, but I realized this importance from Putin's remarks at the Valdai Conference in November 2011.'[58] Putin is good at impressing the participants with his 'emotional' performance; Shimotomai recalled how he had been impressed by Putin, 'who enthusiastically criticized the environmental pollution caused by the shale gas revolution in the United States.'[59]

Furthermore, a blind worship of Moscow sources is peculiar to the Valdai regulars. For example, Abiru rushed to Moscow immediately after the annexation of Crimea to exchange opinions with 'local experts and journalists' to examine the reasons behind this fateful decision and its impact on Japanese–Russian relations.[60] Abiru argued that Putin did not plan the annexation of Crimea beforehand because both Putin and Lavrov publicly rejected such a scenario in early March and the Russian president changed his mind only after 'the Crimean autonomous government changed the referendum question from 'expansion of autonomy' to 'incorporation to the Russian Federation' and moved the referendum from May 25 to March 16.'[61] After the downing of the Malaysia Airlines MH17 in

---

57   Leaked emails show that Putin launched the comprehensive influence operations (active measures) to thwart Ukraine's aspirations to join the European Union as early as at the beginning of 2013, and that the earliest manifestations of the preparation of the Crimea operation appeared in November 2013. Hosaka, 'The Kremlin's Active Measures Failed in 2013'.
58   Shimotomai, 'Daitoryo senkyo-go no Roshia', p.2.
59   Nobuo Shimotomai, 'Roshia no taiheiyo senryaku to Abe gaiko: Ukuraina kiki de kasoku suru toho shifuto [Russia's Pacific strategy and Abe's diplomacy: the eastern shift accelerating in the Ukraine Crisis]', *Gaiko*, no.24 (2014), pp.31-32.
60   Taisuke Abiru, 'Roshia "toho shifuto" de nitchu tenbin [Russia's "east shift" balancing between Japan and China]', *Facta*, vol. 9, no. 5 (2014), p.63.
61   Abiru, 'Ukuraina kiki o kaibo', p.13. The intercepted phone conversation between Sergei Glaz'ev and Sergei Aksenov shows that the change of the

Eastern Ukraine in July 2014, citing 'a Russian expert well-versed in the situation in Ukraine,' Abiru speculated that President Putin decided to provide the pro-Russian insurgencies in Ukraine with weapons in order to encourage 'political dialogue between the Ukrainian government and pro-Russian forces.'[62] Abiru concluded that Putin's remarks right after the crash of MH17 ('if military operations had not resumed in Eastern Ukraine on June 28, this tragedy probably could have been avoided') reflected his 'true intention.' But 'President Poroshenko refused that.'[63]

In the autumn of 2014, Shimotomai cited an interview with 'former foreign minister and prime minister Yevgeny Primakov' (who could be introduced otherwise, as a former KGB agent and Russian foreign intelligence chief), who said that Russia had attempted to incorporate Crimea 'by political means, asking the will of residents.' According to Primakov (and quoted by Shimotomai) Russia 'demanded that an international conference including Ukraine be held, but Ukraine blocked it, which ultimately led to what happened in March.' Aleksei Venediktov of *Ekho Moskvy* radio hinted to the Japanese scholar that before the deployment of Russian troops into Eastern Ukraine, 'there seems to have been secret negotiations with Turkey.'[64] In 2019, Shimotomai, citing 'Russian political scientist Dmitrii Trenin' (who is a 'former' GRU officer) argued that the Orthodox Church in the US, taking control of the personnel policies within the Ukrainian Orthodox Church, was orchestrating the independence of Ukrainian Orthodox Church to bring 'the quarrel between the brothers' — Russia and Ukraine —

'referendum' question and date was initiated by the Kremlin (Conflict Intelligence Team 2016). Conflict Intelligence Team, 'Kto Est' Kto v Proslushke Peregovorov Sergeia Glaz'eva [Who Is Who in the Wiretapping of the Negotiations of Sergei Glazyev]', 23 August 2016, https://citeam.org/glazyev-whoiswho/.
62 Taisuke Abiru, 'Ukuraina tobu mareshia kokuki gekitsui jiken ga yurugasu kokusai josei [The world shaken by the downing of the Malaysian aircraft in Eastern Ukraine]', *Sekai* (September 2014), p.22.
63 Abiru, pp.20-24.
64 Shimotomai, 'Futatsu no kirisutokyo sekai', p.147.

over Crimea to the point of an ultimate division between the two countries.⁶⁵

Ukraine—An 'Imagined Community'

As a historian, Shimotomai explained the origin of the word 'Ukraine,' albeit in Russian propagandistic terms: although 'Ukraine' as a common noun has the meaning of 'frontier' in Slavic languages, 'the word Ukraine was first used as a proper noun in Russia after the Russo-Japanese War, so it has a history of about a hundred years.'⁶⁶ Elsewhere, citing Russian historian Alexey Miller, the Japanese Russianist argued that 'Ukraine' had been the word favored by Poles to divide the antagonistic Russian empire and noted that 'Ukrainians were referred to as *khohly*.'⁶⁷

According to the Japanese historian, the country now known as Ukraine is an 'imagined community' created by Soviet leaders Vladimir Lenin and Joseph Stalin after the revolution by cobbling together the 'half-Polish' world and the 'Russian' world called *Novorossiia* ('New Russia')⁶⁸ Shimotomai's narratives align perfectly with so-called 'Russian historical propaganda.'⁶⁹ Back in 2009, in a Japanese leading thinktank report, Shimotomai rejected the genocide characterization of the famine in Ukraine (1932–33), calling

---

65 Nobuo Shimotomai, 'Shikai furyo chitai Roshia to Ukuraina tairitsu shinka no haikei ni shukyo bunretsu puchin kensei e Beikoku ga anyaku [Poor visibility zone; religious division behind the deepning conflict between Russia and Ukraine; the United States keeping Putin in check]', *Ekonomisuto*, vol.97, no. 1 (2019), p.87.
66 Shimotomai, 'Futatsu no kirisutokyo sekai', pp.149, 155.
67 Shimotomai, 'Kiki no haikei', p.40. For a critical review of Miller's interview to *Novaya gazeta* of 16 April 2014, see Hrytsak, 'Ignorance Is Power', p.221. According to Hrytsak, Miller's characteristic thesis is: 'Ukraine is not a subject but an object in a game' run by 'anyone except Ukrainians.'
68 Shimotomai, 'Kiki no haikei', p.40; Nobuo Shimotomai, *Ukuraina, roshia, shinsekaichitsujo (?): Nihonkogyokurabu mokuyo koen-kai koen yoshi [Ukraine, Russia, New World Order(?): The Industry Club of Japan Thursday Lecture Abstract]* (Tokyo: Nihonkogyokurabu, 2014), p.14.
69 Volodymyr Yermolenko, ed., *Re-Vision of History. Russian Historical Propaganda and Ukraine* (Kyiv: K.I.S., 2019), pp.66–67.

Ukraine's argument on the Holodomor a 'half-truth.'[70] For Shimotomai, Ukraine is thus part of the *Russkii mir* (Russian World). Relations between Russia and Ukraine are 'brotherly,' and their conflict would entail what he compared to 'fratricide.'[71] Consequently, there is no doubt that 'Ukraine's future lies only in improved relations with Russia.'[72]

'No Evidence' of Russian Military Involvement

The participants of the Valdai Club consistently claimed that there was no evidence for the presence of Russian troops in Eastern Ukraine, thus portraying the conflict as 'civil war.' In July 2014, Abiru argued that 'the objective fact' was that 'neither the interim Ukraine government nor the Obama administration has provided any evidence to prove the connection between the pro-Russian groups in eastern Ukraine and the Russian special forces.' Thus, Abiru subscribed to the storyline promoted by Russian 'journalists.'[73]

> It is hard to say that Russia is not involved in the current situation in eastern Ukraine, but it would be unreasonable to assume that Russia is leading this [pro-Russian groups in Eastern Ukraine].[74]

---

70   Nobuo Shimotomai, '"Kuhaku" to "kioku": Ukuraina kikin to rekishi ninshiki ["Blank" and "Memory": Ukraine famine and historical perception]', *Kokusaimondai*, no. 580 (April 2009), pp.1–3.
71   Shimotomai, 'Kiki no haikei', p.42.
72   Shimotomai, 'Futatsu no kirisutokyo sekai', p.157. Shimotomai attributes this statement ('Ukraine's future lies only in improved relations with Russia') to then Japanese foreign minister Fumio Kishida, who became prime minister in 2021. However, I have been unable to locate any records of Kishida having made any such remark.
73   For example, in 2014, Oleg Kashin argued that Aleksandr Borodai, the 'prime minister of Donetsk People's Republic,' was a Russian ultranationalist acting independently of Moscow: 'This is not the hand of Moscow, it's just Borodai.' Oleg Kashin, 'Iz Kryma v Donbass: Priklyucheniya Igorya Strelkova i Aleksandra Borodaya [From Crimea to Donbass: Adventures of Igor Strelkov and Alexander Borodai]', *Slon*, 19 May 2014, https://republic.ru/posts/41009. Kashin's view was widely circulated by the mainstream western media. See e.g., Sabrina Tavernise, 'In Ukraine War, Kremlin Leaves No Fingerprints', *The New York Times*, 31 May 2014, https://www.nytimes.com/2014/06/01/world/europe/in-ukraine-war-kremlin-leaves-no-fingerprints.html?_r=0.
74   Abiru, 'Ukuraina kiki o kaibo', p.15.

Likewise, Shimotomai argued that the Kremlin was not involved in the events in Eastern Ukraine, blaming 'the half-demolished Ukrainian government structure and armed forces' and 'oligarch rule:'

> Relatively poor people in eastern Ukraine, dissatisfied with oligarch rule, probably appealed for the establishment of the people's republics. This situation was used by pro-Russian forces advocating federalization. Russian nationalistic groups and siloviki are seen occasionally, but the Kremlin has not been in direct control of them.[75]

After the downing of MH17 in Eastern Ukraine, a genetic fallacy brought Shimotomai to blame what he believed to be Western anti-Russian sentiments: 'Russia bashing would be fine. Jumping on the bandwagon by joining American sanctions would also be fine. But again, there is no smoking-gun evidence that a pro-Russian group shot down the Malaysian aircraft.'[76] Similarly, Abiru argued that even though 'the international media overwhelmingly supported the Obama administration's claim,' it would be 'premature' to make a final judgment on this matter.[77] However, both scholars have remained strangely silent about the evidence later demonstrated by the Joint Investigation Team (JIT) for Russia's direct involvement in the downing of the MH17 by transporting the BUK system from the 53rd Anti-Aircraft Missile Brigade, a unit of the Russian armed forces in Kursk, the Russian Federation, as well as Moscow's direct control and orchestration of 'people's republics.'[78]

Support for 'Federalization'

The notion of 'federalization' that surfaced in political discourse in February 2014 as a solution to the turmoil in Ukraine was a euphemism for divide-and-rule by Moscow. Insisting on the federalization of Ukraine, Russia aimed to subordinate its eastern part to Russia's control in order to block Ukraine's pro-Western foreign

---

75   Shimotomai, 'Futatsu no kirisutokyo sekai', p.157.
76   Shimotomai, *Nyuenerugi koen*, p.34.
77   Abiru, 'Ukuraina tobu mareshia kokuki', p.21.
78   Politie, 'Witness Appeal June 2019'; Hosaka, 'Welcome to Surkov's Theater'.

policies.⁷⁹ Among many Japanese Russianists, only a few, including the two Valdai members, expressed explicit support for Moscow's concept of blatant interference in Ukraine's sovereign affairs. In May 2014, Abiru argued that Russia's annexation of Crimea had become 'an established fact,' shifting attention from Crimea to eastern Ukraine:

> Russia's call for 'federalization of Ukraine' is broadly in line with the spirit of the February 21 Agreement [on settlement of the political crisis in Ukraine] in terms of respecting the interests of eastern Ukraine. Therefore, it would be an ideal development if Europe and Russia would be able to agree on that, and then the US will join it.⁸⁰

A similar proposal came from Shimotomai, who characterized Ukraine as 'a failed state': 'A compromise may be to turn Ukraine into a federal state and give autonomy to its east following the earliest possible ceasefire, as suggested by Chancellor Angela Merkel [sic].'⁸¹ However, a Berlin-based Japanese journalist Toru Kumagai, with an accurate understanding of Putin's support for federalization, criticized the Japanese Russia experts who advocated Ukraine's federalization as a solution to the crisis. According to the journalist, 'such a solution would not be acceptable in Western Europe, especially Germany.'⁸² Indeed, Merkel clarified that what Berlin called 'federalization' was not what Russia proposed, but was rather a matter of 'decentralization.'⁸³

---

79   Hosaka, 'The Kremlin's Active Measures Failed in 2013', p.361.
80   Taisuke Abiru, Kazuhiko Fuji, and Masumi Motomura, 'Kinkyu zadan-kai: Ukuraina kinpaku de towareru Abe seiken no enerugi senryaku [Roundtable: Ukraine tension challenges Abe administration's energy strategy]', *Enerugiforamu*, vol.60, no. 713 (2014), p.34.
81   Shimotomai, *Nyuenerugi koen*, p.34.
82   Toru Kumagai, 'Ukuraina kiki ga oshi yusaburu tairo seisaku de doitsu ni jirenma [The Ukraine crisis shakes Europe: dilemma in Germany's policy towards Russia]', *Journalism*, no. 289 (2014), pp.142–49.
83   'Germany's Vice-Chancellor Backs "federalization" in Ukraine', *Reuters*, 23 August 2014, https://www.reuters.com/article/us-ukraine-crisis-germany-gabriel-idUSKBN0GN08X20140823.

Keep Good Relations with Russia
(Ukraine Gets in the Way)

In August 2014, during an address to the Japanese energy sector elite, Shimotomai argued that 'unstable Japanese-Russia relations will drive Russia more and more toward China. It is against the national interests of Japan and the US.' Calling attention to Russia's pivot to Asia, he stressed:

> Furthermore, in May of this year [2014], after the International Economic Forum in St. Petersburg, [Putin] sent a very important message to Japan: 'In the Japan-Russia negotiations, when it comes to islands, there are not only two but four.' ... Putin mentioned '4' [islands] first time during his 15-year rule.[84]

Shimotomai concluded that 'for a stable energy supply mechanism in East Asia, dialogue with Russia will be inevitable,' and hence Japan should not be drawn into the Ukraine crisis. In other words, Japan should promote cooperation with Russia, irrespective of the developments in Ukraine.[85] In December 2014, delivering a speech to the Japanese industrial elites, Shimotomai further shared his hermeneutical reading of 'Russia's mind,' expressing ungrounded optimism for a resolution of the Northern Territories dispute: 'while Putin settled the historical dispute on Crimea by recovering what Russia thought to be its lost territory, I think that Putin may make a certain decision on the Northern Territories, which Russia does not consider its own at the back of its mind.'[86]

A similar optimism was shared by Abiru, who argued, citing 'a Russian expert,' that Putin, who had achieved high popular support with the annexation of Crimea, would now be able to 'take a

---

84 Shimotomai, *Nyueneruqi koen*, p.35. It should be noted that despite what Shimotomai called Putin's 'important message,' the 27 bilateral meetings held between the Japanese prime minister and Vladimir Putin did not produce any progress in the territorial issue; instead, Russia rhetorically replaced the territorial dispute between the two countries with the issue of a peace treaty. Hosaka, 'China-Russia "Alliance": Lessons from Japan's Failed "Detachment" Strategy'.
85 Shimotomai, *Nyueneruqi koen*, pp.34–35.
86 Shimotomai, *Ukuraina, roshia, shinsekaichitsujo (?)*, p.40.

dramatic decision on the Northern Territories.'[87] In fact, many other Japanese experts say the opposite: a nationalist Putin would not compromise on the territorial issue.

According to Abiru, the fact that Tokyo had taken a softer position on the sanctions compared to the EU and the US signaled to Moscow its intention to 'maintain a good relationship.' The Japanese expert maintained, 'unless the situation escalates into the Russian military invasion of eastern Ukraine, we should see Russia as a reliable partner,' recommending that Japan actively promote the realization of bilateral projects with Moscow.[88] After Russia's full-fledged military invasion of eastern Ukraine in the summer of 2014, Abiru continued to advocate the improvement of relations with Russia, only adjusting his rhetoric in April 2015 when he argued, 'to ensure Putin's visit to Japan, regardless of the further development of the situation in eastern Ukraine, it would be necessary to prepare a 'Plan B'.'[89] To support his point, Abiru, citing the *Foreign Affairs* article 'Pointless Punishment,' argued that there was an argument even among Americans that the US-led sanctions on Russia should not prevent Japan from developing relations with Moscow.[90]

Aspiration for 'Alternatives'

Narratives of scholars on the Ukraine crisis reveal their epistemological aversion to the Western mainstream discourse. This is closely linked to an aspiration inherent in critical, often 'progressive,' scholars to present alternative explanations, and/or rests on the perception of what they believe to be Western 'Russophobia.' In extreme cases, the combination of these epistemological concerns entails an astonishing degree of empathy with Russian suffering.

---

87   Abiru, 'Roshia "toho shifuto"'.
88   Abiru, Fuji, and Motomura, 'Kinkyu zadan-kai', pp.36–37.
89   Taisuke Abiru, 'Ukuraina teisen goi puchin ga nerau "funso toketsu jotai" [Ceasefire agreement in Ukraine, Putin's goal "frozen conflict"]', *Facta*, vol.10, no.4 (2015), p.74.
90   Taisuke Abiru, 'Ukuraina kiki go no Rochu kankei [Russia-China Relations after the Ukrainian Crisis]', in *Erina Report* (Niigata: The Economic Research Institute for Northeast Asia, 2015), p.11.

Empirical Enthusiasm — 'Bottom-Up Story'

A good illustration of scholars' aspiration for alternative discourse is the Ninth World Congress of the ICCEES (Makuhari, Japan, August 2015), which hosted as many as 15 panels on the Ukraine crisis. According to Kimitaka Matsuzato, secretary-general of the congress organizing committee, the significance of hosting the ICCEES in Japan lay in the fact that 'diverse views were expressed;' this would not have been possible had the congress been held 'in Europe or the US, where Russia is overwhelmingly seen as a villain.'[91]

Matsuzato personally facilitated a special symposium on the Ukraine crisis titled 'Did They Have Alternatives? The Ukrainian Turmoil from Local Perspectives,' inviting Serhiy Kudelia of Baylor University, who was, according to Matsuzato, a 'participant from North America but gave a critical view on the Euromaidan Revolution,'[92] Vladimir Dzharalla of the 'Crimean parliament,' and Kirill Cherkashin of 'Donetsk University.' Matsuzato stressed the academic importance of the event for two reasons. First, none of the international conferences on 'the Second Ossetia War in 2008' had invited researchers from South Ossetia, a principal party to the conflict, due to the difficulties involved in obtaining visas for

---

91 'Organizing Committee [Organizing Committee for the Ninth World Congress of ICCEES', 2016, pp.26–27, https://www.l.u-tokyo.ac.jp/makuhari2015/images/ICCEES2015_report.pdf. Matsuzato, who stayed in Simferopol and saw no military personnel on the day of the Crimea 'referendum,' asserted: 'Western media reports on "the referendum at gunpoint" are a lie.' Kimitaka Matsuzato, 'Kurimia no naisei to seihen (2009-2014 nen) [Crimean Internal Politics and Political Change (2009-14)]', *Gendai shiso*, vol.42, no.10 (2014), pp.99–100.

92 Kudelia is one of those Western scholars who argue the armed conflict in Eastern Ukraine was an internally motivated, 'homegrown' phenomenon, failing to see Russia's central role in this conflict. See Serhiy Kudelia, 'Domestic Sources of the Donbas Insurgency', *PONARS Eurasia Policy Memo*, 29 September 2014, http://www.ponarseurasia.org/memo/domestic-sources-donbasinsurgency; Andreas Umland, 'In Defense of Conspirology: A Rejoinder to Serhiy Kudelia's Anti-Political Analysis of the Hybrid War in Eastern Ukraine', *PONARS Eurasia*, 30 September 2014, https://www.ponarseurasia.org/in-defense-of-conspirology-a-rejoinder-to-serhiy-kudelia-s-anti-political-analysis-of-the-hybrid-war-in-eastern-ukraine/; Sanshiro Hosaka, 'Enough with Donbas "Civil War" Narratives? Identifying the Main Combatant Leading "the Bulk of the Fighting"', in *Civil War? Interstate War? Hybrid War? Dimensions and Interpretations of the Donbas Conflict in 2014-2020*, ed. Jakob Hauter, Soviet and Post-Soviet Politics and Society (Stuttgart: ibidem-Verlag, 2021).

researchers from the non-recognized republic. Second, he argued that it was 'wrongly believed that South Ossetia, Abkhazia, Crimea and Donbas are all Russian puppets, hence no need for giving them the floor.'[93]

In his article on the Donbas war, Matsuzato criticizes the 'renewed Cold War perception' among Western scholars. He argued that such a view involves the stereotypical reduction of Ukrainian politics to vacillation between pro-Western and pro-Russian and fails to see relationships between local actors as well as social discontent as domestic sources of the conflict. This view is in stark contrast to the ontological dichotomy between the West and Russia held by the Valdai members discussed above. Matsuzato called for scholars to examine different domestic and local actors in the 'civil war,' including the 'DNR' leaders.[94] However, after the 'DNR'-arranged visit to 'one ruined and two destroyed but restored schools' in Donetsk City suburb in August 2017, Matsuzato called Ukrainian president Petro Poroshenko a war criminal in his article awarded with a prize for the best article published in *Nationalities Papers* in 2019: 'Putting aside President Poroshenko's undisputable war crime of shelling children, I often explain to Donetsk citizens that, even under cruel Japanese militarism, children were evacuated from urban areas in the last months of World War II.'[95] Besides his multiple fieldwork trips to the 'DNR,' Matsuzato hailed a visit made by a fellow member of his research team to 'DNR' territory as 'an advantage for Japan's Ukrainian studies,' arguing that 'researchers from other countries tend not to enter the separatist area for political and security reasons.'[96]

Matsuzato's view was echoed by the guests invited by him to the ICCEES special symposium in Japan. Cherkashin, a representative of the 'Donetsk People's Republic (DNR),' pointed out later in

---

93 'Organizing Committee', pp.26–27.
94 Kimitaka Matsuzato, 'The Donbass War: Outbreak and Deadlock', *Demokratizatsiya: The Journal of Post-Soviet Democratization*, vol.25, no.2 (2017), p.177.
95 Kimitaka Matsuzato, 'The Donbas War and Politics in Cities on the Front: Mariupol and Kramatorsk', *Nationalities Papers*, vol.46, no.6 (2018), pp.1012–13.
96 'Fiscal Year Annual Research Report', 2015, https://kaken.nii.ac.jp/en/report/KAKENHI-PROJECT-15H03309/15H033092015jisseki/.

an outlet published by 'DNR' academia that a considerable part of Western researchers at ICCEES adhered to 'objective positions,' regarding it 'not entirely correct' to understand the issue simply as 'Russian aggression' and Ukraine as an 'innocent victim.' The Donetsk native stated that the representatives of the 'DNR' and Crimea had been invited to the conference because of a 'pre-existing academic connection,' and thanked Matsuzato for his efforts to 'ensure the presence of representatives of the regions of the former Ukraine at the conference,' which allowed them to 'convey to the international academic community the point of view of the majority of residents' of Donetsk and Crimea.[97]

Another speaker, Vladimir Dzharalla, a would-be 'independent expert from Crimea,' after taking part in the conference in Makuhari, correctly noted in the Russian media that 'in the academic community, there is an urgent need for independent sources of information about what is happening in these regions [Crimea and Donbas], without the mediation of the mass media.' Responding to the questions from the floor on reports of coercion and harassment during Russia's annexation of Crimea, Dzharalla managed to change the audience's attitude 'from distrust to contemplation on what they had just heard' from him. He concluded with satisfaction that an 'information breakthrough' had taken place.[98]

In order to ascertain to what extent the views of Cherkashin and Dzharalla did represent the 'majority of residents' in Donetsk and Crimea, we should place these views under a microscope alongside their dubious track records. In 2012, Cherkashin was a speaker at the conference titled 'Donbas in the Eurasian Project' organized by Andrei Purgin of the public organization 'Donetsk Republic,' a future 'deputy prime minister' of the 'DNR.' The conference was attended by guests from Moscow and local fringe intellectuals influenced by Aleksandr Dugin's *geopolitika*, Eurasianism, and

---

[97] K.V. Cherkashin, 'Vizit delegatsii uchenykh DNR i Kryma v Yaponiiu', in *Visit of Donetsk People's Republic and Crimea scientists' delegation to Japan*, vol. 2, 2015, p.109.
[98] Anastasiya Leonova, 'Krymskii politolog prorval informatsionnuiu blokadu v Yaponii" [Crimean politolog broke through information blockade in Japan', 2015, https://www.crimea.kp.ru/online/news/2135920/.

anti-liberalism.⁹⁹ During the Russian–Ukrainian war, as the Surkov leaks show, Cherkashin joined the ranks of the illegally formulated 'Supreme Soviet of the DNR,' the membership of which was reported by its 'Chairman' Denis Pushlin to Moscow's handler Vladislav Surkov in June 2014.¹⁰⁰

Similarly, Dzharalla is exposed in other leaked emails, namely the Frolov leaks.¹⁰¹ In November 2013, the Russian-based CIS Institute, which actively enlisted local agents for subversive activities in Crimea, seriously considered the recruitment of Dzharalla as the most likely candidate for 'speaker' of a new Russian political technology project in Crimea. An internal document describes him as a 'talking head' on a local TV show and 'light infantry' carrying out assignments in social and political events. The same document justifies Dzharalla's candidacy because of his 'exotic' Iranian-Persian origin, his lack of affiliation with any local 'clan,' and the fact that Dzharalla 'ardently' but carefully spoke 'for Russia' at the meeting of young Russian compatriots in Sevastopol.¹⁰² Although the leaked emails do not provide confirmation that this recruitment took place, it is at least obvious that Dzharalla has been a mouthpiece in political technology projects.

The collaboration between scholars and local political technologists to explore 'alternative' views on the Ukraine crisis was criticized for the biased selection of guest speakers. One attendee of the

---

99 'V Donetske Proshla Mezhdunarodnaia Nauchno-Prakticheskaia Konferentsiia "Donbass v Evraziiskom Proekte"', in *The International Scientific and Practical Conference "Donbas in the Eurasian Project" Was Held in Donetsk*]. *Russkii Mir* (Ukraina, 2012), http://russmir.info/pol/3362-v-donecke-proshla-mezhdunarodnaya-nauchno.html.
100 dnrpdv@mail.ru, e-mail to prm_Surkova@gov.ru, 'Shtat Verkhovnogo Soveta Donetskoi Narodnoi Respubliki', 13 June 2014. For the details of the Surkov leaks, see Hosaka, 'Welcome to Surkov's Theater'.
101 For the details of the Frolov leaks and the subversive activities the Russian CIS Institute conducted in Ukraine, see Hosaka, 'The Kremlin's Active Measures Failed in 2013'; Hosaka, 'Welcome to Surkov's Theater'.
102 institute@materik.ru to frolov_moskva@mail.ru and geomant-rus@yandex.ru, 'Fwd: Dzharalla', 2 December 2013.

symposium in Tokyo remarked that it should have invited participants from outside Crimea and the 'DNR.'[103]

After the end of the Cold War, the growing number of smaller localized ethnopolitical conflicts prompted scholars to research domestic societal-level explanatory variables.[104] It is, however, plausible that supposedly autonomous local actors do not have actual power over the political process, which is clandestinely controlled by the center of the patron state. In such cases, the propensity of researchers to demonstrate 'alternative' local perspectives runs the high risk of overestimating the political subjectivity of seemingly indigenous movements if they are ill-equipped to examine the genuine, mostly concealed, relationship between a patron state and its puppets.

The Donbas war is an excellent illustration of this hidden power relation. Although the lively accounts of relations between 'local' actors—'Novorossianists' (Kimitaka Matsuzato) and 'Russian Spring actors' (Anna Matveeva)—may reveal interesting details of the adventure of Russian 'volunteers' or local 'warlords,'[105] these bits and pieces obfuscate the most significant variable in unraveling the cause of the war—Moscow's central role. Similarly, Nadiia Koval' points out that French researchers of local conflicts in the post-Soviet space (especially, Moldova, Georgia, Ukraine) tend to ignore Russia's leading role in provoking and sponsoring

---

103 'Organizing Committee', 43. For first-hand observations of this congress from the perspective of a Ukrainian scholar, see Olga Bertelsen's contribution to this volume.
104 Jack S. Levy, 'The Causes of War and Conditions of Peace', *Annual Review of Political Science*, vol.1, no.1 (1998), p.160. Another problem endemic to scholars, which I will discuss elsewhere, is an awkward application of familiar theories to the Donbas war. Tymofii Brik, 'The Donbas and Social Science: Terra Incognita?', in *Civil War? Interstate War? Hybrid War? Dimensions and Interpretations of the Donbas Conflict in 2014-2020*, ed. J. Hauter (Stuttgart: ibidem-Verlag, 2021), pp.201–2. For example, Rogers Brubaker's triadic nexus framework runs the risk of reducing the complicated reality of post-Soviet Ukraine to a simple relationship between Ukraine as a nationalizing state, Russians in Ukraine as a national minority, and Russia as the external homeland. Volodymyr Kulyk, 'The Politics of Ethnicity in Post-Soviet Ukraine: Beyond Brubaker', *Journal of Ukrainian Studies*, vol.26, no.1–2 (2001), pp.197–221.
105 Matveeva, *Through Times of Trouble*; Matsuzato, 'The Donbass War: Outbreak and Deadlock'.

the conflicts, with their willingness to study 'de facto states' as a political feature of the region.[106]

Scholars' Mission to Counter 'Russophobia'

Another core tenet stemming from the epistemological aversion to mainstream discourse is the image of the West perpetually 'blaming' or 'demonizing' Russia, leading scholars to abstain from 'blaming' and instead take what Zhuk calls a conformist approach.[107] Scholars accusing the West of 'Russophobia' often confuse the latter with criticism of Putin's politics,[108] rejecting negative information about Russia as 'Cold War stereotypes.'[109]

The rhetoric that Western (and Japanese) mainstream discourse vis-à-vis Russia is biased or simply 'anti-Russian' is shared not only by the Valdai members but by a wide range of leading Japanese scholars of Russia, at times leading to assertions that Russia's negative image was allegedly created in the US-led 'information war.'[110] These scholars believe that the US has aimed to weaken

---

106 Nadiia Koval, 'Vichne povernennya do "vichnoyi Rosiyi": vyklyky "ukrayins'koyi kryzy" dlya frantsuz'koho intelektual'noho dyskursu [Eternal return to "eternal Russia": challenges of "Ukrainian crisis" for French intellectual discourse]', in *Interpretatsiyi rosiys'ko-ukrayins'koho konfliktu v zakhidnykh naukovykh i ekspertno-analitychnykh pratsyakh [Interpretation of the Russian-Ukrainian Conflict in Western Scientific and Expert-Analytical Works]*, ed. Volodymyr Kulyk, Kulyk (Kyiv: IPiEND im. I. F. Kurasa, 2020), p.148.
107 Zhuk, 'Ukrainian Maidan'.
108 Gretskiy, 'Lukyanov Doctrine: Conceptual Origins of Russia's Hybrid Foreign Policy—The Case of Ukraine', pp.4–5.
109 Phrases such as 'Russophobia' and 'anti-Russian sentiments' are Moscow's last resorts to defend itself against well-grounded criticism from foreign partners (Putin's accusations about a Western 'containment' policy fulfil a similar function). Predictably, the use of these phrases by the Russian foreign ministry and propaganda media increased dramatically after March 2014. Ben Nimmo, '#PutinAtWar: How Russia Weaponized "Russophobia"', *Medium*, 15 February 2018, https://medium.com/dfrlab/putinatwar-how-russia-weaponized-russophobia-40a3723d26d4. This technique based on a genetic fallacy is reminiscent of the Soviet propaganda labeling any worrisome tendencies as 'anti-Soviet.'
110 Similarly, some Western scholars of journalism studies see the mainstream 'western' media as the source of the US government propaganda, calling for reducing dependency on the mainstream media by using 'alternative media' (e.g., Boyd-Barrett 2017). See e.g., Oliver Boyd-Barrett, 'Ukraine, Mainstream Media and Conflict Propaganda', *Journalism Studies*, vol.18, no. 8 (2017), pp.1016–34, https://doi.org/10.1080/1461670X.2015.1099461.

Russia's international position since the end of the Cold War in order to render Russia incapable of challenging US hegemony; they dismiss the Western sanctions on Russia as 'Russia bashing.'[111] In an emotional interview, Ikuo Kameyama, a scholar of Russian literature and president of Nagoya University of Foreign Studies, expressed his resentment of Western intellectuals who draw parallels between Putin's annexation of Crimea and Hitler's Anschluss, arguing that such an analogy is humiliating for Russians who made a huge sacrifice during the war against Nazi Germany (ignoring other Soviet nationalities, such as Ukrainians and Belarusians, who suffered far more). He explained his empathy with Russian suffering as that of a 'person who has been engaged in Russian literature and culture as well as deeply interested in Russian politics for 45 years, or who has, in a sense, identified himself with a Russian mentality.'[112]

Toshihiko Ueno, professor of Russian politics and then president of the Japanese Association for Russian and Eastern European Studies, reflecting on the Ukraine crisis, maintained that the role of scholars should be to 'illuminate the historical background, analyze various events with concrete data and figures' but not to 'blame one party to a conflict or make a superficial comment.'[113] Similarly, Mitsuyoshi Numano, an experienced scholar of Slavic literature, criticized his US colleagues accusing Russia of interference in Ukraine for lacking 'cultural and historical perspective.'[114]

A pitfall of this epistemology, peculiar to Russianists, is that their aspiration to elucidate the historical and cultural background of the phenomenon often ends in a hermeneutical reading of Russian motives, endorsing Putin's talking points and sentiments.

---

111 See e.g., Nobuaki Shiokawa and Mitsuyoshi Numano, '"Ukuraina kiki no shinso o yomu" [Interpret the depths of the Ukraine crisis]', *Gendai Shiso,* vol.42, no.10 (2014), p.49; Ikuo Kameyama, 'Roshia wa doko e mukau ka? [Where is Russia going?]', *Gendai Shiso,* vol.42, no.10 (2014), pp.31–32; Kiichi Mochizuki, 'Puchin No Kyokuto Shiko to Ukuraina Soran [Putin's Far East Orientation and Ukrainian Uprising]', *Roshia Yurashia No Keizai to Shakai,* no. 985 (2014), pp.11–31.
112 Kameyama, 'Roshia wa doko e mukau ka? [Where is Russia going?]', p.29.
113 Ueno, 'Ukuraina kiki ni yosete [Ukrainian crisis and our stance]', p.1.
114 Shiokawa and Numano, '"Ukuraina kiki no shinso o yomu" [Interpret the depths of the Ukraine crisis]', p.39.

Thus, in his article for a Eurasian studies journal, Ueno wrote, 'although the referendum was held, [Russia's] incorporation of Crimea contradicts the Ukrainian Constitution and international law.' However, he continued, 'there are good reasons for Russia's incorporation of Crimea.' The Japanese professor argued that from Napoleon to the two world wars, Russia was invaded by Western Europe and that this historical memory constitutes the basis of Russia's threat perception that will never tolerate NATO enlargement, let alone Ukraine's entry into it. Ueno further speculated that it is disputable what represents post-Soviet Ukraine, with its 'extremely artificial' border established after World War II.[115] Likewise, Numano pointed out that notwithstanding its political attribution, Crimea has been a mythical and divine place for Russian literature since the end of the 18th century, arguing that 'it is not easy to draw borders and decide on the attribution of such a historically and culturally diverse territory.'[116] Putin's theses on Khrushchev's 1954 'illegal' handover of Crimea to the Ukrainian SSR, Ukrainian nationalists' and Bandera's collaboration with Nazis, and *Novorossiia* that includes even Sloboda Ukraine (which was never included in the historical *Novorossiya*) were all repeated and elaborated with hardly any criticism by scholars seeking 'historical background.'[117]

On the contrary, during the conference of the Japanese Association for Russian and East European Studies in the autumn of 2014, Shigeki Hakamada, a scholar of Russian politics, criticized the special session on 'The Crisis in Ukraine and International Relations' for downplaying Russia's flagrant violation of international law, and highlighting instead the annexation of Crimea and the situation in Eastern Ukraine only from historical, religious, political, and military perspectives.[118] Similarly, Hiroshi Kimura, a scholar of Russian politics, issued a reminder that Russia had recognized the

---

115 Toshihiko Ueno, 'Ukuraina mondai o kangaeru shiten" [Ukraine Problems: From Some Points of View', *Yurashia kenkyu*, no.51 (2014), p.6.
116 Shiokawa and Numano, '"Ukuraina kiki no shinso o yomu" [Interpret the depths of the Ukraine crisis]', p.40.
117 See e.g., Shimotomai, 'Kiki no haikei'; Shimotomai, 'Futatsu no kirisutokyo sekai'.
118 Yoko Hirose et al., 'Panel Discussion: The Crisis in Ukraine and International Relations', *Roshia Touou Kenkyu*, vol.43 (2014), pp.65–66.

sovereignty and territorial integrity of Ukraine in return for Ukraine's abandonment of nuclear weapons in the 1994 Budapest Memorandum, asserting that 'the Crimean peninsula is doubtless Ukrainian.' Kimura further drew parallels between Crimea and Japan's Northern Territories as both territories have been under occupation by Russia, suggesting that Japan spearhead Western sanctions on Russia.[119] Hiroshi Ishida, a Rome-based correspondent of a major Japanese newspaper, who was dispatched to Kyiv during the Ukraine crisis and critically covered Russia's annexation of Crimea, recalled that his articles and tweets had been labeled as 'Western perspectives' by those 'skeptical of the Western media' although he had not written anything to praise Europe or the United States.[120]

Conclusion

This article has demonstrated the positionality of Area Studies scholars in their knowledge production, and two different, though to some degree intertwined, paths down the rabbit hole of Russian narratives on the Ukraine crisis: a shortcut from Russia-centered ontology and a detour via epistemological aversion to Western mainstream discourse. A few notes of caution are due here.

First, scholars trapped in a Russia-centered ontology are not passive actors, as derogatorily described as 'useful idiots,' but proactive actors who know their role as communicators very well. Japanese participants of the Valdai Discussion Club not only sympathize with Putin's Russia but also aspire to improve Japan's relations with Moscow in the belief that their sacred mission is to serve as a bridge between the two countries, thus trying to bring Russia, 'a close but far' country, truly closer to Japanese domestic

---

119 Hiroshi Kimura, 'Ukuraina Kiki to Nihon No Tairo Seisai: Kurimia to Hopporyodo Wa Dokon, Abe Seiken Wa Kizento Taio Subeki" [The Ukraine Crisis and Japan's Sanctions against Russia: Crimea and Northern Territories Have the Same Roots, Abe Administration Should Respond Resolutely', *Interijensu Repoto,* no.75 (2014), pp.4–17.
120 Takashi Kida and Hiroshi Ishida, 'Genchi no media jokyo to shuzai kankyo [Local media situation and coverage environment]', *Shinbunkenkyu,* no. 755 (2014), pp.47–51.

audiences.¹²¹ However, their goodwill aimed at rectifying the knowledge deficit on Russia appears to be offered at the expense of Russia's neighbor — Ukraine — by negating the latter's history and culture, agency in international politics, and ultimately its importance for Japan.

Second, resonating with Russian narratives does not necessarily require scholars to be pro-Russian and explicitly dependent on Moscow. As is the case with the 2015 ICCEES symposium, an epistemological aversion to mainstream discourse, turning their passion for alternative local stories into vulnerability to information manipulation, may expose scholars to the pernicious influence of Russian narratives.

On the one hand, scholars of Russian studies (and some scholars of Ukrainian studies) tend to see their role in providing alternatives to dominant worldviews in the West as well as the world's mainstream English-language information. Often, opponents of US hegemony pin their hopes on Russia as a counterbalance.¹²² Scholars with such an epistemological inclination are tempted to increase their value and fill a niche in the academic market by differentiating their views from major Western discourse. On the other hand, concentrating on searching for 'double standards' or 'hypocrisy' in US policies towards Russia blinds them to Russia's wrongdoings and

---

121 According to a poll held by Pew Research Center in 2013, Russia was viewed in a mostly negative manner in Japan: 64% unfavorable against 27% favorable. 'Russia's Global Image Negative amid Crisis in Ukraine' (Pew Research Center, 9 July 2014), https://www.pewresearch.org/global/2014/07/09/russias-global-image-negative-amid-crisis-in-ukraine/.

122 It is noteworthy, as an extreme example, that a group of Western scholars critical of the 'US hegemony' and supportive of the 'multipolar world' visited the Russia-occupied Crimea in July 2014 and signed the 'Yalta Declaration of the Assembly of Citizens of Ukraine' that accuses the Ukraine government of 'a brutal military assault in the southeast of the country' and demands 'direct talks between Kiev and the representatives of Donetsk and Lugansk republics' exactly in line with Moscow's disinformation points. This 'declaration' was published in a Taylor & Francis peer-reviewed journal..Radhika Desai, Alan Freeman, and Boris Kagarlitsky, 'The Conflict in Ukraine and Contemporary Imperialism', *International Critical Thought*, vol.6, no.4 (2016), pp.489–512, https://doi.org/10.1080/21598282.2016.1242338. At least, among signers from 'locals' can be found Vladimir Rogov, the Zaporizhian head of the People's Front of the Southeastern Regions, which was directly controlled by Surkov's office Hosaka, 'Welcome to Surkov's Theater', p.759.

covert operations against its neighbors. As Thompson points out, although Western intellectuals are eager to deconstruct western colonialism, Russian colonialism somehow slips away from their view.[123]

Lastly, Russian disinformation targeting scholars is perhaps most effective when these ontological and/or epistemological preconditions are met. This article has not addressed how the object of scholars' attention, Russia, in turn, views the role of international academia. However, historical research indicates that both Soviet and foreign scientists were a useful channel for the Soviet secret services to convey the Kremlin's narrative to targets in 'capitalist' countries.[124] Moreover, the Soviet intelligence tradition suggests that authoritative Russian thinktanks remain at the forefront of such operations, or in carrying out what is referred to in the Soviet and Russian parlance as 'political espionage from the territory [politicheskaya razvedka s territorii].' As discussed above, scholars are not 'useful idiots' who simply disseminate false information according to instructions from Moscow. Disinformation operations through academia require more sophisticated approaches from their suppliers—Russian intelligence officers and their agents, who take careful account of the ontological and epistemological foundations of the worldviews of potential consumers. More comprehensive research is required to explain how each actor defines their mutual interests and gains, and to uncover the intricacies of the supply-and-demand relationship which makes cooperation between intelligence services and academics particularly 'fruitful.'

---

123 Thompson, *Imperial Knowledge: Russian Literature and Colonialism*, p.15.
124 See e.g., Sanshiro Hosaka, 'Repeating History: Soviet Offensive Counterintelligence Active Measures', *International Journal of Intelligence and CounterIntelligence*, vol.35, no. 3 (022): 15, https://doi.org/10.1080/08850607.2020.1822100.

Propaganda Targeting Foreign Audiences
A Comparative Analysis of Soviet and Russian Propaganda in the Czechoslovak Socialist Republic / Czech Republic

Veronika Krátka Špalková

Introduction

In his famous 1924 essay, *Why I Am Not a Communist*, the Czech writer Karel Čapek wrote:

> The method of Communism is an attempt on a large scale to create international misunderstanding; it is an attempt to split into isolated pieces. What is good on one side is not good and must not be good on the other; as if there were not on both sides people morally and physiologically identical[1].

What Čapek calls the "method of Communism" could just as well be called the method of the Soviet Union and later the method of the Russian Federation under the rule of Vladimir Putin. The Soviet authorities used propaganda as an instrument for consolidating their position in Czechoslovakia, seeking to convince people that anything other than communism was wrong, and to provoke hatred towards the liberal and democratic West. The Putin regime, with its propaganda, is likewise trying to divide Czech society today, to disrupt social ties, and incite hatred.

The two countries have different names, borders, ideologies, and political, economic, and social systems, and yet in many respects their practices are similar and their foreign policies have pursued similar goals. The Soviet Union, like the Russian Federation under Vladimir Putin, pursued a foreign policy towards Central and Eastern Europe in the name of spreading its sphere of influence. Manipulating citizens has been part of the strategy used to this end in both cases. While in communist Czechoslovakia

---

1 Karel Čapek, 'Proč nejsem komunistou,' *Přítomnost,* vol.1, no.47 (1924), pp.737–39.

propaganda was used to strengthen the power position of the communist pro-Kremlin party, in the contemporary Czech Republic it is an attempt to influence the electoral behavior of citizens so as to create a situation in which the Czech Republic will gradually turn its back on its Western allies and yield to Russian influence.

Propaganda can be defined from different angles, and has been defined in different ways in different historical periods. Kateřina Prokopová, a Czech scholar who focuses on propaganda, offers an overview of how scholarly views on propaganda have changed over time, with propaganda variously defined as a tool used by governments to form democratic views; a technique of social control; or a means of influencing and manipulating people[2].

Philosopher and media studies scholar Nancy Snow has defined propaganda as "sponsored information that uses cause- and emotion-laden content to sway public opinion and behavior in support of the source's goals"[3]. For my purposes, this definition is especially useful for its inclusion of the concept of "sponsorship" as a key aspect of propaganda.

In this project, I am interested specifically in sponsored information produced for foreign audiences. During the Soviet period, a number of specialist institutions were created and funded by the state for this purpose[4]. Similarly, there are currently several Russian propaganda channels that are aimed primarily at foreign audiences, such as the English-language channel *RT* and the

---

2 Kateřina Prokopová, *Propaganda a persvaze* (Olomouc: Univerzita Palackého, 2014).
 The scholarly literature on propaganda is rich and extensive. For a useful recent contribution, including detailed typologies and discussion on methodologies for the analysis of propaganda, see Garth S. Jowett, Victoria O'Donnell, *Propaganda and Persuasion*, (USA: SAGE Publications, 2014); see also Stanley B. Cunningham, *The Idea of Propaganda: A Reconstruction*, (USA: Praeger Publishers, 2002); Oliver Thomson, *Historia propagandy*, (Warszawa: Książka i Wiedza, 1999); and Frederick Elmore Lumley, *The Propaganda Menace*, (New York: The Century, 1933).
3 Nancy Snow, 'Propaganda' In: Tim Vos, Folker Hanusch, Dimitra Dimitrakopoulou, Margaretha Geertsema-Sligh, Annika Sehl eds., *International Encyclopedia of Journalism Studies* (Hoboken: John Wiley & Sons, 2019).
4 Martin Dewhirst, Robert Farrell, eds, *The Soviet Censorship* (Metuchen: Scarecrow Press, 1973).

international project *Sputnik*, which publishes in more than thirty languages. These projects are fully funded by the Russian government and are an essential part of the Russian propaganda ecosystem[5].

A useful perspective on foreign propaganda is provided by Ladislav Bittman, a former Czechoslovak State Security agent, subsequent critic of the Soviet-led invasion of Czechoslovakia in 1968 who later emigrated to the United States. Bittman's reflections on this topic focus on the techniques and strategies used in the production of propaganda for foreign audiences:

> International disinformation campaigns are a language of false views that parasitize on existing prejudices. The content and phraseology are chosen to confuse people's opinions, insult people's national pride or religious feelings, and give the impression that an external enemy is behind all the existing problems[6].

The focus of my analysis is news media propaganda created and disseminated as part of the foreign policy of the USSR/Russian Federation with regard to the Czechoslovak Socialist Republic/the Czech Republic. Propaganda is a very broad and interdisciplinary topic; therefore, the aim of this work is not to examine or explain propaganda in all its aspects. Rather, I set out to offer a deep analysis focused on two specific and narrowly defined cases of limited period and scope.

The first case concerns the Soviet invasion of Afghanistan, which began in December 1979 and the subsequent Soviet–Afghan War. I examine how these events were narrated in the Czechoslovak Socialist Republic in articles published in *Rudé právo* between December 1979 and February 1984.

The second case examined is the March 2014 Russian annexation of the Crimean Peninsula. Here I examine articles on this event published by the Czech version of Russian *Sputnik* between January

---

5   U.S. Department of State, 'RT and Sputnik's Role in Russia's Disinformation and Propaganda Ecosystem,' *state.gov*, January 20, 2022. Available at https://www.state.gov/wp-content/uploads/2022/01/Kremlin-Funded-Media_January_update-19.pdf.
6   Ladislav Bittman, *Mezinárodní dezinformace: černá propaganda, aktivní opatření a tajné akce* (Praha: Mladá fronta, 2000).

2015 (when Czech *Sputnik* first became operational) and February 2019.

In both cases, I analyze articles published during a 50-month period,[7] with a view to investigating whether Russian propaganda is currently present in the Czech Republic and if so, whether and to what extent it is comparable to Soviet-type propaganda that operated there during the previous regime.

My hypothesis was the following: *There is a continuous relationship between the propaganda techniques in news media used by the USSR against the Czechoslovak Socialist Republic at the turn of the 1970s–'80s and the propaganda techniques used in news media by the Russian Federation against the Czech Republic today.*

Rudé právo functioned as the main press organ of the Communist Party of Czechoslovakia and, far from striving for objective journalism, published information that fit into the Soviet narrative. It was founded in 1920 and was published daily. During the communist period, television, press, and radio media were owned by the state, which was controlled by the communist party. The media was thus directly controlled by the ruling Communist Party of Czechoslovakia, which was in turn controlled by the Communist Party of the Soviet Union.

Sputnik is the only Russian government-funded information medium in the Czech area publishing in the Czech language. Its main headquarters are in Moscow. At the beginning of 2015, the news agency and the radio station *Sputnik* replaced the original Russian state radio station *The Voice of Russia,* which had been broadcasting since 1929. *Sputnik* broadcasts and publishes in more than 30 languages with a focus on the countries of the former Eastern bloc.[8] The Czech version of *Sputnik* also started operating in 2015.

---

7   The time frame was determined by how long *Sputnik* had been operating in the Czech Republic at the time the research was conducted, that is, 50 months (from *Sputnik*'s launch in January 2015 until March 2019, when the research was conducted). In order to balance the research cases, the same length of time was used for the first case, tracking coverage in the 50 months following the Soviet invasion of Afghanistan in December 1979.

8   Neovlivní, 'Hlas Ruska/Sputnik: ozvěny Kremlu v ČR,' *Neovlivní,* May 16, 2015. Available at https://neovlivni.cz/hlas-ruskasputnik-ozveny-kremlu-v-cr/.

The events covered in the two cases — the Soviet invasion of Afghanistan and the Russian annexation of Crimea — likely shared similar motivations from a geopolitical and strategic point of view. Although these are geographically different territories whose relations with the USSR/Russia were very different, a common and significant point where the cases intersect is their bearing on the security of the Russian border. While debates over the history of both these sets of events are still ongoing, border security is one of the most frequently mentioned motivations for both interventions.[9]

In the case of Afghanistan, the situation was exacerbated by the ongoing Cold War. In Afghanistan, there was a struggle not only for a sphere of influence, but above all for a territory that at that time served an irreplaceable function for the USSR as a

---

9 Many experts have joined the debate on the USSR's motivations for invading Afghanistan. The discussion changed after new documents were released that offered insight into the decision-making processes of the Soviet Communist Party, especially thanks to the Cold War International History Project based at the Woodrow Wilson Center in Washington, D.C. as well as additional Soviet materials available from the National Security Archive (NSA), also in Washington, D.C. Until then, there was a general notion that the USSR had intervened in Afghanistan as a response to a growing terrorist threat which had begun spilling over from Afghanistan into the Soviet Union. However, after the publication of the new documents, the majority opinion shifted to the view that this was a defensive step taken in order to prevent Afghanistan from moving into the US sphere of influence, as argued by David N. Gibbs (David N. Gibbs, 'Reassessing Soviet Motives for Invading Afghanistan. A Declassified History,' *Critical Asian Studies*, vol.38, no.2 (2006), pp. 239–63). Many analysts have also taken part in the discussion about Russia's motivations for annexing Crimea, including, for example, the prominent international relations theorist John Mearsheimer, who in his article (2014) blames the West and its alleged expansionism (John Mearsheimer, 'Why the Ukraine Crisis is the West's Fault,' *Foreign Affairs*, September/October, 2014. Available at https://www.foreignaffairs.com/articles/russia-fsu/2014-08-18/why-ukraine-crisis-west-s-fault).
Various motivations are also discussed by Daniel Treisman in his article "Why Putin Took Crimea: The Gambler in the Kremlin" (2016). Treisman attaches some importance to the security of the Russian border but does not consider it to be Putin's main motive for the annexation of Crimea. However, he admits that the Russian naval base in Sevastopol plays an irreplaceable role for Russia (Daniel Treisman, (2016) 'Why Putin Took Crimea: The Gambler in the Kremlin,' *Foreign Affairs*, vol.95, no.3 (2016), pp.47–54.).

southern buffer zone. An Afghanistan on friendly terms with the United States would be a strategic disaster for the USSR.[10]

Similarly, the events in Ukraine cannot be considered only as a struggle for sphere of influence, because for modern Russia, created after the collapse of the USSR, its Black Sea Fleet in Sevastopol in Crimea played and continues to play an irreplaceable role, without which Russia would not be able to effectively protect its southern border.[11] Even if we disregard all the other reasons why Ukraine is important to Russia (economic, political, and cultural interconnectedness), we will still have security issues. The question of what would happen to the Russian Black Sea Fleet if Ukraine became a member of the EU (whether Ukraine would extend the lease of the Sevastopol base or not) remains a topic for counterfactual history.

There are, of course, many editorial, control, and organizational differences between *Rudé právo* and *Sputnik*. Their positions on the market are also different, and the social and political context for the two publications is almost incomparable due to regime change. Nevertheless, I find many similarities, especially in how the publishing activities of the two organizations operate. Many articles published in the Czech version of *Sputnik* are taken from the Russian version and simply translated from Russian into Czech. In both cases articles are often published that contain the same information and offer nothing new; they are issued only for the purpose of spreading and reinforcing the Soviet/Russian perspective on the given event.

Rudé právo often published shorter articles that did not contain any new information and merely repeated the Soviet line on the situation. The aim of such articles was to repeat the Soviet narratives, which allowed no alternative views or interpretations. In the case

---

10 David N. Gibbs, 'Reassessing Soviet Motives for Invading Afghanistan. A Declassified History,' *Critical Asian Studies*, vol.38, no.2 (2006), pp. 239–63.

11 Boris Toucas, 'The Geostrategic Importance of the Black Sea Region: A Brief History,' *Centre for Strategic & International Studies*, February 2, 2017. Available at https://www.csis.org/analysis/geostrategic-importance-black-sea-region-brief-history. John, Biersack, Shannon O'Lear, S, 'The Geopolitics of Russia's Annexation of Crimea: Narratives, Identity, Silences, and Energy,' *Eurasian Geography and Economics*, vol.55, no.3 (2014), pp.247–69.

of the invasion of Afghanistan, a standard template was often repeated, condemning "American interference" and "expressing support for the April Revolution, which the imperialist forces are trying to destroy." Immediately after the invasion, in January 1980, three such articles were published in one edition, for example. In connection with the Russian annexation of Crimea, several articles with almost identical content were published each day on the *Sputnik* website during the whole examined period. Both media have in common a complete lack of the objectivity that is crucial for quality and impartial reporting.

However, my goal is not to compare these two information platforms as such. I am not trying to prove that *Sputnik* occupies the position of *Rudé právo* in the current Czech Republic. Both media serve me as a means through which I obtain objects of analysis that are based on the text itself. The primary goal of this analysis is to find out whether there is currently Russian propaganda in the Czech Republic which is similar to the Soviet propaganda in the Czechoslovak Socialist Republic. *Rudé právo* undoubtedly published content carrying Soviet propaganda, so it is very suitable for the analysis. If Russian propaganda is currently active in the Czech Republic, there is no more suitable object of analysis in the Czech media than *Sputnik*, which publishes in Czech, has a social impact on hundreds of thousands of citizens, and whose main information and all financial sources come from Russia.

I awarded each article points based on content analysis, aimed at determining how much of the article constituted propaganda. At the same time, I categorized all articles according to the topics they addressed.

Two datasets were created — one for each case — and these were then compared. By setting different criteria, it is possible to monitor which propaganda techniques were used most frequently. By tracking the frequency of topics, it is possible to specify similarities or differences in the process of creating news texts.

I used so-called multidimensional methods which allow comparative research to be carried out at the statistical level and to reveal any similarities or differences that may not be visible at first glance. To make sure that the results generated were not merely coincidental, several analyses were performed using different types of these techniques, namely: principal component analysis; multidimensional scaling; and t-Distributed Stochastic Neighbor Embedding (t-SNE).

News Media Propaganda Techniques

There is no comprehensive work that deals with communist language as a linguistic phenomenon in the Czechoslovak Socialist Republic. There are several overviews that deal with Soviet communist language in general, such as Lenore A. Grenoble's *Language Policy in the Soviet Union* (2003)[12] or *Newspeak: The Language of Soviet Communism* (1989)[13] by François Thom, but none of these works deals specifically with the Czechoslovak language. The phenomenon of the communist language in the Czech Republic has thus been studied only rather marginally, although there has been a significant shift in recent years. Based on the corpus of the communist language from 1948–89, the *Dictionary of Communist Totalitarianism* was created in 2010 by a team of scholars at the Institute of the Czech National Corpus of the Faculty of Arts, Charles University. Věra Schmiedtová, a long-time scholar of this topic, hailed this project as the first major attempt to describe the totalitarian language of the Czechoslovak Socialist Republic.[14] These efforts have since been further developed within the Czech National Corpus project (see for example Schmiedtová 2014[15]).

Given that the research on this topic is still in its infancy, there was no predetermined range of propaganda techniques that I could take over and apply in my research. I chose the set of propaganda techniques to be analyzed based on a range of theoretical works on

---

12   Lenore A. Grenoble, *Language Policy in the Soviet Union*, (New York: Kluwer Academic Publishers, 2003).
13   François Thom, *Newspeak: The Language of Soviet Communism*, (London: Claridge, 1989).
14   Věra Schmiedtová, 'What Did the Totalitarian Language in the Former Socialistic Czechoslovakia Look Like?,' *Research Gate*, 2006. Available at https://www.researchgate.net/publication/
15   Věra Schmiedtová, 'Srovnání kolokací totalitního jazyka v bývalém Československu s jazykem současným,' *Časopis pro moderní filologii*, vol.96, no.2 (2014), pp.165–79.

propaganda. These include the work of Czech pedagogue, philosopher, and psychologist, František Marek. In his 2016 article[16] on the psychology of propaganda, Marek provides a list of propaganda techniques that have been useful for my study.[17]

Edvard Lotko ranks linguistic propaganda techniques involving the use of persuasive expressions, which can also be used very effectively in written propaganda. These include: 1) the use of euphemisms which are related to a general effort not to call things by their real names (for example, *certain illegal groups* instead of *political opposition*); 2) the use of metaphors, especially those related to sports and war (for example, *being on the front line*); 3) presupposition which allows us to express more than what is written (for example, *we will not let anyone disrupt our economy*); 4) frequent use of evaluative words, usually with emotional coloring (for example, *provocative speech*); 5) slogans that do not allow replication, do not allow dialogue, and are non-negotiable and unverifiable (for example, *we will win because we are stronger*); and 6) negations, which are more impressive and serve to express contrast (for example, *we can't disagree…*).[18]

The most valuable work for the criteria generation phase of my research was James A. C. Brown's book *Techniques of Persuasion* which lists and explains the specific techniques used in propaganda. Brown points out that these are the most effective techniques that follow the simplest basic knowledge of human consciousness, such as: 1) the use of stereotypes; 2) the replacement of names (comparable to the euphemisms described by Lotko as a

---

16 František Marek, 'Psychologie propagandy X.—Slovo mluvené a psané,' *Manipulatori.cz*, January 23, 2016. Available at https://manipulatori.cz/psychologie-propagandy-x-slovo-mluvene-a-psane/.
17 These include: proving something other than was supposed to be proven and refuting what no one is saying *(ignoratio elenchi)*; abuse of ambiguity of words *(equivalence)*; unclear grammatical constructions of sentences *(amphibole)*; concealment of circumstances that contradict evidence *(saltus in probando)*; proving claims in a vicious circle using words other than in a statement *(circulus vitiosus)*; proving statements with something that would first have to be proved *(petitio principii)*; and the application of random properties and circumstances to a general rule *(fallacia accidentis)* (Marek 2016).
18 Edvard, Lotko, *Kapitoly ze současné rétoriky* (Olomouc: Univerzita Palackého, 2004).

propaganda technique); 3) selection (the propagandist selects information that is in accordance with his/her goals and then works with them, intentionally ignoring other facts); 4) outright lying; 5) repetition; 6) non-specific statements (the propagandist uses flat messages with zero informativeness to support his/her version); 7) pointing to the enemy; and 8) referring to authority.[19]

Research Parameters and Methodology

For my analysis, I have selected only those articles that relate to selected cases: the Soviet invasion of Afghanistan as a historical case and the Russian annexation of the Crimean Peninsula as a contemporary case. The aim of this work is to determine whether there is continuity between the past tactics of foreign policy propaganda of the USSR towards the Czechoslovak Socialist Republic and the present strategy of the Russian Federation towards the Czech Republic.

The keywords used for selecting articles in the historical case were the terms that most likely indicated reports on the situation in Afghanistan, i.e., Afghanistan; its derived words (Afghan); and the name of the capital Kabul. I searched for articles that contained at least one of the terms listed. To analyze the articles, I used a digital archive that contains all editions of *Rudé právo*.

Similarly, for the contemporary case, the keyword used was Crimea (Crimean) in combination with the word Russia and its inflected forms. Since *Sputnik* is not published as a printed medium in the Czech Republic and is only published online, the analysis of its content is simpler. To filter the articles relevant to my study I used the Monitora application, which is used for comprehensive monitoring of online, print, and audio-visual media in the Czech Republic. The application allows users to filter articles of a specific medium in a given time period containing selected keywords.

The analysis was performed in two dimensions: the criteria generated from theories of propaganda and communication

---

[19] James Alexander Campbell Brown, *Techniques of Persuasion. From Propaganda to Brainwashing* (Harmondsworth: Penguin Books Ltd., 1963).

(Marek 2016,[20] Lotko 2004,[21] Brown 1963[22]); and the trends that have emerged over time with regard to the topics of articles. In terms of topics, I draw on the work of Roy Godson and Richard Shultz, who, based on extensive research, defined five areas that emerged as propaganda themes and that were typical of Cold War-era Soviet foreign policy, supported by other active measures: 1) to secure, strengthen and expand security in areas that fall within the Soviet sphere of influence; 2) to divide the West, drive a wedge between countries and divide alliances; 3) to maintain the Soviet Union's primacy in the communist world; 4) to promote "proletarian internationalism" and "national liberation movements"; and 5) to minimize risk and avoid serious involvement in more than one open conflict at a time.[23]

While creating the datasets, I identified eight topics for each event that occurred most frequently, and around which the structure of a specific text was built. The topics were not assigned a point value; I only recorded whether they appeared in each article or not. In the data language this means that if the topic appeared in an article, the number 1 was marked for it, and if the topic did not appear in the article, the number 0 was marked for it. The value of these numbers does not matter. Five of these topics are the same or comparable in both cases, and the other three are different for each event. The topics are set out in Table 1 below.

Table 1. List of Topics.

Topics common to both cases	
Topic 1 (T1)	Laying the blame on the US/West
Topic 2 (T2)	Emphasis on referendum (in the case of Crimea) or revolution (in the case of Afghanistan), highlighting the

---

20   František Marek, 'Psychologie propagandy X. – Slovo mluvené a psané,' *Manipulatori.cz*, January 23, 2016. Available at https://manipulatori.cz/psychologie-propagandy-x-slovo-mluvene-a-psane/.
21   Edvard, Lotko, *Kapitoly ze současné rétoriky* (Olomouc: Univerzita Palackého, 2004).
22   James Alexander Campbell Brown, *Techniques of Persuasion. From Propaganda to Brainwashing* (Harmondsworth: Penguin Books Ltd., 1963).
23   Roy Godson, Richard Shultz, '"Active Measures" in Soviet Strategy' In: Erik Hoffman and Robin Laird eds., *Soviet Foreign Policy in a Changing World* (New York: Aldine Publishing Company, 1986).

	popularity of said referendum/revolution and implying strong legitimacy for citizens' decisions
Topic 3 (T3)	Russian aid to and protection of Russian-speaking Crimeans/Soviet aid to and protection of revolutionaries and local communists
Topic 4 (T4)	Emphasis on improving the living conditions of Afghans/Crimeans after the Soviet/Russian intervention
Topic 5 (T5)	Article is neutral and informative (this is a control topic)
Topics specific to *Rudé právo*	
Topic 6 (T6)	Emphasis on world peace
Topic 7 (T7)	Critique of China and its efforts to achieve hegemony
Topic 8 (T8)	Imperialism and capitalism as enemy
Topics specific to *Sputnik*	
Topic 6 (T6)	Highlighting the fact that the Crimean Peninsula belonged to Russia in the past
Topic 7 (T7)	laying the blame on the European Union
Topic 8 (T8)	Pointing out the injustice of sanctions against Russia, calling for their abolition and questioning their effectiveness

Source: all tables and graphs in the article were produced by the author.

The second dimension of the analysis is criteria. The lowest possible number of points obtained for all criteria is 0, with 12 being the highest possible number. The higher the number of points, the more propagandistic the article. Points were awarded in six categories representing selected individual propaganda techniques that appear most often in the news media, with a maximum of 2 points possible per category. Thus, the point scale ranges from 0 to 2, with 0 meaning that the propaganda technique does not occur in the article; 1 point meaning that it occurs there, but only once or weakly and marginally; and 2 points indicating that a particular technique dominates in the article or occurs there more than once (e.g., multiple euphemisms used in a given article. I devised the following evaluation categories focused on news media propaganda techniques:

> **Criterion 1 (K1):** Replacing names, terms (euphemism). This is a propaganda technique that replaces popular or unpopular names, terms that have some emotional connotation, with other, neutral ones. An example might be

the replacement of the word "communist" with the word "red," or "union bosses" instead of "union presidents," etc.[24] At present, for example, the designation of the president as "elected by the people" rather than "directly elected" could be included in this category, which (unlike previous examples) would turn an emotionally unnamed term into an emotionally colored term emphasizing the legitimacy of the president.

Criterion 2 (K2): Exaggeration or trivialization of a phenomenon. This technique focuses on modifying the illocutionary power of a statement, that is, the purpose of its use is either to discredit the phenomenon and arouse doubt in the reader about its importance or give the impression that an insignificant thing can negatively or positively affect the life of the reader himself. There are various means by which such a goal can be achieved, including through supplementary questions, vague expression, hyperbole, hesitation, conditioning, etc.[25] For example, one might pose a follow-up question in order to cast doubt on a previous message: *They do not want to disclose other names. Or perhaps they're unable to do so?* This use of the interrogative sentence at the end also hints at secrecy and thus adds more importance to the whole topic.

Criterion 3 (K3): Finger pointing and blaming the "enemy." This propaganda message works best if, in addition to the information itself, it also involves a clear enemy which causes frustration for those to whom propaganda is primarily aimed. The most famous and frightening example of this technique is the Nazi blaming of Jews.[26] A current example might be the frequent use of the term "Brussels" by Euro-sceptical and anti-EU politicians/commentators in connection with EU issues.

Criterion 4 (K4): Appeal to authority. This is a technique that seeks to support its message by appealing to someone or something that is a socially accepted authority. This trick is often used in the advertising industry where it is quite typical that a product is said to be "recommended by doctors".[27] It is typical for the use of news media propaganda as one of the foreign policy tools that something is "claimed by security experts" or "confirmed by military experts," without their profile being specified.

Criterion 5 (K5): A change in the nature or circumstances of the phenomenon, or a complete change of one state for another. This is a technique employed to confuse the reader. By simply swapping a time or place, or replacing one phenomenon with another, several different versions of what might

---

24 James Alexander Campbell Brown, *Techniques of Persuasion. From Propaganda to Brainwashing* (Harmondsworth: Penguin Books Ltd., 1963).
25 Kateřina Prokopová, *Propaganda a persvaze* (Olomouc: Univerzita Palackého, 2014).
26 James Alexander Campbell Brown, *Techniques of Persuasion. From Propaganda to Brainwashing* (Harmondsworth: Penguin Books Ltd., 1963).
27 *Ibid.* 28

have happened are created. The aim is to make the reader uncertain about what is and is not true.

Criterion 6 (K6): The use of "new words," emotionally colored words, vulgar expressions. This represents an attempt to draw the reader into the story more fully and to stigmatize persons or phenomena, for example through the use of value-laden expressions such as "sinister," etc.

Multidimensional Analysis

Most of the data acquired in any field is multidimensional. Usually, it is not enough to find out only one feature of a given object for research. In order to be able to understand the researched issue comprehensively we need various characteristics or variables. Rarely is it enough for us to analyze only one variable separately because to fully understand the relationships between subjects we must analyze at least most and preferably all variables simultaneously. This is done by multidimensional methods that can analyze, display, and describe multidimensional data. In the vast majority of cases, it is not possible to solve these methods manually because the computational demands are too high. For this reason, it is necessary to use software tools. There are several of these available, not all of which are suitable for all types of multidimensional analysis. Commercial software tools include, for example, SPSS or STATISTICA software which are generally among the most popular due to their graphical user interface. For the purposes of this analysis, however, I used the freely available software R, which has the widest range of multidimensional methods available.

Principal Component Analysis (PCA)

The PCA method is one of the oldest and most widely used methods of multidimensional analysis. The input data in PCA are the original vectors in n-dimensional space.[28] The aim of the method is mainly to simplify the description of a group of mutually linear dependents. Technically, the original characters are linearly transformed into new, uncorrelated variables which we call the main

---

28 Ingwer Borg, Patrick Groenen, *Modern Multidimensional Scaling. Theory and Applications* (USA: Springer, 2005).

components, with each main component being a linear combination of the original characters. The basic characteristic of each main component is its variability or variance. The main components are arranged from the largest to the smallest variance and most of the information on the variability of the original data is contained in the first main component, while the least information is contained in the last component.[29]

This method is very convenient for displaying multidimensional data. New variables (original linearly transformed data) are simpler, there are fewer of them, they have much more suitable features and capture almost the entire variability of the original data (transformation occurs with very little loss of information). There is a reduction of variables which are then worked with so that multidimensional data can be graphically visualized. When this method is used correctly, so-called latent variables are identified (hidden features that are not visible at first glance), data dimensionality is reduced to be visualizable, and correlations between variables are identified.[30]

Multidimensional Scaling (MDS)

MDS is one of the exploratory statistical methods based on the reduction of multidimensional space and solves similar tasks to PCA. It is a technique of creating a diagram of the relative location of objects in the plane of a two-dimensional graph based on data of distances between objects, the so-called proximity matrix.[31] This method first calculates a metric classical or non-metric solution and is based either directly on experimental values of X, a correlation matrix R or a matrix of similarities S or distance D.[32] The distance

---

29 Milan Meloun, Jiří Militký, *Statistická analýza experimentálních dat* (Praha: Akademia, 2004).
30 Alboukadel Kassambara, *Practical Guide to Principal Component Methods in R. PCA, (M)CA, FAMD, MFA, HCPC, factoextra* (USA: CreateSpace Independent Publishing Platform, 2017).
31 Jan de Leeuw, Patrick Mair, (2009) 'Multidimensional Scaling Using Majorization,' *Journal of Statistical Software*, vo.31, no.3 (2009), pp.1–30.
32 Michael Cox, Trevor Cox, *Multidimensional Scaling* (Boca, Raton, London, New York, Washington, D.C.: Chapman & Hall/CRC, 2001).

between the two objects is Euclidean and is calculated by the Pythagorean theorem. The goal of MDS is to find meaningful dimensions that allow us to explain the observed distances (dissimilarities) or similarities between objects. This means that the multidimensional scaling method takes a set of differences and returns a set of points so that the distances between the points are approximately the same as the differences in the original data.[33]

MDS is suitable for processing all types of data measured on nominal, ordinal, interval, and ratio scales. Data enter the operation in the form of a matrix of distances (dissimilarities) or similarities between objects. The result is a representation of the observed relationships between objects in reduced space, e.g., in a two-dimensional or three-dimensional graph.[34]

T-Distributed Stochastic Neighbor Embedding (t-SNE)

The t-SNE method is one of the latest methods used to reduce dimensions and transform high-dimensional data into low-dimensional data. Its basic goal is therefore the same as for PCA and MDS. The main difference lies in the sensitivity of this technique. PCA and MDS are linear techniques that focus on keeping low-dimensional representations of different data points far apart. For high-dimensional data that lie directly on or near low-dimensional, nonlinear varieties, it is usually more important to keep low-dimensional representations of very similar data points close together, which is typically not feasible with linear mapping. What t-SNE does is to find a way to design data into low-dimensional space so that it retains its properties typical of the particular cluster in which it is located in high-dimensional space. The t-SNE method is able to capture very well most of the local structure of high-dimensional data and at the same time reveal a global structure, such as the presence of clusters on several scales.[35]

---

33 Ibid. 12
34 Joseph Kruskal, Myron Wish, *Multidimensional Scaling* (USA: SAGE Publications, Inc., 1978).
35 Laurens van der Maaten, Geoffrey Hinton, 'Visualizing Data Using t-SNE,' *Journal of Machine Learning Research*, vol.9, no.86 (2008), pp.2579–605.

PROPAGANDA TARGETING FOREIGN AUDIENCES 213

Soviet Propaganda

In general, Soviet propaganda is highly inconsistent, which is a consequence of its flexibility and change over time. For example, early Soviet propaganda was characterized by an ardent emphasis on the subject of the world revolution and the inevitable triumph of communism over capitalism. This was subsequently refuted in a speech by Soviet People's Commissar for Foreign Affairs Georgii Chicherin at the 1922 Genoa conference where he spoke of the merging of two social systems of a given historical epoch.[36] The vision of the world revolution was later resurrected by Leonid Brezhnev in a speech to mark the 100th anniversary of Lenin's birth on 22 April 1970.[37]

However, according to American communications theorist and political scientist Harold Lasswell, we can find one very important in common feature across Soviet propaganda which lies in a common strategic goal which is to "maximise the power of Russian ruling individuals and groups at home and abroad".[38] Soviet propaganda was an instrument of total politics along with diplomacy, economics, and military forces, and political propaganda entailed the management of mass communication for the needs of power. The main task of the Soviet propaganda strategy was to get the timing right in relation to the specific dangers and opportunities that might influence the power position of the Soviet elite.[39]

In the USSR, propaganda fell into the category of so-called "active measures" which included, for example, efforts to influence the policies of other governments, undermine the self-confidence of their leaders and institutions, disrupt their relations with other countries, discredit government and non-governmental opponents,

---

36 Harold D. Lasswell, 'The Strategy of Soviet Propaganda,' *Academy of Political Science*, vol.24, no.2 (1951), pp.66–78.
37 Jan Wanner, *Brežněv a východní Evropa* (Praha: Institut mezinárodních studií fakulty sociálních věd Univerzity Karlovy, 1995).
38 Harold D. Lasswell, 'The Strategy of Soviet Propaganda,' *Academy of Political Science*, vol.24, no.2 (1951), pp.66–78.
39 *Ibid.*
    Pavel Verner, *Propaganda a manipulace* (Praha: Univerzita Jana Amose Komenského, 2011).

and distort people's perception of reality. Active measures were undertaken through officially sponsored foreign propaganda channels, diplomatic relations, and cultural diplomacy. Hidden political techniques included the use of "black propaganda," oral and written disinformation, secret radio, and much more.[40] In practice, these techniques have been interconnected and coordinated and, under certain circumstances, have been used by all states. However, the way propaganda was used by the Soviets was quite different in both quantitative and qualitative terms: covert Soviet techniques were controlled centrally, were much more intense, and were conducted in an organized manner on a global scale.[41] Roy Godson and Richard Shultz[42] observed that few (if any) Western countries have imitated this strategy in peacetime. According to them, Soviet leaders had world ambitions and approached world politics as a continuous state of conflict and war.

The fact that propaganda was one of the basic components of Soviet foreign policy is also demonstrated by the fact that since the 1950s, active measures were coordinated by at least three organizations: 1) the International Department of the Central Committee of the CPSU;[43] 2) the International Information Department;[44] and 3)

---

40 John Barron, *KGB. The Secret Work of Soviet Secret Agents* (New York: Reader's Digest Press, 1974).
41 Herbert Romerstein, 'Disinformation as a KGB Weapon in the Cold War,' *Journal of Intelligence History*, vol.1, no.1 (2001), pp.54–67.
42 Roy Godson, Richard Shultz, '"Active Measures" in Soviet Strategy' In: Erik Hoffman and Robin Laird eds., *Soviet Foreign Policy in a Changing World* (New York: Aldine Publishing Company, 1986).
43 The International Department of the CPSU was created in 1943 to coordinate all "inputs" related to Soviet foreign policy and active measures undertaken by the Ministry of Foreign Affairs. It controlled a number of think tanks under the Academy of Sciences and other communist, national, etc. movements around the world. It also coordinated secret radio stations that broadcast in the non-communist world. For more information see Leonard Schapiro, 'The International Department of the CPSU: Key to Soviet Policy,' *International Journal*, vol.32, no.1 (1976/1977), pp.41–55.
44 The International Information Department was established in 1978 to coordinate open propaganda aimed at foreign audiences such as foreign operations of TASS, Novosti, international radio broadcasting, periodicals and books sent abroad, and embassy information departments. For more information see Roy Godson, Richard Shultz, '"Active Measures" in Soviet Strategy' In: Erik

the KGB's First Chief Directorate.[45] It is estimated that 10,000 and 15,000 people worked in this "field" in the late 1970s with a budget of US$3-4 billion a year.[46]

Rudé právo *and the Soviet Invasion of Afghanistan*

The communist daily *Rudé právo* was founded in 1920 in the era of the first Czechoslovak Republic (1918-38) when the structure of the press was created in close connection with the development of political parties and readers' demand. At that time political parties communicated with their voters mainly through the party media and therefore often published (in addition to the central press) a number of regional papers with different areas of focus and periodicity.[47] At the end of the 1960s, pro-democratization tendencies emerged in Czechoslovakia and were originally based in the moderate wing of the Communist Party of Czechoslovakia itself. This resulted in the period of the so-called Prague Spring, which was characterized by a temporary relaxation of totalitarian conditions and the overall democratization of society. As a result, however, on 21 August 1968, Warsaw Pact troops intervened in Czechoslovakia and a period of so-called normalization began. The tightening of Soviet communist supervision was definitively decided upon in Moscow with the signing of the so-called Moscow Protocol. Oldřich Švestka, a former *Rudé právo* editor-in-chief, took part in this event.

Hoffman and Robin Laird eds., *Soviet Foreign Policy in a Changing World* (New York: Aldine Publishing Company, 1986).
45 The KGB's First Chief Directorate was in charge of espionage and active measures directly abroad. In the 1950s the scope of the KGB was expanded, and Department D (for Dezinformatsiia) was created and then changed to Service A (active measures) — this group helped so-called KGB "residents" (agents located directly abroad) to more easily participate in covert active measures with the secret services of other Eastern Bloc countries. For more information see Herbert Romerstein, 'Disinformation as a KGB Weapon in the Cold War,' *Journal of Intelligence History*, vol.1, no.1 (2001), pp.54–67 and Martin Dewhirst, Robert Farrell, eds, *The Soviet Censorship* (Metuchen: Scarecrow Press, 1973).
46 Roy Godson, Richard Shultz, '"Active Measures" in Soviet Strategy' In: Erik Hoffman and Robin Laird eds., *Soviet Foreign Policy in a Changing World* (New York: Aldine Publishing Company, 1986).
47 Petr Bednařík, Jan Jirák, Barbara Köpplová, *Dějiny českých médií. Od počátku do současnosti* (Praha: Grada Publishing, 2011).

The period of normalization also affected the media. As early as 30 August 1968, the Press and Information Office was established in Czechoslovakia.[48] The law allowed for preliminary censorship (stricter than the original 1966 law), established the institution of proxies, and expanded the system of sanctions against publishers. *Rudé právo* set an example to all other media in this regard and strictly adhered to all the directives issued by the censorship office since the date of their publication.[49]

The price of the newspaper was uniform; regardless of the number of pages, one copy cost 30 haléřů[50] on weekdays and 50 haléřů on Sundays.[51] The daily circulation was around one million. In the 1980s it increased slightly year by year; in 1980, its print-run was 942,000 copies, and in 1987, 1,025,300 copies.[52]

The analysis of articles from *Rudé právo* set out below presents the basic processing of data into graphs that show how the use of individual criteria and topics has changed.

A total of 394 articles were analyzed in which the keyword *Afghanistan* (or its derivative *Afghan*) or the keyword *Kabul* appeared and which were published between December 1979 and February 1984. The first article in which the Soviet invasion is mentioned was published on 29 December 1979. It was entitled "Helping the Afghan Revolution" and described *Soviet military aid to Afghanistan*. Over time, many different phrases were used for the Soviet invasion and military operations, such as: *fraternal assistance to the Afghan people; efforts to defend the achievements of the April Revolution; active support for the PDPA's*[53] *policy, necessary support in the fight against counterrevolutionaries;* or *defense against imperialist efforts to control Afghanistan against its will.*

---

48 Jakub Končelík, Petr Orság, Pavel Večeřa, *Dějiny českých médií 20. století* (Praha: Portál, 2010).
49 Národní muzeum. 'Média od ledna 1968 do začátku normalizace 1969.' Available at http://dvacatestoleti.eu/data/files/MH_ML_10_leden1968_duben19 69.pdf.
50 There were 100 haléřů to the Czechoslovak Koruna or "Crown" in English.
51 Petr Bednařík, Jan Jirák, Barbara Köpplová, *Dějiny českých médií. Od počátku do současnosti* (Praha: Grada Publishing, 2011).
52 Národní muzeum. 'Média od ledna 1968 do začátku normalizace 1969.' Available at http://dvacatestoleti.eu/data/files/MH_ML_10_leden1968_duben19 69.pdf.
53 People's Democratic Party of Afghanistan.

The following tables show the basic analyses that can be calculated from the created datasets. For the sake of clarity and partly also aesthetics, the full names of criteria and topics are not included in the tables and graphs. Abbreviations are explained directly below the tables/graphs. The maximum possible number of points obtained for each of the criteria was 788 (in the event that all articles received 2 points for a given criterion). No such situation occurred, however, the percentages given are calculated from 788 points.

Table 2.   *Rudé právo* Use of Propaganda Techniques in Percentages.

	K1	K2	K3	K4	K5	K6
Number of points earned	519	352	440	229	491	337
Percentage share	65.86%	44.67%	55.84%	29.06%	62.31%	42.77%

K1 = Replacing names, terms
K2 = Exaggerating or downplaying a phenomenon
K3 = Pointing and assigning guilt to an "enemy"
K4 = Appealing to authority
K5 = Changing the nature, circumstances of a phenomenon or complete exchange of one status for another
K6 = Use of "new words," emotionally colored words, vulgar expressions

Table 2 shows that the most commonly used propaganda technique in *Rudé právo* articles is a technique in which names and terms that have some emotional connotations are replaced by less neutral ones, and vice versa. A typical example is the use of the label *fraternal aid to Afghanistan* — the word *fraternal* adds information with positive sentiment, while exchanging the terms *invasion* or *occupation* with the word *aid* reduces negative sentiment. The aim is to confuse the reader and to create the impression that the events taking place in Afghanistan are not only necessary but even desirable.

The second most commonly used propaganda technique was the use of "new words," emotionally colored words. This is mainly due to the huge frequency of terms such as *bandits* and *counterrevolutionaries*. The least used technique was that of appealing to authority. In percentage terms this technique was present to a similar degree in the case of *Sputnik* (to be discussed in more detail below). Its low frequency indicates a certain degree of unpopularity. In *Rudé právo*, the authors of the articles seldom invoke any higher authority. Only in a limited number of cases does an article invoke the notion of anonymous sources or security "experts," as a means of underlining the reliability of the information reported.

The following graph shows the presence of individual topics. The vast majority of articles were built around at least one of the monitored topics. In the whole sample of 394 articles only 12 were found which did not contain any of the monitored topics, and at the same time were not neutral — i.e., these 12 articles are propagandistic and contain some of the observed propaganda techniques, but their content is not built around any of the monitored topics.

Graph 1.
Number of articles in which individual topics appeared

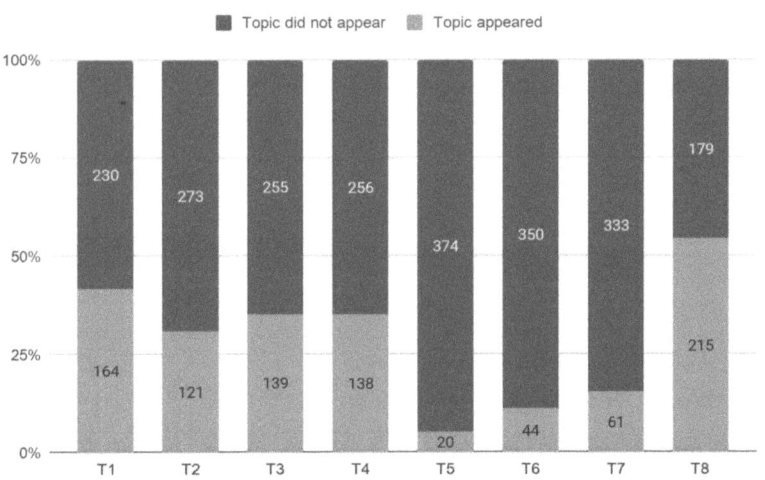

T1 = assigning blame to the US/West
T2 = emphasis on referendum/revolution (popularity of both — strong legitimacy)
T3 = Soviet/Russian aid/protection of Russian-speaking Crimeans/revolutionaries
T4 = emphasis on improving the living conditions of Afghans/Crimeans after Soviet/Russian intervention
T5 = neutral, informative
T6 = emphasizing world peace
T7 = negative about China.
T8 = imperialism as an enemy.

The above graph shows that the most used topic was T8 (imperialism as the enemy) and the second most used topic was T1 (blaming the US/West). This result reflects the fact that these two topics are interrelated. According to Soviet propaganda, it was the US and the West that represented the hated imperialism that was portrayed as something extremely negative. Often the two topics appeared in articles together.

The smallest number can be seen at T5 which indicates neutral, informative articles. T5 served as a control topic in this analysis. This means that the result of all analyses was clearly assumed for T5 and, if confirmed, the accuracy of the analysis was also confirmed. The result shown by the graph was assumed and is desirable. Only 20 articles from the analyzed sample can be described as neutral and informative, which means they do not contain any of the monitored propaganda topics.

Contemporary Russian Propaganda

Thanks to social networks, the spread of propaganda is easier and faster than ever before. However, because it is a public and completely open space, the propaganda media leave traces that can be documented. At present, we are no longer talking about impressions or assumptions that a propaganda campaign is taking place. Thanks to the ability to analyze social networks, we know that it is taking place and we have hard facts that prove it.[54]

---

54 There are a number of studies and analyses that focus on specific political events such as elections and examine the degree of Russian influence on them. These include the US Senate report, *Putin's Asymmetric Assault on Democracy in Russia and Europe: Implications for U.S. National Security* (2018); a study by the digital and communications agency 89up on Russian interference in the pre-Brexit campaign, *Russian Media Interference in The EU Referendum worth up to £4 million* (2018); Chavier Lesaca's study of the activities of Russian and pro-Russian media in Spain in relation to the Catalan crisis, *Why Did Russian Social Media Swarm the Digital Conversation about Catalan Independence?* (2017); and a case study by the European group EU DisinfoLab focused on the activity of Russian and pro-Russian media before the Italian parliamentary elections in 2018: *Developing a Disinformation Detection System and Sourcing it Live: The Case Study of the 2018 Italian Elections* (2018). In 2018, the NATO Strategic Communications Center of Excellence published a detailed analysis called *Robotrolling* (2018), which mapped how Russia seeks to compromise NATO's integrity by spreading false news, especially in places and countries where there is a strong Russian diaspora.

Moscow is adapting very quickly to the development of information technology and is using the new opportunities presented by online and social media to wage an information war unprecedented in scale and complexity. Russia is investing considerable money in this area, spending $1.1 billion on mass media in 2014. A year later spending on internationally oriented media such as the *Russia Today* platform or the *Rossiya Segodnya* agency, which sponsors the *Sputnik* media project, also increased. Russia's social media campaign cannot be separated from information operations involving traditional media as the two phenomena are closely interlinked; classic stories and articles are created by traditional media but are now taken over by social networks and disseminated with immense speed.[55]

The issue of so-called trolls[56] is also related to the dissemination of news and articles on social networks which is described in detail in the NATO Strategic Communications Centre of Excellence study entitled "Robotrolling".[57] Notoriously, a so-called troll farm was even discovered in St. Petersburg, Russia, employing 250 people who were paid to produce and spread false news. The Russian government invested a total of $2.2 million in the farm which went mostly on wages.[58]

---

55 Todd C. Helmus, Elizabeth Bodine-Baron, Andrew Radin, Madeine Magnuson, Joshua Mendelsohn, William Marcellino, Andriy Bega, Zev Winkelman, *Russian Social Media Influence: Understanding Russian Propaganda in Eastern Europe* (Santa Monica: RAND Corporation, 2018).
56 A troll is a person who controls fake accounts on social networks (most often on Facebook in the Czech context) and whose task is to spread specific information through these accounts, write hateful and controversial comments under opposition posts or write laudatory comments under posts which share his or her worldview. The aims are to arouse emotions, to divide society, to give the impression that extremist views are needed in society but are suppressed, etc. (Monika Evstatieva, Jolie Mayers, 'Meet the Activist Who Uncovered the Russian Troll Factory Named in The Mueller Probe,' *npr.org*, March 15, 2018. Available at https://www.npr.org/sections/parallels/2018/03/15/59406288 7/some-russians-see-u-s-investigation-into-russian-election-meddling-as-a-so ap-ope?t=1555587923612&t=1615717347251).
57 stratcomcoe.org, 'Robotrolling', *stratcomcoe.org*, November 22, 2018. Available at https://stratcomcoe.org/pdfjs/?file=/publications/download/web_robotr olling_2008-003.pdf?zoom=page-fit.
58 Oliver Carroll, 'St Petersburg 'Troll Farm' had 90 Dedicated Staff Working to Influence the US Election Campaign,' *Independent*, October 17, 2017. Available

PROPAGANDA TARGETING FOREIGN AUDIENCES 221

In the Czech Republic, the topic of Russian propaganda has been widespread in recent years, mainly due to some controversial statements by Czech President Miloš Zeman. For example, during his visit to China in 2014, Zeman gave an interview to the local media where he called the conflict in eastern Ukraine a "civil war," in line with the Kremlin's narrative on this.[59] The Czech Security Information Service has been warning of the dangers of Russian disinformation and influence operations in the Czech Republic in its annual reports since 2014.[60] In connection with the phenomenon of disinformation and foreign influential operations, the Centre against Terrorism and Hybrid Threats was established in the Czech Republic. The Centre, which has been in operation since 1 January 2017, falls under the Ministry of the Interior. Its website states that it was founded on

> a recommendation based on the preliminary conclusions of several chapters of the National Security Audit which assesses various types of hybrid threats, including terrorism and other forms of radicalization or influential and disinformation campaigns from abroad as a serious threat. For the

---

at https://www.independent.co.uk/news/world/europe/russia-us-election-donald-trump-st-petersburg-troll-farm-hillary-clinton-a8005276.html

59 Daniel Macek, 'Zemanův čínský rozhovor: Mohu vám ukázat Jen-šu, vynikající vývozní artikl,' *Lidové noviny*, November 11, 2014. Available at https://www.li dovky.cz/domov/chci-se-priucit-jak-stabilizovat-spolecnost-rekl-zeman-v-cin e.A141101_120320_ln_domov_ele

60 Annual report of Czech Security Information Service from 2014 (https://www.bis.cz/public/site/bis.cz/content/vyrocni-zpravy/2014-vz-cz.pdf); Annual report of Czech Security Information Service from 2015 (https://www.bis.cz/public/site/bis.cz/content/vyrocni-zpravy/2015-vz-cz.pdf); Annual report of Czech Security Information Service from 2016 (https://www.bis.cz/public/site/bis.cz/content/vyrocni-zpravy/2016-vz-cz.pdf); Annual report of Czech Security Information Service from 2017 (https://www.bis.cz/public/site/bis.cz/content/vyrocni-zpravy/2017-vz-cz.pdf); Annual report of Czech Security Information Service from 2018 (https://www.bis.cz/public/site/bis.cz/content/vyrocni-zpravy/2018-vz-cz.pdf.pdf); Annual report of Czech Security Information Service from 2019 (https://www.bis.cz/public/site/bis.cz/content/vyrocni-zpravy/2019-vz-cz.pdf); Annual report of Czech Security Information Service from 2020 (https://www.bis.cz/public/site/bis.cz/content/vyrocni-zpravy/2020-vz-cz-2.pdf).

internal security of the state, it recommends that similar workplaces be established at all relevant authorities.[61]

Sputnik *and the Russian Annexation of Crimea*

At the beginning of 2015 the Russian state news agency and the radio station *Sputnik* replaced the original Russian state radio station *Voice of Russia* which had been broadcasting since 1929. *Sputnik* broadcasts and publishes in more than 30 languages and its main target is the countries of the former Eastern bloc.[62] The Czech version of *Sputnik* also started operating in 2015. It is an official Russian state project, which is financed by Russian money.

The number of articles analyzed on the *Sputnik* website is significantly higher than in the case of the *Rudé právo*. The combination of keywords to search for articles was Crimea (and its inflected forms) along with the word Russia. A total of 1,074 articles were analyzed which contained the keywords and were published between January 2015 and March 2019. The higher number of articles is due to the fact that, unlike *Rudé právo*, *Sputnik* is an online information medium that is not limited by place, paper, or anything else.

This source base includes a number of striking features. Many of the articles were very brief, comprising three paragraphs of a few sentences in length, two of which essentially repeated the same thing.[63] Very typical were articles that at first seemed non-propagandistic and purely informative, but concluded with a paragraph such as the following:

> Crimea and Sevastopol became Russian regions after a referendum on 16 March 2014 in which the majority of participants voted for unification with Russia. Moscow emphasizes that the organization of the referendum in Crimea complies with the norms of international law and the UN Charter.[64]

---

61   CTHH, 'Centrum proti terorismu a hybridním hrozbám,' *mvcr.cz*, April 18, 2019. Available at https://www.mvcr.cz/cthh/clanek/centrum-proti-terorismu-a-hybridnim-hroz- bam.aspx

62   Neovlivní, 'Hlas Ruska/Sputnik: ozvěny Kremlu v ČR,' *Neovlivní*, May 16, 2015. Available at https://neovlivni.cz/hlas-ruskasputnik-ozveny-kremlu-v-cr/.

63   'Putin: Rusko udělá vše pro to, aby Ukrajina co nejrychleji překonala složité období, '*Sputnik*, March 18, 2015. Available at https://cz.sputniknews.com/svet/20150318126309/.

64   'Porošenko sestavil seznam sankcí proti Rusku,' *Sputnik*, June 5, 2015. Available at https://cz.sputniknews.com/svet/20150605513760/.

PROPAGANDA TARGETING FOREIGN AUDIENCES   223

There were dozens of articles with an identical or very similar final paragraph. Reports mentioning the support of a foreign (repeatedly German, French, or Italian) politician or political party were also very common.[65] As in the case of the invasion of Afghanistan, there were many different ways to name and frame the Russian annexation of Crimea: *the involvement of Crimea in the composition of Russia; Crimea is ancient Russian territory and cannot return to Ukraine;* or *Ukraine's connection to the Russian Federation*, etc.

The following tables show the basic analyses that can be calculated from the created datasets. As with the previous event the full names of the criteria and topics are not inscribed in the tables/graphs. Abbreviations are always explained directly below the table/graph. The largest possible number of points obtained in each of the criteria was 2148. Such a situation did not occur, however, from the number 2148, the percentages were calculated and are shown in the following table.

Table 3. *Sputnik* Use of Propaganda Techniques in Percentages.

	K1	K2	K3	K4	K5	K6
Number of points earned	950	1015	591	611	1123	701
Percentage share	44.22%	47.26%	27.51%	28.45%	52.28%	32.64%

K1 = Replacing names, terms
K2 = Exaggerating or downplaying a phenomenon
K3 = Pointing and assigning guilt to an "enemy"
K4 = Appealing to authority
K5 = Changing the nature, circumstances of a phenomenon or complete exchange of one status for another
K6 = Use of "new words," emotionally colored words, vulgar expressions

The table shows that the most frequently used technique in the case of *Sputnik* was K5: changing the nature or circumstances of a phenomenon or exchanging one status for another. In the case of the

---

65   'Premiér Bavorska pochybuje o nutnosti sankcí EU proti Rusku, '*Sputnik*, December 18, 2015. Available at https://cz.sputniknews.com/nazory/201512 181962765-premier-bavorsko-rusko-sankce/.

Russian annexation of Crimea, this technique sought to create several different versions of what really happened, for example, by denying the presence of Russian soldiers; emphasizing the legitimacy of the supposedly free "referendum" in which 83% of eligible voters allegedly participated (with well over 90% of them supposedly voting in favor of joining Russia[66]); or pointing out that Crimea had "always" been Russian and that in 1991, after the collapse of the USSR, it had actually been "annexed" by Ukraine, etc.

The least frequently used technique was pointing at and blaming the enemy. There were several cases in which Ukraine or the EU were blamed for the events, but much more often a nationalist motif focused on Russian unity emerged. It can be assumed that this approach was also preferable for Putin in terms of his self-promotion as this strategy had also worked for him in the past.

The following graph shows the presence of individual topics. The majority of articles were built around at least one of the monitored topics. In the whole sample of 1074 articles, 183 did not contain any of the monitored topics, and at the same time were not neutral., i.e., these 183 articles are propagandistic and contain some of the observed propaganda techniques, but their content is not built around any of the monitored topics. This comprises 17% of the articles from the examined sample which is more than in the case of *Rudé právo* where these articles accounted for only 3% of those examined. However, such a difference is to be expected given the different formats of the individual media.

---

66 The figures given by Moscow regarding the Crimean referendum cannot be confirmed because no international independent observer took part. The legitimacy of the referendum is questioned for many reasons and is not recognized as valid by the West or Ukraine. In addition, a member of Putin's Human Rights Council reportedly said that turnout in the Crimean referendum was in fact around 30%, and that only about half of those voters voted to join the Russian Federation (Steven Pifer, 'Five Years after Crimea's Illegal Annexation, The Issue is No Closer to Resolution,' brookings.edu, March 18, 2019. Available at https://www.brookings.edu/blog/order-from-chaos/2019/03/18/five-years-after-crimeas-illegal-annexation-the-issue-is-no-closer-to-resolution/).

Graph 2.

Number of articles in which individual topics appeared

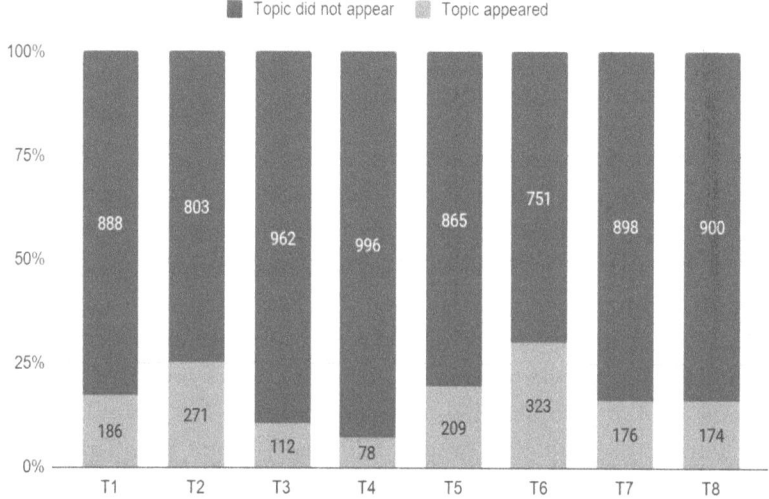

T1 = assigning blame to the US/West
T2 = emphasis on referendum/revolution (popularity of both — strong legitimacy)
T3 = Soviet/Russian aid/protection of Russian-speaking Crimeans/ revolutionaries
T4 = emphasis on improving the living conditions of Afghans/Crimeans after Soviet/Russian intervention
T5 = neutral, informative
T6 = Crimea was originally Russian
T7 = assigning blame to the EU
T8 = critical of sanctions imposed on Russia by the EU and the US

The theme T6 most often appears in the articles which represent the narrative contending that Crimea has always been Russian. This is in line with the fact that this narrative was indeed very strongly promoted as part of Russia's disinformation campaign on the events in Ukraine and Crimea in 2014. The same applies to the second most frequently used topic, T2, which highlights the referendum in Crimea.

The least used topic was T4 which emphasizes the improvement of the living conditions of Crimean citizens after the Russian annexation. This is probably not due to the fact that this topic was unpopular; rather, it started to be used later, in response to specific changes in Russian actions. This topic remained in use in subsequent years, for example, after the completion of the bridge over the Kerch Strait which connected Crimea to Russian territory.

Comparison of the Cases using Multidimensional Analyses

As described above, multidimensional methods are used to analyze, display, and describe multidimensional data. Most of the data acquired in any field is multidimensional because it is usually not enough for us to find out only one feature of a given subject for research. In order to be able to understand the researched issue comprehensively we need various characteristics or variables. In the case of this analysis, six criteria were examined representing individual propaganda techniques and eight topics representing the trends most often appearing in propaganda articles around which the text itself is built. For comparability, only topics T1 to T5, which are the same for both cases, were included in the multidimensional analyses.

Multidimensional methods examine both datasets at the same time (the data were combined into one file and distinguished by the letters R for *Rudé právo* articles and S for *Sputnik* articles in the article ID which are called *rownames* in the programming language). The methods were selected according to the nature of the data and the objectives: Principal Component Analysis (PCA), Multidimensional Scaling (MDS), and the t-Distributed Stochastic Neighbor Embedding (t-SNE) method.

Principal Component Analysis (PCA)

Principal component analysis is one of the most basic and widely used multidimensional methods. Its biggest benefits are that it: reduces the number of original variables so that they can be represented graphically; identifies hidden latent relationships; and at the same time identifies correlations between variables.

The following graph shows the processing of data from the *Rudé právo* and from *Sputnik* by the PCA method. The graph visualizes work with unique data.[67]

Graph 3. PCA with Unique Data.

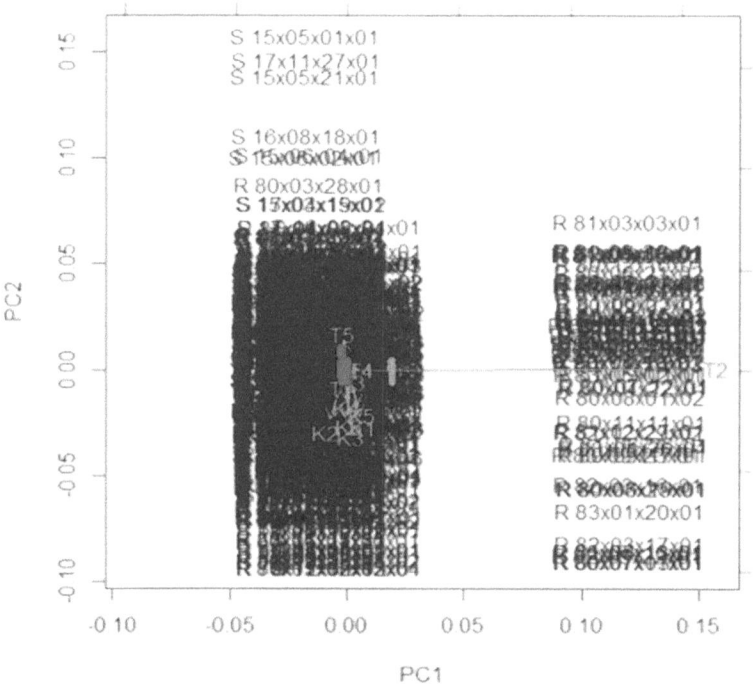

Most data are concentrated in one place. However, it is clear from the graph that a small group of articles from *Sputnik* deviates and concentrates in the upper-left corner, whereas slightly more articles from the *Rudé právo* deviate and cluster in the right-hand section, which means that certain articles from the dataset are similar to each other and together they differ from most. Interestingly, the

---

67 The *unique* function in R – unique (), eliminates duplicate elements/lines from a vector, data frame, or array. Therefore, this function eliminates all duplicate rows (that is, rows that contain identical data) and works only with unique data. In some cases, this allows us to see relationships that would not otherwise be seen.

separate groups collect articles almost exclusively from either *Rudé právo* or *Sputnik*.

Graph 4. PCA with All Data (Not Only Unique).

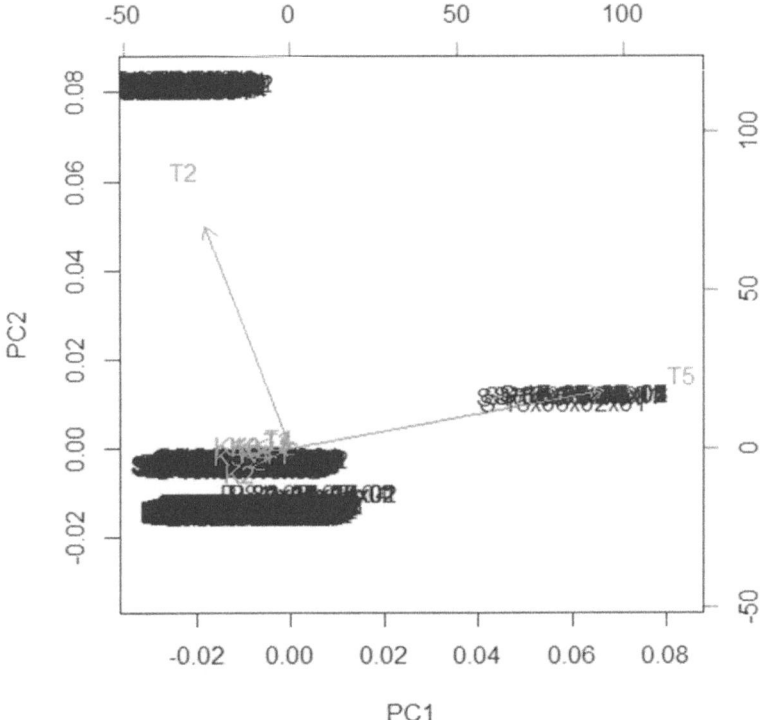

If we look at Graph 4, which works with all data and not only with specific information, we also notice the same trend as in the previous example, though with much more decisive results. The vast majority of data is concentrated in one place and is very similar. The data on the right side of the graph are articles from *Sputnik* whose biggest difference is caused by T5 which represents neutral, informative articles. This is most probably due to the fact that neutral, informative articles about the Russian annexation of Crimea were published in *Sputnik* much more often compared to neutral, informative articles on the Soviet invasion of Afghanistan in *Rudé právo*. The difference is appreciable in the number of articles (which is obvious given that more articles from *Sputnik* were analyzed) but also in the percentage distribution within the individual datasets. The data which are clustered in the upper-left corner show *Rudé právo* articles that differ mainly in T2 which represents emphasis on the referendum/revolution (popularity of both—strong legitimacy). The most likely reason for this is that great emphasis was placed in the whole examined sample of articles on the April Revolution in Afghanistan from 1978. The referendum in Crimea was also relatively strongly emphasized, but not to the same extent as the revolution.

Multidimensional Scaling (MDS)

Multidimensional scaling works much like PCA. The original data are processed so that their differences or similarities are roughly the same as the distances between points on the resulting graph. This means that the multidimensional data and the dimensions in which they occur are reduced so that they can be visualized in the simplest possible graph.[68] In this case, the graph is two-dimensional. The MDS method can be calculated at different distances/similarities. If we use the classical MDS technique, which considers the Euclidean distance, we should get the same result as when using PCA. The choice of distance to be calculated is usually decided by the analyst him/herself.[69] In this case, calculations were performed with Euclidean, Cosine,[70] and Manhattan[71] distances in order to compare the results and confirm that these were not coincidental.[72] Therefore, the following graph (Graph 5) was generated using the classical MDS method with Euclidean distance for control and

---

68 Forrest Young, *Multidimensional scaling: history, theory, and applications* (New Jersey: Lawrence Erlbaum Associates Publishers, 1987).
69 Florian Wickelmaier. 2003. 'An Introduction to MDS,' *Sound Quality Research Unit*, May 4, 2003. Available at http://citeseerx.ist.psu.edu/viewdoc/download?doi=10.1.1.495.4629&rep=rep1&type=pdf
70 Cosine similarity is a measure of the similarity between two vectors of the inner space of a product that measures the cosine of the angle between them (Manuel Martín-Merino, Alberto Muñoz, 'Visualizing Asymmetric Proximities with SOM and MDS Models,' *Neurocomputing*, vol.63, no.2 (2005), pp.171–92.)
71 Absolute distance between two vectors
72 David I. Warton, Stephen T. Wright, Yi Wang, 'Distance-based Multivariate Analyses Confound Location and Dispersion Effects', *Methods in Ecology and Evolution*, vol.3, no.1 (2012), pp.89–101.

comparison. The circles represent articles published on the *Sputnik* website, and the squares represent articles published by *Rudé právo*.

Graph 5. MDS with Euclidian Distance.

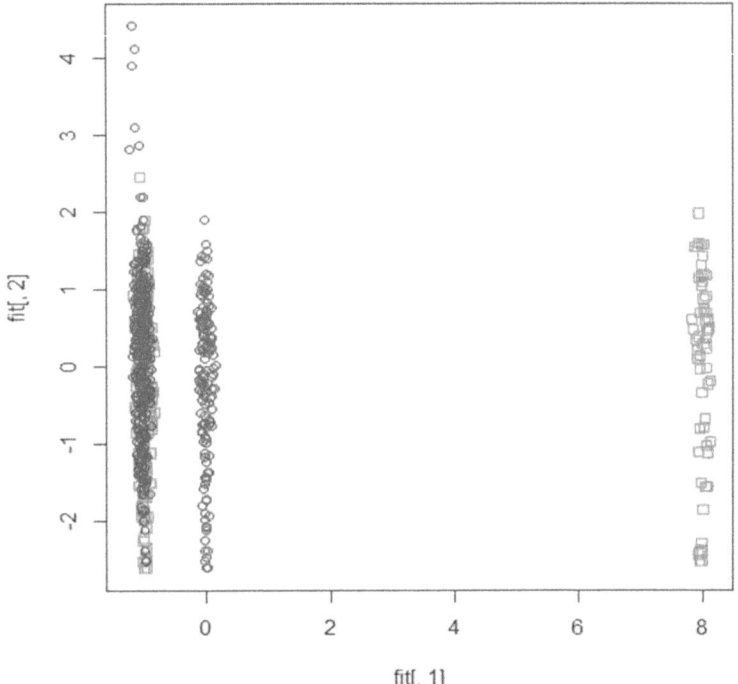

It is clear from the graph that the results are the same as in the case of PCA. Most articles are very close and cluster in one place. The X-axis always shows the main component that has the greatest influence on the data, while the Y-axis is the second main component. Thus, according to the main component, the largest group of data is very similar (almost identical) and differs only slightly from the second major component (which shows their scattering along the Y-axis). The group of articles from *Sputnik* deviates considerably from the formula, while the group of articles from *Rudé právo* deviates significantly less. Graphs that are generated by the MDS method but with a different distance are provided in the appendix.

T-Distributed Stochastic Neighbor Embedding (t-SNE) method

The t-SNE method is one of the newest methods used for the reduction of high-dimensional data and their visualization in low-dimensional space. Its task is very similar to that of the PCA and MDS methods, however, t-SNE works much more sensitively and is designed so that data does not lose any information. This means that the use of this method reveals even the subtlest differences between clusters.[73] It was included because it is currently best able to confirm whether the results of previous analyses produce coincidences and thus definitively prove the results of analyses that compare the two cases examined. Graph 6 shows the results of the comparison of the dataset from *Rudé právo* with the dataset from *Sputnik* using the t-SNE method where perplexity[74] = 10.

---

[73] Laurens van der Maaten, Geoffrey Hinton, 'Visualizing Data Using t-SNE,' *Journal of Machine Learning Research*, vol.9, no.86 (2008), pp.2579–605.
[74] Perplexity (proximity) is a standard measure of the performance of statistical models of natural language (Thomas Griffiths, Mark Steyvers, 'Finding Scientific Topics,' *PNAS, vol.*101, no.1 (2004), pp.5228–235).

Graph 6. t-SNE with perplexity = 10.

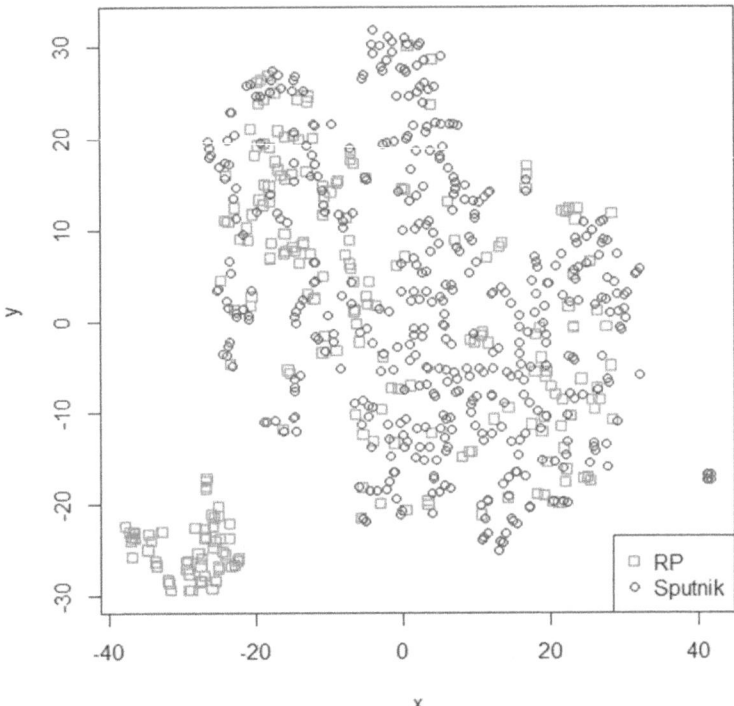

The graph shows that the t-SNE method produces a very similar result to the PCA and MDS methods. Most of the articles are grouped in one place which means that they are similar, regardless of whether they deal with the Soviet invasion of Afghanistan and come from *Rudé právo* or deal with the Russian annexation of Crimea and were published on the *Sputnik* website. Exceptions are a small group of *Rudé právo* articles which is grouped outside the main cluster, and an even smaller group of *Sputnik* articles which are also clustered nearby. All multidimensional analyses have shown that clusters of articles that deviate are strictly divided according to where they came from. In the case of *Sputnik*, these are neutral, informative articles of which there were significantly more than in *Rudé právo*. The *Rudé právo* articles that differ are the ones which emphasize the popularity of the April Revolution and thus the legitimacy of the government of the Marxist People's Democratic Party of Afghanistan which, according to this logic, was to emerge from the people.

Conclusion

This analysis was devoted to propaganda and the role which it has played, and continues to play, in the foreign policy of the USSR and Russia respectively. Soviet foreign policy was associated with propaganda from the very beginning of the Soviet state's existence as the communist regime was one of two totalitarian regimes (along with the Nazi one) that began to use language as an instrument of power in ways that were truly Orwellian in nature and scope.

The aim of this analysis was to find out whether propaganda occupies a similar position in the foreign policy of the Russian Federation and more specifically whether there is continuity between Soviet propaganda targeting the Czechoslovak Socialist Republic during the communist regime and Russian propaganda aimed at the Czech Republic at present.

The hypothesis was therefore as follows: *There is a continuous relationship between the propaganda techniques in news media used by the USSR against the Czechoslovak Socialist Republic during communism at the turn of the 1970s and '80s and the propaganda techniques used in news media by the Russian Federation against the Czech Republic today.*

The historical contexts surrounding the events in Afghanistan and Crimea are very different, as are the relationships between the USSR and Afghanistan on the one hand, and the Russian Federation and Crimea, on the other. However, the two cases intersect in important ways when it comes issues around the security of the Soviet/Russian southern border. From a security point of view, the motivations of the Soviet and Russian officials were very similar. In the context of the Cold War, it was essential for the USSR to ensure that Afghanistan did not enter the American sphere of influence because this would mean that in the event of a conflict erupting, the United States would have an important strategic advantage. The annexation of Crimea was based on a similar logic given the importance of Russia's Black Sea fleet base in Sevastopol for effectively protecting Russia's southern border. Through the annexation of the Crimean Peninsula, Putin sought to eliminate the possibility of increased cooperation between Ukraine and the EU jeopardizing the extension of the lease on the base in the future.

Rudé právo and Sputnik are different information platforms in many ways, making them difficult to compare. Nevertheless, their selection was based on certain similarities. *Rudé právo* was the main printed communication channel of the Communist Party whose task was to strengthen totalitarian power in the state and project the Soviet worldview. The selection of articles was based on the position of the USSR in the international system and its attitude to world events. For research into Soviet printed propaganda as a tool of foreign policy *Rudé právo* is the most suitable written periodical. *Sputnik* is the only information platform in the Czech Republic to be directly and openly financed by the Russian Federation which also publishes in the Czech language. The Czech version of *Sputnik* works to disseminate the Russian perspective on important world events among Czech citizens. Additional topics for discussion and analysis would include Russia's motivation for maintaining a media platform in the Czech Republic at the present moment, and whether it has any real impact on citizens' views — these are important questions, but they lie beyond the scope of the present article.

The multidimensional methods used for this study were selected as appropriate with respect to the nature of the data and the objectives of the following: Principal Component Analysis (PCA), Multidimensional Scaling (MDS), and the t-Distributed Stochastic Neighbor Embedding (t-SNE) method. All these techniques focus on finding similarities or differences between multidimensional data using calculations that reduce the data to a low-dimensional representation with very little loss of information, and all ultimately generate very similar results.

My findings show that articles on the Soviet invasion of Afghanistan published in *Rudé právo* and the articles on the Russian annexation of the Crimean Peninsula published on the *Sputnik* website are, in the vast majority of cases, very similar or the same. In all the graphs that produced multidimensional analyses, this was evident from the fact that almost all the examined articles clustered in one place in the form of points. There were only two exceptions: The first was articles from *Sputnik* which were neutral and informative, which is quite logical given that *Sputnik* produced many more neutral and informative articles than *Rudé právo*. The second exception is *Rudé právo* articles which emphasized the popularity and legitimacy of the Afghan April Revolution of 1978, a topic emphasized strongly in the newspaper articles examined. No other significant differences were noted.

Based on the results of the above analyses, I conclude that the hypothesis can be confirmed. The abovementioned anomalies do not weaken this statement significantly. The articles from *Sputnik* which were out of place fall into the so-called control sample because the topic of informative, neutral articles was included precisely for this reason. It was quite obvious that the connection of this topic with the criteria would be zero, but it served to verify the correctness of the methods that were used for the analysis. That is, diametrically different results on this topic were expected and if such results came out in analyses, this would confirm their accuracy, which is exactly what happened. The small group of *Rudé právo* articles that differed from the others is just a small sample in a dataset containing data from a total of 1468 articles. This result was quite striking and there is scope for exploring further in more detail at the qualitative level the topic of the propaganda emphasis on the popularity and legitimacy of the revolution.

From the analysis it is possible to draw specific conclusions with relevance to the current situation in the Czech Republic. Immediately after the collapse of the USSR the Russian Federation recorded a brief moment in Russia's long history when the local environment relaxed in all spheres. However, with Vladimir Putin's rise to power, the strategies used by the USSR began to return at many levels. The Russian Federation now uses propaganda as a tool of power perhaps even more effectively than its Soviet predecessor. Thanks to social media networks, Russian propaganda manages to penetrate the information space of foreign countries, including the Czech Republic, much more effectively than the Soviet Union did. Another difference here is that the current Russian propaganda is less recognizable to citizens because it does not come from a single and well-known source, as was the case with the *Rudé právo*. In order to combat such propaganda, it is first necessary to know it well and identify the strategies it uses. In my analysis, I was able to prove that the strategies used by the Russian Federation in creating propaganda are no different from the strategies used by the Soviet Union. Thanks to this, we as a society can now skip this first necessary step in the form of strategy identification. The strategies turned out to be the same, which is good news, because we already know the Soviet propaganda strategy. Currently, the problems associated with the so-called disinformation campaigns, which are comparable to propaganda, are being publicly discussed. We are in the favorable position of being able to move straight to the point where we analyze the new environment where propaganda is spreading, rather than re-inventing the wheel when it comes to identifying the methods and strategies employed in the creation and dissemination of propaganda.

Even though the hypothesis was confirmed, the work has its limits. A larger number of propaganda techniques and topics could be included in the research. The point range could be also wider, as could the range of events and media platforms that deal with them. This would result in a more detailed analysis that would show more similarities and/or differences than an article of this length is able to cover. From this point of view the possibilities for such research are almost inexhaustible.

A closer qualitative evaluation would also benefit the analysis, not only in terms of arriving at a deeper understanding of the topics used but also in terms of the linguistic classification of specific words and phrases that were most often used for the needs of propaganda techniques. This is certainly an area that deserves further research, given that the communist totalitarian language is still practically unexplored in the Czech Republic. The Czech National Corpus project is doing pioneering work on this front. Future research, ideally through interdisciplinary cooperation with linguistic experts, might fruitfully explore this topic further in the context of Soviet/Russian international relations and foreign policy.

Collusion and Conspiracy Theories
US Domestic Politics and Russian Active Measures

Andrei Znamenski

Between 2016 and 2021, the United States mainstream media saw the avalanche of print and internet materials on the "Russian collusion," which either directly or indirectly suggested that the former President Donald Trump came to power with the assistance of Vladimir Putin's authoritarian regime.[1] Moreover, some authors stretched out this thesis to its extreme, arguing that Trump was Putin's agent of influence who had been compromised by KGB that allegedly blackmailed the US president.[2] Yet, the underlying message was that Trump, an outsider who, because of his billionaire status, narcissistic demeanor, and isolationist mindset, did not care about established ways of governmentality, including liberal internationalism in foreign policy,[3] did not belong to established political circles and was an illegitimate president. In fact, that narrative was internalized to such an extent that many on the left and liberal[4] side of the US political spectrum came to view conservative political interests in US in general or any politician for that matter who disagreed with the abovementioned line of thought as Putin's puppet.

The most grotesque example of such attitude was the 2019 Hillary Clinton claim that former US Congress representative from Hawaii Tulsi Gabbard, who became a successful Democratic

---

1 Richard Sakwa, "Greater Russia: Is Moscow out to Subvert the West?" *International Politics* 58 (2021): 334.
2 Craig Unger, *American Komplomat: How the KGB Cultivated Donald Trump, and Related Tales of Sex, Greed, Power, and Treachery* (New York: Dutton, 2021).
3 Valentina Aronica and Inderjeet Parmar, "Domestic Influences on Foreign Policy Making," in Michael Cox and Doug Stokes, eds., *US Foreign Policy* (Oxford: Oxford University Press, 2018), 136-137.
4 Here I use the word "liberal" in its American meaning that signifies what Europeans usually label by such expressions as "social-democratic."

contender during the 2020 presidential campaign, and libertarian politician Jill Stein were Russian assets whom Putin's regime groomed as third-party spoiler candidates.[5] On a "grass root level," political bloggers and provincial reporters routinely took it for granted that either Russia and the Koch brothers brought Trump to power or that Putin had some compromising materials on Trump.[6] In his seminal *The Paranoid Style in American Politics* (1954), which deals with the history of conspiratorial thinking in the United States, including anti-communist hysteria in the 1950s, Richard Hofstadter remarked that not infrequently the paranoid style drew not only on manufactured events but also on actual facts: "What distinguishes the paranoid style is not, then, the absence of verifiable facts [...] but rather the curious leap of imagination that is always made at some critical point in the recital of events."[7] Furthermore, he stressed that such a style, which is based on ascribing gigantic and demonic powers to an adversary, represented an old and recurrent mode of political life of various nations. Hofstadter enumerated long-term and well-known paranoias regarding the "conspiracies" on the part of Jesuits, Freemasons, international Jewry, international capitalists, and communists.[8]

Now let's shift for a moment to the other side of the Atlantic, where in Russia, since the early 2000s, mainstream media and the greater part of the establishment have been increasingly insisting that any democratic reforms supported by the domestic opposition was a project instigated by sinister Western and especially

---

5 Matt Taibbi, "Everyone Is a Russian Asset: America Laughed at Hillary Clinton's Remarks about Tulsi Gabbard, but Her Ideas Fit Perfectly in the Intellectual Mainstream," *Rolling Stone*, October 21 (2019), https://www.rollingstone.com/politics/political-commentary/clinton-gabbard-russian-asset-jill-stein-901593/.
6 See, for example, James P. Lenfestey, "Russia, Elections, Money and Minnesota," *Minnesota Star Tribune*, June 28 (2017), https://www.startribune.com/russia-elections-money-and-minnesota/431408853/; Herb Rothschild Jr., "Say It: Trump is a Russian Agent," *Oregon Mail Tribune*, November 23 (2019), https://www.mailtribune.com/columns/2019/11/23/herb-rothschild-jr-say-it-trump-is-a-russian-agent/
7 Richard Hofstadter, *The Paranoid Style in American Politics and Other Essays* (New York: Vintage, [1954] 1964), 37.
8 Hofstadter, *The Paranoid Style in American Politics*, 5-6.

COLLUSION AND CONSPIRACY THEORIES 239

American intelligence and diplomatic services.[9] Thus, President Putin and the Russian propaganda industry claimed Alexey Navalny, the chief critic of the corrupt regime who also dared to express a wish to run as a presidential candidate, was a foreign agent and American plant. Moreover, as part of its ongoing campaign of targeted repressions, the Russian secret police attempted to poison him. When caught red-handed, Putin publicly claimed that Navalny himself orchestrated the incident with the help of the CIA. With hardly any opposition media to challenge that fake narrative and with the massive eradication of civic and independent political organizations, Putin's propaganda machine convinced a significant segment of the Russian population that the domestic opposition was working on behalf of the CIA and US State Department. In fact, such sentiments in current Russia manifested themselves in the emergence of a popular *Gosdep* (State Department for short in Russian) meme as a handy reference to any political opposition inside the country that was not officially vetted by Putin's regime.[10]

That meme has been also increasingly used to explain away various economic and political setbacks in the domestic life of the

---

9   Since the Russian invasion of Ukraine miserably failed to accomplish its ambitious original goals, the Putin regime amplified that anti-American (and more broadly anti-Western) narrative to such an extent that now Russian officials present their aggressive war against Ukraine as a existential civilizational fight between "highly spiritual" "collectivist" "traditionalist" Russia and the "corrupt" "decadent" "individualistic" West.

10 See, for example, Ilia Zar, "Rossiei pravit gosdep SShA [US Syaye Department Rules Russia]," *Maxpark*, March 23 (2013), https://maxpark.com/user/2454 892180/content/1900885; Elena Stafeeva, "Pochemu gosdep SShA na vyborakh v Rossii topit za kommunistov [Why US State Department Supports Communists during Russian Elections]," *Life.ru*, September 16, 2020, https://life.ru/p/1436046; Alexei Ivanov, "Gosdep SShA vozglavit globalist-rusofob [A Globalost-Rusophobe Will Head the US State Department]," *Zavtra*, November 25, 2020, https://zavtra.ru/events/gosdep_ssha_vozglavit_evrej_(globalist-rusofob)_pravnuk_kievskogo_literatora_pisavshego_na_idish; A. Usanin, "Gosdep SShA vydelil $70 millionov dlia sverzhenia Vladimira Putina [US State Department Allocated $70 Million to Topple Down Vladimir Putin]," *Russkoe agenstvo novostei*, March 7, 2018, путин.ru-an.info/новости/госдеп-сша-выделил-70-млрд-для-свержения-владимира-путина/; Alla Sergeevna, "Chto takoe Gosdep I kak s nim borotsia [What is the US State Department and How to Fight It]," *Newsland*, November 10, (2018), https://newsland.com/community/5166/content/chto-takoe-gosdep-i-kak-s-nim-borotsia/6541700

Russian Federation, where, since Soviet times, economic and social drawbacks have been frequently viewed as the result of interference by malicious external forces. On a lower bureaucratic level, such notions not infrequently have acquired grotesque manifestations. Thus, in 2016, in response to a question from a female worker when a local practice of regular salary delays would be stopped, angry Samara governor Nikolai Merkushkin, blamed her in being a transmitter of US State Department and CIA disinformation campaigns. Moreover, in a next equally paranoid act, this Putin appointee and an apparatchik with a provincial mindset whose career went back to the Soviet times accused a local government-friendly Communist Party leader, who spoke against reinstalling transportation fees for local retirees of being "an acting agent of the US State Department in the Samara Region."[11] Casting what one can observe in Russia on an ongoing basis for the past three decades against what the world saw in the United States between 2016 and 2021, one must to keep in mind that, unlike authoritarian countries where political paranoias routinely linger for decades, in democratic countries bouts of political hysteria usually represent short-term phenomena, which tend to evaporate being muted by the independent opposition and uncensored mass media.

The goal of this chapter is twofold. First, I will provide a brief review of major book-length popular and scholarly texts dealing with the "Russian Collusion." Second, while critically reviewing that literature published by 2022, I want to draw attention to US domestic politics that heavily contributed to the emergence of the "Russian Collusion" narrative. Particularly, I want to emphasize the role of the governmental institutional culture, including foreign and security policy makers, whose mindsets were shaped, on the one hand, by Cold War legacy practices, and, on the other hand, by

---

11 Yelena Plotnikova and Robert Coalson, "Samara Governor Offers A Stark Choice: United Russia Or The CIA," September 10, 2016, *Radio Free Europe/Radio Liberty*, https://www.rferl.org/a/russia-samara-governor-merkushkin-united-russia-cia/27978955.html; Sergei Kurt-Adzhiev, "Gubernator Samarskoi oblasti ne dogovorilsia s kommunistami," *Park Gagarina*, March 16, 2017, https://parkgagarina.info/index.php/politika/24815-gubernator-samarskoj-oblasti-ne-dogovorilsya-s-kommunistami.html

societal and political changes in the 1960s and 1970s, particularly by the New Left cultural turn that made deep inroads into the American mainstream.

In both democratic and authoritarian regimes political elites become hostages of domestic politics, existing political cultures, and institutional cultures of bureaucracies responsible for conducting foreign policy and espionage work. There is extensive literature about domestic influences on American foreign policies.[12] We also have publications on how KGB culture, which can be traced to Soviet times, has shaped present-day Russian foreign and security policies.[13]

Since the publication of the seminal Hofstadter's *The Paranoid Style in American Politics*, scholars have extensively researched conspiracy theories related to foreign policy and "external forces" that have been informing political movements and trends on the conservative right-wing side of the US political spectrum. Yet, we do not have sufficient research that analyses similar trends in the left-liberal thought collective. This also concerns the above-mentioned "Russian Collusion" narrative. The first scholar who attempted to briefly address the conspiracy traits in the "collusion" media was political scientist Joseph E. Uscinski. In 2017, prior to several

---

12 For a comprehensive discussion of domestic politics' influence on foreign policies, see Ryan K. Beasley et. al., ed., *Foreign Policy in Comparative Perspective: Domestic and International Influences on State Behavior* (Mountain Oaks, CA, and London: Sage/CQ Press, 2013); Aronica and Parmar, "Domestic Influences on Foreign Policy Making," 125-140; Daniel S. Hamilton and Teija Tiilikainen, eds., *Domestic Determinants of Foreign Policy in the European Union and the United States* (Washington, DC: Center for Transatlantic Relations and Finnish Institute of International Affairs, 2018); Liam Kraft and Melissa Ballard, "Where Domestic Meets Foreign: Domestic America and U.S. Foreign Policy," *The International Scholar*, April 29, 2020, https://www.theintlscholar.com/periodical/domestic-meets-foreign-domestic-america-us-foreign-policy.

13 For samples of the most recent writings on this topic, see Kimberly Marten, "The 'KGB State' and Russian Political and Foreign Policy Culture," *The Journal of Slavic Military Studies* 30, vol. 2 (2017):131-151; Michael McFaul, "Putin, Putinism, and the Domestic Determinants of Russian Foreign Policy," *International Security*, 45, vol. 2 (2020): 95–139; Marcin Kaczmarski, "Domestic Power Relations and Russia's Foreign Policy," 2014; *Demokratizatsiya: The Journal of Post-Soviet Democratization*, 22, vol. 3 (2014): 383-409; Brookings Institution, *The Domestic Context of Russian Foreign Policy* (2016), https://www.brookings.edu/wpcontent/uploads/2016/07/Chapter-One-12.pdf.

scholars whose writings I will examine later in the chapter, he placed that event (along with the "deep state" meme that is popular with the right-wing) in the context of American and world political history that has been influenced by conspiracy theories.[14]

I built on the scholarship of the scholars who have argued that one of the chief reasons for the emergence and development of the "Russian Collusion" narrative between 2016 and 2020 was the unwillingness of the left-liberal establishment to face US domestic social and political circumstances that had triggered the Trump movement. Although a pro-Kremlin British academic, Richard Sakwa has correctly stressed that "the Russiagate affair demonstrates, Russia acts as the scapegoat for problems generated by domestic contradictions."[15] Moreover, I want to expand this argument by stressing that in a spontaneous manner the "collusion" narrative acquired an additional value for the anti-Trump resistance because the standard racism accusation that was routinely levelled at the president and his supporters was losing its potency. In fact, given Trump's colorblind approach and his declared civic nationalism, the left "anti-racist" rhetoric was becoming meaningless. This became obvious during the 2020 elections, when, in addition to "white" working class people, small business owners, and evangelicals, which were Trump's core social base, he received the highest share of "non-white" vote than any other republican candidate since 1960.[16] In this context, the external "Russian Collusion" factor provided another powerful leverage for the resistance movement against the "illegitimate" president. In other words, the "Russian Collusion" narrative empowered the loose and broad anti-Trump

---

14 Joseph E. Uscinski, "The Election was Rigged, the News is Fake, and the Deep State is Out to Get Us," *Eurozone*, 28 September 2017, https://www.eurozine.com/the-election-was-rigged-the-news-is-fake-and-the-deep-state-is-out-to-get-us/
15 R. Sakwa, "Greater Russia: Is Moscow out to Subvert the West?" 355.
16 Zachary Evans, "Trump Won Highest Share of Non-White Vote of Any Republican Since 1960, Exit Polls Show," *Yahoo News*, November 4, 2020, https://www.yahoo.com/now/trump-won-highest-share-non-164843048.html

coalition that could not completely rely on the anti-racism cliches and related rhetoric in its polemics with the right.[17]

What is also important to keep in mind is that Putin's KGB mafia state, which turned out to be very weak from an economic standpoint, has been intentionally seeking to amplify its worldwide menacing imagery through bizarre geopolitical demands, signature assassinations of anti-Putin political figures inside and outside the country, and through hacking and cyber warfare. Such posturing by the Moscow regime provided a convenient backdrop for the emergence of the "Russian Collusion" narrative. Finally, the above-mentioned Cold War legacy mindset (Russians versus Americans) most likely became an additional contributing factor; the fact that Chinese espionage activities, which have been conducted on the same and even greater scale, did not receive adequate government and media attention, seems to support this thesis.[18]

---

17   Blaming their opponents in being racists escalated on the left since Obama's coming to office in 2008. Trying to morally disarm the republican opposition, democrats found it convenient to link any objections to their social and economic agenda to the alleged animosity of their opponents toward the first "black" president. Incidentally, this partially helps explain such paradox in the US current affairs as the coexistence of the increased racial and cultural tolerance in society on a grass-root level and the aggressive cry racism woke hysteria in mass media (Wilfred Reilly, *Hate Crime Hoax: How the Left is Selling a Fake Race War* (Washington, DC: Regnery, 2019). By now, in the US political discourse the label of "racism" has been so worn out and overused that it might follow the fate of expression "fascism" that by the end of the last century had lost its meaning and become a cliche curse word for everything someone disliked in surrounding political and social life.

18   Even those media outlets that accepted the "collusion" narrative had to admit that "talk to former intel officials, and many will say that China poses an equal, if not greater, long-term threat. They have all the time in the world, and all the patience in the world." Also, "Chinese intelligence employs a more decentralized strategy than Russia does. China draws from a much larger population pool to achieve its objectives — using opportunistic businessmen, ardent nationalists, students, travelers and others alike." Zach Dorfman, "How Silicon Valley Became a Den of Spies," *Politico*, August 27, 2018, https://www.politico.com/magazine/story/2018/07/27/silicon-valley-spies-china-russia-219071/. Just as Russia, China dramatically increased her espionage activities in US since the early 2000s. For more about the latter, see Evan Burke et. al., "Survey of Chinese Espionage in the United States Since 2000," Center for Strategic and International Studies (CSIS), 2020, https://www.csis.org/programs/technology-policy-program/survey-chinese-linked-espionage-united-states-2000

Not only in authoritarian states like Russia, China or Iran but also in democracies, established governmental elites who face sudden challenges to their institutional culture, as took place in the US in 2016-2020,[19] tend to look for an external factor to explain away their economic blunders and political setbacks: "Paranoid disposition is mobilized into action chiefly by social conflicts that involve ultimate schemes of values that bring fundamental fears and hatreds, rather than negotiable interests, into political action. Catastrophe or the fear of catastrophe is most likely to elicit the syndrome of paranoid rhetoric."[20]

Instigated by elites and media, political hysteria can captivate masses for a short while and then quickly evaporate, leaving a psychological residue that continues to shape popular and elites' mindsets. In US history, one of the first popular paranoias was the so-called Bishop Controversy in the 1760s, when the Protestant majority in then still British North America, who had been harboring strong anti-Catholic ("antipapist') sentiments since the 1517 Protestant Reformation, were caught in a false rumors frenzy that the English king was going to put them under the heel of Roman Catholic bishops.[21] Incidentally, this fear was a factor in spearheading the eventual secession of the colonies from the mother country. One can also point to the popular anti-Communist frenzy in the US in the 1950s, when on a grassroot level, some extremely "vigilant patriots" linked such routine practices as fluoridation of water to attempts by external forces to promote socialism under the guise of public health.[22]

---

19 Aronica and Parmar, "Domestic Influences on Foreign Policy Making," 139.
20 Hofstadter, *The Paranoid Style in American Politics*, 39.
21 For more about this pivotal political and religious paranoia, see Carl Bridenbaugh, *Mitre and Sceptre: Transatlantic Faiths, Ideas, Personalities, and Politics, 1689-1775* (New York: Oxford University Press, 1962); Peter W. Walker, "The Bishop Controversy, the Imperial Crisis, and Religious Radicalism in New England, 1763-74," *The New England Quarterly*, 90, no. 3 (2017): 306-343.
22 Hofstadter, *The Paranoid Style in American Politics*, 6.

Domestic Politics' Influence on Foreign Policy and Institutional Culture

The effect of institutional culture on foreign policy becomes visible when established elites face sudden challenges in domestic policies. Thus, Putin and his circle ascribed the dramatic rise of civic activities in Russia, the Navalny phenomenon, and the domestic effect of color revolutions to US machinations. As discussed earlier, the Russian establishment and a large segment of the populace internalized this narrative.

In the United States, such challenge was represented by the unexpected victory of Trump along with his attempt to move away from "liberal internationalism" in international affairs and regime change overseas and to make a shift towards isolationism. Incidentally, this was precisely the policy that attracted the attention of the Putin regime that interpreted the declared change in US international priorities as an opportunity to create a "safe space" for the Kremlin's geopolitical games in the near abroad and beyond.[23] As subsequent events showed, this was a false expectation. Bombarded by the "collusion" accusation, Trump had to demonstrate his anti-Putin stance, which resulted in an increase in some NATO members military budgets, the unblocking of military assistance to Ukraine, and targeted missile strikes against the Syrian army and Russian Wagner mercenaries.

The emergence of Trump shell-shocked left, liberal, and neoconservative establishments who felt deeply suspicious of and threatened by the politician with a reckless style and no links to policy-making circles. He not only threatened to disrupt established economic links with China and to antagonize Iran but, in his domestic policies, also sought to debase the security and the lifestyles of established federal bureaucracy in Washington DC (the infamous "drain the swamp" populist slogan),[24] undermine business

---

23 Sakwa, "Greater Russia: Is Moscow out to Subvert the West?", 343, 348.
24 On average, 90% of voters in the Washington DC area, the district with the highest concentration of federal employees, routinely choose democrats, "District Of Columbia, 2020 Elections," https://www.270towin.com/states/District_of _Columbia.

interests that depended on cheap labor of illegal aliens, and dismantle the entire "diversity" industry in favor of civic nationalism. Russian espionage activities in the US that were widely discussed in the media during the second Obama administration, Trump's early visit to Russia along with his abortive bizarre plan to erect a Trump Tower in Moscow, and clumsy attempt of the Trump election campaign to gather dirt on their democratic opponents from Russian sources[25] triggered FBI surveillance of the Trump team in 2016-2017 and naturally convinced many on the losing side of the 2016 presidential elections that the sudden ascent of the unvetted politician could not have happened without some malicious influence of foreign forces. Those who lost in 2016 were unwilling to analyze various social and economic circumstances that brought Trump to power. For them the "Russian Collusion" became a convenient and easy alternative explanation. Those circumstances included the decline and migration of manufacturing industry abroad; uncontrolled immigration; frustration with financially wasteful support given to foreign clients that frequently peddled an anti-American agenda; and a disgust with the ideological agenda of "diversity" policies and multiculturalism that were seen as leading to the balkanization of US society.

When discussing the domestic agenda affecting foreign policy making, one usually deals with public opinions. Evidence suggests that US public indifference towards foreign policy questions frequently opens a door of opportunity for elites to experiment in foreign affairs. Yet, on the contrary, when we deal with a fixation of a large segment of population on a specific foreign policy issue, that window of opportunity shrinks. For example, in our case, because of the emergence of the "Russian Collusion" factor, liberal internationalist political forces (i.e., so-called neoliberals and neoconservatives) in the federal government and media not only effectively paralyzed the declared Trump isolationist project but also forced him

---

25 As we know, the Hillary Clinton team was simultaneously working on gathering dirt on their Republican opponents, similarly relying on Russian sources (the infamous false "Steele dossier") that FBI utilized to justify their surveillance of the Trump team.

to play by their rules, provoking the president to intensify a neo-containment policy and to show how tough and assertive he was in relations with Russia, Syria and beyond.[26]

Although the US public may not clearly articulate its opinions regarding foreign policy, it does often send signals to elites about enduring core values in the form of changing moods. These can refer to such notions as isolationism, anticommunism, non-appeasement, neutrality, or anti-imperialism.[27] As applied to present-day China and Russia such core values revolve around great power identity, whereas for Venezuela, Bolivia, and Iran it is anti-imperialism. Or, as in the case of the Unites States and Canada, it can be the promotion of democracy, human rights, and a diversity multicultural agenda.

Powerful ideas that are shared by members of the public, government bureaucracy, and opinion makers set boundaries within which leaders must remain or risk public opposition or the loss of their influence. In democratic countries there are often contesting groups pushing back against certain foreign policies. For example, in the United States, it could be a competition between liberal internationalists (who are focused on the promotion of global human rights and enforcing diversity), neoconservatives (well known for being supporters of regime change), and isolationists. At the same time, as several students of comparative international politics have reminded us, one should not exaggerate differences between the processes of foreign policy making in democratic and authoritarian governments. Foreign policy decisions are not as diffused and constrained in democracies as we sometimes assume. In contrast to domestic policy matters, decisions regarding external affairs are often highly centralized at the senior levels of the government's hierarchy.[28]

In these circles, people frequently become prisoners of existing corporate cultures in foreign and intelligence service agencies that

---

26 Sakwa, "Greater Russia: Is Moscow out to Subvert the West?" 353.
27 Juliet Kaarbo, Jeffrey S. Lantis, and Ryan K. Beasley, "The Analysis of Foreign Policy in Comparative Perspective," in Beasley, *Foreign Policy in Comparative Perspective*, 14.
28 Ibid., 17.

"develop their own sense of identity or organizational mission."[29] These experiences may set bounders and constrain elites' behavior by inherited values and ways or informal moral codes. Finally, the mindsets of foreign and espionage decision-making actors are not infrequently shaped by their personal experiences, such as family backgrounds or the specifics of their education and professional work. In this chapter I am concerned with institutional culture and the behavior of foreign policy and security actors. Particularly, I would like to draw attention to two factors: the recent ideological fixation of US domestic and foreign bureaucracies on "anti-racism" and "diversity" and to the enduring legacy of US Cold War practices (that were amplified by the Putin's aggressive posturing), which had singled out the Soviet Union as major threat to US national security. I intend to demonstrate that both factors played a pivotal role in the emergence of the "Russian Collusion" narrative.

Russian *Siloviki* and US Liberal Multiculturalists

It is common knowledge that people often ignore or distort information that contradicts what they already believe. This is especially relevant in situations when we already have strong stereotypes about how other countries and cultures behave.[30] Maryia Omelicheva, who drew attention to educational, professional, and cultural socialization of foreign policy makers, writes: "Individual leaders are products of their environment. Therefore, placing their views and perspectives on foreign policy inside the broader context of national culture, identity, and ideology may be beneficial to understanding their foreign policy choices."[31] She has noted such an obvious fact as the KGB conspiracy mindset that was fixated on security matters, which Putin and his cronies brought to both foreign and domestic policies. As a result, they have been viewing entire societal life and foreign policy through the distorted lenses of their espionage training and experiences.

---

29 Ibid., 17
30 Ibid., 19.
31 Mariya Omelicheva, "Russian Foreign Policy: A Quest for Great Power Status in a Multipolar World," in Beasley *Foreign Policy in Comparative Perspective*, 108.

The corporate culture of foreign policy making in Russia is heavily influenced by the KGB and its successors (Federal Security Service [FSB], External Intelligence Service [SVR]) as well as interest groups and law enforcement circles that depend on them. They represent the so-called *siloviki* who in the 1990s replaced in power communist party apparatchiks of the old Soviet Union. Russia's "new nobility" consists of active and retired officers of the KGB (FSB, SVR), military and law enforcement personnel along with former KGB (FSB) and existing informers (termed "trusted assistants"). Planted in all key fields of policymaking, they form a thought collective that is obsessed with foreign and domestic conspiracies and convinced that the surrounding world can be controlled by a group of powerful puppeteers. They are fixated on surveillance, support a centralized omnipotent state, and prioritize order and stability above everything else. They also view the United States and NATO with suspicion and aspire to reinstate Russia's sphere of influence in the former republics of the Soviet Union. Moreover, the most popular and officially sanctioned opposition, which is represented by the Communist party, shares their anti-Western conspiratorial values.

The heavy influence of security service interest groups in the government originates in the KGB's Cold War ethos and a general frustration within Russian elites who concluded that the West was not treating Russia with the respect due to a great power. This led to the emergence of powerful anti-Western and especially anti-American tendencies in Russian foreign policy and among espionage actors, who were deeply rooted in the Soviet past. After his 2004-2007 famous statements, in which Putin challenged the alleged American condescending explanation of how "natives" should behave,[32] the anti-colonial rhetoric that the Putin regime employed began to expand.[33] In fact, after World War II, such rhetoric

---

32   Quoted after Thomas Ambrosio, *Authoritarian Backlash: Russian Resistance to Democratization in the Former Soviet Union* (Farnham, UK and Burlington, US: Ashgate, 2009), 79.
33   Again, this "anti-colonial" narrative was greatly amplified by the Putin regime after its invasion of Ukraine. Edyta Bojanowska, "Putin's Anti-Colonial Agenda?" *The Jordan Center for the Advanced Study of Russia News*, December 13

became a standard "progressive" tool in the hands of many non-Western countries that sought to justify their nationalism and xenophobia in foreign policy or a crackdown on the opposition within their own countries. At the same time, since the 1960s, a similar anti-colonial and anti-Western rhetoric entered the European and North American cultural and political mainstream, having captivated the minds of Western intellectual elites.[34] Incidentally, such discourse also permeates the Russian vague ideology of so-called Eurasianism which suggests that in her domestic policies Russia follows "organic" collectivist tradition, and in her foreign policy she successfully harmonized relations with its subject countries — unlike Western countries that are based on "rotten" individualism, racism, materialism, and colonial expansion.

Incidentally, communist China, which was among the first to employ Third World anti-colonial narratives as early as the 1950s-1960s, has thrown back the "evil racist US" narrative at American liberal internationalists. Thus, in March of 2021, during their first encounter with the Biden administration, Chinese delegates humiliated them by bombarding the Americans with the mantra of "anti-racism" (Black Lives Matter (BLM) propaganda and the "systemic racism" meme), aiming to shut down US criticism of forced labor camps in Western China and suppression of national minorities by the Chinese Communist Party and secret police. Trapped in their own anti-Western ideology of "diversity, inclusion, and equity," which the American left and liberals supported and amplified since the summer 2020 urban disturbances, the US delegation had to walk on eggshells to avoid these toxic issues.[35]

(2022), https://jordanrussiacenter.org/news/putins-anti-colonial-agenda/#.Z FW3pXbMIuX

34 Roger Kimball, *The Long March: How the Cultural Revolution of the 1960's Changed America* (San Francisco: Encounter Books, 2000).

35 Lara Jakes, "In First Talks, Dueling Accusations Set Testy Tone for U.S.-China Diplomacy," *New York Times*, March 18, 2021, https://www.nytimes.com/2021/03/18/us/politics/china-blinken-sullivan.html. Carol M. Swain and Christopher J. Schorr, *Black Eye for America: How Critical Race Theory is Burning Down the House* (La Vergne, TN: Be the People Books, 2021), 16-17. For more on the corrosive effect of the "anti-racism" CRT ideology, see James Lindsay, *Race Marxism: The Truth about Critical Race Theory and Practice*

Ironically, despite their mutual suspicions, Chinese "national socialists," Russian "Eurasianists," and US "liberal multiculturalists" are often unanimous in showing their contempt for the traditional guiding myths of Western civilization that are focused on individual liberty, equality of opportunities, colorblind justice, constitutionalism, and free market. All three groups blame the West for colonialism and racism, simultaneously praising a centralized benevolent state and collectivist "tribal" ethos (such as equity at the expense of equality in the US, spirituality (*duhovnost'*) and collectivism (*sobornost'*) in Russia, and socialism with national characteristics in China). .

Furthermore, despite their slight differences, in the United States, "liberal internationalists" and "neoconservatives," who have been defining the mainstream consensus in foreign policies, promoted a regime change and "democratic values" in foreign affairs. In domestic policies, they have been pledging their commitment to "diversity" ideology fixated on "anti-racism" and critique of Western "white" values. As in the case of the US elite in general, the ethos of the greater part of American foreign policy and security elites was shaped by the 1960s-1970s campus culture that had been heavily influenced by New Left ideas that revolved around identity issues with an emphasis on race, gender, and culture. Scholars on the left and on the right have repeatedly stated this to be the case.[36]

The dramatic decline of manufacturing industries that moved out of the US, the growing popularity of civic nationalism in domestic life, frustration with "diversity" quotas and political correctness, and support for isolationism in international politics eventually brought Trump to power. Although those attitudes germinated over the previous decade, their sudden ascent to the political Olympus caught the establishment by surprise, and it resorted to familiar ideological tools to explain these sudden changes. Thus, in

---

(Orlando, FL: New Discourses, 2022); John McWorther, *Woke Racism: How a New Religion Has Betrayed Black America* (New York: Portfolio/Penguin, 2022).

36   For a left-wing perspective, see Michael Kazin, *American Dreamers: How the Left Changed a Nation* (New York: Knopf, 2011) and Eric Davin, *Radicals in Power: The New Left Experience in Office* (Lanham, MN: Lexington Books, 2012). For the right-wing view of that phenomenon, see Kimball, *The Long March.*

domestic politics millions of conservative and libertarian supporters of the new president were all labeled as racists even though in 2016 Trump received more minority votes than any other Republican presidential after 1964. Moreover, he was able to further increase the number of his minority supporters during the 2020 elections.[37]

Incidentally, the family and college background of Obama is one of the best examples of how the cultural left ethos had been internalized by US political elites that matured between the 1960s and the 1980s. Groomed by radical leftist Marshal Davis during his college years, Obama had rubbed shoulders with leftist professors and radical students involved in discussions of neocolonialism, Franz Fanon, Eurocentrism, and patriarchy.[38] He cooperated with Black Power activists, eventually becoming a lawyer for ACORN. Among other issues, this now defunct social justice organization was specialized in the 1990s in forcing banks to grant home mortgages and credit to financially unsustainable people.[39] In the White House, in addition to the traditional realist approaches to foreign policy, Obama introduced an anti-colonialist "post-American" view of the world where the US was expected to apologize for its imperialism and Eurocentrism.[40]

---

37 Matthew Impelli, Trump Wins Highest Percent of Nonwhite Voters of Any Republican in 60 Years, Doubles LGBTQ Support From 2016," *Newsweek*, November 5 (2020), https://www.newsweek.com/trump-wins-highest-percent-nonwhite-voters-any-republican-60-years-doubles-lgbtq-support-2016-1545294; Ashitha Nagesh, "US Election 2020: Why Trump Gained Support Among Minorities," *BBC News*, November 22, 2022, https://www.bbc.com/news/world-us-canada-54972389.
38 Barack Obama, *Dreams from My Father: A Story of Race and Inheritance* (New York: Random House, 2007), 100.
39 Stanley Kurtz, Stanley, *Radical-in-Chief: Barack Obama and the Untold Story of American Socialism* (New York: Simon and Schuster, 2010), 197-218.
40 Dinesh D'Souza, "How Obama Thinks," *Forbes*, September 9 (2010); idem: Barack Obama: the Last Anti-Colonialist, *Standpoint*, October 21, 2010, https://standpointmag.co.uk/features-november-10-barack-obama-the-last-anti-colonialist-dinesh-d-souza/; However, some authors have questioned that narrative, insisting that Obama's approach in international relations was completely devoid of any cultural left post-colonialist traits. Robert Singh, *Barack Obama's Post-American Foreign Policy: The Limits of Engagement* (London: Bloomsbury Academic, 2012). As always, the truth is most probably somewhere in the middle.

COLLUSION AND CONSPIRACY THEORIES 253

Hillary Clinton, another important actor, has a similar background. In her youth as a college student, she belonged to a class of people whom Americans usually call the "limousine left," a well-to-do person who toyed from time to time with hype radical ideas to fit the popular trend, later assimilating traits from these ideas into her professional career behavior. In this manner, in the late 1960s, Clinton corresponded with Saul Alinsky, a radical cultural left community organizer who authored the notorious handbook *Rules for Radicals*. The young Clinton wrote a thesis *"There Is Only the Fight . . . ": An Analysis of the Alinsky Model* (1969) endorsing Alinsky's struggle and agenda. Although she disagreed with him about the need to completely dismantle the "oppressive" US system, Clinton nevertheless argued that the same goals one could reach by working within that system.[41]

Still, like many people of the 1960s generation who entered power structures, by becoming a mainstream center-left democratic politician, she internalized some of the New Left ideas regarding race, gender, and culture, particularly the vision of US society as divided into "oppressed" (i.e., race and gender minorities, non-Western cultures) and "oppressors" (i.e., white, male, Western). It is appropriate to remark here that, like Clinton, CIA Director William Brennan, who was one of the major spearheads of the "Russian Collusion," was heavily involved in New Left political culture at the end of the 1970s. In fact, he went even further beyond the mainstream cultural left by voting for Gus Hall, the Community Party USA presidential candidate in 1980. Moreover, in 2016, Brennan hinted that past left-wing activism should not be a stumbling block during a CIA recruitment process.[42]

Like Hillary Clinton, Susan Rice, National Security Advisor in the Obama administration, became a mainstream democratic

---

41 David Blankenhorn, "Clinton's Alinsky Problem—and Ours," *American Interest*, October 11, 2016, https://www.the-american-interest.com/2016/10/11/clintons-alinsky-problem-and-ours/; Stanley Kurtz, "Why Hillary's Alinsky Letters Matter," *National Review*, September 22, 2014, https://www.nationalreview.com/corner/why-hillarys-alinsky-letters-matter-stanley-kurtz/

42 Tal Kopan, "Polygraph Panic: CIA Director Fretted His Vote for Communist," *CNN Politics*, September 15, 2016, https://www.cnn.com/2016/09/15/politics/john-brennan-cia-communist-vote/index.html

politician and eventually a career diplomat. In her youth, as a college student and beyond, she apprenticed with a Black Power identity group and internalized some of its ethos. Moreover, at one point, along with a group of educators, she produced a brochure that propagated how to introduce black studies into elementary and secondary schools across the United States and how to "make white students learn black history."[43] This 1980s guidebook and similar contemporary products prepared the ground for the ongoing "progressive" woke agenda that seeks to debase Western "white" values, condemn all American institutions as "systemic racism," replace the rule of law with "racial justice," and balkanize society into the "oppressed" and "oppressors."

Rice had worked for the Bill Clinton administration in the 1990s as his advisor for African Affairs. In this position she became notorious in promoting "anti-colonial" African autocrats and endorsing their tribal politics.[44] According to her own admission, she had "lingering fears" that her accomplishments would be diminished by people who attributed them to affirmative action programs. Although the Black Power establishment viewed her as part of the "assimilated black elite," she clearly internalized some of the "anti-colonial" mindset.

Mainstream social scholarship on American Foreign Policy hardly discusses the abovementioned matters. For example, *Ideologies of American Foreign Policy* (2019) by John Callaghan, Brendon O'Connor, Mark Phythian is one of the seminal monographs in the field and deals with the Cold War period and anti-communist discourse in US domestic and foreign policies. By covering multiple approaches in American foreign policy throughout history (American exceptionalism, realism, neoconservatism, classical liberalism, nationalism, isolationism and so forth), the study has somehow managed to avoid the analysis of the effect of New Left and postcolonial agenda on US policy makers. Moreover, the book skipped

---

43 Susan E Rice, Loretta M Butler, Barbara Patterson, and Gwen Thompson, *A History Deferred: A Guide for Teachers* (Washington, DC: Black Student Fund, 1986).
44 Bret Stephens, "Susan Rice Was a Diplomatic Disaster," *New York Times*, 10 August 2020, https://www.nytimes.com/2020/08/10/opinion/susan-rice-africa.html.

the discussion of the Obama administration that was steeped in that agenda.[45] Limiting the foreign policy ideological trends to what he characterized as a "liberal-realist approach," O'Connor only noted that Obama brought US foreign policy back to the FDR era of the 1930s.[46]

There is also an economic backdrop that provided a window of opportunity for the emergence of the "Russian Collusion" narrative. In contrast to the close economic relations between US and China and the enormous size of US-Chinese trade ($600 billion in 2017), Russian-American trade relations are minuscule ($35 billion in 2019). Holding China responsible for escalating acts of espionage and violations of human rights (e. g., crackdown on Hong Kong autonomy and labor camps for Muslim minorities in Western China) could have had economic repercussions. In contrast, challenging the aggressive geopolitical posturing of Putin's regime in the near abroad and its hybrid warfare activities in the West brought about few economic risks. Soil and platinum accounted for sixty percent of Russian export to the US in 2019, which the US always could sanction and instead import from the Middle East. In contrast, any political disruptions in US-Chinese relations could inflict serious damage to the American economy.

"Russian Collusion" and "Russiagate" in Popular Non-Fiction

Since the "Russian Collusion" is a recent event, book-length comprehensive scholarly studies of that phenomenon are still few. Existing literature on the topic is mostly represented by journalistic trade books designed to ride the narrative about Trump conspiring with the Russians. These texts have been authored by writers, reporters, and scholars with left and liberal leanings. Among them one could find, for example, Seth Abramson, who is a former

---

45 John Callaghan, Brendon O'Connor, Mark Phythian, *Ideologies of American Foreign Policy* (Abingdon, UK: Routledge, 2019),
46 Brendon O'Connor, "Ideology and the Foreign Policy of Barack Obama: A Liberal-Realist Approach to International Affairs," *Presidential Studies Quarterly*, 51, no.3 (2021): 635-666.

criminal defense attorney and social justice journalism scholar, teaching legal advocacy and cultural theory (a "woke" methodology that people on the right label as Cultural Marxism) at the University of New Hampshire.

Among these texts one can also find the one produced by Howard A. DeWitt, a professional retired historian of the 1960s generation with strong left-wing sympathies, whose specialty is the history of rock and roll and ethnic studies. Among the first authors who wrote on the topic one can see Luke Harding, a British journalist at *The Guardian*, fiction writer Malcolm Nance, former intelligence officer and counter-terrorism analyst for NBC News and MSNBC Craig Unger, and career journalist at *Vanity Fair* and the *New Republic* Greg Miller, who is also a national security reporter for the *Washington Post*. Incidentally, Miller was one of the newspaper's reporters who was awarded the 2018 Pulitzer Prize for stories on Trump's "links" to Kremlin agents. Finally, Peter Strzok, a former FBI official who was one of the top intelligence bosses to initiate surveillance of the Trump team, too produced a book-length text on the same "collusion" topic.[47]

An advertisement for the paperback edition of Harding's *Collusion*, which was built on the fake Steele dossier, dramatized "the biggest scandal of the modern era" and described his book as follows: "An explosive exposé that lays out the story behind the Steele Dossier, including Russia's decades-in-the-making political game to upend American democracy and the Trump administration's ties

---

47 Seth Abramson, *Proof of Conspiracy: How Trump's International Collusion Is Threatening American Democracy* (New York: St. Martin's, 2019); idem, *Proof of Collusion: How Trump Betrayed America* (New York: Simon & Schuster 2018); Howard A. DeWitt, *Trump's Plot To Destroy Democracy* (Scottsdale, AZ: Horizon Books 2021); Luke Harding, *Collusion: Secret Meetings, Dirty Money, and How Russia Helped Donald Trump Win* (New York: St. Martin's 2017); Malcolm Nance, *The Plot to Betray America: How Team Trump Embraced Our Enemies, Compromised Our Security, and How We Can Fix It* (New York and Boston: Hachette Books, 2019); Craig Unger, *American Kompromat: How the KGB Cultivated Donald Trump, and Related Tales of Sex, Greed, Power, and Treachery* (New York: Dutton, 2021); Greg Miller, *The Apprentice: Trump, Russia and the Subversion of American Democracy* (New York, NY: Custom House, 2018); Peter Strzok, *Compromised: Counterintelligence and the Threat of Donald J. Trump* (Boston: Houghton Mifflin Harcourt, 2020).

to Moscow." The *New Republic* commended Harding for presenting "a powerful case for Russian interference, and the Trump campaigns collusion, by collecting years of reporting on Trump's connections to Russia and putting it all together in a coherent narrative." Nance's *The Plot to Betray America* is presented as a text that "reveals exactly how Trump and his inner circle conspired, coordinated, communicated, and eventually strategized to commit the greatest act of treachery in the history of the United States. Seduced by the promises of riches dangled in front of them by Putin, the Trump administration eagerly decided to reap the rewards of the plan to install a Kremlin-friendly crony in the Oval Office."

In his *Trump Against The World*, DeWitt employed the "anti-colonial" and "critical theory" narrative of the cultural left, which I discussed earlier, suggesting that Trump was a racist and his foreign policy was racist as well. After this, he dissected "the Russian influence upon Trump," using as one of the major "proofs" of the "collusion" Russian propaganda media (e.g., RT) that spoke favorably about Trump's isolationist foreign policy. On the basis of this "evidence," DeWitt concluded that "the president has made a deal with the devil." Incidentally, in a similar manner, an inquisitive reader might claim "Chinese collision" because Chinese communist government propaganda spoke more favorably about Biden during the 2020-election cycle because Trump had disrupted US-China economic relations that had worked in China's favor. Moreover, in his second book *Trump's Plot To Destroy Democracy*, DeWitt made a bizarre argument that Trump endangered First Amendment freedoms contrary to the fact that after 2016, it was conservative and libertarian media outlets that were de-platformed by such internet giants as Facebook, Twitter, and YouTube (Google). Enjoying legal immunity under Section 230 of the 1996 Internet Decency Act they eventually removed Trump and his supporters from all their platforms. Moreover, it was later revealed that Twitter literally partnered with the FBI to remove popular US-based accounts that were critical of the left agenda. It is notable that, although imprisoned by the Putin regime, the leading Russian dissident Alexei Navalny took efforts to reach out to media to call those Twitter activities "an unacceptable act of censorship."[48]

Unlike other "collusion" texts that suggested Trump was an agent of influence or Putin's useful idiot, in *American Kompromat* Unger analyzed "documentary" evidence and came to a definitive conclusion that Trump was a Russian asset. The writer unfolded a convoluted story about how Trump had been "spotted" by the KGB, how the latter had cultivated him as an asset, arranging his trip to Moscow and even providing him with talking points. Drawing on the speculations of one Yuri Shvets, a perestroika era KGB defector and currently a popular video blogger, Unger suggested that because of routine KGB protocol activities with regards to the 1987 Trump visit to Moscow, the Soviets caught the would-be president in their espionage web. Moreover, Unger and Shvets speculated that the Soviets might have turned Trump into a "special unofficial contact" for the KGB. In this capacity he was to become an intelligence asset whose role was to be what the late Soviet-friendly industrialist Armand Hammer had played for pre-Gorbachev Soviet governments.

On the other side of the political spectrum, we have literature produced by conservative writers. In response to the massive left-liberal campaign of resistance that aimed to arrest the advance of the Trump movement, conservative media and right-wing grassroots created their own conspiracy narrative about a sinister and omnipotent "deep state" that conspired to destroy the American republic and constitution and that included the US intelligence services, state department, and the mainstream media. Challenging the "Russian Collusion" narrative, this print and internet media began to popularize the "Russiagate" narrative.

---

48 Mary Kay Linge and Jon Levine, "Latest Twitter Files shows CIA, FBI Have Spent Years Meddling in Content Moderation," *New York Post*, December 24, 2022, https://nypost.com/2022/12/24/latest-batch-of-twitter-files-shows-cia-fbi-involved-in-content-moderation/; Jon Levine Benjamin Wallace-Wells, "What the Twitter Files Reveal About Free Speech and Social Media," *The New Yorker*, January 11, 2023, https://www.newyorker.com/news/the-political-scene/what-the-twitter-files-reveal-about-free-speech-and-social-media

Among the conservative writers who came to challenge the "collusion" narrative with their own popular trade books we can find Andrew C. McCarthy at the *National Review*; Fox News contributor, writer and contributor to *Federalist* Julie Kelly; Roger Stone, a publicity seeking political trickster who was part of Trump's 2016 presidential campaign; George Papadopoulos, a former Trump advisor who became an object of FBI surveillance; Brent Bozell, who heads the conservative watchdog Media Research Center; Matthew G. Whitaker, a conservative attorney who worked at the Department of Justice on behalf of Trump; Gregg Jarrett, a political analyst at Fox News; and finally Michael Savage, one of the most popular talk show hosts.[49]

Among existing publications, Dan Kovalik's and Rebekah Koffler's texts stand out. The first one, which has been produced by a progressive author and a labor/human rights lawyer, has tried to redirect the whole "collusion" narrative by utilizing the old left-wing ideological genre — blaming the US. This was in a sharp contrast to the behavior of current left-liberal mainstream thought collective that changed its attitudes after 2016 by warming to the CIA and FBI (which had earlier served as a manifestation of the "great Satan" for the New Left) and to the power of the existing bureaucratic state. Particularly, Kovalik examined how the US spent billions of dollars by meddling widely in other countries elections.[50]

---

49 Andrew C. McCarthy, *Ball of Collusion: The Plot to Rig an Election and Destroy a Presidency* (San Francisco: Encounter Books, 2019); Julie Kelly, *Disloyal Opposition: How the Never Trump Right Tried And Failed To Take Down the President* (San Francisco: Encounter Books, 2020); Roger Stone, The Myth of Russian Collusion: The Inside Story of How Donald Trump Really Won (New York: Skyhorse, 2019); George Papadopoulos, Deep State Target: How I got Caught in the Crosshairs of the Plot to Bring Down President Trump (New York: Diversion Books, 2019); Brent Bozell and Tim Graham, *Unmasked: Big Media's War Against Trump* (West Palm Beach, FL: Humanix Books, 2019); Matthew G Whitaker, *Above the Law: the Inside Story of How the Justice Department Tried to Subvert President Trump* (Washington, DC: Regnery, 2020); Gregg Jarrett, *Witch Hunt: The Story of the Greatest Mass Delusion in American Political History* (New York: Broadside Books, 2019); Michael Savage, *Stop Mass Hysteria: America's Insanity from the Salem Witch Trials to the Trump Witch Hunt, from the Red Scare to Russian Collusion* (New York: Center Street, 2018)

50 For more on a specific case of meddling of the Clinton administration into the 1996 Russian elections on behalf of Boris Yeltsin, see David Strickland,

In her turn, Koffler, a conservative-leaning and Soviet-born former CIA officer, challenged the narrative about Trump being Putin's agent by separating Russia's espionage activities in the US and Trump's agenda. Her thesis is that Putin in fact did not have any "party preferences." Instead, the Russian dictator simply sought to undermine the political system in US by creating chaos and pitching democrats and republicans against each other.[51]

Scholarly Insights into the "Russian Collusion"

Stephen Cohen, an editor of the left-wing *Nation* magazine, has produced the first book-length scholarly study that, among other topics, addressed the "Russian Collusion" factor that, incidentally, he has labeled "Russiagate."[52] Although a committed leftist, Cohen has always sided with Russian imperialists over Ukraine and has adopted Russian imperial nationalist and the Kremlin's paradigms when analyzing Ukraine's regional diversity. In his *War with Russia? From Putin & Ukraine to Trump & Russiagate* (2019), Cohen, although himself a left-winger, challenged the left-liberal narrative "Russiagate" while simultaneously rejecting apologetic pro-Trump "deep state" arguments. This was undertaken at the same time as presenting Putin's Russia's foreign policy, including towards Ukraine, in a very favorable light.

Discussing both the situation surrounding Ukraine and "Russiagate," Cohen has downplayed domestic policy factor and focused exclusively on external factors and foreign policies, which has undermined his analysis. Thus, he has neglected the roots of the 2014 Euromaidan Revolution against a corrupt, authoritarian leader, Viktor Yanukovych, and made absurd claims that the Maidan protestors were CIA puppets. Cohen also insisted that the

---

"Overriding Democracy: American Intervention in Yeltsin's 1996 Reelection Campaign," *Footnotes: A Journal of History*, vol. 4 (2020), https://journals.uair.arizona.edu/index.php/UAHISTJRNL/article/view/23567/22426

51 Dan Kovalik, *Plot to Control the World* (New York: Hot Books, 2018); Rebekah Koffler *Putin's Playbook: Russia's Secret Plan to Defeat America* (Washington, D.C: Regnery, 2021).

52 Stephen F. Cohen, *War with Russia: From Putin & Ukraine to Trump & Russiagate* (New York: Skyhorse, 2019).

killings of the protestors was a false flag operation by Ukrainian nationalists.

One of the first scholars to draw attention to the domestic sources of the "collusion" narrative was historian of the Soviet Union Stephen Kotkin. As early as 2019, commenting on the results of the Mueller investigation, when the "collusion" campaign reached its heights, he noted, "The obsession with Russian interference and the madcap speculation that Trump is a Kremlin asset have helped exclude many of the domestic problems that made Trump's homegrown victory possible."[53] Particularly, Kotkin drew on the above-mentioned Hofstadter "paranoid style" metaphor to address both the obsessive fixation in Putin's Russia on the CIA and State Department's "omnipotent" anti-Russian forces and the craze regarding the "Russian Collusion" in the United States. Kotkin attempted to briefly outline the whole US domestic context that made the "collusion" narrative possible. Thus, he noted the attempt on the part of FBI to investigate possible Trump-Russian links — an operation that was caught in the crossfire[54] of the heated 2016 presidential campaign, where both sides sought to gather dirt on each other.

In a snowball effect, as Kotkin suggested, the Russia "collusion" narrative acquired a life of its own and led to an avalanche of media accusations, while Hillary Clinton and many Democrats who were shell-shocked by their loss, declared Trump an

---

53 Stephen Kotkin, "American Hustle: What Mueller Found and Didn't Find About Trump and Russia," *Foreign Policy*, July/August (2019): 72.
54 Ironically, the surveillance operation that FBI initiated regarding Trump and members of his team was called "Hurricane Crossfire." For more on this operation from the conservative perspective, see Julian Sanchez, "The Crossfire Hurricane Report's Inconvenient Findings," *Just Security*, December 11, 2019, https://www.justsecurity.org/67691/the-crossfire-hurricane-reports-inconvenient-findings/. For more about the same operation from an anti-Trump perspective, see the memoirs of special assistant to FBI director: Josh Campbell, *Crossfire Hurricane: Inside Donald Trump's War on the FBI* (Chapel Hill, North Carolina: Algonquin Books of Chapel Hill, 2019). See also United States. Congress. Senate. Committee on Homeland Security, *Congressional oversight in the face of executive branch and media suppression: the case study of Crossfire Hurricane*: 116th Congress, 2nd session, December 3, 2020 (Washington: U.S. Government Publishing Office, 2020).

illegitimate president;[55] ironically, with the Democrats' victory in 2020, the right came up with a similar accusation, arguing the election was stolen through the machination of "deep state" bureaucrats and left-wing activists.[56] Seeking to exonerate himself, Trump, dragged his political insecurities into the international arena, which led to episodes that were embarrassing for US international standing. Thus, during the Trump-Putin Helsinki meeting, the US president tried to publicly involve Putin into debunking the collusion myth. Essentially, the US foreign policy became a hostage of American domestic political squabbles.

Kotkin also drew attention to the fact that traditionally wide espionage activities that the Soviets and Russians have been conducting in the United States since the 1930s were suddenly amplified for American domestic consumption between 2016-2020. In the meantime, the emerging narrative "conveniently ignores countless other instances of countries doing just that."[57] Kotkin also stressed that, in a backlash reaction, the political tug-of-war between Republicans and Democrats, along with revelations about FBI surveillance of the Trump team in 2015-2017, led many on the right to

---

55 Colby Itkowitz, "Hillary Clinton: Trump is an 'Illegitimate President," *Washington Post*, September 26, 2019, https://www.washingtonpost.com/politics/hillary-clinton-trump-is-an-illegitimate-president/2019/09/26/29195d5a-e099-11e9-b199-f638bf2c340f_story.html; Terry Gross, "Clinton Won't Rule Out Questioning 2016 Election, But Says No Clear Means To Do So," *NPR Fresh Air*, September 18, 2017; Ashe Schow, "The Left's Miraculous Change of Heart on Accepting Election Results," *Observer*, November 28, 2016, https://observer.com/2016/11/the-lefts-miraculous-change-of-heart-on-accepting-election-res ults/; Dan Mangan, "Democratic Party Files Suit Alleging Russia, the Trump Campaign, and WikiLeaks Conspired to Disrupt the 2016 election," *CNBC*, April 20 (2018), https://www.cnbc.com/2018/04/20/democratic-party-files-suit-alleging-russia-the-trump-campaign-and-wikileaks-conspired-to-disrupt-the-2016-election-report.html; Andrew Prokop, "Be Very Skeptical of Stolen Election Claims," *Vox*, November 23, 2016, https://www.vox.com/2016/11/22/13721426/election-hacked-stolen-trump-russia; Betsy Sinclair, Steven S. Smith, and Patrick Tucker, "'It's Largely a Rigged System': Voter Confidence and the Winner Effect in 2016," *Political Research Quarterly*, 71, no. 4 (2018): 854-868.
56 Susan Milligan Nov. 16, 2021 "Republicans Cling to Voter Fraud Claims—at Their Own Peril," *US News and World Report*, November 16, 2021, https://www.usnews.com/news/politics/articles/2021-11-16/republicans-cling-to-v oter-fraud-claims-at-their-own-peril
57 Kotkin, "American Hustle," 72.

accept their own conspiracy theory about powerful "deep state" forces and an elusive "cabal" of government and intelligence bureaucrats, who, in their view, had banded together to topple Trump as early as 2015.[58]

What the "deep state" narrative proponents viewed as an organized sinister plot was in fact a spontaneous and uncoordinated resistance of the government bureaucracy, transnational monopolies, left-wing groups, and liberal and neoconservative think tanks that did not want to accept as president an unvetted politician who had no political experience and who wanted to drastically steer the country away from liberal internationalism toward civic nationalism and isolationism. Kotkin also remarked that the actual "deep state" that might have thwarted the efforts of the "inconvenient" president was Trump's own team whose members sought to mute parts of the abovementioned agenda they considered too reckless and dangerous.[59]

So far, the only comprehensive study of the "collusion" topic has been produced by left-leaning pro-Russian British scholar Sakwa.[60] He has compared the "collusion" (like Cohen, Sakwa refers to it as "Russiagate") with the 1919 Red Scare and McCarthyism in the 1950s, arguing that the left-liberal establishment, frustrated at the results of the 2016 elections, sought to discredit their legitimate political opponents by tying them to an external enemy.[61] Sakwa argued that the setbacks that the liberal mainstream experienced in 2016 prompted it to look beyond US borders for explanations: "As the Russiagate affair demonstrated, Russia acts as the scapegoat for problems generated by domestic contradictions. In that case, Russian meddling helped explain how the most

---

58 The best example of such conspiracy theory approach was demonstrated by a conservative political science scholar and independent journalist Jerome R Corsi, *Killing the Deep State: the Fight to Save President Trump* (West Palm Beach, FL: Humanix Books, 2018).
59 Kotkin, "American Hustle," 66.
60 Sakwa's research on this topic, can be found both in his article and book that has been simultaneously published in 2021. Since his book was not yet available during my work on this article, I relied on his paper: Sakwa, "Greater Russia: Is Moscow out to Subvert the West?"
61 Ibid., 337.

improbable of candidates was able to win against an experienced politician, Hillary Clinton, with a long record of public service."[62]

Regarding temporary alliances that Putin's regime sought to strike with Western right-wing populists and that were frequently presented as evidence of collusion, Sakwa dismissed them as an occasional marriage of convenience. He also has stressed that Russia was not the main instigator and beneficiary of the "nationalist and populist insurgency" in Europe and North America.[63] Although he has correctly debunked those authors who insisted that populist nationalists in Europe and North America are fundamentally anti-Western, unfortunately, Sakwa has not explained the dramatic change of the identity of the right-wing since the 1960s, which in fact reveals fundamental differences, especially in domestic policies, between Putin's regime, which seeks to curtail classical liberal values, and most of the current mainstream Western right-wing that aspires to defend them. More careful reading of the ongoing conservative, nationalist, and libertarian "insurgency" would have shown that, despite their strong anti-globalist sentiments (which in fact transgresses the existing left-right ideological divide), the Western right are now more focused on defending classical liberal values (individualism, rule of law, constitutionalism), civic nationalism, and local autonomy.

What is clearly missing in the current right-wing mainstream in the West and especially in North America is racism, xenophobia, and "fascism" (state worship, collectivism, and corporativism), traits that had indeed been widespread on the right prior to the 1960s and that establishment figures and opinion makers on the left-liberal spectrum continue to ascribe to it. Incidentally, the best litmus test here is attitudes toward freedom of speech and the rule of law. In opposition to the current right, the present-day left-liberal mainstream in the United States calls for the eradication of "harmful" and "hate" speech, simultaneously promoting so-called equity (equality of outcomes) by trying to tilt the existing legal, social, and economic system toward greater "racial and gender "justice."

---

62 Ibid., 355.
63 Ibid., 345.

Conclusions

The story of the "Russian Collusion" proves that conspiracy theories do not simply emerge out of thin air. They frequently appear spontaneously when societies undergo a dramatic socio-economic transformation and when established elites feel that ideology and familiar rhetoric that they use to shield their own interests and control societies suddenly lose their effect. Under these circumstances, elites spontaneously search for and fall back on other convenient and familiar narratives they inherited as part of their mainstream upbringing and establishment culture. Since 2008, the left-liberal establishment successfully shielded President Obama by dismissing any criticism of his social and economic policies as manifestations of racism on the part of retrograde Republicans. That potent rhetoric was effective for a long while because it appealed to American historical memory. In fact, by the early 2000s, that rhetoric was already utilized on a wide scale as a political weapon both on the left and on the right. Essentially, it became part of the American mainstream because a large part of the US elite (the left, liberals, and neoconservatives) had matured in the 1960s-1980s, being saturated with the New Left political culture of "diversity." For example, the American left and liberals never missed c chance to accus their opponents of being anti-black and anti-Hispanic, whereas the latter routinely blamed their opponents for being anti-Semitic and anti-Asian. At the same time, between 2008 and 2016, that rhetoric was monopolized and amplified by Democrats to shield their social, economic, and political agenda.

When against all expectations the non-systemic and unvetted presidential candidate—Trump—won the 2016 elections, the shell-shocked establishment began feverishly looking for explanations. Although by default that old anti-racism rhetoric continued to persist in the left-liberal mainstream, it did not affect Trump whose populist message of civic nationalism and isolationism transgressed ethnic and racial borders; some media also attempted to smear Trump supporters as misogynists who hated Hillary Clinton because she was a woman, yet this label could not compete in its potency with the cry racism narrative that too somewhat became worn out and started losing its popularity. Under these circumstances, the "Russian Collusion" emerged as a handy and effective propaganda weapon against conservatives.

The anti-American and anti-Western sentiments of the Putin regime that were escalating since 2007 provided the ready ammunition that could be used to confirm "Russian Collusion." Meanwhile, the Kremlin promoted its own conspiracy theories about US and NATO plots through color revolutions to undermine the core spiritual values of Russia and her geopolitical interests. Russia's interference into American politics during the Obama era, Cold War legacy practices that permeated the US foreign policy and security apparatus, and finally Trump's flamboyant isolationism provided a fertile background for the emergence of the "Russian Collusion" narrative. In this atmosphere, widely circulated stories about Trump being a Russian agent and the "Steele dossier," which was promoted by the Democrats to smear him in the elections, appeared credible to a large segment of the American public. Finally, the United States having little to lose during a potential confrontation with the Putin regime made it easy to railroad the "Russian Collusion" narrative.

German Self-Images and Russia's Influence

Andreas Heinemann-Grüder

The worldview of German politics over the last fifty years collapsed with Russian President Vladimir Putin's invasion of Ukraine. The justifications for special relations with Russia have seemed increasingly bizarre in recent years. However, in order to say goodbye to one's own beliefs and wishful thinking, the unambiguity of a war was needed. When the Green Party introduced a motion in the Bundestag in June 2021 for a change of course in Germany's Russia policy, the bill was rejected in a direct vote by a majority of the Christian democrats (CDU/CSU), the social democrats (SPD), the nationalist-populist *Alternative für Deutschland* (Alternative Germany [AfD)] and *Die Linke* (The Left) against the vote of *Bündnis 90/Die Grünen* (Alliance 90/The Greens), with the liberal Freie Demokratische Partei (Free Democratic Party [FDP]) abstaining.[1] There was cross-party consensus on the policy of appeasement, including Greens, who did not want to supply Ukraine with weapons for self-defense until the invasion. Putin's regime should not be snubbed by criticism under any circumstances because this could lead to war and damage business. The self-image of German policy up to the war can be summarized in three formulas: "Never again war with Russia, even if its victims stand alone," "Values are nice, business is more important," and "In case of war—without me."

In May 2021, Nikolay Mitrokhin and I wrote in the monthly magazine *Osteuropa*:

> "The policy of the Federal Republic of Germany towards Russia needs a fundamental reorientation, starting with a clear definition of its own priorities, certainty about its own values and an illusionless understanding of the authoritarian character of the Russian political system. The Russian regime is a rival in the competition between socio-political systems, a security risk and a threat to the free democratic world. German policy toward Russia must strengthen resistance to anti-democratic influences in Germany and the EU,

---

1 https://www.bundestag.de/dokumente/textarchiv/2021/kw23-de-russland-politik-843426.

protect security in eastern Europe, advocate freedom of choice of the political system and foreign and security alliances of neighboring states, and vigorously assist those who are victims of repression."[2]

The appeal remained without any response.

German *Ostpolitik* had always been guided by a supposed realism, namely the possibility of a balance of interests between different social orders. Germany's policy of détente toward the Soviet Union and later Russia was based on a belief in its own "civilian power," on business interests dressed up as "change through trade," on a preference for Russia over the other victims of Nazism, and on a resentment toward the United States among the left, the social democrats, parts of the CDU, and the extreme right. Russia, notwithstanding the radicalization of its autocracy, stood for the possibility of a convergence of systems. Ultimately, however, German policy toward Russia was guided only by a Stockholm syndrome. If Putin were not provoked by military maneuvers, arms deliveries to Ukraine or sanctions, he could be somehow tamed.

The Legacy of the Policy of Détente

Those wishing to examine the influence of Russian policy toward Germany must understand the background to its openness to Russian overtures. In the last fifty years, German policy towards Russia has seen itself as a bridge-builder towards the Soviet Union, then towards Russia. Feelings of guilt due to Nazi crimes committed in World War II, a frontline position in the Cold War, a romantic affinity to Russia since the 19th century, gratitude for President Mikhail Gorbachev's enabling of German unity, pacifism and anti-Americanism are mixed with the special relationship with Russia. Germany's *Ostpolitik*, by which Germany's Russia policy was defined, was credited with bringing about change through rapprochement and thus overcoming East-West confrontation, even with inspiring Gorbachev's perestroika. Before and during the Cold War, relations with Russia were characterized by the supposed second-

---

2   Andreas Heinemann-Grüder, Nikolay Mitrokhin, 'Für eine neue Russland-Politik' *Osteuropa*, 3 (2021): 91-98.

rate status of countries in *Mitteleuropa* (Middle Europe), which had historically been divided between the great powers. Although there were early analyses and warnings of authoritarian regression in Russia, German policy cooperated with a deeply corrupt and authoritarian regime, allowing it access to critical infrastructures in Germany; namely *Gazprom* and its subsidiaries.

After 1989, German self-image vis-à-vis Russia could be presented as a civilian power. Germany should never again pose a threat to world peace, and its neighbors to the east and west should have no reason for security fears. Russia was to become part of a "Common European Home" and a pan-European peace order was to include Russia, based on the OSCE Charter of Paris adopted in 1990, the Council of Europe and its Convention on Human Rights. Regardless of whether Russia would democratize, it was too big to be included in the EU or NATO.

For many Western Europeans, Russia is distant and present only through the ubiquity of its consumers with purchasing power. Politically, Europe's borders since 1945 have always been defined by its relationship to the West. When Russians, Central Asians, Ukrainians or the people of the South Caucasus speak of Europe, they mean an ideal Europe, a European value area. In Germany, Russia was always the counterweight to a rejected or only half-completed orientation toward the West. German perceptions of Russia changed from Bismarck to the Treaty of Rapallo to the Hitler-Stalin Pact, from German partition to the policy of détente, from Gorbachev to Putin. For Germany's politicians, with the exception of Adenauer's CDU and the Bündnis 90/Die Grünen party, the "long road to the West" was never fully completed or only halfway. After Adenauer, "value-based" foreign policy always found a limit with the need for a policy of balance, if not equidistance from the great powers. After 1989, most Eastern Europeans were therefore ideally much more Western than Germany, which saw itself as a mediator between East and West. Germany wanted to be a bridge builder to Russia, but in doing so it contributed to the division of Europe.

Since the Ukraine crisis in 2014, the German population as a whole has been more critical of Russia than the political and economic elites. In March 2015, an Allensbach opinion poll pointed to the German public's clear position on who was primarily responsible for the conflict in Ukraine. Fifty-five per cent of respondents blamed Russia while only 20 per cent blamed Ukraine. Only 17 per cent said the USA was responsible—a revealing statistic given the anti-American streak in German public opinion. Sixty-one per cent believed Russia was seeking to conquer Ukraine. At the same time, only 8 per cent of respondents said they had a positive view of Putin, down from 43 per cent in 2001.[3] The overwhelmingly critical attitude, however, was time and again followed by a quest for appeasement. In a YouGov poll in late 2019, 54 per cent of respondents said they favored cooperation over deterrence in dealing with Russia while 55 per cent wanted Europe to be responsible for its defense without the USA.[4]

Pro-Russian Positions in Academia

The vast majority of German experts on Eastern Europe and Russia at universities and think tanks, especially renowned historians and political scientists, take a critical stance toward Russia's autocracy and aggression. Among established scholars, there are only a few *Putinverseteher* (Russia Understanders). Among law experts, there is only one notable exception. The jurist Reinhard Merkel, professor emeritus of criminal law, denied Russia had annexed Crimea because the majority of Crimean inhabitants had wanted to join Russia. However, under international law, secessionism in eastern Ukraine was allegedly a gray area. Merkel disputed Ukraine's right to use force against separatists.[5] The position of Merkel, who is not an expert on international law, was often quoted by sympathizers of Russian policy, but remained a confused single position. Even Norman Paech, an international law expert who is otherwise very

---

3 John Lough, *Germany's Russia Problem. The Struggle for Balance in Europe* (Manchester: Manchester University Press. Kindle Version, 2021). 160.
4 Ibid, 161.
5 Reinhard Merkel, *Internationales Völkerrecht – eine juristische Sicht auf die Krim und den Donbass* (2014), https://www.internetz-zeitung.eu/index.php/2597-völkerrechtsprofessor-merkel-krim-einverleibung-durch-russland-war-keine-annektion; https://www.rubikon.news/artikel/Die Krim und das Völkerrecht | Rubikon.

critical of the United States and who was for a time a member of the Left Party in the Bundestag, considered the annexation of Crimea to be unconstitutional and contrary to international law.[6]

Political scientist Johannes Varwick initiated an appeal in December 2021, hoping to find a way out of the "spiral of escalation" through dialogue with Russia. The appeal called for a permanent security conference, refraining from deploying additional troops on either side of the Russian border, transparency in military maneuvers, reviving the NATO-Russia Council, and deepening economic ties. A decline of energy exports from Russia could lead to political instability, the appeal warned.[7] The appeal was signed by a number of military officials, as well as a former German ambassador to Moscow and political science professors who have traditionally been supporters of détente. At the same time on December 17, 2021, Russia submitted a draft security guarantees treaty with NATO, that expected it to refrain from stationing troops and weapons in the member states who had joined after May 1997. NATO was also asked to commit itself to not accept new members and to not engage in military activities in Eastern Europe, Ukraine, the South Caucasus, and Central Asia. In addition, no short- or medium-range missiles were to be stationed in areas that could reach the territory of the other side.[8] Ultimately, Russia demanded a reversal of NATO enlargement and recognition of the former Warsaw Treaty area as Russia's sphere of influence. Russia expected NATO not to support Ukraine militarily while imposing no obligation on itself to renounce force.

These Russian demands were so unrealistic that even in the Kremlin their implementation was never expected. Why should NATO concede to Russia the entire former USSR and Eastern Europe as its exclusive sphere of military influence? The appeal by

---

6   Norman Paech, *Wem gehört die Krim? Die Krimkrise und das Völkerrecht, Norman Paech – Völkerrecht I* (norman-paech.de), Krimkrise und Völkerrecht 07-14.pdf (2014).
7   https://www.gsp-sipo.de/news/news-details/aufruf-zur-verbesserung-der-beziehungen-zu-russland.
8   Agreement on measures to ensure the security of The Russian Federation and member States of the North Atlantic Treaty Organization, 17 December 2021 13:26; https://mid.ru/ru/foreign_policy/rso/nato/1790803/?lang=en.

Varwick and his co-signers relied on confidence-building measures, assuming Russia would back down from its maximum demands at an OSCE conference.

Peace and conflict researchers occupy a special position in the German academic community. The German peace research institutes publish a peace report once a year, which is presented in the Bundestag, at the Federal Press Conference and in a number of ministries, and finds resonance in the media. If there was a permanent dispute among the participating institutes from Frankfurt, Hamburg, Duisburg and Bonn, it was over the Federal Republic of Germany's policy toward Russia. The positions of Putin Understanders were often enforced by ultimatums. Russia's annexation of Crimea, for example, was not allowed to be described as an annexation. In March 2022, the four directors of the Peace Research Institutes wrote a paper that was presented to the German Foreign Office. The paper placed blame equally on both parties to the conflict. Sanctions should not hit Putin's regime, only defensive weapons should be delivered, and sanctions relief should be promised, all without any conditions.[9]

The pro-Russian positions of peace and conflict research institutes serve the expectations of those who belonged to the peace movement in the 1980s. In the present, these are predominantly older people in the Protestant Church and the Catholic Church or pacifist organizations close to them. In 2017, Mathias Dembinski and Achim Spanger of the Hessian Foundation for Peace and Conflict Research, Germany's largest peace research institute in Frankfurt, called on German policymakers to change course toward Putin.[10] According to Spanger and Dembinski, the expansive, even aggressive West has expanded and Russia was portrayed as a victim of Western expansion. According to Spanger and Dembinski, Russia distances itself from the colonialism of "liberal peace," refusing to be treated in a subaltern manner. The authors wrongly

---

9 The paper, which was presented to the Foreign Ministry of Germany, was not published, but the author holds a copy.
10 Matthias Dembinski, Hans-Joachim Spanger, 'Pluraler Frieden. Leitideen für eine neue Russlandpolitik,' *Osteuropa* 3-4 (2017), 87-96.

reinterpreted the Charter of Paris (1990), the normative foundation of the post-Cold War world. From the very beginning Russia was allegedly only concerned with equality and security policy rather than democracy and human rights. Russian policy was no longer interpreted as a departure from a previously shared normative order, but as a liberation from a "liberal peace" that supposedly bore colonial features.

Spanger and Dembinski's theses amount to a reinterpretation of the past. Yet, "the West" by no means imposed perestroika and regime change on the Soviet Union. Gorbachev was not the result of Western expansion. On the contrary, it was the Russian elites who recognized the advantages of market reforms. The plutocracy of Russia's current rulers was not imposed on them by a "liberal peace" of the West, but was in the interest of Russia's state-capitalist elites and oligarchs

Spanger and Dembinski tie this in with the policy of détente, which recognized neither East European opposition movements nor the legitimacy crisis of the communist regime. The détente policy was state-fixated, assuming the sovereignty of states as if they possessed ultimate decision-making powers.[11] Spanger and Dembinski argued for recognition of Russian interests without legitimation; their plea for a "plural peace" amounted to acceptance of Russian spheres of influence, especially in the form of a veto right for Russia over future EU and NATO membership of post-Soviet states. The call for a "plural peace" meant a peace that recognized Russian predominance in the post-Soviet space and no longer relied on democracy and the rule of law. Talk of "plural peace" was not based on the sovereignty of peoples or "sovereignty as responsibility", it did not even return to the primacy of state sovereignty. Indeed, the definition of sovereignty in "plural peace" was left to Russia, because it was supposed to be able to decide how "plural" a country like Ukraine may be.

The political scientist and publicist Herfried Münkler, who is well-known in Germany, also argued from a supposedly "realistic"

---

11   Timothy Garton Ash, *In Europe's Name: Germany and the Divided Continent* (New York: Knopf Doubleday 1994).

perspective. Russia should have been assured of Ukraine's neutrality before the war, combined with security guarantees for Ukraine. Münkler, however, left unmentioned who should have provided security guarantees to Ukraine. Immense destruction and tens of thousands of deaths could allegedly have been avoided. "Perhaps the territorial integrity of Ukraine, as it existed at the beginning of the war, could have been secured," Münkler surmised. "And, for that matter, a European level of prosperity."[12] Ukraine must remain a non-aligned buffer state, Münkler declares. At the same time, he recognizes that Putin is concerned with the renewal of empire (i.e., not only with neutrality). For Münkler, Ukraine is merely the battleground of a confrontation between Russia and the West. Münkler's argument culminates in the key sentence where Ukraine should not inflict high casualties on Russia, because high casualties would make it more difficult for Russia to exit the war: "That would be understandable in collective psychological terms, but strategically and geopolitically a disaster." Münkler thus varies the thesis according to which Russia should not be provoked by military resistance. Münkler leaves unanswered, why Russia would become willing to negotiate if there was no resistance by Ukraine. For Münkler, Ukraine's sovereignty is ultimately negligible and negotiable. Münkler expresses himself incoherently. His supposed "realism" clings to the old delusion that Putin is concerned with limited (i.e., negotiable, security policy goals).

German Political Parties on Russia

Understanding and sympathy for Putin's policies are articulated in Germany by the Left Party (especially Sahra Wagenknecht, Oskar Lafontaine, and Wolfgang Gehrcke-Reymann) and, on the right, by the AfD (namely Alexander Gauland). Among the ruling parties that solicited understanding for Putin's regime, the SPD stands out. Former SPD Chancellor Helmut Schmidt (a Wehrmacht officer who participated in the blockade of Leningrad) found Russian actions in Crimea "quite understandable." He considered sanctions "stupid

---

12 Interview with Herfried Münkler: Die Ukraine wird unter die Räder kommen, wie immer die Sache ausgeht, *Neue Zürcher Zeitung* 19 May 2022.

stuff." The situation in Ukraine was dangerous, he said—but he blamed the West.[13] Schmidt criticized the West for using human rights as a political weapon, as if human rights were nothing more than an aggressive term for interference in the internal affairs of a country.[14] In 2014, Egon Bahr, the intellectual "father" of the policy of détente under Chancellor Willy Brandt, called for "respect" for the annexation of Crimea.[15] Like Helmut Schmidt, ex-Chancellor Gerhard Schröder spoke out against sanctions and in favor of "dialogue" with his friend Putin. Immediately after being voted out as chancellor in 2005, Schröder became chairman of the shareholders' committee of the pipeline company Northstream, in which Gazprom holds a 51 percent stake and Wintershall (a wholly owned BASF subsidiary) and EON who each held 15.5 percent.[16]

Matthias Platzeck, former prime minister of Brandenburg and for a time chairman of the SPD, has argued for years that Russia's fear of encirclement should be taken seriously, and that we are in a community of fate with Russia. He called for the annexation of Crimea to be settled under international law.[17] The late SPD politician Erhard Eppler, who had joined the NSDAP at the age of 16, reproached the U.S. for being interested in the Ukraine conflict, saying Russia's behavior should not be branded as aggression. There were supposedly no Russian troops in the Donetsk and Luhansk regions. The Ukrainian government installed as a result of the Maidan had sought confrontation with Russia, according to Eppler.[18]

---

13   https://www.spiegel.de/politik/ausland/helmut-schmidt-verteidigt-in-krim-krise-putins-ukraine-kurs-a-960834.html.
14   https://www.youtube.com/watch?v=fetPiGwnqNM.
15   https://www.stern.de/politik/ausland/ukraine-konflikt--egon-bahr-fordert--respektierung--der-krim-annexion-3242510.html.
16   Susanne Spahn, *Das Ukraine-Bild in Deutschland. Die Rolle der russischen Medien. Wie Russland die deutsche Öffentlichkeit beeinflusst* (Berlin, Institut für Strategie-, Politik-, Sicherheits- und Wirtschaftsberatung, 2016), 51.
17   Matthias Platzeck Interview Deutschlandfunk, 17 Nov. 2014, http://www.deutschlandfunk.de/europa-und-russland-wir-sollten-es-uns-nicht-zu-leicht.694.de.html?dram:article_id=303403; Platzeck fordert Anerkennung der Krim-Annexion, Zeit online, 18 Nov. 2014, http://www.zeit.de/politik/ausland/2014-11/platzeck-russland-ukraine.
18   Erhard Eppler: Einen Sieg wird es nicht geben. *Süddeutsche Zeitung* 11 February 2015, https://www.sueddeutsche.de/politik/ukraine-konflikt-einen-sieg-wird-es-nicht-geben-1.2344320.

Klaus von Dohnanyi, former federal minister and SPD mayor of Hamburg, also viewed the U.S. as the culprit in the conflict with Putin's Russia:

> "There are people in the establishment in Washington who have had nothing else on their minds for decades but to push Russia back further. That may be in their geopolitical interest, but it is not in Europe's interest. And we would have to make that clearer in Washington for once."[19]

These SPD politicians are united by a deep-seated anti-Americanism, a preference for economic interests over human rights, a self-image as a therapist for the wounded Russian soul, and a romantic, transfiguring view of Russia.

In an appeal published on December 5, 2014 by more than 60 personalities from politics, business, culture and the media, the signatories warned against a war with Russia and called for a new policy of détente. In the appeal "War again in Europe? Not in our name!" the signatories, who included former Chancellor Gerhard Schröder and former German President Roman Herzog, complained the United States and Canada were driving the European Union and Russia toward war.[20] The appeal spoke of the West's "expansion eastward, threatening to Russia, without a simultaneous deepening of cooperation with Moscow" — this narrative then served as an explanation for Russia's annexation of Crimea. Although Russia had annexed Crimea and invaded the Donbass, it was declared, "the Russians' need for security is as legitimate and pronounced as that for the Germans, the Poles, the Balts, and the Ukrainians." The perpetrator was re-declared to be a victim.

In contrast, a counter-call by renowned experts on Eastern Europe declared,

> "German policy on Eastern Europe should be based on empirical values, factual knowledge and the results of analysis, and not on pathos, forgetfulness of history and sweeping judgments. No one favors a military confrontation with Russia or wants to break off dialogue with the Kremlin.

---

19 Klaus von Dohnanyi, *Nationale Interessen. Orientierung für deutsche und europäische Politik in Zeiten globaler Umbrüche*, München.
20 https://www.zeit.de/politik/2014-12/aufruf-russland-dialog.

However, the territorial integrity of Ukraine, Georgia and Moldova cannot be sacrificed to the "prudence" of German (and Austrian) Russian policy."[21]

After February 24, 2022, Putin sympathizers were at first silent. Two months later, however, some of them again commented with an open letter to Chancellor Scholz, in which they said, on the one hand, that there must be resistance to aggression, but on the other hand, they called on the German chancellor to not supply Ukraine with heavy weapons.[22] Otherwise, Germany would contribute to escalation. In other words, only a weakening of Ukraine would lead to de-escalation. Moreover, arms deliveries would increase the suffering of the Ukrainian population (not Russian military attacks). The chancellor was addressed as a representative of universally valid norms; in contrast to the Ukrainian president, who was implicitly accused of representing particular interests.

Under the cloak of pacifism and a self-attested moral universalism, the signatories called on the German government to deny military support to Ukraine, hoping to be spared from a nuclear war by Putin. The "logic" was in line with the old thinking: Whoever does not provoke Putin will receive peace from him as a gift. The fact that this cynical "pacifism" of German celebrities is willing to sacrifice Ukraine for their own peace of mind bears colonial traits and orientalism. Among the signatories was the aforementioned law expert Merkel. His brother, political scientist and member of the SPD's Basic Values Commission, Wolfgang Merkel, was also among them. For a long time, Wolfgang Merkel had classified Putin's autocracy as a "defective democracy".

Although there was sharp criticism of this appeal, it made it clear that the ghosts of the past had not yet fully disappeared as a result of Putin's war. An appeasement policy toward autocrats is deeply rooted in social democracy, but also in the Christian Democratic Party, showing the continuity from the Leonid Brezhnev regime to the present. The "policy of détente" had always preferred elite understandings at the expense of civil society and sovereignty.

---

21 https://www.tagesspiegel.de/politik/gegen-aufruf-im-ukraine-konflikt-osteuropa-experten-sehen-russland-als-aggressor/11105530.html.
22 https://www.emma.de/artikel/offener-brief-bundeskanzler-scholz-339463.

Russian-Speaking Community in Germany

A total of about 3.5 million people lived in Germany in 2019 with an immigrant background from the former Soviet Union, most of whom speak Russian as their first or second language. 2.4 million voters in Germany have a Russian-speaking background. Politically and culturally, these post-Soviet migrants and their descendants are heterogeneous. The Russian-speaking community in Germany is divided in its attitudes toward Putin's Russia, especially between the older generation, which consumes Russian media, and the younger ones, who did not live through their formative years in the Soviet Union. Some Russians with German roots felt perceived and marginalized as Russians, rather than accepted as native Germans, most prefer to communicate among themselves in Russian. The national-populist AfD caters to conservative, illiberal, and chauvinistic values in this community. Putin's image of a strong man reactivated authoritarian and illiberal views among those who had grown up in the Soviet Union. The AfD saw an opportunity to speak to this alienated group and to attempt to attract its support. As early as 2013, Alexander Gauland, the co-founder of the AfD, called for reconnecting with the nineteenth-century Prussian tradition of cultivating close relations with Russia. The party reinforced its anti-establishment credentials by voicing Russia-friendly positions in contrast to the government's support for sanctions.[23]

Since March 2002, motorcades in support of Putin's Russia have been organized worldwide with the support of Russian embassies: including in Serbia, Cyprus, Greece, Montenegro, Italy, France, and Germany. Since March 2022, motorcades have been held in major German cities, such as Berlin, Cologne, Stuttgart, Lahr, Würzburg, Heilbronn, Lörrach, Dresden, Lübeck and Hanover with Russian flags, the St. George ribbon, Soviet flags, the flag of the Black Sea Fleet or flags in black, yellow and white with the double-headed eagle (the emblem of the Tsarist Russian Empire).

Pro-Russian motorcades have been a common feature in Germany since 2017, mostly around commemorative days such as May

---

23 Lough (2021), op. cit., 168.

9. Several hundred Russian-speaking participants from the catchment area of major cities usually take part in the motorcades. The slogans are similar to those used by media loyal to the Kremlin: "Russia feels cornered," "The West is only concerned with economic interests," "We are against discrimination of the Russian population," or "You need denazification in Ukraine."[24] Even though the participants usually speak out in favor of "peace," they gather to demonstrate their solidarity with Putin's war on Ukraine. When asked how they arrive at these assessments and where they receive their information, many demonstrators point to social networks such as Telegram. By contrast, they distrust the traditional German media.

The pictures of German Russians are supposed to show support from Germany to the Russian television audiences. The response from the German population to the "Putinists" is mainly negative, especially since many pro-Ukrainian counter-demonstrations have taken place. Some motorcades were cancelled after pro-Russian organizers feared negative consequences for their business. Their license plates and faces can be photographed and thus identified. One organizer in Berlin, for example, had placed a Star of David at the head of the demonstration with the inscription "Russian" and the question "Soon we too?" The police removed it. The display of the "Z" as a symbol of Russian warfare, visible during some early motorcades, was also prohibited by the German police.

The simultaneity of the motorcades and the uniform slogans suggest there is a central organizational apparatus. The organizers of the pro-Russian motorcades include Russian biker clubs, the association *Pamiat* (Memory), representatives of the Russian foundation *Russkoe pol'e* (Russian Field), the foundation *Russkij Mir* (Russian World) and local groups of the *Bessmertnyi polk* (Immortal Regiment). Soldiers who died in the Great Patriotic War (rather than in the Second World War) are remembered at these motorcades in order to strengthen patriotism for Putin's Russia, to call for German-

---

24 https://www.alamy.de/stockfoto-zuschauer-mit-der-flagge-von-russland-mit-einem-marine-sp"eichern-der-russischen-schwarzmeerflotte-in-sewastopol-kein-model-release-140637117.html.

Russian unity against Ukraine and to win young people over to a militaristic culture. Russia and Germany should stick together, the Germans should not follow the Americans, the British or NATO, but should cultivate German-Russian friendship. Germany would suffer from sanctions and make itself a satellite of the USA. Finally, the motorcades attempt to appeal to a pacifist audience by criticizing military support for Ukraine.

Refugees from Ukraine in Germany in particular feel provoked by pro-Russian motorcades. Russia's war against Ukraine is admittedly causing support for Putin to wane among the Russian-speaking population in Germany, because the longer it goes on the more it is impossible to close one's eyes to what is happening in the war.[25] In almost all major German cities, there were counter-demonstrations by pro-European Russians.

Pro-Russian Publicists and the Media

The German media are strongly fixated on Putin as a person. The number of journalists accredited from Germany in Russia has steadily declined, and working conditions have dramatically deteriorated.[26] Major German newspapers and weeklies, such as *Frankfurter Allgemeine Zeitung, Süddeutsche, Die Zeit, Der Tagesspiegel, Die Welt, Der Spiegel* and *Focus* have for years criticized authoritarian regression in Russia and appeasement policy towards Putin.

More pro-Russian coverage can be found in the *Berliner Zeitung, Neues Deutschland* (formerly the organ of the Socialist Unity Party of the GDR), and *Junge Welt* (formerly the newspaper of the Free German Youth in the GDR). Until the Russian invasion, pro-Russian media in Germany also included *RT Deutsch* and *Sputnik* (German branches of Russian state media), radio stations, such as Ken FM (on the air until 2021), *Compact Magazine* (run by the former extreme left and now populist nationalist Jürgen Elsässer), and

---

25 Natalie Klauser, *Russlanddeutsche im Generationenkonflikt?* (Konrad-Adenauer-Stiftung, 19 April 2022), https://www.kas.de/de/kurzum/detail/-/content/russlanddeutsche-im-generationenkonflikt.

26 Gemma Pörzgen, Das Russlandbild in den deutschen Medien (Bonn, Bundeszentrale für politische Bildung, 2018), https://www.bpb.de/themen/europa/russland/47998/das-russlandbild-in-den-deutschen-medien/.

Seewald TV. Pro-Russian German-language publicists included the self-styled "peace researcher" Daniele Ganser based in Switzerland, as well as the Austrian-based auf1.at TV. Clips from these pro-Russian channels were also distributed in Germany through social media networks. Their pro-Russian rhetoric repeated standard stereotypes such as whataboutism with constant references to US imperialism and NATO expansion. Arms supplies to Ukraine are criticized and the economic consequences of sanctions are lamented. For years, the former editor-in-chief of RT Deutsch, Igor Rodionov, and Dmitry Tulchinsky, bureau chief at RIA Novosti in Berlin, were invited to prominent German talk shows to present the official Russian position in a spirit of pluralism.

A number of Germans or German-Russians regularly appear as "reporters" on Russian TV channels. Their pro-Russian propaganda is presented as the authentic voice of Germany, especially to Russian television audiences. These include the former presenter of RT Deutsch, Lea Frings, and the blogger Thomas Röper (also calling himself Tomas Reper), who has lived in St. Petersburg since 1998. However, Lea Frings, as "the face" of RT Deutsch, left the channel following the station's xenophobic coverage. Alina Lipp, a German-Russian who claims to be a "peace journalist," spreads Putin's version of the liberation and denazification of Ukraine through the Telegram social media app with 130,000 subscribers. She was previously an activist at Querdenker (covid conspiracy theorists) demonstrations in Berlin.[27] Röper appears on Russian television as a witness for Russia's war narrative, "reporting", for example, from the destroyed city of Mariupol. Röper is accredited to the *Inforos* news agency and runs an "anti-Spiegel" portal dedicated to revelations about the German magazine *Der Spiegel*. Röper attributes the massacres of Bucha and Mariupol to the Ukrainians as a false flag operation. The aforementioned journalist-actors serve the Russian war narrative, sweepingly criticize the "mainstream" media, complain of Russia-bashing, and spread conspiracy theories and xenophobia.

---

27 https://www.t-online.de/nachrichten/ausland/id_91759336/alina-lipp-auf-telegramm-einst-bei-den-gruenen-jetzt-putins-infokriegerin-.html.

Publicist and lobbyist Alexander Rahr, who is a frequent voice on Russian TV, worked for the German Council on Foreign Relations until 2012 and is one of the best-known Russia "experts" in Germany. Rahr sat on the steering committee of the Petersburg Dialogue from 2004 to 2015 and has been project director of the German-Russian Forum since 2012. He oversees the "Potsdam Encounters" and the "Lisbon-Vladivostok Common Space" working group. From 2012-2015, he was Senior Advisor to Wintershall Holding GmbH, which has a stake in Northstream, and advisor to the president of the German-Russian Chamber of Commerce Abroad. Since 2014 he was deputy chairman, then member of the advisory board of the Association of Russian Business in Germany. Since 2015, he has in turn been an advisor on EU affairs to Gazprom in Brussels.

Rahr is not active in the academic world, but for years he spoke out in favor of the construction of Northstream I and II Baltic Sea gas pipelines on various television channels. He has always advocated the primacy of German economic interests and opposed NATO's eastward expansion. Germany, he said, was losing its reputation with the Russians through "presumption."[28] Although he used to work for Radio Liberty, Rahr consistently argues from an anti-American position.

Former journalist Gabriele Krone-Schmalz was a correspondent for the ARD station in Moscow from 1987-1991. She appeared regularly on popular talk shows until the war. She has been a member of the steering committee of the Petersburg Dialogue, a government-financed forum with Russian partners, since December 2000 and an Honorary Trustee of the Deutsch-Russisches Forum e. V. since 2021. She thus prominently featured in official German-Russian "dialogue" formats. In books such as *What's Happening in Russia?* (2007) and *Understanding Russia. The Struggle over Ukraine and the Arrogance of the West* (2015), Krone-Schmalz lamented the alleged demonization of Putin. On a talk show, Krone-Schmalz opined the EU caused the war against Ukraine through the Eastern

---

28   Alexander Rahr, *Anmaßung. Wie Deutschland sein Ansehen bei den Russen verspielt* (Berlin: Das neue Berlin, 2021).

Partnership's Association Agreement.[29] Furthermore, a plethora of groups on social networks, including Putinists (German Friends of Vladimir Putin), glorify Putin and his policies and advocate cooperation between Germany and Russia.[30]

Russian television (and Russian social media) likes to feature "experts" from Germany who are completely unknown in Germany. For years, a certain "Professor" Lorenz Haag, head of an "Agency for Global Communication" in Germany, has been acting as a defender of Russia's Ukraine policy. But he does not teach at any German university, there is no academic proof of his professorial title, and his agency does not exist.[31] However, although he has been promoted as a German "expert" by the Russian news agency ITAR-Tass since 2007 in fact his office and title are fictitious.[32]

> "Major Russian media corporations such as *Russia Today* (now RT) and *Sputnik* are well established in Germany, as indicated by their significant social media following and web traffic. They are known for heavily biased, often factually inaccurate reporting critical of the German government, former Chancellor Angela Merkel, and the European Union. However, mirroring the findings of the German intelligence investigation... it is hardly illegal to an extent that would justify censorship or filtering."[33]

According to Neudert's investigation into Russian influence on the 2017 federal elections in Germany, pro-Russian content played only a minor role in internet propaganda and social media. An intelligence officer interviewed by Neudert in 2017 estimated that 10-15 percent of the German population held pro-Russian views, which

---

29 https://www.focus.de/kultur/kino_tv/menschen-bei-maischberger-bei-talk runde-ueber-putins-plaene-fliegen-die-fetzen_id_4500809.html.
30 Spahn (2016), op. cit. 37f.
31 Gesine Dornblüth: *Moskaus Imagearbeit. Professor Haag lobt Russland*, 23 May 2022, https://www.deutschlandfunk.de/moskaus-imagearbeit-professor-haag-lobt-russland-100.html.
32 https://euromaidanpress.com/2014/10/11/wer-sind-sie-professor-haag/.
33 Lisa-Maria N. Neudert, 'Germany A Cautionary Tale,' in *Computational Propaganda. Political Parties, Politicians, and Political Manipulation on Social Media*, edited by Samuel C. Woolley and Philip N. Howard, (Oxford: Oxford University Press, 2017), 173.

were accompanied by skepticism toward the United States and NATO.[34]

Conclusions

Germany's self-image was based on its role as a bridge-builder between Eastern Europeans, traditionally critical of Russia, and the Kremlin, between the bellicose USA and a traumatized Russia. German policy recommended itself as a mediator between the emotionally charged actors, as if Germany stood aside from conflicts and existed on a higher level of perennial peace. Historians will continue to argue about the contribution Germany made to enabling Putinism, as well as about the signals that were missed due to its wishful thinking. Former détente politicians currently feel disavowed; they are preoccupied with amnesia, self-absolution and fending off accusations from Ukraine. Hesitant arms deliveries to Ukraine since February 24, 2022, which have always been made only in response to external pressure, smack of an inability to come to terms with dramatic changes brought about by Russia's invasion.

The war destroys the illusions of German politics. The supposedly "difficult partnership" with Putin's Russia has turned into a dispute that is not based on misunderstandings, communication errors or a lack of consideration for Russia's legitimate security interests, but the irreconcilability of imperialism and international law, of dictatorship and democracy, of liberal and fascist values. With a regime that periodically threatens the use of nuclear weapons in order to be able to wage a war of annihilation against Ukraine undisturbed, there is currently no "cold war" possible, only antagonism. With Putin's regime, there will be ceasefires at best, but no more peace in Europe. The Russian regime is structurally incapable of peace; therefore there will be peace in Europe only after the end of Putin's regime.

---

34 Neudert (2017), op. cit., 151; Camilla Kohrs, 'Russische Propaganda für deutsche Zuschauer,' *CORRECTIV*, 4 January 2017, https://correctiv.org/re cherchen/neue-rechte/artikel/2017/01/04/medien-RT-RTdeutsch-russia-to day/.

The Russian-controlled world and the rest of Europe will be permanently divided. The war is changing Europe; economically by cutting off its ability to be blackmailed by Russian energy supplies, politically by reaffirming Europe's community of values in the face of the Russian threat, and security-wise by remaining dependent on U.S. security guarantees (rather than EU strategic autonomy). Without NATO, there is no security in Europe. The beginning of the end for the Russian petro-state business model has begun. However the Ukraine war ends, Russia will emerge weakened. Russia's future influence in the post-Soviet space (and beyond) will also be diminished by China, Turkey, Iran, the U.S. and the EU.

Germany not only loses its image as a bridge builder between East and West, but also as a power within the EU. A disastrous lack of strategic foresight, the policy of appeasement toward Putin, and hesitation and dithering after February 24 have done lasting damage to Germany's soft power. The supposed equidistance and balance policy vis-à-vis the great powers has been replaced by band wagoning. After the Merkel era, Germany mutated from a crisis manager and diplomatic purveyor of the status quo to that of a band wagoner.

Empire, Sonderwege and Russia
The German Historical Debate about Ukraine

Martin Schulze Wessel

To gauge the extent of Germany's misconceptions about Ukraine, one must go back to the 2014 crisis. The West reacted to the annexation of Crimea and Moscow's continued military intervention in eastern Ukraine with mild sanctions, while at the same time allowing its own energy dependence on Russia to increase. Disregarding Ukraine's concerns, Berlin and Moscow built Nord Stream 2. Part of the historical discussion took a similarly Russophile course. Quite representative of this trend was the stance taken by Berlin historian Jörg Baberowski. When Russia occupied Crimea and supported separatism in Donetsk and Luhansk with military force, Baberowski came up with the thesis that Ukraine was "a child of Soviet nationality policy." He maintained that a fundamental memory-cultural divide ran between the west and the east of Ukraine and asked, "Why should it be ruled out for all time that the eastern part of Ukraine separates from the western part?"[1] Other historians such as Ulrich Schmid and Andreas Kappeler, who unlike Baberowski had extensively studied the history of Ukraine, disagreed. They pointed to the history of the Ukrainian national movement in the nineteenth century and cited the high approval ratings that the foundation of the independent Ukrainian state had found in the east of the country in the wake of the USSR's disintegration. Nevertheless, Baberowski's thesis found its way into political discourse. Fourteen days after the publication of his text, former German Chancellor Helmut Schmidt was quoted in *Die Zeit* on March 27, 2014, immediately after the annexation of Crimea, saying: "It is disputed among historians whether there is a Ukrainian nation at

---

1   Jörg Baberowski. 'Zwischen den Imperien', *Die Zeit*. 2014. No. 12. March 13. https://www.zeit.de/2014/12/westen-russland-konflikt-geschichte-ukraine/komplettansicht.

all."[2] Schmidt would be no doubt surprised to hear he is repeating the same views as Russian imperial nationalists in the Kremlin who deny the existence of Ukraine and Ukrainians.

Now Baberowski has spoken out again after the launch of Russia's invasion of Ukraine in February 2022, this time in the *Frankfurter Allgemeine Zeitung*.[3] He does not explicitly admit his 2014 thesis was mistaken but at least no longer insists on the cultural contrast between western and eastern Ukraine. Somewhat ironically, Baberowski now attributes this claim solely to Putin, who does not understand that "even in the east of the country, citizens have come to terms with the state order because they have been able to find a place in it."[4] While Baberowski no longer insists Ukraine is a failed or fragile nation state, he still does not fully accept reality by suggesting Ukrainians have merely "come to terms" with their nation-state. This is a remarkable understatement that does not capture the new cohesion of Ukrainian society that has shown an extraordinary spirit of resistance after months of military aggression by Russian forces, first concentrating along the border for many months and eventually staging an invasion. Despite immense pressure, local governments in the east of the country showed no inclination to change allegiance and voluntarily accept Russia's rule.

Baberowski becomes more informative when it speaks not about Ukraine but discusses the nature of war in general. Above all, the text is a remarkable historical source documenting the transition announced by Chancellor Olaf Scholz in his special address to the Bundestag on February 27, 2022, that was a *Zeitenwende* (Change of Eras).[5] Turning times are more complex than they seem

---

2 Matthias Naß. '"Putins Vorgehen ist verständlich." Helmut Schmidt über Russlands Recht auf die Krim, die Überreaktion des Westens und den Unsinn von Sanktionen', *Die Zeit*. 2014. No. 14. March 27. https://www.zeit.de/2014/14/helmut-schmidt-russland.
3 Jörg Baberowski. 'Schwieriger Abschied vom Imperium: Der Krieg verändert alles, auch den Angreifer. Was in Zeiten der Gewalt dennoch auf Frieden hoffen lässt', *Frankfurter Allgemeine Zeitung*. 2002. No. 50. March 1. P. 9.
4 Ibid.
5 Rachel Tausendfreund. 'Zeitenwende – The Dawn of the Deterrence Era in Germany', *The German Marshall Fund of the United States*. 2022. February 28. https://www.gmfus.org/news/zeitenwende-dawn-deterrence-era-germany.

at first glance. New realities emerge as some things in the past are adapting to the changed situation, while others that have become outdated persist in the shadow of events and may later unfold with new efficacy. One such remnant in Baberowski's text is the idea the disintegration of the Soviet Union had made Russian life quasi-existential. In a 2015 essay, Baberowski explained the Soviet Union was the "homeland" (*Heimat*) for the Russians.[6] The conventional understanding of home as one's intimate and familiar environment seems at odds with the idea that it can be applied to the entire territory of the largest state in the world with its diverse multicultural populations. Yet, such an overstretched application of the home metaphor provides some justification for Russia's claims for revising its borders. Baberowski has now replaced the word "*Heimat*" with the synonym "*Zuhause*", so the old idea reemerges in the new essay in a different wording: "For most Russians, the Soviet Union was a home (*Zuhause*) they liked to live in. For they had no other."[7]

This sentimental understanding of Russia was strikingly off-key in 2015 and is unbearable today, as Ukrainians have their homes quite literally destroyed by Russian shells and missiles, whole cities razed, and their inhabitants forced to flee in incalculable numbers. This horrible war of aggression was not only looming when Baberowski published his essay, it had already begun one year earlier. By emotionalizing and thus humanizing the alleged empire of memory as "home", Baberowski assigns it an existential meaning, which is quite close to Putin's emotional way of instrumentalizing history. Baberowski cites Putin's televised speech of February 24, 2022, legitimized the war on Ukraine, in which "the otherwise coolly calculating technician of power" went berserk and expressed "rage at the loss of empire." This collectivist explanation, in which Russian cultural patterns, "many Russians," and President Putin merge, diverts attention from individuals to social groups. There is simply no empirical evidence that the restoration

---

6   Jörg Baberowski. 'Der Westen kapiert es nicht', *Die Zeit*. 2015. No. 11. March 12. https://www.zeit.de/2015/11/ukraine-krieg-fehler-usa-europa-putin-treue-russland/komplettansicht.
7   Baberowski. 'Schwieriger Abschied vom Imperium'.

of Soviet borders would have had existential significance for Russians today, either scholarly or by personal anecdote. I heard my interlocutors speaking about such existential desires as freedom and prosperity, or about respect towards the history and culture of Russia, but never about the restoration of old borders. Baberowski himself admits the instrumentalization of imperial nostalgia loses its power and concludes his essay on an uplifting note: "I believe in Russia and its people..." This phrase obviously resonates with the famous line by Russian poet and conservative publicist Fyodor Tyutchev (1803–1873): "In Russia you can only believe."[8]

It is high time to ditch this pseudo-religious Russian kitsch. Putin is recolonizing Eastern Europe. The answer to this must lie in a consistent decolonization of our concepts.[9] In historiography, for example, this requires overcoming the still widespread conventional nineteenth century imperial nationalist scheme of "Russian history." This leads from "Kievan Russia" via Muscovy to the Russian Empire and obscures other narratives, such as the work of the Ukrainian historian Mykhailo Hrushevsky, who as early as in 1904 outlined an alternative historical framework. Hrushevsky's framework included Kyivan Rus as the first Ukrainian state which, after the Mongol invasion in 1240, continued in the Galician-Volhynian Principality, and later in the Polish–Lithuanian republic of nobles — not Muscovy and the Russian Empire. Modern histories of Ukraine, published in Ukraine and in North America since the 1980s, use Hrushevsky's framework.[10] Ukrainian public opinion polls also show that a high majority of Ukrainians view Kyiv Rus as the first

---

8   Fyodor Tyutchev. *Polnoe sobranie stikhotvorenii. Vol. 2*. Moscow, 1994, p. 181.
9   Marina Mogilner. 'There Can Be No "Vne"', *Ab Imperio*. 2021. No. 4, pp. 24–26.
10 Andreas Kappeler. *Ungleiche Brüder: Russen und Ukrainer vom Mittelalter bis zur Gegenwart*, (Munich: C.H. Beck, 2018). For example, Orest Subtelny, *Ukraine. A History*, (Toronto: University of Toronto Press, 1988, 1994, 2000, 2009); Serhii Plokhy, *The Gates of Europe: A History of Ukraine*, (New York: Basic Books, 2015); Paul R. Magocsi, *A History of Ukraine*, (Toronto: University of Toronto Press, 1996) and *A History of Ukraine. The Land and Its People* (Toronto: University of Toronto Press, 2010).

Ukrainian state[11] — not as a state which gave birth to an eastern Slavic pan-Russian people.

Furthermore, it is time to rethink the concept of empire. It has been very productive in historical scholarship over the past decades and undoubtedly has great potential to incorporate different perspectives. At least in the German tradition, it is also associated with certain legacies from the interwar period. When the multiethnic empires in Eastern Europe began to collapse a century ago, many intellectuals of the newly emerging nation states of East Central Europe saw this moment as the fulfilment of a historical promise: Russia, the Habsburg Monarchy, the Ottoman Empire, and Prussia-Germany were regarded by them as soulless and prisons of nations. The Czech philosopher Tomáš Masaryk summed up this view when he wrote the pamphlet "The New Europe (The Slav Standpoint)" in Petrograd in 1917. The most important task after the war was "the reorganization of Eastern Europe" on a national basis because humanity was not something supranational, but the organization of individual nations.[12]

The collapse of empires at the end of World War I brought about not only joy over the destruction of the prisons of nations. Soon the defunct empires became the subject of melancholic contemplation, even among the victorious powers which made the decision to dissolve the Habsburg Monarchy. Remarkable is the case of James Headlam-Morley, member of the British delegation to the peace conference, who anticipated empire nostalgia before the act of the dissolution of the Habsburg Monarchy: "What we have to do is not merely end the war, but to arrange the liquidation of the Austro-Hungarian Monarchy" which he described as "one of the oldest, the greatest and most extensive states of the continent of Europe."[13] More influential became empire nostalgia in the German

---

11　Taras Kuzio, *Russian Nationalism and the Russian-Ukrainian War: Autocracy-Orthodoxy-Nationality*, (London: Routledge, 2022), p.82.
12　Thomas G. Masaryk. *The New Europe (The Slav Standpoint)*, (London: Eyre & Spottiswoode, 1918), p.10.
13　J. W. Headlam-Morley. 'Note on the Draft of Austrian Treaty (May 26, 1919)', cited in: Natasha Wheatly. 'Central Europe as Ground Zero of the New International Order', *Slavic Review*. 2019. Vol. 78. No. 4, p.902.

speaking countries. Joseph Roth's novel *Radetzkymarsch* (1930), which recounted the decline of the Habsburg monarchy in the fateful relationship between the emperor and a lieutenant from a Slovenian peasant family, evoked the empire as a world unto itself in which diversity was ordered and contradictions reconciled. Tolerance and multiculturalism are qualities that are often unreflectively attributed to empire, in contrast to the compulsive unambiguity and the "invention" of history by nation states. In Germany, this has a problematic conservative and revisionist tradition that became especially virulent in the interwar period and still has consequences today. A recent example is the representation of the German expellee associations and *Landsmannschaften* in the new exhibitions in Berlin and Munich. They present empires as the framework for a fruitful coexistence of imperial nations, whereas Czech and Polish nationalisms are depicted as the cause of the destruction of supposedly harmonious worlds, leading almost determinedly to ethnic cleansing and expulsion.[14]

There is no direct connection between the public use of history and scholarly studies about empires and nations. However, empires have been reevaluated in scholarship too, albeit much more subtly than in the public sphere. Over the past several decades, scholars have stressed the viability of empires in modern times. Recent studies have left behind the old opposition of the categories of nation and empire and focused on examining the connections and transitions between the two forms of rule. Speaking only of a few German examples, I should mention the edited volume by Jörn Leonhard und Ulrike von Hirschhausen which challenged the dichotomy of the categories of empire and nation and emphasized the achievements of the historical multiethnic empires.[15] No less than nation states, empires in the nineteenth century were committed to

---

14 This is true especially for the Sudetendeutsches Museum in Munich (https://www.sudetendeutsches-museum.de/). See also the exhibition of the "Stiftung Flucht, Vertreibung, Versöhnung" in Berlin (https://www.flucht-vertreibung-versoehnung.de/en/home).
15 Jörn Leonhard and Ulrike von Hirschhausen (Eds.). *Comparing Empires: Encounters and Transfers in the Long Nineteenth Century*, (Göttingen: Vandenhoeck & Ruprecht, 2011).

the modernization of their technological, economic, and military infrastructures. In many respects empires adapted techniques of governance that were developed by European nation states. Empires and nation-states alike were part of an intensive competition which took place in the framework of the modern international system. From the perspective of the long nineteenth century, empires were in the center of global modernizing processes. This narrative of the modernity of empires has been emphasized both with regard to the Russian and the Habsburg Empire. In the latter case Pieter Judson's, *The Habsburg Empire* has been especially influential.[16] Other scholars have supported the opposite narrative of the anachronistic empire. Thus, Steven Beller notes the Habsburg Monarchy "despite all the changes and transformations, liberalization, nationalization and modernization" was perhaps "bound to disappear in any case, given its anachronistic structures and style."[17]

The ability of empires to manage diversity is emphasized especially when it comes to diaspora nations in Eastern Europe with their far-reaching networks. For them, large empires seemed to have been a better home than the small-scale, often xenophobic nation states. Dan Diner has argued along this line about the Jewish communities of the Habsburg monarchy.[18] Pieter Judson and Jana Osterkamp have written histories of the Habsburg Monarchy which also stress their integrative potential.[19] The same trend can be observed with regard to the Russian Empire. Robert Crews has made a similar argument about the Russian Empire and the Muslims. Not only antagonism but also interactions and interdependence shaped the relationship between the imperial state and

---

16   Pieter Judson. *The Habsburg Empire: A New History*, (Cambridge: Cambridge University Press, 2016).
17   Steven Beller. *The Habsburg Monarchy, 1815–1918*, (Cambridge: Cambridge University Press, 2018), pp.276, 286.
18   Dan Diner. *Cataclysms: A History of the Twentieth Century from Europe's Edge*, (Madison, WIS: University of Wisconsin Press, 2008).
19   Judson. *The Habsburg Empire*; Jana Osterkamp. *Vielfalt ordnen: das föderale Europa der Habsburgermonarchie (Vormärz bis 1918)*, (Göttingen: Vandenhoeck & Ruprecht 2020).

Muslim communities.[20] The trend of deconstructing narratives of imperial rule over national minorities is fundamental also for Paul Werth's interpretation of Russia's "multi-confessional establishment" into which minorities such as Jews, Muslims, Catholics, and Evangelicals were integrated to different degrees. Werth argues that Jews and Muslims had the most to gain from their integration into the imperial bureaucratic structure that, after serious onslaughts on their religion over the eighteenth century, provided them with a degree of toleration.[21]

In contrast to the historiography of European maritime empires, the prevailing interpretation of the Russian Empire and the Habsburg Monarchy is very positive. This approach underlines an empire's ability to accommodate diversity, placing relatively little emphasis on the colonial character of imperial rule, which was formative in Russia in Central Asia and in the Habsburg Monarchy in Bosnia-Herzegovina. Ricarda Vulpius advanced a balanced interpretation of the imperial and colonial patterns of Russian rule in the eighteenth century. Combining an analysis or the concept of "civilization" in eighteenth century Russia with research into state practices in various political fields, she concludes that the discourse of civilization was a highly influential concept which shaped imperial and colonial policy in the south and east of the empire.[22] Alexander Morrison highlights the importance of the ideas of civilizational and racial superiority for Russian policy in Central Asia in the nineteenth century. He notes a "growing arrogance and intolerance that played an important role in stimulating and justifying imperial expansion and dominion" in the maritime powers, as well as in Russia.[23] More symbiotic relationships between Russians and

---

20 Robert Crews. 'Empire and the Confessional State: Islam and Religious Politics in Nineteenth-Century Russia', *The American Historical Review*. 2003. Vol. 108. No. 1, pp.50–83; Robert Crews. *For Prophet and Tsar: Islam and Empire in Russia and Central Asia* (Cambridge, MA: Harvard University Press, 2006).
21 Paul W. Werth. *The Tsar's Foreign Faiths: Toleration and the Fate of Religious Freedom in Imperial Russia*, (Oxford: Oxford University Press, 2014), esp. pp. 46–73.
22 Ricarda Vulpius. *Die Geburt des Russländischen Imperiums. Herrschaftskonzepte und -praktiken im 18. Jahrhundert*, (Vienna: Böhlau, 2020).
23 Alexander Morrison. *The Russian Conquest of Central Asia: A Study in Imperial Expansion, 1814–1914*, (Cambridge: Cambridge University Press, 2020), p.25.

"Asiatic" or "native" states, as well as with local elites were framed in terms of overwhelming European cultural and eventually racial superiority. Compared with the maritime powers Russian imperialism was not a milder variant of colonialism in the East.[24]

A sense of cultural and racial superiority was also an essential precondition for crimes against humanity committed by the Soviet Union, especially in its southern and eastern regions. German scholars have contributed a number of studies to the international historiography of Soviet rule in Central Asia and the Far East, which underscores a colonial character of Russian rule.[25] It is all the more striking that this literature has almost nothing to say on the subject of the 1933 *Holodomor* (To Kill by Starvation) in Ukraine, despite an overall very well-established historiography of Stalinism in Germany and despite the fact that there are some good German studies on the history of violence in Ukraine in the twentieth century, including that committed during the Nazi occupation of Ukraine.[26]

Why no major studies on the *Holodomor* have emerged in Germany cannot be clearly explained. Certainly, the politicization of the Ukrainian diaspora in post-war Germany played a role, which somewhat discouraged left-wing and liberal historians from exploring this topic. More important is the question of whether

---

24   Moritz Florin. 'Zentralasien und die Dekolonisierung der Osteuropaforschung. Gedanken anlässlich des russischen Überfalls auf die Ukraine', *Zeitgeschichte-online*. 2022. April 21. https://zeitgeschichte-online.de/themen/zentralasien-und-die-dekolonisierung-der-osteuropaforschung.

25   See for example: Moritz Florin. 'Beyond Colonialism? Agency, Power and the Making of Soviet Central Asia', *Kritika. Explorations in Russian and Eurasian History*. 2017. No. 4, pp.791–805; Idem. *Kirgistan und die sowjetische Moderne: 1941–1991*, (Göttingen: Vandenhoeck und Ruprecht, 2015); Jörn Happel. *Nomadische Lebenswelten und zarische Politik. Der Aufstand in Zentralasien 1916*, (Stuttgart: Steiner, 2010); Robert Kindler. *Stalins Nomaden. Herrschaft und Hunger in Kasachstan*, (Hamburg: Hamburger Edition, 2014); Sören Urbansky (Ed.). *"Unsere Insel." Sowjetische Identitätspolitik auf Sachalin nach 1945*, (Berlin: Be-bra Wissenschaftsverlag, 2013).

26   About the history of memory of the Holodomor in Ukraine and the famine in Kazakhstan: Robert Kindler. 'Opfer ohne Täter. Kasachische und ukrainische Erinnerung an den Hunger 1932/33', *Osteuropa*. 2012. Vol. 62. No. 3, pp.105–120; Guido Hausmann and Tanja Penter. 'Instrumentalisiert, verdrängt, ignoriert. Der Holodomor im Bewusstsein der Deutschen', *Osteuropa*. 2020. No. 3–4, pp.193–214.

research on the *Holodomor* will be encouraged in Germany in the future. The main obstacle to the study of the *Holodomor* is not a discussion over historical interpretations. According to one, it was not a Russian but a Bolshevik project. This assessment is supported by the fact the famine took place not only in Ukraine but also in other areas such as Kazakhstan and southern Russia. According to the opposite view supporting the genocide thesis, the fact that Soviet power in Ukraine combined terror by hunger with a campaign against national cultural and intellectual elites testifies to the intention to undermine the very existence of the Ukrainian nation. But it is not this dispute about the genocidal character of the *Holodomor* that is at stake now. It is a political argument that connects the *Holodomor* and the legitimacy of the Ukrainian nation-state. For example, according to one such interpretation, the entire *Holodomor* agenda is a result of an "invented" national xenophobic traditions since 1991 which has cultivated the myth of genocide to forge a Ukrainian nation.[27]

Regardless of one's position in the historical debate on the nature of *Holodomor*, its perception as only a post-Soviet nationalist myth is an example of reductionism that denies the need of the descendants of victims to come to terms with the injustice committed. In this context, it also makes a difference to the individual who remembers whether the *Holodomor* was a mere catastrophe or was deliberately exacerbated by Moscow and linked to an anti-Ukrainian cultural war. The politicized version of the *Holodomor* debate reverberates with the current war and its political assessment as genocide.[28] What is certain is that this approach devalues everyone's needed to come to terms with the past on the individual level and supports the taboo on the study of the perpetrators. Moreover, it also obstructs the possibilities for postcolonial critical research.

---

27 Baberowski. *Zwischen den Imperien*.
28 As Baberowski put it in an interview with the *Neue Zürcher Zeitung*, "Ukrainians must finally emancipate themselves from this legacy, from which they cannot seem to get away. There will only be peace if people learn to forget..." "Die Greuel des Krieges wachsen aus der Schwäche". Interview with Jörg Baberowski, *Neue Zürcher Zeitung*. 2022. April 4.

Poland and the Russian Question Prior to the 2014 Crisis
Between Naïve Pragmatism and Accusations of "Russophobia"

Michal Wawrzonek

One of the important tools with which the goals of Poland's policy towards Russia and the methods of achieving them were conceptualized was the concept of "Russophobia". The main aim of the chapter is to analyze the way this appeared in debates conducted by Polish elites involved in the conduct of foreign policy in 2007-2014 and the practical consequences of this. The logical starting point for this analysis of Polish policy is 2007 when President Vladimir Putin presented his infamous speech to the Munich Security Conference.[1] Moreover, it was in that year that the process of shaping and formalizing the conceptual principles of the Kremlin's policy towards the post-Soviet area and towards the West entered a decisive phase. This concerned the concept of *Russkij Mir* (Russian World), which became the basic tool with which the administration of President Putin began to define Russia's place in international relations.[2] At the same time, in 2007, a new government coalition was established in Poland, which set for itself the goal of "normalizing" and "warming" relations with Russia. It was supposed to be a "new opening" after a period of tension under PiS (Law and Justice). The final turning point was 2014. It was then that, after the annexation of Crimea and the outbreak of the conflict in Donbas,

---

1 'Speech and the Following Discussion at the Munich Conference on Security Policy', February 10, 2007. Available at http://en.kremlin.ru/events/preside nt/transcripts/24034
2 Marlene Laruelle *The "Russian World" Russia's Soft Power and Geopolitical Imagination,* (Washington: Center on Global Interests, 2015); Michał Wawrzonek, Nelly Bekus, Mirella Korzeniewska-Wiszniewska *Orthodoxy versus Post-communism? Belarus, Serbia, Ukraine and the Russkiy Mir,* (Newcastle upon Tyne: Cambridge Scholars Publishing, 2016), pp. 37-70.

the illusions related to the possibility of "normalizing" and "warming" relations with Russia were finally buried in Poland. Former promoters of this approach were at the forefront of criticism directed at Russia's actions — at least on the verbal level. At the same time, between 2007 and 2014, the discursive distinction between "pragmatists" and "Russophobes" became an important way of drawing dividing lines in Polish politics between "good" and "bad" political forces respectively.

The chapter consists of two parts. The first one contains an analysis of the activities undertaken in the sphere of historical policy and the policy of memory which led to "Polish-Russian reconciliation". This is a case study that will show the consequences of attempts to implement a policy free from alleged "Russophobia" in relations with Russia. The second part will present examples of the use of the concept of "Russophobia" in public discourse with respect to Polish-Russian relations and Polish foreign policy. The subject of the analysis will be the statements of the main participants in Polish politics during parliamentary debates in 2007-2014 and in connection with key political events, such as elections to the European Parliament and presidential elections.

A separate section is devoted to attempts to adjust the ambitious goals of the Polish "Eastern foreign policy" to the fear of "Russophobia" common in the EU. They resulted in the Eastern Partnership initiative, based on wishful thinking towards Russia and its political goals.

The phenomenon of Russophilia in Poland is not common. When it comes to politics, it can be found among far-left and far-right fringe groups and nationalist movements. These circles were potentially vulnerable to Russian propaganda and soft power. Some fringe parties like *Zmiana* (Change) or fringe actors like former MEP and current MP Janusz Korwin-Mikke were "either infiltrated or courted to echo and legitimize pro-Russian narratives of a "fascist coup" in Kyiv, or the need for fruitful cooperation with Russia despite the war in Ukraine".[3]

---

3   Łukasz Wenerski, Michał Kacewicz *Russian soft power in Poland — The Kremlin and pro-Russian organizations*, (Budapest: Political Capital, 2017), p. 9, available

However, generally pro-Russian propaganda and the promotion of Russophilia as tools to influence political discourse and political practice in Poland have been of only marginal importance. In the case of the Polish political mainstream, this function was successfully performed by the concept of Russophobia. Russophobia would mean a tendency to cause conflicts and problems in relations with Russia, both bilaterally and in the regional and pan-European levels. This inclination would result from an irrational dislike of Russia, built on negative stereotypes and prejudices.

The concept of "Russophobia" as a tool of "intellectual and conceptual support" of the Russian government appeared in the first half of the 19th century.[4] Under Stalin "Russophobia" entered "the lexical resources of the Russian language".[5] In Soviet times, the issue of Russophobia "was a constant concern of academic analysis and political journalism". This was supposedly a way of discrediting both Soviet dissidents and Western critics of the USSR, such as Richard Pipes and Friedrich Hayek.[6] After the collapse of the USSR, informational activities based on the Russophobic stereotype continued. They became a "way of communication between Russia and individual countries, forcing them to adjust their critical stance towards the Kremlin's policy".[7] Russia used the concept of "Russophobia" to discredit the governments and political elites of other countries critical of the Kremlin's policy.[8] Thus, at various times, the concept of "Russophobia" was used to implement various policy objectives both within and beyond the Russian state; to discipline the rebellious peoples of the Russian Empire; to combat "global Zionism"; to consolidate society; and also as an argument against the enlargement of NATO and the EU.[9]

---

    online: https://www.politicalcapital.hu/pc-admin/source/documents/PC_NED_country_study_PL_20170428.pdf.
4   Jolanta Darczewska, Piotr Żochowski *Russophobia in the Kremlin's strategy. A weapon of mass destruction*, (Warszawa: Ośrodek Studiów Wschodnich im. Marka Karpia, 2015), p. 9.
5   Jolanta Darczewska, Piotr Żochowski *Russophobia* ..., p. 10.
6   Jolanta Darczewska, Piotr Żochowski *Russophobia* ..., p. 11.
7   Jolanta Darczewska, Piotr Żochowski *Russophobia* ..., p., 8.
8   Ibidem.
9   Jolanta Darczewska, Piotr Żochowski *Russophobia* ..., p. 6.

Russophobia as a conceptualization of relations between East European countries and Russia has been deeply internalized in the West "An allegation of Russophobia" is "a frequent rebuttal by apologists of Putin's policies, in debates on Western approaches to Eastern Europe".[10] *Putinverstehers* (Putin Understanders) "accuse the critics of Moscow's recent foreign and domestic policies of a lack of empathy for, or even of xenophobia towards, the Russian nation, as well as its traditions, concerns, and views.[11] However, the problem of perceiving relations between Eastern European countries and Russia through the prism of Russophobia does not only concern the apologists of Putin. There are reasons to believe that professional Western diplomats dealing with Eastern Europe also acquired a way of thinking that was determined by the axiom of Russophobia prevailing in the region. For example, in February 2009, the US ambassador to Poland, Victor Ashe, describing the situation under the PO-PSL coalition, reported to the then Secretary of State Hillary Clinton: "Poles make a lot of demands, but they are our consistent and strong allies (...) Although they are less Russophobic than their predecessors, it is Radosław Sikorski and Donald Tusk who persistently insist on moving European and transatlantic institutions to the East".[12] If you take a closer look at this statement and its context, it turns out that any attempts by Poland to pursue a more active policy towards the post-Soviet area could have been interpreted not only by Russian, but also by Western diplomats, as a manifestation of "Russophobia".

The concept of Russophobia has many meanings. One of them is especially targeted at Western European political and intellectual elites. It is based on the presumption that Russophobia is a manifestation of intolerance towards "an alien system of values". Accordingly, "adherence to Russophobia is contrary to democratic

---

10 Andreas Umland, *The Putinverstehers' Misconceived Charge of Russophobia: How Western Apology for the Kremlin's Current Behavior Contradicts Russian National Interests,* https://isnblog.ethz.ch/international-relations/the-putinverstehers-misconceived-charge-of-russophobia-how-western-apology-for-the-kremlins-current-behavior-contradicts-russian-national-interests.
11 Ibidem.
12 Radosław Sikorski *Polska może być lepsza,* (Kraków: Znak, 2018), p. 157.

values".[13] An alleged baseless Polish Russophobia is one of the elements of "a set of propaganda messages aimed at influencing Poles and foreign audiences".[14] According to this narrative, "Poles have an anti-Russian complex. Without Russia there would be no Polish patriotism, which is based on anti-Russian uprisings from the nineteenth century."[15]

Over time, the problem of "Russophobia", as a fetish that allowed Western discourse on Russia to be manipulated, attracted the attention of analysts dealing with the Russian information war. Among others, at the turn of 2018 and 2019, a team led by Dmitry Gorenburg monitored Russian and Western media and found a set of ten narratives frequently used by officials discussing Russian foreign policy. One of them is "Russophobia".[16] In 2016, Katri Pynnöniemi asserted, that "The terms anti-Russian and Russophobic" have become part of the Kremlin's "official parlance".[17]

The Policy of "Normalization" in Practice

Before 2014, that is, before the annexation of Crimea and the outbreak of armed conflict in Donbas, the possibility of building relations with Russia, free from Russophobia, was an implicit criterion for assessing Poland as a reliable partner in European politics. Under these conditions, the Polish government attempted to implement the strategy understood as "realism" in its approach to

---

13 Jolanta Darczewska, Piotr Żochowski *Russophobia* ..., p. 15.
14 Joanna Kwiecień, 'Poland through Eurasian Eyes: Russian Propaganda Messages in the Media', *The Warsaw Institute Review*, No. 3. (2017) Special edition, p. 72.
15 Joanna Kwiecień, 'Poland through..., p. 73.
16 Dmitry Gorenburg, 'Strategic Messaging: Propaganda and Disinformation Efforts', In: Graeme P. Herd ed., *Russia's Global Reach: A Security and Statecraft Assessment*, ed. (Garmisch-Partenkirchen: George C. Marshall European Center for Security Studies, 2021). Available at https://www.marshallcenter.org/en/publications/marshall-center-books/russias-global-reach/chapter-15-strategic-messaging-propaganda-and-disinformation-efforts
17 Katri Pynnöniemi, András Rácz *Fog of Falsehood, Russian Strategy of Deception and the Conflict in Ukraine*, (Helsinki: The Finnish Institute of International Affairs, 2016). Available at: https://www.fiia.fi/wp-content/uploads/2017/01/fiiareport45_fogoffalsehood.pdf. see also: *Appealing to the Lowest Feelings*, https://euvsdisinfo.eu/the-russophobia-myth-appealing-to-the-lowest-feelings/

Russia. It was expressed in the idea of cooperation "with Russia as it is" as announced by Prime Minister Tusk.[18] It was about recognizing that Russian native traditions and "cultural codes" cannot be reconciled with the values on which the European Union was built. If so, then, as the head of the Ministry of Foreign Affairs, Sikorski, argued, "we must be satisfied" to base "EU-Russian cooperation on the agreed rules of the game".[19] Thus, as understood, "realism" was supposed to be an antidote to the policy of "ineffective non-forgiveness", which was associated with the opposition at that time, whose core was PiS.[20] The reasons for this "irreconcilability" were seen in alleged "Russophobia" which characterized opponents and critics of the "realistic" approach to relations with Russia.

One of the areas where opportunities were sought to improve relations with Russia in the realm of memory politics. The key element became the issue of Polish-Russian reconciliation. The achievement of this was goal was establishing Poland and its ruling political camp in the eyes of Western partners as a serious player in European politics, free from "Russophobia". The actions that were taken in connection with this aim took place on two levels: at the level of official interstate relations and within the framework of public diplomacy. The joint visit of Prime Ministers Tusk and Putin to Katyn was supposed to signify a culmination of official relations, while the counterpart to this event in the sphere of public diplomacy was a joint message signed by representatives of the Roman Catholic Church in Poland and the Russian Orthodox Church. A more detailed analysis of the aforementioned activities will make it possible to show quite clearly what effects were brought about by the strategy of building relations with Russia based on "pragmatism" free from Russophobia.

---

18 transcript of the parliamentary session from November 23 2007. Available at https://orka2.sejm.gov.pl/StenoInter6.nsf/0/6372FE4B9619C127C125739D00 53E245/$file/2_a_ksiazka.pdf, p. 24
19 'Sprawozdanie Stenograficzne z 15 posiedzenia Sejmu Rzeczypospolitej Polskiej w dniu 7 maja 2008 r.' Available at https://orka2.sejm.gov.pl/StenoInter 6.nsf/0/8FFBB2BA0A916821C1257444000289F9/$file/15_a_ksiazka.pdf, p. 8
20 ibidem

Katyn and the Politics of Polish-Russian Reconciliation

The key issue when it comes to the past in Polish-Russian relations is that of commemorating the victims of the Katyn massacre (i.e. the murder, as ordered by the Soviet authorities in 1940, of Polish officers and other Polish uniformed services who were imprisoned by the USSR after September 17, 1939). In the early 1990s, the Russian authorities made a number of gestures that contributed to documenting and acknowledging this crime. In 1990, the Soviet Premier Mikhail Gorbachev handed President Wojciech Jaruzelski some documents from the NKVD files concerning Polish prisoners, spanning the years 1939–1940. In 1992, President Boris Yeltsin in turn "declassified files demonstrating the responsibility of the highest Soviet authorities for the Katyn crime and handed them over to the Polish side". Moreover, a year later, Yeltsin placed a wreath under the Katyn cross in the Warsaw Powązki cemetery, the first Russian leader to do so. However, contrary to what is widely believed in Poland, no official apology was offered on that occasion.[21]

From the beginning of the 1990s, the Polish side took steps to accurately determine the resting place of the victims. Subsequently, efforts were made to establish war cemeteries in the area where mass graves had been identified. This case was also the subject of political arrangements between the Russian Federation and Poland.[22] In 1996, the Russian authorities decided to create "memorial complexes" in Katyn and Miednoje (i.e. places where "Polish and Soviet citizens – victims of totalitarian repression" are buried).[23]

It is worth emphasizing that this was the first time the Russian authorities officially engaged in actions to commemorate the crimes of Stalinist totalitarianism, also with respect to citizens of the former

---

21 Katarzyna Pełczyńska-Nałęcz, *How far do the borders of the West extend? Russian/Polish strategic conflicts in the period 1990-2010*, (Warszawa: Ośrodek Studiów Wschodnich im. Marka Karpia, 2010), p. 65

22 *Umowa między Rządem Rzeczypospolitej Polskiej a Rządem Federacji Rosyjskiej o grobach i miejscach pamięci ofiar wojen i represji, sporządzona w Krakowie dnia 22 lutego 1994 r.*, https://isap.sejm.gov.pl/isap.nsf/DocDetails.xsp?id=WDU19941120543

23 Постановление от 19 октября 1996 г. N 1247 „О создании мемориальных комплексов в местах захоронений советских и польских граждан – жертв тоталитарных репрессий в Катыни (Смоленская область) и Медном (Тверская область), https://docs.cntd.ru/document/9031087

Soviet Union. It can be assumed that it was forced to do so by the work carried out on the site of the mass murders in Katyn and Miednoje by Polish teams. It was Polish specialists who provided the Russian side with a map with the location of the graves of Soviet citizens who were also shot in the Katyn forest.[24] In the 1990s, during the negotiations concerning the conditions and manner of commemorating the victims of the Katyn massacre, the Russian side insisted on building joint "memorials" because, as its representatives claimed, "you cannot divide the victims after death". Polish negotiators did not want to agree to this approach. They emphasized the "special meaning and symbolic dimension" of this crime, which was committed "in the majesty of Soviet law." The Polish side was of the opinion that the construction of cemeteries for the murdered victims was "the only form of commemoration close to Christian or national Polish traditions".[25] Przewoźnik, who participated in these talks, stated that "in general, the Russian side did everything not to perform searches and exhumations, without which the construction of cemeteries could not be completed".[26]

Ultimately, the Polish War Cemetery was established as part of the joint Polish-Russian "memorial complex" as specified in the aforementioned 1996 resolution and completed in 2000. At that time, the Russian part of the complex was officially opened. However, for many years to come, it was "practically undeveloped" and the Polish War Cemetery was the only "fully completed part" of it. On the Russian side, only the Orthodox cross was placed, and the areas of mass graves remained "unmarked in any way".[27]

On October 21, 2004, the Russian Military Prosecutor's Office, contrary to the expectations of the Polish side, discontinued the investigation into the murder of Polish citizens in Katyn, and the justification for this decision was classified as confidential. Polish

---

24　Andrzej Przewoźnik, 'Polskie cmentarze wojenne w Katyniu, Charkowie i Miednoje. Zamierzenia, projekty i perspektywy realizacyjne' In: Marek Tarczyński ed. *Ku cmentarzom polskim w Katyniu, Miednoje i Charkowie*, (Warszawa: Niezależny Komitet Badania Zbrodni Katyńskiej, 1997), p. 9
25　Andrzej Przewoźnik, *Polskie cmentarze...*p. 8
26　ibidem
27　https://katynpromemoria.pl/polski-wojenny-w-katyniu/

victims were also denied the right to rehabilitation.²⁸ Contrary to the expectations of the Polish side, the crime was not recognized as genocide, and 116 out of the 183 volumes of files were classified.²⁹ These decisions made it difficult to overcome the trauma of the "Katyn affair" in Polish-Russian relations.

At the same time, the actions of the Russian side to commemorate Soviet citizens who were murdered in Katyn gained momentum. In 2005, the then Metropolitan of Smolensk and later Moscow Patriarch Kirill consecrated the cornerstone for the construction of the Church on the site of the "memorial complex" in Katyn.³⁰

The issue of building a Church in the immediate vicinity of the Polish war cemetery became a source of controversy in Polish-Russian relations. Pursuant to the 1994 Polish-Russian agreement, changes to the arrangement of "places of memory and rest" required the consent of both parties. Undoubtedly, the construction of the planned Church violated the agreed shape of the symbolic space in the "memorial complex". Due to the protests of the Polish side, the location of the Church was changed and moved to the area adjacent to the complex. The problem, however, was that, according to the new location, the Church was to be built at the entrance to the "memorial complex". Even if it were formally erected off-site, it was clear that it would become the dominant feature of the surrounding landscape. Obviously, such a solution was contrary to the wishes of the Polish side.

In the meantime, after the change of power resulting from the 2007 elections, a new government under Tusk was established and began an effort to improve relations with Russia. This also concerned the issue of commemorating the victims of the Katyn massacre and broadly understood Polish-Russian "reconciliation". At the same time, however, the Polish Ministry of Foreign Affairs still

---

28 'Komunikat w sprawie Zbrodni Katyńskiej oraz informacja o stanie śledztwa', https://ipn.gov.pl/pl/dla-mediow/komunikaty/9958,Komunikat-w-sprawie-Zbrodn i-Katynskiej-oraz-informacja-o-stanie-sledztwa.html
29 Katarzyna Pełczyńska-Nałęcz, *How far* ... pp. 65-66
30 Митрополит Кирилл заложил камень в основание нового храма на территории мемориала «Катынь», May 16 2005, http://www.patriarchia.ru/db/text/11226.html

"had reservations" about an Orthodox Church being built in Katyn, because, as discussed in talks with the Russian side, "the place of national memory of both nations in Katyn should maintain its confessional balance, without giving preference to any religion".[31] However, representatives of the Russian Federation stated that, due to the change in the location of the Church and its relocation outside the designated area of the "memorial complex", Polish concerns were groundless.

On April 7, 2010, Tusk's meeting with Putin in Katyn was described by Sikorski as a "milestone" in bilateral relations. At the same time, he stressed, "it was entirely Putin's initiative".[32] During the meeting, Prime Minister Tusk and Putin laid the cornerstone for the construction of the Church. This happened despite the fact the Polish side kept raising objections to the controversial Church through diplomatic channels. The joint laying of the cornerstone by Prime Ministers Tusk and Putin meant that further negotiations concerning this matter no longer made sense.

The Polish side believed the demonstrated flexibility in the commemoration of the Katyn massacre would give rise to a real partnership in relations with Russia. Two days before Prime Minister Tusk's visit to Katyn, Andrzej Przewoźnik, the head of the institution, who takes care of memorial sites on behalf of the Polish state and who played a key role in efforts to commemorate the victims of the Katyn massacre, stated that "we are slowly gaining a very significant ally in the [Russian] Orthodox Church. An institution is emerging that has a kind of government of souls in Russian society, which alludes to God and faith, and which says openly: we condemn Stalin and all that Stalinism represented".[33]

Ultimately, in 2011, "after considering the Russian arguments, the Polish side decided to withdraw its opposition to the

---

31 'Odpowiedź podsekretarza stanu w Ministerstwie Spraw Zagranicznych — z upoważnienia prezesa Rady Ministrów — na interpelację nr 22424 w sprawie budowy cerkwi w pobliżu polskiego cmentarza w Katyniu'. Available at https://orka2.sejm.gov.pl/IZ6.nsf/main/128E68BB.
32 Radosław Sikorski, *Polska...*, p.122
33 'Andrzej Przewoźnik, April 05 2010. Available at https://dzieje.pl/node/46128

construction of the Church".³⁴ In fact, this objection was already pointless at that time, as the case had been resolved by events which transpired during Tusk's visit to Katyn a few months earlier. In spite of this, Polish diplomacy still counted on some concessions in the symbolic sphere from the Russian side. This can be confirmed by the statement of the Polish Ministry of Foreign Affairs, who, in the previously mentioned reply to the parliamentary question regarding the issue of the Church in Katyn, justified the actions of the Polish government. The official stated that the Polish side, having withdrawn its opposition to the construction of the Church, expected this "gesture would be appreciated in the context of the request of the Catholic community in Smolensk for the return of the local Church and other Churches in Russia, which had not yet been resolved".³⁵

The controversial Church at the entrance to the Polish-Russian "memorial complex" was completed in 2012. During the dedication ceremony on June 15, 2012, Patriarch Kirill finally noted with satisfaction that the change of location was "providential." The body of the Church with a high tower dominates the area, and as the Russian Orthodox Church head said, "today nobody who comes close to Katyn has any doubt that this is where people died in large numbers. The majestic Church that stands at the entrance to the Katyn military training ground is a great monument to those who died here".³⁶ In Patriarch Kirill's speech, during the ceremony of the consecration of the aforementioned Church, the goals of memory politics in Russian-Polish relations were presented quite well. The Orthodox hierarch said that Katyn, next to the training ground in Butowo and the Solovetsky Islands, "is one of our Russian Golgothas". The head of the Russian Orthodox Church also mentioned the "Polish officers" murdered there. What is very characteristic, however, he noted they were there "as a result of hostilities in the territory of the USSR" and not as a result of the annexation of the

---

34   'Odpowiedź podsekretarza...
35   'Odpowiedź podsekretarza...
36   'Слово Святейшего Патриарха Кирилла после Божественной литургии в новоосвященном храме-памятнике Воскресения Христова в Катыни', July 12 2012. Available at http://www.patriarchia.ru/db/text/2346187.html

territory of the Polish state by the Soviet Union. Moreover, Kirill emphasized that Katyn is a "terrible symbol of our common" — Polish and Russian — "tragedy".[37] The thread of "common tragedy" and "one common sacrifice" appeared in Kirill's speech several times.

It can therefore be seen that the Russian side was openly returning to the narrative it had been pushing against the intentions of Polish negotiators in talks at the beginning of the 1990s. Nevertheless, two months later, Patriarch Kirill visited Poland. During this visit, not only was a solemn joint declaration on historic Polish-Russian reconciliation signed. President Bronisław Komorowski also publicly thanked the head of the Russian Orthodox Church for the erection and dedication of the Church in Katyn.[38]

At the same time, in the case of the Katyn massacre, the Russian side, apart from the symbolic gesture of Prime Minister Putin during the meeting with Tusk in Katyn, did not take any specific actions that would meet Polish expectations. It was primarily about such issues as the initiation of court proceedings in the case of the Katyn massacre, the trial of specific perpetrators, and seeking redress for the victims. In 2011 Włodzimierz Marciniak, who was a member of a special Polish-Russian Group for Difficult Matters (i.e. a body of experts who were to moderate the dialogue on the common past), recalled in one of the interview that already in the early 1990s a group of Russian "experts, prosecutors, and scientists", at the request of the Russian military prosecutor's office, prepared a ruling in which it clearly stated that "the Katyn massacre should be tried and should be subject to court proceedings". Marcinak emphasized that "this group recommended what should be in the indictment of the Russian prosecutor's office. In fact, the matter is clear and obvious, the case could be brought to court, a verdict issued and the problem closed. For over 15 years, the Russian

---

37 Ibidem,
38 'Patriarcha Cyryl I w Polsce', August 19 2012. Available at https://www.ekai.pl/patriarcha-cyryl-i-w-polsce/

authorities have been trying to do something instead of the obvious," said the Polish expert.[39]

The hopes for an improvement in the situation of Catholic communities, which was critical after the Polish side had come to terms with the construction of the Church, also failed. This applies both to the general situation of Catholic communities in Russia and the parish in Smolensk. In 2017, the secretary general of the Russian Catholic Bishops' Conference, Igor Kowalewski, stated that "the real situation of the Catholic community in Russia allows us to speak, if not about direct persecution, then at least about disregarding and diminishing [its] rights, which sometimes occur".[40] The Church in Smolensk was not returned, and on May 26, 2021 the Council of the Smolensk *oblast* declared that "in the foreseeable future" there was no provision for the return of the Church. Moreover, the Russian Orthodox Church diocese of Smolensk did not support the efforts of local Catholics.[41]

Russian Orthodox Church as a Partner in Dialogue About the Past

On 5-6 May 2009, the then head of the Polish Ministry of Foreign Affairs, Radosław Sikorski, paid an official visit to Moscow. Among other things, he visited the Butów cemetery near Moscow. This is the place where the victims of Stalinist repression were shot by the NKVD. The Orthodox Church caught the attention of the Polish minister, which was built, inter alia, to commemorate the representatives of the Orthodox clergy murdered in this place. "I found out while I was there," relates Sikorski, "that Putin visits it regularly." It was then that the head of the Polish Ministry of Foreign Affairs came to understand, "the Orthodox Church may be our ally in deconstructing the Stalinist historical narrative that is still in force in

---

39 'Katyń: postęp czy unik', February 10 2011. Avaliable at https://www.polskie radio.pl/7/158/Artykul/309932,Katyn-postep-czy-unik
40 'Katolicy są dyskryminowani przez władze Rosji', August 23 2017. Available at https://www.ekai.pl/katolicy-sa-dyskryminowani-przez-wladze-rosji/
41 ibidem

Russia".[42] The idea was to involve the hierarchy of the Polish Roman Catholic Church and the Russian Orthodox Church in dialogue on past Polish-Russian relations.

The Russian side skillfully managed this dialogue from the very beginning. After the visit of then Prime Minister Putin to Poland in 2009, it was Russia who initiated work on the "Common message to the nations of Poland and Russia".[43] The document was solemnly signed on August 17, 2012 by Patriarch Kirill and Archbishop Józef Michalik. For this purpose, the head of the Russian Orthodox Church paid an official visit to Poland. The ceremony related to the signing of the document took place at the Royal Castle in Warsaw.[44] The Roman Catholic Church in Poland engaged its authority in the promotion of this event. The most important Polish hierarchs and the Apostolic Nuncio took part in the ceremony. In addition, a week after the ceremony, the Council of Bishops of the Roman Catholic Church in Poland decided the document would be read on 9 September 2012 in all Churches in Poland. The Polish authorities were also involved; for example, through the presence of the deputy prime minister, ministers and the marshal of the senate at the ceremony in the Royal Castle. A day earlier, then President Komorowski hosted Patriarch Kirill for a gala dinner, during which he expressed the hope "the joint message to the Nations of Poland and Russia would become an important step in rapprochement between Poles and Russians".[45]

The "Common Message" had two threads. The first was a call to "dialogue and reconciliation" and to "rebuild mutual trust" in the name of a "peaceful future free from violence and wars".[46]

---

42 Radosław Sikorski, 'Polska..., p. 107
43 Katarzyna Chawryło, Jadwiga Rogoża, 'Patriarch Cyril in Poland: the policy of the Orthodox Church and the policy of the Kremlin' https://www.osw.waw.pl/en/publikacje/analyses/2012-08-22/patriarch-cyril-poland-policy-orthodox-church-and-policy-kremlin
44 'Wspólne przesłanie do narodów Polski i Rosji', August 17 2017. Available at https://www.niedziela.pl/artykul/98720/nd/Wspolne-przeslanie-do-narodow-Polski-i
45 'Spotkanie prezydenta z Cyrylem I', August 16 2012. Available at https://www.prezydent.pl/kancelaria/archiwum/archiwum-bronislawa-komorowskiego/aktualnosci/wideo/spotkanie-prezydenta-z-cyrylem-i,214
46 'Wspólne przesłanie...,

However, as analysts at the Warsaw-based Center of Eastern Studies noted,

> "the general tone of the visit and the signed declaration is in line with the Kremlin's historical and foreign policies. Russia is presented as a constructive partner and initiator of dialogue, although any such dialogue is to be conducted on Russian terms, and aims to encourage the closure of existing disputes, rather offer than any explanation for them".[47]

The second thread was a call to cooperate in the fight against societal challenges faced by the signatories of the "Common Message" and its addressees. In the light of the cited document, these are "religious indifferentism and progressive secularization", as well as the protection of "basic moral values" in social life. The authors of the "Message" declared that they recognize the "autonomy of secular and ecclesiastical authorities", but at the same time stated the need to establish "cooperation" between both of them, "in the field of family care, education, social order and other issues important for the good of society." The text of the document strongly opposed "the promotion of abortion, euthanasia, and single-sex relationships, which proponents try to present as a form of marriage" and the propaganda of the "consumerist lifestyle".[48] Patriarch Kirill said during a dinner with President Komorowski: "The Polish and Russian nations must be together especially now, when our common foundation of tradition resulting from Christianity is under threat. The moral norms that have always served as the glue of society are being challenged." Therefore, according to the head of the Russian Orthodox Church, "in view of this great task, we should forget about our past conflicts so that Poland and Russia can become allies in the work of promoting Christian order across the continent".[49]

In the following year, the Russian side skillfully used the theme of a "Common Message" to confirm its point of view on the Polish-Russian "difficult past" and to promote itself as the patron of the movement in defense of traditional values in Europe. Another opportunity was the conference organized in Warsaw on

---

47 Katarzyna Chawryło, Jadwiga Rogoża, , *Patriarch Cyril* ...,
48 'Wspólne przesłanie ...,
49 Spotkanie prezydenta...

November 28 – December 1, 2013 on the topic: "The Future of Christianity in Europe. The Role of the Churches and Nations of Poland and Europe". This event was to show that dialogue for Polish-Russian reconciliation, initiated a year previously with the solemn "Message", was still being continued. The event was held under the patronage of President Komorowski, and the Polish ministry of foreign affairs financially supported the organization of the event. Again among the participants were the marshal of the senate of the Republic of Poland and the upper hierarchy of the Roman Catholic Church in Poland.[50]

The head of the Russian delegation that attended the conference was the Metropolitan of Volokama, Hilarion who is responsible for the Russian Orthodox Church's external relations. In his statements at the conference forum, Metropolitan Hilarion devoted much of his message to criticism of the European integration process. According to Metropolitan Hilarion, its ideology would be reduced to a "secular paradigm", which was deprived of "the necessary connection with moral imperatives" and which was based "solely on freedom, democracy and the supremacy of the law".[51] Metropolitan Hilarion stated that "a whole series of Western countries" support legislative initiatives aimed at equalizing the status of traditional family and same-sex relationships, and this is undertaken "against the will of the people" and without a "serious and free" social debate on the subject.[52] The Russian Orthodox Church hierarchy also called for the creation of a network to defend "traditional Christian values" so that it could organize "joint actions together with social organizations, engage in projects on a pan-European level and cooperate with religious and political leaders".[53]

---

50 'Konferencja „Przyszłość chrześcijaństwa w Europie. Rola Kościołów i narodów Polski i Rosji"', November 20 2013. Available at http://www.lasbielanski.pl/content/konferencja-przyszłość-chrześcijaństwa-w-europie-rola-kośc iołów-i-narodów-polski-i-rosji
51 'Новые вызовы христианскому миру: перспективы совместных действий Церквей', November 29 2013. Available at http://www.patriarchia.ru/db/text/3404662.html
52 'Новые вызовы…
53 ibidem,

Despite the fact the activities involved the Polish government and the Catholic Church, which is one of the most important institutions in Poland's social life, they did not change the way Poles perceive Russia and Russians. Opinion polls clearly show this. In 2012, 80 percent of respondents were convinced Russia had an unfriendly attitude towards Poland in international relations. Two years later, 82 percent of respondents held this opinion.[54] The same respondents were also asked how, in their opinion, Russians perceived Poland. In 2012, most of the respondents were convinced they perceived Poland as friendly (61 percent), while two years later only 46 percent of the respondents held this opinion.[55]

Public opinion polls on Polish-Russian relations, conducted by the Polish Public Opinion Research Center since the second half of the 1980s, also provide a good perspective. Initially, the Tusk governments appeasement policy brought about some positive changes in the social perception of Polish-Russian relations. However, the decisive and long-term impact on this was the Smolensk air crash in 2010. In the first weeks after this tragedy, there was a radical increase in positive opinions, which resulted from symbolic gestures made by representatives of the Russian government (i.e., declaration of national mourning, participation of President Medvedev at the funeral ceremonies of President Kaczyński and his wife). However, subsequent events, such as the controversy over the causes of the catastrophe and in particular the report of the Russian commission, which blamed the Polish side for the tragedy, caused a radical and lasting deterioration of Polish opinions about Polish-Russian relations. This trend could in no way be reversed by the "Common Message".

Russian involvement in the preparation and promotion of this document was an example of practical implementation of the strategy of "weaponizing" values and culture. Its goal was "challenging Western (liberal) moral assumptions and axioms that almost everybody takes for granted". It was an element of "the fight for

---

54 *Polska-Rosja. Diagnoza społeczna 2020*, (Warszawa: Centrum Polsko-Rosyjskiego Dialogu i Pojednania 2020), p. 9
55 *Polska-Rosja…* , p. 11

ideological hegemony against the West".⁵⁶ In the guise of the *Russkij Mir* concept, it became an officially recognized and intensively promoted element of Russian foreign policy agenda since 2007. It was then that the *Russkij Mir* foundation was established on the basis of a decree by President Putin. In 2009, Patriarch Kirill signed a cooperation agreement with the foundation's board on behalf of the Russian Orthodox Church. Kirill himself and other Russian Orthodox Church clergy became active propagators of the *Russkij Mir* ideology both in Russia and abroad. In this respect, one can speak of a close partnership between the Russian Orthodox Church and the Russian Ministry of Foreign Affairs.⁵⁷

"A common message to the Polish and Russian nations" can be considered one of the results of this cooperation. The theme of reconciliation was used as a pretext to promote Russia's new international identity as an ally of all opponents to the Western model of a liberal social and cultural order. The content of the "Message" harmonized with the image of Putin as a defender of Christianity and traditional Christian values in the contemporary world. It was promoted in a campaign before the presidential election, which took place several months before the ceremonial signing of the "Message".⁵⁸

The aforementioned conference in 2013 and the events related to the signing of the "Message" earlier that year were very good examples of the practical implementation of the strategy of "weaponizing" values and culture as part of the confrontation with the West. The Polish Roman Catholic Church and Polish authorities were used to give credibility to Russian actions taken in this area. This was to help promote the new image of the country as a potential patron and partner in the defense of traditional values in the life of European societies. These values and their "defense" were only

---

56 Péter Krekó, Lóránt Győri, *The Weaponization of Culture: Kremlin's traditional agenda and the export of values to Central Europe*, (Budapest: Political Capital Institute, 2016), p. 5
57 Michał Wawrzonek, Nelly Bekus, Mirella Korzeniewska-Wiszniewska, *Orthodoxy versus...*, p. 46
58 Clare Morris, 'Vladimir Putin Vows to Defend Christianity Worldwide', February 12, 2012. Available at https://www.christianpost.com/news/vladimir-putin-vows-to-defend-christianity-worldwide.html

a pretext with the conference organized in Warsaw a platform to criticize the process of European integration.

These orchestrations were initiated at a pivotal moment. A few days earlier, as a result of many months of pressure from Russia, President Yanukovych withdrew from signing an agreement on Ukraine's association with the EU. During the conference, on November 30, 2013, the first brutal pacification of demonstrations by supporters of Ukraine's integration with the EU took place in Kyiv. In this way, a rather awkward situation arose, because on the one hand, Poland had consistently advocated on behalf of Ukraine in the EU for many years, and on the other, the Polish authorities and social elites allowed themselves to be realigned in support of Russia's actions to disavow the value system under which European integration was taking place.

Nevertheless, the Polish authorities consistently maintained the illusion of partnership in the dialogue for Polish-Russian reconciliation until as late as Spring 2014. The statement by Metropolitan Hilarion during the conference in Warsaw in 2013 is a good stage in this dialogue. He then stated, "history is not only a collection of objective facts, but also a subjective way of interpreting them by participants and their descendants. We cannot impose our attitude towards this or that historical period on others, just as we cannot renounce our understanding of the past".[59]

The Polish strategy can be gauged from statements made by Minister of Foreign Affairs Sikorski. In 2011, he argued in the *Sejm*, the lower house of Poland's parliament, that "our philosophy has proved successful: make a positive gesture, and then act according to the principle of reciprocity".[60] However, the reconstructed course of events shows that during past official Polish-Russian dialogue the Russian authorities, as stated above by Metropolitan Hilarion, "cannot", and at least, did not intend to abandon "their own understanding of the past". Despite the lack of expected

---

59 'Новые вызовы...
60 'Sprawozdanie Stenograficzne z 87 posiedzenia Sejmu Rzeczypospolitej Polskiej w dniu 16 marca 2011 r.', https://orka2.sejm.gov.pl/StenoInter6.nsf/0/CD0C11E6036E3398C125785A0051F0B2/$file/87_a_ksiazka.pdf, p. 11

"reciprocity", Polish representatives gave way to their Russian partners on subsequent issues. Even 5 days before his death in the Smolensk catastrophe, Przewoźnik consistently promoted the image of the Russian Orthodox Church as an "ally" of Poland in relations with Russia, despite the fact that the Polish side had previously signaled its reservations about the initiative to build a Church in Katyn. Prime Minister Tusk took part in placing the cornerstone in the foundations of the Church in Katyn and thus not only authenticated the illusion there was harmony in Polish-Russian relations, but also legitimized Russia's "understanding of the past". Interestingly, even in retrospect, Sikorski argues that on the day of Prime Minister Tusk's visit to Katyn on April 7, 2010 "we were approaching Russia on European soil as "two great nations" and he was convinced, "the Russians wanted to normalize relations with Poland, to start acting in our common interest, and they were ready to pay for it with concessions in memory politics".[61]

Russophobia in the Policy Debate Concerning Russia

Russophobia as a tool to describe reality was seized upon, inter alia, during parliamentary debates, especially in the realm of Polish foreign policy. In February 2009, during the annual debate on Polish foreign policy in parliament, Jolanta Szymanek-Deresz, a representative of the SLD (Democratic Left Alliance) party, was convinced "Russia wants to talk to us" and therefore, "we should make broad use of this offer."[62] The SLD deputy referred to the recent visit by Russian Minister of Foreign Affairs Sergei Lavrov to Warsaw which took place only a few weeks after the crisis related to the Russo-Georgian war. During this conflict, President Lech Kaczyński became extremely involved in the defense of Georgia's sovereignty and in his speech in Tbilisi, he warned against Russian neo-imperialism. In this context, the left-wing leader expressed the conviction, "Russia cares about further contacts with Poland and

---

61 Radosław Sikorski, *Polska...*, p. 123
62 'Sprawozdanie Stenograficzne z 35 posiedzenia Sejmu Rzeczypospolitej Polskiej w dniu 13 lutego 2009 r.', https://orka2.sejm.gov.pl/StenoInter6.nsf/0/5B70D5B230689B20C125755C00704CFB/$file/35_c_ksiazka.pdf, p. 264

the European Union", but on the Polish side it meets with an "unequivocally anti-Russian position" of President Lech Kaczyński's Russophobia.[63]

Jerzy Szmajdziński, Deputy Speaker of the *Sejm*, on behalf of the SLD, spoke to the media using a similar tone about the presidential visit to Georgia in 2008 and he disavowed President Kaczynski's speech in Tbilisi described it as a "political mistake". According to Szmajdziński, this is how Kaczyński "entered the list of leaders characterized by Russophobia".[64]

Jolanta Szymanek-Deresz, in the above-mentioned speech in Sejm in February 2009, regretted that in the European Union "the perception that we are Russophobic is unfortunately widespread".[65] In this way, the SLD deputy referred to the common belief in the West about the ontologically negative attitude of most Polish political elites towards Russia. Szymanek-Deresz also emphasized that "fortunately" this unfavorable image is saved by "the alternative foreign policy, represented by Prime Minister Tusk's government" who the SLD deputy described as representing a "civilized Russophobia". In using this term, the MP was referring to the opinion of Mikhail Leontyev,[66] a high-profile Putin political technologist.[67] The fact that he was mentioned during the parliamentary discussion on foreign policy as an authority showed how strongly Russian propaganda influenced the political debate in Poland, in both domestic and foreign policy.

During the debate on the attitude of the Polish president in relation to the Russian-Georgian war, PiS leader Jarosław Kaczyński stated, inter alia, that "in Poland, there is a powerful Russian lobby"; that is, "people in Poland who represent not Polish, but Russian interests". Jarosław Kaczyński also stated that

> "you do not need to pursue an anti-Russian policy, but a Polish one, which consists of defending everything that happened in Poland and in the world

---

63 Ibidem,
64 'SLD: Kaczyńskiego cechuje rusofobia', August 13, 2008. Available at https://tvn24.pl/polska/sld-kaczynskiego-cechuje-rusofobia-ra67616-3714268
65 'Sprawozdanie Stenograficzne z 35 posiedzenia…,' p. 264
66 Ibidem
67 https://www.spisok-putina.org/en/personas/leontyev/

after 1989, because thanks to this, Poland is independent, and there is a union between the independence of Poland and Georgia, and only a complete idiot does not see this connection".[68]

Referring to this statement, the then head of the Civic Platform parliamentary club, Zbigniew Chlebowski, stated that "not for the first time Jarosław Kaczyński shows his own phobias towards Russians. He does not hide his emotions and negative attitude".[69]

This strategy was important because it belonged to one of the then leaders of the ruling PO-PSL (Civil Platform—Polish People Party) coalition which formed the Tusk government in 2007 which had decided to "attempt normalization" in Poland's relations with Russia. As explained by Sikorski, who was the minister of foreign affairs for almost the entire period of the PO-PSL coalition government, the aim was to create "an image of Poland as a serious player, a country that can rise above post-colonial fears and prejudices".[70] Therefore, the Polish side focused its efforts on the area of, among others, memory politics. One of the important stages of this policy was to be the joint visit of Prime Ministers Tusk and Putin to Katyn on April 7, 2010. A day later, the Polish Minister of Foreign Affairs Sikorski, opening the debate on Polish foreign policy in the *Sejm*, described the event as a "historic moment" and stated, "our Polish and Russian approach to the 70th anniversary of the Katyn massacre is a test of how normalized our relationship has become".[71] Sikorski's optimism had no basis.

However, for the representatives of the then ruling coalition, the symbolic effect of Tusk's meeting with Putin in Katyn was very important. Using the language of Kremlin propaganda, he was supposed to show progress in the process of "civilizing" Polish Russophobia. In other words, a key goal of Polish pragmatism in its relations with Russia was to lead to a positive image of Poland in

---

68 *Tylko kompletny idiota nie rozumie*, November 26, 2008. Available at https://tvn24.pl/polska/tylko-kompletny-idiota-nie-rozumie-ra77969-3719513
69 Ibidem
70 Radosław Sikorski, *Polska...*, p. 124.
71 'Sprawozdanie Stenograficzne z 64 posiedzenia Sejmu Rzeczypospolitej Polskiej w dniu 8 kwietnia 2010 r.', https://orka2.sejm.gov.pl/StenoInter6.nsf/0/DB4E6ACDE5210284C125770000482791/$file/64_b_ksiazka.pdf, p. 139

the West. One day after the event, one of the leaders of the Civic Platform and the head of the parliamentary foreign affairs committee, Andrzej Halicki, emphasized in parliament that "the effects of Polish foreign policy are related to what our partners noticed and what the world noticed, which was emphasized yesterday live on the BBC stations or CNN (...). Well, [Poland's] confrontational foreign policy is gone".[72]

The leading SLD expert on international affairs, Tadeusz Iwiński, agreed with this opinion, stating that following PiS rule, which was full of "Euroscepticism, anti-German and anti-Russian phobias", there was a need for "normalization".[73] However, according to his fellow party member Jolanta Szymanek-Deresz, this positive image was still shadowed by the bad attitude of "some of our leaders", who, in her opinion, "see Moscow as a constant and serious threat". The SLD deputy suggested that "part of the Polish right needs a Moscow which is evil and terrible" and warned that "the world is beginning to look at our phobia of Russians with increasing astonishment".[74] The context of the statements implied that the political circles associated with President Lech Kaczyński and the opposition centered around PiS at the time were to remain a problem.

On April 10, 2010, in a parliamentary debate the second part of the celebrations commemorating the 70th anniversary of the Katyn massacre was to take place. In connection with this, a delegation headed by President Lech Kaczyński travelled to Katyn, but they all perished in the plane crash near Smolensk. Among the victims were both the president and first lady and representatives of all the most important political parties, senior members of the Polish military high command, and heads of key state institutions.

Early elections were brought about by the death of Lech Kaczyński. During the election campaign, Bronisław Komorowski, who ran on behalf of the PO, made a characteristic attempt to discredit his main rival, Jarosław Kaczyński by accusing him of having

---

72 'Sprawozdanie Stenograficzne z 64 posiedzenia..., p. 147
73 'Sprawozdanie Stenograficzne z 64 posiedzenia..., p. 167
74 'Sprawozdanie Stenograficzne z 64 posiedzenia..., p.154

a "Russophobic attitudes" and "xenophobic traits and views", which should disqualify him from participating in "Polish-Russian reconciliation".[75]

The Smolensk catastrophe shocked the Polish political scene and was of fundamental importance to the further development of Polish-Russian relations. It made it more difficult to continue with a "pragmatic" foreign policy towards Russia. In 2018, Sikorski summed this up as follows: "Before Smolensk, Europe was beginning to say that pragmatism in Polish-Russian relations and the seeds of reconciliation could become an inspiration for Russia's difficult relations with most of its neighbors."[76] The former head of the Polish Ministry of Foreign Affairs lamented that "unfortunately Smolensk returned everything to the old, familiar ruts, resulting in a net loss for both countries".[77] However, his comments contrasted both with what Sikorski had himself publicly said about Polish-Russian relations when he was Minister of Foreign Affairs, and with the statements made by the PO-PSL coalition and opposition SLD leaders. Throughout this time, until the annexation of Crimea and the beginning of the armed conflict in eastern Ukraine, they focused, contrary to the prevailing circumstances, on creating a positive image of a pragmatic Polish-Russian partnership.

In 2011, Minister of Foreign Affairs Sikorski had convinced parliamentarians that "while there have been differences in terms of both motives and assessments, despite the difficulties related to the Smolensk investigation, the balance of the last three years of Polish-Russian relations is positive".[78] Sikorski emphasized that "the fact that we do not have major quarrels with Russia only strengthens our position in Europe".[79] Tadeusz Iwiński, one of the SLD leaders, also spoke in a similar tone. In his assessment, "the

---

75 'Polacy nie zapomnieli o rusofobii Kaczyńskiego', May 17, 2010. Available at https://tvn24.pl/polska/polacy-nie-zapomnieli-o-rusofobii-kaczynskiego-ra 134198-3585270
76 Radosław Sikorski, Polska..., p. 124
77 ibidem.
78 'Sprawozdanie Stenograficzne z 87 posiedzenia Sejmu Rzeczypospolitej Polskiej w dniu 16 marca 2011 r.', https://orka2.sejm.gov.pl/StenoInter6.nsf/0 /CD0C11E6036E3398C125785A0051F0B2/$file/87_a_ksiazka.pdf
79 ibidem

past year, despite the Smolensk tragedy, was marked as a period of acceleration of the difficult and historically delayed process of understanding and reconciliation with Russia".[80]

Even more optimistic in this regard was Robert Tyszkiewicz, representing the PO party. He stated that in Polish relations with Russia,

> "the will to cooperate and the will to repair them withstood the test of the Smolensk catastrophe (...). However, if we look at the balance, starting with the economy, intense growth in trade, and ending with the extremely important historical policies or the sphere of relations related to memory politics (...) it can be seen that on both sides, not only on the Polish, there is an interest in developing these relations and building constructive conditions for cooperation".[81]

In 2014, Robert Tyszkiewicz was chosen as one of the top ten MPs in a poll organized by journalists at the opinion-forming *Polityka* weekly which rated "as a very good and very substantive vice-chairman of the Parliament Foreign Affairs Committee" and as a parliamentarian "well versed in Eastern politics", "important commentator" and "source of knowledge for journalists".[82]

It is quite characteristic that in 2013, the head of the Polish Ministry of Foreign Affairs in his annual speech before parliament drew a picture of dynamically developing Polish-Russian economic relations and argued that Poland and Russia are "able to speak with one voice on important and difficult historical matters."[83] These assurances by Sikorski had little to do with reality, but they corresponded to the expectations of the "European mainstream". As Grzegorz Schetyna, chairman of the PO party, reported, "Herman Van Rompuy said that in the case of Russia, we must move from partnership by necessity to partnership by choice." Polish

---

80 'Sprawozdanie Stenograficzne z 87 posiedzenia..., p. 19
81 Ibidem
82 'Biedroń, Kamiński, Olejniczak... Kogo jeszcze wyróżniliśmy za dobre posłowanie?', September 11, 2014. Available at https://www.polityka.pl/tygodnikpolityka/kraj/1592275,1,biedron-kaminski-olejniczak-kogo-jeszcze-wyrozniliismy-za-dobre-poslowanie.read
83 'Sprawozdanie Stenograficzne z 36 posiedzenia Sejmu Rzeczypospolitej Polskiej w dniu 20 marca 2013 roku', https://orka2.sejm.gov.pl/StenoInter7.nsf/0/48239696DF9135D8C1257B350004E792/%24File/36_a_ksiazka.pdf, p. 9

diplomacy, in the name of reinforcing the "image of Poland as a serious player" among its Western partners, had no choice but to adjust to the elections made in Brussels. Hence, G. Schetyna declared, "here in Warsaw it is worth fighting for and it is worth building such an approach to this problem." He added while, "there is a long road ahead of us, but there is no other".[84] Thus, the official Polish foreign policy position, backed by the EU, was that there was no alternative to Polish-Russian "pragmatic" relations.

Efforts were made to create a positive image of relations with Russia, "with whom we do not have any major quarrels." This happened even though on the most important issue in Polish-Russian political relations (i.e., the Smolensk catastrophe), public opinion polls showed something completely different. Most Poles, regardless of their political sympathies, were convinced, "the Russians hid the evidence, blurred the traces of the flight controllers' errors and irregularities in the work of the airport service".[85]

In March 2014, when Russia violated the territorial integrity of Ukraine, Tusk considered it necessary to point out that Poland is a partner that "has no prejudices and does not work because it is Russophobic."[86] The then prime minister emphasized that in this respect, the politics of the PO-PSL coalition "when it comes to eastern issues, is something exactly the opposite of what the Kaczyńskis proposed".[87] Tusk also speculated that if Kaczyński had been in power at that moment, he would have "tried to force a radically anti-Russian stance on the countries in the region". Such a policy would obviously have disqualified Poland as a reliable partner because, in Tusk's opinion, "only a government that has made efforts to cooperate with Europe and Russia is credible, because only such a government is competent in the eyes of the West. (...) If Poland were to proceed as proposed by Jarosław Kaczyński, we would lose the chance to influence the common behavior of the entire

---

84 'Sprawozdanie Stenograficzne z 36 posiedzenia..., p. 16).
85 *Komunikat z badań BS/85/2012*, (Warszawa: Centrum Badań Opinii Społecznej, 2012), p. 3. Available at: https://cbos.pl/SPISKOM.POL/2012/K_085_12.PDF.
86 'Tusk zarzuca PiS rusofobię', March 18, 2014. Available at https://tvrepublika.pl/tusk-zarzuca-pis-rusofobie,5013.html
87 Ibidem

European Union". Most EU countries do not want any argument with Russia, "the head of the Polish government emphasized".[88]

Another opportunity emerged to construct a discourse on Polish foreign policy according to the model of competence and responsibility versus Russophobia during the campaign before the May 2014 elections to the European Parliament. During this campaign, one of the leaders and an MP from the PO Andrzej Halicki argued that "the Civic Platform will win elections to the European Parliament, because Poles will notice that the Civic Platform conducts a responsible foreign policy." At a time when war had already begun in eastern Ukraine, Halicki incredulously emphasized that "no one needs Russophobic quixoticism".[89] The supporters at that time of a "competent and responsible" policy towards Russia radically changed their rhetoric only during the debate on Polish foreign policy in the *Sejm* on May 8, 2014. While opening the debate, Minister of Foreign Affairs Sikorski referring to "Russia's actions in Ukraine", said that "Moscow is issuing a challenge" of "ideological confrontation".[90] The head of Polish diplomacy also noted that "Russia does not accept the rules that the international community has painstakingly worked out over the course of decades, remembering the enormity of the tragedy of two world wars." Moreover, Sikorski concluded that "the Russian state seems to have its own vision of the world". Considering this perspective, the collapse of the Soviet Union was a catastrophe and a humiliation, and the choice of independence by the nations of the former Soviet republics a historical injustice.[91]

Minister of Foreign Affairs Minister Sikorski also informed the deputies in his speech that "modern Russia has recognized itself as the center of Orthodox civilization, as the only heir of old [Kyiv]

---

88 Ibidem,
89 'Halicki: Polacy nie chcą rusofobów. PO wygra wybory do Europarlamentu', March 23, 2014. Available at https://www.gazetaprawna.pl/wiadomosci/arty kuly/785745,halicki-polacy-nie-chca-rusofobow-po-wygra-wybory-do-europa rlamentu.html,komentarze-najstarsze,1
90 'Sprawozdanie Stenograficzne z 67 posiedzenia Sejmu Rzeczypospolitej Polskiej w dniu 8 maja 2014 roku', https://orka2.sejm.gov.pl/StenoInter7.nsf/0 /757955B50A87A1BDC1257CD3000B2502/%24File/67_b_ksiazka.pdf, p. 183
91 Ibidem,

Rus. Thanks to this, it grants itself the right to "gather Ruthenian lands", as did the Moscow princes in the late Middle Ages. Sikorski stressed that "if we accept the Russian point of view, international relations in the 21st century should be governed by the law of the stronger. The post-Soviet area would be Russia's exclusive sphere of influence".[92]

In turn, Grzegorz Schetyna stated that

> "the intensity of Moscow's propaganda and the policy of lies exceeded all expectations. Starting with pressure on Ukraine and on the Ukrainian leadership, and ending with — in recent days, we can see it very clearly — supporting separatists or directly sending troops to the territory of a neighboring country, Russian actions demand a condemnation in our country and a call for a reaction from Europe and the entire democratic world".[93]

A statement by one more leader of the ruling camp, Jacek Rostowski, stated that in Russia "a certain ideology is growing", which "puts national egoism over the rule of international law, which puts the rights of people with Russian nationality over the rights of their neighbors, who, moreover, are mostly, even in the eastern regions of Ukraine, Ukrainian" and which prioritizes "national egoism" as the goal and justification of the actions of the Russian Federation.[94]

Halicki, who had warned about "Russophobic quixoticism" two weeks earlier, now stated emphatically that there are only two paths for European integration. The first leads to "an autocratic world that some politicians are trying to build for themselves." The second, on the other hand, "ensures civil rights, which must be fought for, provides a sense of security, and also builds a sense of energy and economic security." Halicki twice emphasized that "there is no third way" and that "Putin is the only alternative to the European path".[95]

---

92 Ibidem,
93 'Sprawozdanie Stenograficzne z 67 posiedzenia..., p. 189
94 'Sprawozdanie Stenograficzne z 67 posiedzenia..., p. 208
95 'Sprawozdanie Stenograficzne z 67 posiedzenia..., p. 228

The Eastern Partnership and a Trap of Wishful Thinking

In 2009, EU policy towards the post-Soviet space gained a new institutional shape. The eastern dimension developed out of the European Neighborhood Policy and became the Eastern Partnership (EP). Poland was one of the main promoters of this change and the Eastern Partnership was recognized as a key instrument of Polish foreign policy in the east. On May 7, 2009, a special debate on this topic was held in the Sejm of the Republic of Poland. Foreign Minister R. Sikorski presented this project as "the first Polish initiative that has been implemented in the EU's external policy".[96] Sikorski metaphorically characterized the main goal of the Partnership as enabling "many countries to leave post-Soviet civilization and enter European civilization".[97] Of course, the most important recipient of the post-Soviet states invited into the Eastern Partnership was Ukraine.

However, the Eastern Partnership was "a child of its time". At the time of its announcement, US President Barack Obama declared a "reset" in relations with the Kremlin after the Russian invasion of Georgia, "the EU continued to pursue a 'strategic partnership" with Russia, and a company headed by former German Chancellor Gerhard Schröder headed the Gazprom Nord Stream project" with Nord Stream II launched only less than two years after the Eastern Partnership in 2011.[98] Presumably, the creators of the Eastern Partnership concept were aware of the danger of "Russia's destructive tendencies" but chose to ignore them.[99] However, they assumed that over time it would become clear that "the positive agenda for cooperation with the EU that was presented to partner countries may be available not only to them, but also to their great neighbor"

---

96 'Sprawozdanie Stenograficzne z 41 posiedzenia Sejmu Rzeczypospolitej Polskiej w dniu 7 maja 2009 r. (drugi dzień obrad)', https://orka2.sejm.gov.pl/StenoInter6.nsf/0/C97CEB4E5C6B7BBFC12575AF007D7FDF/$file/41_b_ksiazka.pdf, p. 148
97 Radosław Sikorski, *Polska...*, p. 24
98 Taras Kuzio, 'Ukraine between a Constrained EU and Assertive Russia,' *Journal of Common Market Studies*, vol.55, no.1 (January 2017), p 109
99 Radosław Sikorski, *Polska...*, p. 24

[i.e., Russia].[100] During the debate on the EP, Danuta Jałowiecka from the ruling Civic Platform emphasized in a very characteristic way that "particularly important in the partnership is its extension to include Russia's participation in some activities of the entire initiative".[101] It was therefore assumed that Russia would at least not interfere with the Western modernization of its neighborhood, and perhaps even the Kremlin would be interested in joining these activities and benefiting from them.

The then Polish government's "pragmatic" assessment of the political and security situation in Eastern Europe was addressed not only to the Russian authorities, but also to Western decision-makers, who were also under illusions about the prospects of Russia's democratization. Moreover, this approach overlooked the fact that Russia's international identity was increasingly determined by its supposed ontological confrontation with Western values and principles which Putin made abundantly clear in his February 2007 speech to the Munich Security Conference. In addition, Putin's turn to imperial nationalism and adoption of the mantle of 'Gatherer of Russian Lands" was evident when he returned through the use of blatant election fraud to the presidency in 2012. The evolution of Putin and the Kremlin towards White Russian émigré imperial nationalism was evident since the 2004 Orange Revolution and launch of the *Russkiy Mir* in 2007 but the Polish government and EU had ignored them.

Sikorski wrongly claims that Russia "did not oppose" the EP at the beginning and the initiative had a chance to develop "smoothly".[102] In August 2008, President Dmitri Medvedev declared Eurasia to be

> "regions in which Russia has privileged interests. These regions are home to countries with which we share special historical relations and are bound together as friends and good neighbours. We will pay particular attention to our work in these regions and build friendly ties with these countries, our

---

100 'Sprawozdanie Stenograficzne z 41..., p. 150
101 'Sprawozdanie Stenograficzne z 41 posiedzenia..., p. 151
102 Radosław Sikorski, *Polska*..., p. 25

close neighbours. These are the principles I will follow in carrying out our foreign policy."

Medvedev was merely re-affirming long-standing Russian demands the West recognize Eurasia as its exclusive sphere of influence. Exactly a year later Medvedev sent a vitriolic open letter to President Viktor Yushchenko demanding corrections in Ukrainian domestic and foreign policies. In 2010, Putin launched his signature CIS Customs Union, the embryo Eurasian Economic Union, as Putin's competitor to the EP and where the Kremlin expected all Eurasian states, especially Ukraine, would belong.

Nevertheless, the Polish government and EU's inability to comprehend the growth of imperial nationalism in Russia continued because they wrongly believed, "Putin's inflammatory rhetoric towards the West and over Ukraine and Russia's invasion of Georgia had not influenced Western policies to Russia and they continued with business as usual".[103] Sikorski personally, and the government of which he was a member, sought to prove their "Europeanness" and therefore tried to adapt to the dominant trends in EU policy towards Russia. The EP had ambitious goals premised on very low budget. Especially at the beginning, it received relatively weak support from key EU members who were involved in business joint ventures with Russia. Under these conditions, to the EU (and Polish government) the EP resembled a harmless public relations project that had the possibility of shaping a positive image of the EU abroad rather than a program of real action that could bring changes unfavorable for Russia. After all, the EU believed, they were only offering integration and not membership in the EP which Russia should not oppose. This ignored the fact that EP integration gave access to the EU Customs Union. Countries can be only members of one customs union and thereby joining the EU Customs Union meant EP members in Eurasia (such as Ukraine) could not also join Putin's pet project, the CIS Customs Union.

The Polish government and EU also chose to ignore Russia's long-standing claim to exclusive control over Eurasia, or what the

---

103 Taras Kuzio, 'Ukraine between..., p. 109.

Polish foreign minister called "post-Soviet civilization". Russian leaders and political decision-makers gave the non-Russian successor states of the former USSR no independent agency and declared on their behalf "that they do not desire to become a Western-style country".[104] The Kremlin expected all states and societies invited to join the EP to reject it, as Armenia did in 2013 and Russia pressured Yanukovych to do so, and instead follow Russia's leadership at the center of a competing Eurasian civilization. The EP undermined Russia's geo-strategic position in the Eurasian "post-Soviet civilization" and *Ruskiy Mir* and Western challenges to this would be met by force, as in Georgia in 2008.

There was a growing radicalization of anti-Western xenophobia in the Kremlin from the post-Orange Revolution era through to Putin's return to the presidency.[105] Growing imperial nationalism in Russia claimed the country faced the challenge of defending Eurasia and the Russkiy Mir against Western interventions (through color revolutions) and expansion of NATO and the EU. However, the Polish government and its deputies in the European Parliament chose to ignore these important changes in Russia, claiming that skillful dialogue with, and diplomacy towards, Russia would ease Ukraine's integration with the EU. Andrzej Halicki from the Civic Platform, who would become chairman of the *Sejm* Foreign Affairs Committee in 2009, said during the EP debate in the Polish Parliament:

> "The main difference between partnership and all other activities is that partnership is not war. Partnership is cooperation and dialogue for the benefit of citizens. Development and peace. Peace, not war (…) If [Russian Foreign] Minister Lavrov says: I see it and I appreciate it, it means that even in difficult situations, dialogue is better than aggression, and dialogue is better than conflict" (p. 162).

It is worth noting paradoxes and contradictions in the EP from its launch. Members of the EP were treated as independent agents who had freedom to decide whether to take up the EU offer or not; that is, Brussels—unlike Moscow—treated them as sovereign states

---

104 ibidem
105 'Speech and the Following Discussion…

with the right to decide their foreign policy orientations. In 2011, the European Commission and the High Representative of the European Union for Foreign Affairs and Security Policy developed a "Joint Communication" on the challenges facing the EU's Neighborhood Policy. According to this announcement

> "the new approach must be based on mutual accountability and a shared commitment to the universal values of human rights, democracy, and the rule of law. It will involve a much higher level of differentiation allowing each partner country to develop its links with the EU as far as its own aspirations, needs and capacities allow".[106]

Foreign Minister Sikorski repeated the illusion of post-soviet states "free choice" in his March 2013 address to the Polish parliament when he stated: "For us and for Europe in the 21st century, it will be very important which civilizational association will be chosen by nations in the Eastern part of the continent. We are an active promoter of the EU Partnership. However, we are aware that progress towards democracy, the rule of law and modernization largely depends on them".[107] Such an assessment of the situation completely overlooked the importance of the pressure that Russia had already begun to exert on EP participants since Putin returned to the presidency,[108] ranging from economic sanctions to in 2014 the military invasion of Ukraine. In 2013, after heavy pressure Armenia withdrew from the Eastern Partnership and Yanukovych announced Ukraine's withdrawal. Therefore, Armenia turned its back on Europe and joined the Eurasian Economic Union while Yanukovych's action led to the Euromaidan Revolution's mass protests. The Polish government had failed to see that Putin's goal since 2012 had been to pressure Yanukovych to reject the EP in favour of Ukraine joining Russia and Belarus in the *Russkiy Mir* core of the Eurasian Economic Union. Sikorski's 2013 speech showed that after four

---

106 'A new response to a changing Neighbourhood', https://eur-lex.europa.eu/legal-content/EN/TXT/?uri=celex%3A52011DC0303 p. 2
107 'Sprawozdanie Stenograficzne z 36 posiedzenia Sejmu Rzeczypospolitej Polskiej w dniu 20 marca 2013 roku', https://orka2.sejm.gov.pl/StenoInter7.nsf/0/48239696DF9135D8C1257B350004E792/%24File/36_a_ksiazka.pdf p. 8
108 See Karel Svoboda, 'On the Road to Maidan: Russia's Economic Statecraft Towards Ukraine in 2013' *Europe-Asia Studies*, 71: 1685-1704.

years of implementing the EP, its main promoters had not come to an understanding of Russia, did not see the rise of imperial nationalism as a threat to the EP, ignored Putin's obsession with Ukraine and overall remained poorly versed in the security challenges faced by the EU's eastern neighbors.

The EU was therefore unable to adequately respond to the dynamic situation unfolding in its eastern neighborhood. The EU's inability to comprehend the criminal and imperial nationalistic nature of Yanukovych and Russia respectively, continued throughout the 92-day Euromaidan Revolution. During talks in February 2014 between the opposition and the Ukrainian president brokered by the pro-Russian German Federal Minister for Foreign Affairs Frank-Walter Steinmeier, and the Polish and French Foreign Ministers Sikorski and Laurent Fabius, all three representing the EU, they reached a "compromise" whereby Yanukovych would remain in power until December when he would hold pre-term elections[109]. It came after the murder of 100 protestors and there was no trust in Yanukovych (unlike with Sikorski and his two EU co-negotiators) to abide by the agreement and hold elections in December. Nevertheless, Foreign Minister Sikorski insisted: "If you do not support it [the agreement] there will be a state of emergency, the army will be sent in. You will all die.[110]" Euromaidan protesters flatly rejected the "compromise". Sikorski wrote in his memoirs that right after this compromise was presented to the protesters "some crank shouted from the tribune on Independence square, that agreements signed with an assassin are invalid"[111]. Sikorski is still likely to be proud of his activities during Euromaidan, asserting that "the shootings stopped only thanks to the agreement"[112] which he and his colleagues from the EU negotiated with Yanukovych and opposition. He was wrong. Yanukovych fled from Kyiv and from his

---

109 https://archive.ph/20140223081530/http://www.president.gov.ua/ru/news/30117.html
110 'Urging the Maidan Rada, Sikorski says that otherwise all will die', February 21, 2014. Available at https://euromaidanpress.com/2014/02/21/urging-the-maidan-rada-sikorski-says-that-otherwise-all-will-die/
111 Radosław Sikorski, Polska..., p. 9
112 Ibidem

office, Euromaidan Revolutionaries came to power, parliament *de facto* impeached Yanukovych and the Party of Regions disintegrated.

Conclusions

Based on the statements analyzed in this chapter, it can be concluded that some Polish politicians were very aware of the real goals the Kremlin had set for itself in its foreign and security policies. It can be assumed that the architects and promoters of the Polish-Russian partnership and reconciliation policy conducted in 2007-14 were aware of the dangers related to the neo-imperial aspirations of Putin and his Kremlin entourage. Sikorski's diagnosis of Russian foreign and security policies were particularly accurate, referring back to Putin's infamous speech to the 2007 Munich Security Conference. Sikorski summarized the main assumptions of the concept of the *Russkij Mir* which the Kremlin had been promoting since 2007. However, it seems that fears of being accused of "Russophobia" and the resulting loss of identity as a "reliable" partner in European politics meant that only in the face of the crisis in Ukraine, could representatives of the ruling coalition openly criticize Russia. It is no coincidence that during the parliamentary debate on Polish foreign policy in November 2014, Marek Krząkała, the representative of the ruling PO, argued that "it is not true, as the PiS MP said, that we were not critical of Russia. What is more, in the EU we have often faced with the accusation that we are Russophobes".[113]

In debates on foreign policy, representatives of the ruling PO and the opposition SLD both referred to the concept of "Russophobia". Indeed, in the domestic political scene, both groups were "on both sides of the barricade". However, this situation was intersected by another division, which ran independently of the dividing line between the ruling coalition and the opposition parties. The idea was to distinguish between the groups that declared themselves "pro-European" on one hand, and "Eurosceptic" on the

---

[113] 'Sprawozdanie Stenograficzne z 79 posiedzenia Sejmu Rzeczypospolitej Polskiej w dniu 6 listopada 2014 roku' https://orka2.sejm.gov.pl/StenoInter7.nsf/0/ 4D73B67DA7C17F10C1257D8900469881/%24File/79_b_ksiazka_bis.pdf, p. 90

other. The first group included both the ruling PO and the opposition SLD who were sensitive about their "Europeanness". Its key component was a commitment to democratic values.

Meanwhile, in the West, the belief that Russophobia was contrary to democratic values has been firmly established. Shaming someone for his/her adherence to Russophobia has been a means to win allies and supporters of the Kremlin's policy among Western political and intellectual elites.[114] For example, shortly after the aforementioned visit of Lavrov to Warsaw and in the context of publicly formulated warnings against Russian neo-imperialism by President Jarosław Kaczyński, the US ambassador to Poland wrote in a dispatch: "Lavrov's publicly expressed reluctance to meet with President Jarosław Kaczyński strengthens the conviction of international circles that Kaczyński is instinctively too anti-Russian to give him a place at the table at key meetings".[115] Under these conditions, the political forces that identified themselves with being "European" in Poland could not be perceived as Russophobic, because that would disqualify them in the eyes of Western partners.

The concept of "Russophobia" has taken on a certain rhetorical form and become a tool of symbolic violence. With its help, opponents, and critics of the forced policy of "partnership by choice" with Russia were removed from debates at the EU level and in relations between its individual members. From the point of view of the topic under consideration, it should be noted that the concept of "Russophobia" was also willingly used in disputes that took place in the domestic arena. In these cases, Russia gained a virtual tool with which it could destabilize the political system of a given country to its advantage "from the inside" and play on internal conflicts.

Implementing the pattern of "Russophobia" is very damaging to the quality and efficacy of any public debates referring to relations with Russia. Under favorable circumstances, it allows anyone to dismiss their political adversary very easily. At the same time "such actions represent a negation of dialogue by their very

---

114 Jolanta Darczewska, Piotr Żochowski *Russophobia* ..., p. 15
115 Radosław Sikorski, *Polska*..., 119

nature". Therefore, they pervert the customs and political culture on which democratic order should be based.[116]

After 2014, the usefulness of the term "Russophobia" as a tool to eliminate critics of Russia's policy decreased significantly. Due to the dynamic changes in the situation in Ukraine, initiated by the Euromaidan Revolution of Dignity, it was difficult to maintain even the appearance of partnership between Poland and Russia. Moreover, it was becoming less and less necessary as the economic situation on the international stage was changing under the influence of Russia's military aggression against which the EU and the US introduced sanctions. Although *Putinverstehers'* circles were still strong in the West, open criticism of Russia's actions ceased to be a reason for automatic ostracism.

This does not mean that the term "Russophobia" has completely fallen out of use. This is evidenced by the book by Radosław Sikorski *Polska może być lepsza (Poland Could Be Better)* published in 2018. Its author argues, inter alia, that if it were not for the Smolensk catastrophe, Polish-Russian relations "would have been on a different trajectory (...)". However, as it turns out, according to former Minister of Foreign Affairs Sikorski, the problem was not the growing doubts as to the reliability of the method explaining the catastrophe's causes, but the "explosion of verbal Russophobia endorsed by Antoni Macierewicz" who clearly articulated these doubts and reservations.[117] It was this "Russophobia" that was supposed to "destroy the little trust we had gained in each other." Sikorski claimed, "the Russians realized that their controllers could be jointly responsible for the catastrophe" and that is why they began to manipulate the course and results of the investigation.[118] At the same time, Sikorski euphemistically rationalized this procedure as "the priority for Russian defense of their uniform's honor" and argues that if it were not for the aforementioned "Russophobia", the Russian side would not have made it difficult to explain this tragedy.

---

116 Jolanta Darczewska, Piotr Żochowski *Russophobia* ..., p. 8
117 Radosław Sikorski, *Polska*..., p. 124
118 ibidem

This example shows quite clearly the logic of discourse imposed by the concept of Russophobia. It is a tool of symbolic violence, by which means the narrative is transferred from the sphere of rational argumentation to the level of emotional appeal. In so doing, it is also very easy to reverse the status of its participants in the event of a dispute over guilt and perpetration. That is, the perpetrator becomes the victim, and the victim turns out to be at least complicit in the situation. It is this logic that leads to the conclusion that if the Polish side had behaved differently (not Russophobically), Russians would not have been forced to delude themselves and manipulate the facts while explaining the causes of the Smolensk tragedy.

The stereotype of Russophobia prevailing in Poland and Eastern Europe has been deeply rooted in the consciousness of Western elites; at least until Russia's invasion in 2022. Thanks to this, under the pretext of combating extremist behavior, it was possible to paralyze any matter of fact and rational debate on the proper shape of the relationship between the EU, including its individual actors, and Russia. This applied to economic, military, and political issues as well as to the sphere of values.

In practical terms, a policy free from "Russophobia" meant a policy of concessions to Russia in exchange for perceived benefits. The advocates of this strategy, hoping to build partnership relations, fell into the trap of client-patron dependency. Remuneration for tacitly accepting and legitimizing the Russian narrative in memory politics, or for submitting to the fact that Russia does not respect previous joint arrangements and violates the boundaries set by its actions. The potential frustration resulting from unilateral concessions was mitigated by the prospect of a reward in the form of prestige and recognition on the part of Western partners for their ability to pursue a policy towards Russia free from "ineffective nonconciliation".

Attempts at promoting "Polish-Russian reconciliation" were removed from reality, imbued with wishful thinking and driven by an unwillingness to see Russia as it really was. They referred to some of the perceptions about Russia and its political system under Putin that have been disseminated in the West, as well as to wishful thinking about the Kremlin's policy goals. These representations are deeply rooted among some sectors of the Western establishment (i.e., politicians, scientists, analysts). They result from the traditional ignorance of past and ongoing political, social, and civilizational processes in Russia and in Central- Eastern Europe. As a result, the ability to find a "common language" in relations with Russia, or at least the absence of conflicts with Russia, became a sign of how politically mature a person is.

The unexplainable belief the authorities in the Kremlin treated selected Western partners in a serious manner resulted in Polish attempts to join this hypothetical elite club. Polish decision-makers believed that by being members of such a club, they could not only gain a good position in relations with Russia, but also act as a mentor and valued adviser for post-Soviet states like Ukraine that sought closer ties with the West.

This "pragmatism" was based on illusions about Russia that included the playing down of chauvinistic and nationalist discourse, faith in the "rationality" of the Kremlin's decisions, and waiting for signs of reforms, political democratization, and social modernization. It is impossible to ascertain to what extent Polish decision-makers really shared these illusions. Nevertheless, they adapted their policy to the demand for illusionary reforms in Russia to gain recognition from their Western partners they were serious and credible players on the European political scene.

Russia moved to the imperial nationalist right in incremental stages after the 2004 Orange Revolution and Putin's return to the presidency in 2012—both before the 2014 crisis. Putin's 2007 infamous speech explained the Kremlin believed it was at war with the West, not militarily but through other means usually subsumed under hybrid warfare.

As a result, Polish policymakers, like their EU policymaking counterparts, unexplainably and wrongly believed Russia would not oppose the Eastern Partnership in countries such as Ukraine[119] when Russian security policy had consistently opposed since the early 1990s NATO and EU enlargement and UN peacekeeping

---

119 See Taras Kuzio, 'Ukraine between a Constrained EU…, pp. 103-120.

forces in the former Soviet space. Unfortunately, it took Russia's brazen annexation of Crimea and military aggression for Polish pragmatists to wake up from their naïve dreams of "normalizing" relations with a Russia that had long before 2014 been driven by imperial nationalism and anti-Western xenophobia.[120]

---

[120] See T. Kuzio, *Russian Nationalism and the Russian-Ukrainian War: Autocracy-Orthodoxy-Nationality* (London: Routledge, 2022).

Western Russophilism, Russian Disinformation and the Myth of Ukraine's Regional Divide

Petro Kuzyk

Russia's brutal and unprovoked assault on Ukraine and the despicable war crimes committed by the Russian military and security forces on the Ukrainian soil have shocked many in the world.[1] However, the ideological foundations and plans for annihilation of the Ukrainian polity and nation were evident long before these events have actually taken place. The key ideas and myths about Ukraine and Ukrainians, which were used for legitimizing the Russian military attacks, had been carefully bred and spread by Kremlin-affiliated political elites, intellectuals and outright propagandists prior to the launched invasion in February 2022 or illegal annexation of Crimea and occupation of parts of the Donbas in 2014.

Back in 2008, in a conversation with US President George W. Bush, Russian President Vladimir Putin claimed that Ukraine was "not even a state". "What is Ukraine?" maintained Putin, "[p]art of its territories is Eastern Europe, but the greater part is a gift from us."[2] This remark implied some important beliefs that Putin and the Russian elites adhered to regarding Ukraine and were keen to share with their counterparts in the West: Ukraine was an artificial and, therefore, weak political community, which accidentally became a sovereign state; and that it was made up of different parts, many of which "belonged" to Russia.

---

1 Emma Farge, 'Investigation chief says Russia committed war crimes in Ukraine,' *Reuters*, September 23, 2022. Available at https://www.reuters.com/world/europe/un-mandated-inquiry-concludes-war-crimes-were-committed-ukraine-2022-09-23/
2 James Marson, 'Putin to the West: Hands Off Ukraine,' *Time*, May 25, 2009. Available at http://www.themoscowtimes.com/news/article/putin-hints-at-splitting-up-ukraine/361701.html

The subsequent Russia's actions attested that these ideas represented an essential source of the Russian aggressive policy towards Ukraine. They were used for instigating and justifying the 2014 hybrid aggression and annexation of Crimea as well as the recent 2022 invasion, which led to tens of thousands of victims among combatants and civilians. An estimated 50,000 murdered Ukrainian civilians in the destruction of just one port city of Mariupol[3] reveals the scale of killings and devastations these Russian leadership's myths have brought in Ukraine.

Putin used these claims for justifying the illegal annexation of Crimea during the so-called "accession ceremony" in the Kremlin in March 2014. In his formal speech he called Ukraine's southern and eastern regions "the territory of the historic South of Russia", arbitrarily incorporated into the Ukrainian Soviet Socialist Republic by Bolsheviks. In an apparent attempt to portray it as a failed state Putin also insisted on a "permanent political and state crisis in Ukraine" which was allegedly shaking Ukraine.[4]

Likewise, Kremlin used the same ideas in its public narratives aimed at legitimizing Russian imperialistic intentions prior and during the full-scale military aggression against Ukraine launched on the 24 February 2022. In his comprehensive article "On the Historic Unity of Russians and Ukrainians" published in July 2021[5] Putin once argued about an artificial nature of a separate Ukrainian nation, its culture and language. He stressed an illegitimate incorporation of vast inherently "Russian" lands in the Soviet Ukraine. The same claims were once again repeated by Putin in his hour-

---

3 'Ukraine: Mariupol theatre attack was 'a clear war crime' — new investigation,' Amnesty International, June 30, 2022. Available at https://www.amnesty.org.uk/press-releases/ukraine-mariupol-theatre-attack-was-clear-war-crime-new-investigation

4 Vladimir Putin, 'Obrashchenie Prezidenta Rossiiskoi Federatsii,' Prezident Rossiiskoi Federatsii, March 18, 2014. Available at http://kremlin.ru/events/president/news/20603

5 Vladimir Putin, 'Ob istoricheskom iedinstve russkikh i ukraintsev,' Prezident Rossiiskoi Federatsii, July 12, 2021. Available at http://en.kremlin.ru/events/president/news/66181

long televised address on the eve of launching the full scale invasion in Ukraine in February 2022.[6]

These messages, communicated by the Russian leadership both to its own public and the international community, echoed a perception of Ukraine deeply influenced by the Russian imperial legacy. On the one hand, they reiterated an old Russian myth of Ukrainians as a branch of great Russian people incapable of nation-building and separate existence as a sovereign nation-state. On the other hand, these ideas reflected Russia's unhealed nationalist trauma brought about by the break-up of the Soviet Union, which delivered a heavy blow to the Russian imperialist megalomania by degrading political status of the country to a regional power.[7]

The ideas of Ukraine as representing an artificial and failed state formation, arbitrary molded by Russia's enemies out of "stolen" Russian lands and some other territories lying to the west, surely have not been limited to the Russian political class alone. Russia's intellectuals and scholars have played their role in reinforcing and disseminating these myths at home and abroad. In the most repulsive forms these ideas were retranslated by politically influential illiberal thinkers. Aleksandr Dugin, a Eurasianist and fascist ideologue, is probably the best known example whose writings help understand Putin's statements and actions better.[8]

Dugin was an advisor to high-ranking Russian politicians and officials and was implicated in Russia's annexation of Crimea and

---

6 Vladimir Putin, 'Polnyi tekst obrashcheniia po priznaniiu DNR i LNR,' *Komsomolskaia Pravda*, February 21, 2022. Available at https://www.kp.ru/daily/27366/4549244
7 Andreas Kapeller, 'Ukraine and Russia: Legacies of the Imperial Past and Competing Memories,' *Journal of Eurasian Studies*, no.5 (2014), pp. 107-115; Mykola Riabchuk, 'Rosiis'kyi stereotyp ukraintsia: vid impers'koi uiavy do postimpers'koi real'nosti,' *Krytyka*, no.19 (2015), pp.2-11; Taras Kuzio, *Russian Nationalism and the Russian-Ukrainian War: Autocracy-Orthodoxy-Nationality* (London: Routledge, 2022).
8 Anton Barbashin, Hanna Thoburn, 'Putin's Brain: Alexander Dugin and the Philosophy behind Putin's Invasion of Crimea,' *Foreign Affairs*, May 17, 2014. Available at https://www.foreignaffairs.com/articles/russia-fsu/2014-03-31/putins-brain

Novorossia project during the 2014 attack on Ukraine.[9] This odious figure, nevertheless, is best known for his pseudo-scientific writings and particularly his book *"Essentials of Geopolitics"*. In this text Dugin maintained that Ukraine was a fake political formation composed of Russian and some Central-European cultural entities. He also emphasized that a sovereign Ukraine in its contemporary borders presented a threat to Russia and therefore the Ukrainian territory had to be "restructured."[10] While the book was first published in 1997 it has remained an influential ideological text in Russia thereafter.

However, some of the myths regarding Ukraine that formed the conceptual and ideological core of the Russian 2014 and 2022 assaults on Ukraine in fact have been widely shared by Western academic and expert communities. What the latter share in common with the Russian political autocrats and hawkish ideologists in this regard is the stereotypical view of Ukraine as a deeply divided and politically feeble state and society. Since early 1990s and particularly the 2004 Orange Revolution this conceptualization of Ukraine has become a popular stereotype in the West.

Samuel Huntington's portrayal of Ukraine in his *Clash of Civilizations* has been one of the most influential accounts reinforcing this stereotype of Ukraine in the Western political and scholarly discourses.[11] Huntington portrayed Ukraine as positioned between Western and Orthodox civilizations as well as internally split into two parts. "The civilizational fault line between the West and Orthodoxy runs through its heart and has done so for centuries".[12] According to Huntington, the historical dominance of the cultural and

---

9 Andreas Umland, 'Fascist Tendencies in Russia's Political Establishment: The Rise of the International Eurasian Movement,' *Russian Analytical Digest*, no.60 (2009), pp.13-17; Marlene Laruelle, 'The Izborsky Club, or the New Conservative Avant-Garde in Russia,' *The Russian Review*, vol.75, no.4 (2016), pp.626-644; Anton Shekhovtsov, 'Alexandr Dugin's Neo-Eurasianism and the Russian-Ukrainian War' In: Mark Bassin and Gonzalo Pozo, eds., *The Politics of Eurasianism: Identity, Popular Culture and Russia's Foreign Policy* (London: Rowman & Littlefield International, 2017), pp.185-204.
10 Aleksandr Dugin, *Osnovy geopolitiki* (Moskva: Arktogeia, 2000), p.219.
11 Samuel P. Huntington, *The Clash of Civilizations and the Remaking of World Order* (London: Simon&Schuster, 1997), pp.165-168.
12 Huntington, *Clash of Civilizations*, p.165.

religious entities in the respective parts of this 'cleft country' divided between east and west was undermining contemporary Ukraine from within. Hence, he even assumed that "Ukraine could split along its fault line into two separate entities, the eastern of which would merge with Russia".[13]

Such accounts of Ukraine, evoking the stereotypic view of the country as deeply split between eastern and western parts making it a failed state structure with a significant risk of disintegration, continue to influence Western political experts, think tank analysts and scholars. These assertions correlate with the recent allegations voiced by Putin. A combination of traditional Russophilism and decades-long Kremlin's disinformation campaigns in the West seem to have played off. It has also influenced Western scholarly and think tank writing on Ukraine and the view of Western experts and policymakers that Ukraine would be quickly defeated by an invading Russian military force.[14]

This chapter will challenge this stereotypic view of Ukraine by demonstrating that the ideas at its core have significant problems when they are applied to present-day Ukraine. The myths of Ukraine's profound societal divide and weak and incapable state institutions were exaggerated prior to the 2014 crisis but since, as seen in Ukraine's united response to Russian military aggression since the 2022 invasion, is discredited.

The Euromaidan Revolution of Dignity

Claims about Ukraine as a cleft polity have been most effectively questioned by the dramatic events of 2013-2014, 2014 crisis and 2022 invasion. The Euromaidan and, above all, Russian annexation of Crimea, hybrid warfare in the Donbas and invasion put the unity and sustainability of Ukraine to a severe test. Contrary to what could be expected from a "failed state" in such critical conditions, Ukraine demonstrated a strong degree of national solidarity and

---

13   Huntington, *Clash of Civilizations*, p.167.
14   Taras Kuzio, 'Euromaidan Revolution, Crimea and Russia-Ukraine War: Why it is Time for a Review of Ukrainian-Russian Studies,' *Eurasian Geography and Economics*, vol.59, no. (2018), pp. 529-553; Kuzio, *Russian Nationalism*.

endurance with the majority of its Russian-speakers showing an allegiance to Ukrainian (as opposed to Russian World and Eurasian) patriotism.[15] Moreover, it can be argued Russia's military aggression in 2014 and invasion in 2022 has made Ukraine's national integration more consolidated.

A clear sign of the strengthening vibrancy of Ukraine's political community has been its civil society and volunteer movement. The Euromaidan Revolution became a symbol of civic self-organization as well as sacrifice of millions of Ukrainians from all corners of the country. It was the third popular protest which had broken out at critical moments of Ukraine's development. The success of the pro-European and anti-authoritarian protest movement was connected with the spread of ethnic Ukrainian national identity from west to east since the late 1980s and signified another important step towards the national consolidation of Ukrainian society.[16]

The Euromaidan Revolution remained a contentious issue for people living in south-eastern Ukraine. Still in its early phases in December 2013 the Euromaidan Revolution was supported by 30 per cent of the population in the east and just 20 per cent in the south.[17] Nonetheless, a by-*oblast* analysis of attitudes toward the Euromaidan Revolution shortly after its culmination and the flight of President Viktor Yanukovych from Kyiv exposed a tangible

---

15   Volodymyr Kulyk, 'National Identity in Ukraine: Impact of Euromaidan and the War,' *Europe-Asia Studies*, vol.68, no.4 (2016), pp. 588-608; Volodymyr Kulyk, 'Shedding Russianness, recasting Ukrainianness: the post-Euromaidan dynamics of ethnonational identifications in Ukraine,' *Post-Soviet Affairs*, vol.34, no.2-3 (2018), pp. 119-138; Volodymyr Kulyk, 'Identity in Transformation: Russian-speakers in Post-Soviet Ukraine,' *Europe-Asia Studies*, vol.71, no.1 (2019), pp. 156-178; Taras Kuzio, *Putin's War Against Ukraine. Revolution, Nationalism, and Crime* (Toronto: Chair of Ukrainian Studies, 2017), pp.314-357.
16   Taras Kuzio, 'Three Revolutions, One War and Ukraine's West Moves East' In: Pawel Kowal, Georges Mink and Iwona Reichardt, eds., *Three Revolutions: Mobilization and Change in Contemporary Ukraine I. Theoretical Aspects and Analyses on Religion, Memory, and Identity* (Stuttgart and Warsaw: Ibidem and College of Europe, 2019), pp.91-120.
17   'Dva misiatsi protestiv v Ukraini: shcho dali?' Democratic Initiatives Foundation, January 21, 2014. Available at https://dif.org.ua/article/dva-misyatsi-protestiv-v-ukraini-shcho-dali

reconfiguration of public opinion taking place in south-eastern Ukraine.

In April 2014 Donetsk and Luhansk *oblasts* regarded the Euromaidan Revolution as signifying "an armed coup d'état", while either an absolute or relative majority of the public in every other eastern or southern *oblast* (with the exclusion of the already occupied Crimea) preferred to define it as a "civic protest against corruption and oppression of the Yanukovych dictatorship".[18] This reflected post-2014 reality where one powerful pole in the former political and regional dichotomy — the symbolic "east" — had been significantly weakened and ceased to exist in its previous form.[19]

At the same time, the Euromaidan Revolution spread to other regions inciting protests and civic activism outside the Kyiv Maidan. Demonstrations of support took place in many large Ukrainian cities, including in the Donbas and even Crimea before its annexation.[20] The demolishing of Vladimir Lenin monuments and other communist leaders, which had been initiated in Kyiv in December 2013, followed a similar pattern. This continued after the Euromaidan Revolution in the form of mainly spontaneous acts by local activists in central and south-eastern Ukraine and following the adoption of decommunization legislation in 2015 became more structured.[21]

---

18 '*Dumky ta pohliady zhyteliv pivdenno-skhidnykh oblastei Ukrainy: kviten' 2014*,' Kyiv International Institute of Sociology, April 20, 2014. Available at https://www.kiis.com.ua/?lang=ukr&cat=reports&id=302&page=1

19 Tatiana Zhurzhenko, 'From Borderlands to Bloodlands,' *Eurozine*, September 19, 2014. Available at https://www.eurozine.com/from-borderlands-to-bloodlands/; Tatiana Zhurzhenko, 'Ukraine's Eastern Borderlands: the end of ambiguity?' In: Andrew Wilson, ed., *What Does Ukraine Think?* (London, European Council on Foreign Relations, 2015), pp.45-52, https://ecfr.eu/publication/what_does_ukraine_think3026/

20 Kataryna Wolczuk and Roman Wolczuk, 'How Protest and Violence in Ukraine Could Give Way to Unity,' *The Washington Post*, January 28, 2014. Available at https://www.washingtonpost.com/news/monkey-cage/wp/2014/01/28/how-protest-and-violence-in-ukraine-could-give-way-to-unity/; Timothy Snyder, 'Fascism, Russia and Ukraine,' *The New York Review of Books*, March 20, 2014. Available at https://www.nybooks.com/articles/2014/03/20/fascism-russia-and-ukraine/

21 'Za rik v Ukraini znesly pivtysiachi pam'iatnykiv Leninu,' Ukrainian Institute of National Memory, 2015. Available at http://www.memory.gov.ua/news/za-rik-v-ukraini-znesli-pivtisyachi-pam-yatnikiv-leninu; Anna Oliynyk

The participation of south-eastern Ukraine in these revolutionary developments had not occurred either during the Revolution on Granite in 1990 or the Orange Revolution in 2004. The former was a sit-down protest of students against an ailing Soviet regime, while popular backing for the Orange Revolution was largely limited to the western and central regions. The pro-European objectives of the Euromaidan movement as well as intense civic mobilization and the expanded regional and social support base of the protests reflected progress in state and nation-building in the country, strengthened societal cohesion and the increasingly civic nature of Ukraine's national identity.[22]

Following the annexation of Crimea and the Russian-Ukrainian war in the Donbas numerous civic projects and undertakings were initiated throughout Ukraine. These initiatives focused on procurement for the Ukrainian army, improvement of its medical facilities and rehabilitation and providing for the families of the victims of the conflict in the Donbas.[23] An additional problem tackled by the volunteers was assisting almost two million internally displaced people (IDP's) who fled the war-torn Donbas and occupied Crimea and refugees.[24] This volunteerism has again revived, but on a bigger scale, since Russia's invasion.

---

and Taras Kuzio, 'The Euromaidan Revolution of Dignity, Reforms and De-Communisation in Ukraine,' *Europe-Asia Studies*, vol.73, no.5 (2021), pp.807-836.

22 Kulyk, 'National Identity,' pp.588-608; Kulyk 'Shedding Russianness,' pp.119-138; Kulyk, 'Identity in Transformation,' pp.156-178; 'Identychnist Hromadyan Ukrayiny v Novykh Umovakh: Stan, Tendentsii, Rehionalni Osoblyvosti,' Razumkov Center, 2016, http://razumkov.org.ua/uploads/journal/ukr/NSD 161-162_2016_ukr.pdf; 'Konsolidatsiya Ukrayinskoho Suspilstva: Vyklyky, Mozhlyvosti, Shlyakhy,' Razumkov Center, 2016. Available at http://razumkov.org.ua/uploads/journal/ukr/NSD165-166_2016_ukr.pdf; 'Osnovni Zasady ta Shlyakhy Formuvannya Spilnoyi Identychnosti Hromadyan Ukrayiny,' Razumkov Center, 2017. Available at http://razumkov.org.ua/up loads/journal/ukr/NSD169-170_2017_ukr.pdf; Kuzio, *Putin's War*, pp. 314-357.

23 Rosaria Puglisi, *A People's Army: Civil Society as a Security Actor in Post-Maidan Ukraine*, paper no. 23. (Rome: IAI Working Papers, 2015). Available at http://www.iai.it/sites/default/files/iaiwp1523.pdf

24 Maksym Sydorzhevskyi, 'Ukraina potrapyla u spysok rekordsmeniv svitu za kil'kistiu vnutrishnio peremishchenykh osib,' *Deutsche Welle*, May 11, 2016. Available at http://www.dw.com/uk/a-19248485; Natalka Poznyak-Khomenko, ed. *Volontery: Syla nebayduzhykh* (Kyiv: Ukrainian institute for

Crimea and Russia's First Invasion: 2014

The reaction of Ukrainian society to Russia's annexation of Crimea and hybrid war aggression in the Donbas was another significant indicator of Ukraine's growing national integration.[25] In the first place this concerned the moral and human resources the country was able to confront the Russian adversary with despite the disastrous condition of the Ukrainian security forces in the early stage of the war. The Ukrainian army fighting in the Donbas was comprised of soldiers from all parts of the country.

A proportional regional representation of troops in the Ukrainian army prior to the 2022 invasion is indirectly confirmed by a registered death-toll of the Ukrainian security forces in Donbas by place of birth of casualties. The origins of the deceased were fairly evenly distributed throughout western, central, eastern and southern parts of Ukraine. In fact, the eastern Ukrainian Dnipropetrovsk *oblast* and the central Zhytomyr *oblast* have the highest number of Ukrainian military casualties in absolute and relative (as per 100,000 residents) numbers.[26] This has been particularly remarkable in view of that that the city of Dnipropetrovsk/Dnipro has evolved from its status as the heart and soul of Soviet Ukraine[27] to the centre of resistance against Russian military aggression in independent Ukraine.[28]

National Remembrance, 2020) Available at https://uinp.gov.ua/elektronni-vydannya/volontery-syla-nebayduzhyh

25   Olexiy Haran, Maksym Yakovlev, eds. *Constructing a Political Nation: Changes in the Attitudes of Ukrainians during the War in the Donbas* (Kyiv: Stylos Publishing, 2017) Available at https://dif.org.ua/article/894594

26   'Zahybli hromadiany Ukrainy za mistsem narodzhennia v mezhakh Ukrainy,' Knyha Pamiati polehlykh za Ukrainu, 2018. Available at http://memorybook.org.ua/indexfile/statbirth.htm; 'Chysel'nist' naiavnoho naselennia Ukrainy na 1 sichnia 2018 roku,' State Statistics Committee of Ukraine, 2018. Available at http://database.ukrcensus.gov.ua/PXWEB2007/ukr/publ_new1/2018/zb_c hnn2018.pdf

27   Sergei Zhuk, *Rock and Roll in the Rocket City: The West, Identity, and Ideology in Soviet Dniepropetrovsk, 1960-1985* (Washington, DC and Baltimore: Woodrow Wilson Center Press and Johns Hopkins University Press, 2010).

28   Kulyk, 'National Identity,' pp.588-608; Kulyk, 'Shedding Russianness,' pp.119-138; Kulyk, 'Identity in Transformation,' pp.156-178; Ania Voznaia, 'Reasons for Success and Failure of the Revitalization of Ukrainians in Eastern Ukraine,' *Danyliw Research Seminar on Contemporary Ukraine*, University of Ottawa,

As Kuzio wrote: "Ceremonies and speeches at the burials of military casualties and their graves are symbolically important for national identity in every country as military cemeteries become places of pilgrimage and national memory" and "Each panakhyda (requiem mass) becomes a manifestation of Ukrainian patriotism and resolution to stand up to Putin's aggression."[29] Outside the city of Dnipro there is a large military cemetery decorated with Ukrainian flags which has become a place of patriotic pilgrimage. "Putin's military aggression is creating large numbers of military plots in cemeteries throughout eastern and southern Ukraine alongside other graves of Ukrainian soldiers who have died in earlier wars. These deaths are influencing Ukrainian national identity and hastening its divorce from Russia."[30] This trend has accelerated in a major way since Russia's 2022 invasion.

Another notable characteristic of Ukrainian security forces fighting in the Russian-Ukrainian war since 2014 is a strong presence of Russian-speakers in the ranks of the Ukrainian army. The high number of Russian-speakers in the Ukrainian military points to a fairly balanced regional base of support for the Ukrainian army. According to some estimates, Russian-speaking citizens represented more than half the total Ukrainian soldiers in the early stages of the conflict in Donbas.[31] The active involvement of Russian-speakers was evident among the composition of volunteer battalions, such as the Azov Regiment of the national guard as well. The majority of the Azov Regiment's members spoke Russian as their

---

November 9, 2019. Available at https://www.danyliwseminar.com/anna-vo zna; Kuzio, *Putin's war*, pp.314-357; Taras Kuzio, Sergei Zhuk and Paul D'Anieri, eds., *Ukraine's Outpost: Dnipropetrovsk and the Russian-Ukrainian War* (Bristol: E-International Relations, 2022) Available at https://www.e-ir.info/publicat ion/ukraines-outpost-dnipropetrovsk-and-the-russian-ukrainian-war/

29 Taras Kuzio, 'Inconvenient facts: Putin's war is killing Russian speakers,' *Ukraine Alert*, March 1, 2018. Available at https://www.atlanticcouncil.org/blo gs/ukrainealert/inconvenient-facts-putin-s-war-is-killing-russian-speakers/

30 Kuzio, 'Inconvenient facts.'

31 Petro Poroshenko, 'Ukrainu na Donbasse zashchishchali 60% russkoiazychnykh voinov,' *Segodnia*, December 4, 2018. Available at https://www.segod nya.ua/politics/ukrainu-na-donbasse-zashchishchali-60-russkoyazychnyh-vo inov-poroshenko-1194720.html

first language as its units were mainly from south-eastern Ukraine.[32]

This data on Ukrainian security forces fighting in the Donbas confirms a substantial degree of national cohesion and loyalty in Ukraine. Conversely, this challenges the depiction of the Donbas conflict as a "civil war" between Ukrainian-speaking western and Russian-speaking eastern Ukraine—an idea long influential among Western scholars and promoted by Russian information warfare.[33] Just 5 percent of Ukrainian citizens regarded violations of the rights of Russophones to be the cause of the Russian-Ukrainian conflict in the Donbas.[34] Similarly, only two percent of Ukrainians believed Russia's justification for invading Ukraine was to protect Russian speakers.[35]

The patriotic allegiance of the residents of Ukraine's south-eastern regions was one of the decisive factors which helped Ukraine withstand Russian military aggression in 2014 and continues to be the case since the 2022 invasion. The Kremlin's *Novorossia* project to create a Russian-controlled quasi-state formation in south-eastern Ukraine failed in 2014-2015 mainly due to the lack of local support.[36] Eventually, the military conflict was localized to the Donbas until Russia's full-scale invasion.

---

32   Illia Ponomarenko, 'After two years of training, Azov Regiment itches to return to war,' *Kyiv Post*, September 1, 2017. Available at https://www.kyivpost.com/ukraine-politics/two-years-training-azov-regiment-itches-return-war.html; Kuzio, *Putin's war*, pp.251-289.
33   Roy Allison, 'Russian 'Deniable' Intervention in Ukraine: How and Why Russia Broke the Rules,' *International Affairs*, vol.90, no.6 (2014), pp.1262-63; Kuzio, 'Euromaidan Revolution,' pp.529-553.
34   'Identychnist Hromadyan Ukrayiny.'
35   'The fourth national poll of Ukrainians during the war,' Rating Sociological Group, March 15, 2022. Available at https://ratinggroup.ua/en/research/ukraine/chetvertyy_obschenacionalnyy_opros_ukraincev_v_usloviyah_voyny_12-13_marta_2022_goda.html
36   Sergei Loiko, 'The Unravelling of Moscow's 'Novorossia' Dream,' *Radio Liberty*, June 1, 2016. Available at http://www.rferl.org/a/unraveling-moscow-novorossia-dream/27772641.html; Taras Kuzio, 'Russian Stereotypes and Myths of Ukraine and Ukrainians and Why Novorossiya Failed,' *Communist and Post-Communist Studies*, vol.52, no.4 (2019), pp.297-309; Ivan Nechepurenko, 'Death of Novorossia: Why Kremlin Abandoned Ukraine Separatist Project,' *The Moscow Times*, May 25, 2015. Available at https://themoscowtimes.com/articles/

Russian military aggression in 2014 and 2022 are factors facilitating the national unification of Ukrainian society into a civic nation. In the wake of Russia's military invasions, patriotic loyalty to the Ukrainian state prevailed among its citizens in all parts of the country. Since 2014, support for Ukrainian independence has grown to its highest peak since the December 1991 referendum. According to a nation-wide sociological survey, the number of Ukrainians who did not support state independence in a hypothetical referendum accounted to a mere 8 percent.[37] At the same time, a strong majority (72 percent in 2015 and 63 percent in 2018) considered Russia be the aggressor country against Ukraine.[38]

Another important indication of the profound change in worldview as well as growing cohesion of the Ukrainian civic nation has been changing attitudes to foreign policy. For years controversy surrounding the question of whether to follow either a pro-Western or pro-Russian foreign policy course was based on a regionally divided Ukraine. The idea of the pro-Russian East contesting the pro-European West was regarded as a fundamental feature of the country. At least since 2014, however, this stereotypic picture of Ukraine is misleading. Support for integrating into Western political and security organizations is now dominant in Ukrainian society. There has been a tangible increase of popular support for joining NATO and the European Union in Ukraine's south-east. Levels of support for pro-Russian integration into Eurasian structures have plummeted and receive meagre support. Since Russia's 2022 invasion, public support for pro-Russian orientations and policies have disappeared.

This positive dynamic as regards support for European integration has been noticeable since 2014 since when there has been the emergence of a stable majority of Ukrainian citizens supporting

---

death-of-novorossia-why-kremlin-abandoned-ukraine-separatist-project-46 849

37 'Ponad 70% hromadian pidtrymuiut' nezalezhnist' Ukrainy,' *Unian*, August 20, 2015. Available at http://www.unian.ua/society/1113640-ponad-70-groma dyan-pidtrimuyut-nezalejnist-ukrajini-opituvannya.html

38 'Monitorynh elektoral'nykh nastroiv ukraintsiv: Lystopad 2018,' Razumkov Center, 2018. Available at http://razumkov.org.ua/uploads/socio/2018_ razumkov_kmis_reytyng.pdf

joining the EU. In south-eastern Ukraine, support for the Western vector has been traditionally lower than in the rest of the country. Nevertheless, sociological surveys show a large increase in support for European integration as well as a steep decline in support for integration into Russian-led structures in Eurasia.

A similar countrywide trend has recently developed regarding the issue of integrating into international security structures. A direct result of Russian military aggression in 2014 and 2022 has been plummeting support for the idea of joining Russia-led integration projects in Eurasia. This reflects a broad consensus on the impossibility of cooperating with Ukraine's Russian neighbour on security issues. Consistent with this trend, the goal of joining NATO, on the other hand, is now supported by a large majority of Ukrainians, including in the south-east of the country. In a summer 2019 poll, 69 percent of Ukrainians participating in a referendum would support joining NATO.[39] Indeed, changes in support for foreign policy orientations are reflected more broadly in transformative changes in Ukrainian national identity.[40]

Until Russia's 2022 invasion, south-eastern Ukraine demonstrated lower rates of support for joining NATO and the EU. But these differences completely disappeared following Russia's invasion. The collapse of the Russian-oriented foreign and security vector in the once traditionally pro-Russian south-east of Ukraine has been a salient shift of strategic importance. South-eastern Ukraine has ceased to be pro-Russian, gradually after the 2014 crisis and completely since Russia's 2022 invasion. This is a major positive development for Ukraine's societal cohesion which will have far-reaching geopolitical consequences for Europe and Russia's relations with the West.

In view of this analysis and data, it can be argued that claims about Ukraine as a cleft country and failed state are an exaggeration that has nothing to do with reality, as seen in the patriotic response

---

39   'A conflict of Moscow and Kyiv: a window of opportunity, the status quo, or a new round of escalation,' Razumkov Center, August, 2019. Available at https://razumkov.org.ua/uploads/article/2019_Donbass_Italy_Eng.pdf
40   Kuzio, Putin's War, pp.314-357.

of Ukrainians to Russian military aggression in 2014 and 2022. No supposedly failed state could withstand a military attack on its sovereignty and integrity by a powerful international actor such as Russia.

At the same time, it would be foolish to deny that Ukraine is not regionally diverse.[41] The annexation of Crimea and hybrid warfare against the Donbas, coupled with imperial nationalist stereotypes about an "artificial Ukraine", fuelled Russian myths about how easy it would be to occupy Ukraine in 2022. However, the most significant consequence of Russian military aggression and invasion will be the growth of national unity and solidarity and marginalization of the former pro-Russian orientation.

Russia's Invasion and the Myth of Ukraine's Regional Divisions

An unprovoked and brutal full-scale invasion of the Russian Federation against Ukraine in February 2022 has been the hardest test for the Ukrainian polity and nation since its acquisition of independence in 1991. The ability of Ukraine's army, its institutions and people in general to withstand Russian military attacks surprised many in Europe and North America. However, Ukrainian resilience confirmed the main argument put forward in this chapter that stereotypic characterizations of Ukraine as a divided and weak or even failed state were always exaggerated.

The devastating military setbacks of the Russian campaign in Ukraine have many reasons. Yet, they would not have happened without a high degree of national solidarity and unity of Ukrainian society and its determination to repel Russian military aggression. If there was no viable national community or functioning state institutions in place in Ukraine the fate of this sovereign country would have been decided in the early phase of the Russian invasion — as the Kremlin and Western policymakers believed. This undermined the myth of a fragmented Ukrainian nation. The harsh realities of the Russian-Ukrainian war have demonstrated that

---

41 Haran and Yakovlev, *Constructing a Political Nation*.

claims about a fundamental East-West split in Ukraine have been significantly exaggerated.

The underestimation of the potential of the Ukrainian state and civic nation has been rooted in an apparent failure to understand Ukraine's successful state- and nation-building process during the last three decades. These processes, discussed elsewhere and earlier in this chapter, have been key in the integration of southeastern Ukraine with allegations about its cultural belonging to the Russian World and unwavering political attraction to Russia have been proven wrong. In 2014 and 2022, Ukrainians in the Russian-speaking south-east showed their patriotic loyalty to Ukraine and not to the Russian World or Eurasia.

In fact, one of the far-reaching consequences of Russian military aggression has been its indirect facilitation of national integration of Ukrainian society. There is little doubt that without Russian military aggression in 2014 and especially the 2022 invasion, Ukraine's societal cohesion and strengthening of its pro-European democratic community would have been more evolutionary. The war against the Ukrainian state and its people has produced a boomerang effect of the kind that the Kremlin never intended. Contrary to the Kremlin's expectations, the invasion of Ukraine fostered national unity. This has been manifested by the disappearance of the pre-2014 "east" as a pro-Russian ideological and attitudinal pole in Ukraine. Russia's invasion has eradicated once tangible post-Soviet and pro-Russian attitudes and made pro-Russian political forces marginal and unpopular.

Russia's invasion has profoundly reshaped Ukraine's political landscape, especially the former pro-Russian segment of the country's political spectrum. Pro-Russian political forces had been gradually losing their popular appeal and influence in the country since 2014. The murder of the Heavenly Hundred on the Euromaidan, Russia's annexation of Crimea and hybrid warfare against the Donbas led to the collapse of the Party of Regions and reduced electoral support for its successor Opposition Bloc from 45 to only ten percent.[42] The 2022 invasion delivered a crushing blow to pro-Russian political parties, especially when it was revealed some of their members had collaborated with occupation forces. Twelve pro-Russian political parties were subsequently banned.

Apart from the obvious reputational costs inflicted upon pro-Russian forces, the Russian invasion further reduced their already limited support base in south-eastern Ukraine. Russia made south-eastern Ukraine a key target of its military campaign, causing immense human, social and economic costs in these predominantly Russian-speaking parts of Ukraine. In the course of the invasion, Russian forces have been ruthlessly destroying eastern Ukrainian cities, and torturing, raping and killing their inhabitants. In addition, the invasion forced twelve million Ukrainian civilians to flee their homes as IDP's and refugees.[43] While much will depend on the eventual outcome and duration of the war it is, nonetheless, reasonable to anticipate that the political weight of the south-east with its former cultural and ideological distinctiveness will diminish within post-war Ukraine.

The marginalization of pro-Soviet and pro-Russian sentiments in south-eastern Ukraine, just as in the country as a whole, has been an even more important effect of the invasion. Reacting to the Russian invasion and atrocities committed by the Russian army, Ukrainian society has become openly hostile and increasingly skeptical about anything to do with Russia. This attitude also extends to Soviet and Russian historical anniversaries and personalities which are now perceived in Ukraine as symbols and tools of Russia's military aggression against its sovereignty and national identity.

Hence, the mass removals of monuments to Soviet leader Vladimir Lenin (dubbed "Leninopad") in post-Maidan Ukraine is being followed by de-Russification; the removal of monuments, street

---

42 Paul D'Anieri, 'Gerrymandering Ukraine? Electoral Consequences of Occupation,' *East European Politics and Societies*, vol.33, no.1 (2019), pp.89-108.
43 'Ukraine: Millions of displaced traumatized and urgently need help, say experts,' UN OHCHR, May 5, 2022. Available at https://www.ohchr.org/en/press-releases/2022/05/ukraine-millions-displaced-traumatised-and-urgently-need-help-say-experts

names and landmarks to Soviet and Russian figures.[44] These initiatives by local communities and councils have resonated in the Ukrainian parliament and in presidential decrees. Thus, in June 2022 the Ukrainian Parliament voted to impose severe legal restrictions on the playing of music by Russian artists in public and the importing of Russian books.[45]

Spontaneous reactions by civic activists and local and central authorities are rooted in shifts that have occurred in the general political and cultural orientations of Ukrainian society. They reflect tangible attitudinal changes towards such fundamental objects as historical memory, cultural policies and foreign orientations. The unjustified Russian invasion has instigated a nation-wide consensus on many of these formerly divisive issues, such as public attitudes to Ukrainian nationalist groups.

These drastic attitudinal shifts have impacted upon the popular perception of the 9 May Victory Day holiday which held powerful symbolic connection with the Soviet past. Until the Russian invasion, Victory Day was recognized in Ukraine as personally meaningful and a deeply honored anniversary that was shared with the countries of the former USSR, including Russia. This attitude dramatically changed following Russia's invasion when Victory Day became "a relic of the past" (36 percent) or even "a regular day" (23 percent).[46]

---

44 Friedrick Kunkle and Serhii Korolchuk, 'Goodbye, Pushkin. Ukrainians target Russian street names, monuments,' *The Washington Post*, May 23, 2022. Available at https://www.washingtonpost.com/world/2022/05/23/renaming-ukr ainian-landmarks-eliminate-russian-names/?utm_campaign=wp_todays_wor ldview&utm_medium=email&utm_source=newsletter&wpisrc=nl_todayworl d&carta-url=https%3A%2F%2Fs2.washingtonpost.com%2Fcar-ln-tr%2F36eab cb%2F628c59de956121755a8cb68f%2F61ab07e99bbc0f79fd6fb24c%2F38%2F74 %2F628c59de956121755a8cb68f
45 Max Hunder, 'Ukraine to restrict Russian books, music in latest cultural break from Moscow,' *Reuters*, June 19, 2022. Available at https://www.reuters.com/ world/europe/ukraine-restrict-russian-books-music-latest-cultural-break-mo scow-2022-06-19/
46 'The tenth national survey: ideological markers of the war,' Rating Sociological Group, April 27, 2022. Available at https://ratinggroup.ua/en/research/ukra ine/desyatyy_obschenacionalnyy_opros_ideologicheskie_markery_voyny_27 _aprelya_2022.html

It is noteworthy that the determination to part with the remaining historical and symbolic bridges connecting Ukraine with the USSR and Russia are now supported by Ukrainians throughout the country. In this respect, the declining rate of Soviet nostalgia in Ukrainian society serves as an important indication of this general trend. Thus, in April 2022, 87 percent of Ukrainian citizens expressed no regret about the collapse of the USSR in 1991. Just 4 percent in the west and 10 and 15 percent in the centre and south respectively regretted the dissolution of the Soviet Union. Even in the east, a region which had often been associated with Soviet nostalgia, there was no longer disappointment over the collapse of the USSR. 80 percent in Ukraine's east did not regret the disintegration of the USSR compared to 18 percent who still did.[47]

Russia's invasion also accelerated the process of relinquishing Soviet and pro-Russian historic narratives and myths that had continued to persist in Ukrainian society. The intensity and scope of the shift in this area is reflected in the evolution of public opinion regarding recognition of the combatant status of OUN-UPA (Organization of Ukrainian Nationalists-Ukrainian Insurgent Army), demonized in the Soviet Union and present-day Russia. In April 2022 as high a proportion of Ukrainians as 81 percent strongly or tentatively supported the recognition of the status of OUN-UPA as combatants, with a high 73 and 72 percent in the South and East respectively. This marked a significant increase in support of this politically and ideologically symbolic step compared to prior to the 2022 invasion.[48]

Another indication of a closing attitudinal gap between different parts of the country is support for Ukraine's foreign trajectory, a trend that had been taking place since 2014. The previously registered collapse in support of a pro-Russian course in the south and east is accompanied by a growing trend of nationwide support for a Western-bound trajectory. Moreover, since Russia's invasion there is a consensus in Ukraine over this crucial but once contentious aspect of its national identity. In June 2022, 87 percent

---

47 'The tenth national survey.'
48 'The tenth national survey.'

supported joining the EU, including 81 and 75 percent in the south and east respectively.[49]

The extent of the political and ideological cohesion reached in Ukrainian society is demonstrated by public opinion on the formerly highly divisive issue of NATO membership. The level of support for NATO membership in the west (84 percent) is now similar to 79 percent support in the centre and 73 percent in the south, representing tectonic shifts in Ukrainian society. Even in Ukraine's east, where the idea of joining NATO was traditionally the least popular, there has been a remarkable change in this respect with a majority (55 percent) in support of NATO membership.[50]

Ukrainian army's counteroffensives in Autumn 2022 have offered yet another proof that the reality on the ground does not support the image of a helplessly divided Ukraine spread by the Russian propaganda and stuck deep in the Western perception of the country. The myth of a deeply split Ukrainian society, the southeastern part of which is profoundly pro-Russian, has been absolutely shattered by the reports of relief and jubilation on the streets of liberated towns and villages of Kharkiv and Kherson regions upon the return of Ukrainian forces.[51] Scenes of euphorical crowds greeting the arrival of Ukrainian soldiers came from liberated Kherson in particular, the only Ukrainian regional centre that had been captured by the Russian forces in February-March 2022.[52]

This significantly contrasted with the local population's reception of Russian troops during their advances in these regions earlier

---

49 'Thirteenth national survey: foreign policy orientations,' Rating Sociological Group, June 18-19, 2022. Available at https://dif.org.ua/en/article/yak-viyna-vplivae-na-dumku-ukraintsiv-pro-druziv-vorogiv-ta-strategichni-tsili-derzhavi
50 'Thirteenth national survey: foreign policy orientations,' Rating Sociological Group, June 18-19, 2022. Available at https://dif.org.ua/en/article/yak-viyna-vplivae-na-dumku-ukraintsiv-pro-druziv-vorogiv-ta-strategichni-tsili-derzhavi
51 Veronika Lutska, 'Ukrainian forces liberated most of the Kharkiv region in a rapid counter-offensive,' *Russia Invaded Ukraine*, September 18, 2022. Available at https://war.ukraine.ua/articles/ukrainian-forces-liberated-most-of-the-kharkiv-region-in-a-rapid-counter-offensive/
52 Nic Robertson and Amy Woodyatt, 'No water, power or internet—only euphoria in newly liberated Kherson,' *CNN*, November 13, 2022. Available at https://edition.cnn.com/2022/11/12/europe/kherson-city-ukraine-russia-intl/index.html

in the beginning of Russia's military campaign against Ukraine. Thousands of unarmed civilians had bravely confronted the Russian soldiers and tanks[53] and a tangible underground resistance movement had operated in these predominantly Russian-speaking areas during the Russian occupation.[54]

Occupied Ukrainian cities and towns, similar to Crimea and the Donbas after 2014, have witnessed Stalinist-style purges, rapes, looting and mass deportations.[55] Putin and the Kremlin have openly declared their intention to destroy Ukraine and Ukrainian national identity.[56] With the war with Russia continuing indefinitely as Ukraine seeks to liberate all occupied southern and eastern territories, the East-West cleavage is not likely to resurface again in the foreseeable future with relations with Russia remaining poor for decades to come.

Conclusion

The analysis in the present chapter has focused on the often cited "East-West" political and cultural polarization of Ukraine and its alleged frail state institutions and society. This chapter has challenged such stereotypic account of Ukraine disseminated by the Russian political elites and ideologists and also shared by many Western scholars and experts. The latter over-focused on Ukraine's regional divisions, propounding views surprisingly similar to Russian writers and politicians who took this thesis further by alleging Ukraine was a divided, artificial and failed state.

---

53 'Kherson's resistance to Russian occupation continues,' Institute for War and Peace Reporting, March 9, 2022. Available at https://iwpr.net/global-voices/khersons-resistance-russian-occupation-continues

54 Isabelle Khurshudyan and Kamila Hrabchuk, 'Stealthy Kherson resistance fighters undermined Russian occupying forces,' The Washington Post, November 18, 2022. Available at https://www.washingtonpost.com/world/2022/11/18/kherson-resistance-partisans-russia-occupation/

55 Taras Kuzio, 'Vladimir Putin's Ukrainian genocide is proceeding in plain view,' Atlantic Council of the US, June 29, 2022. Available at https://www.atlanticcouncil.org/blogs/ukrainealert/vladimir-putins-ukrainian-genocide-is-proceeding-in-plain-view/

56 Putin, 'Ob istoricheskom edinstve'; Timofey Sergeitsev, 'What should Russia do with Ukraine?' RIA Novosti, April 3, 2022. Available at https://ria.ru/20220403/ukraina-1781469605.html

The conclusions reached in this chapter suggest that these ideas of contemporary Ukraine and Ukrainians were factually incorrect prior to Russian military aggression in 2014 and 2022, and especially since. This chapter has demonstrated that Ukraine's "East-West" cleavage is not as clear-cut and entrenched as was commonly assumed. Conversely, these claims have been undermined by signs of a strengthening political, social and cultural convergence of a Ukrainian civic nation.

Since 1991, Ukraine has experienced an evolutionary growth of societal cohesion displayed by increased cultural and ideological integration of its political and social space. This trend unequivocally revealed itself during the Euromaidan Revolution, annexation of Crimea, hybrid war against the Donbas and the recent Russian full-scale invasion. During these trials and tribulations, the Ukrainian civic nation has shown solidarity and resilience, thereby refuting allegations it was a regionally divided (in the eyes of Western scholars) and artificial and failed state (as promoted by Russian information warfare)

Growing Ukrainian national integration since 2014 has been manifested by strong resilience against Russian military aggression, including by Russian-speaking Ukrainians, high levels of public support for Ukraine's independence as well as significantly increased endorsement of a pro-Western trajectory for the country.[57] Russian military aggression in 2014 and especially Russia's invasion in 2022 have destroyed ties to Russia and pro-Russian orientations in Ukraine for decades to come.

---

57 Tymofii Brik and Jennifer Murtazashvili, 'The Source of Ukraine's Resilience. How Decentralized Government Brought the Country Together,' *Foreign. Affairs*, June 28, 2022. Available at https://www.foreignaffairs.com/articles/ukraine/2022-06-28/source-ukraines-resilience

Russian Narratives, Ukraine, and US Right-Wing Punditry
How Kremlin Propaganda Used a 2021 Washington Think-Tank Debate*

Andreas Umland

Since 2014, Ukraine has—in connection with its pro-Western Euromaidan Revolution as well as following Russia's annexation of Crimea and war with Russia in the Donbas region—become an important issue in U.S. and European Union foreign policies. Ukrainian domestic and foreign affairs had started to have increasingly geopolitical repercussions beyond Eastern Europe, already before the 2022 escalation of Russia's war with Ukraine and acceleration of Kyiv's rapprochement with the EU.[1] These aftereffects have led to a *de facto* return of the Cold War between Russia and the West. They have affected transatlantic relations, European integration, the work of the UN Security Council, international energy affairs, and other vital issues. It was thus unsurprising that controversies about Western policies toward Ukraine grew already before Russia's full-scale invasion of Ukraine on February 24, 2022.[2]

---

* An earlier version of this chapter appeared in the *Policy Studies Yearbook* 12, no. 1 (2021). It is here reprinted, in a revised form, with kind permission by the Policy Studies Organization. A German translation of the earlier version also appeared in the *Zeitschrift für Aussen- und Sicherheitspolitik* (Journal for Foreign and Security Policy) published by the University of Cologne and Springer.
1 Recent larger seminal English-language explorations, submitted for publication before 24 February 2022, include: *Civil War? Interstate War? Hybrid War? Dimensions and Interpretations of the Donbas Conflict in 2014–2020*, ed. Jakob Hauter (Stuttgart: ibidem-Verlag, 2021); Taras Kuzio, *Russian Nationalism and the Russian-Ukrainian War: Autocracy – Orthodoxy – Nationality* (Abingdon, UK: Routledge, 2022); Winfried Schneider-Deters, *Ukraine's Fateful Years 2013-2019*, 2 vols. (Stuttgart: ibidem-Verlag, 2022).
2 First comprehensive assessments, by prominent Ukrainianists, of the escalation since 24 February 2022 include, in chronological order: Gwendolyn Sasse, *Der Krieg gegen die Ukraine: Hintergründe, Ereignisse, Folgen* (München: C. H. Beck, 2022); Taras Kuzio with Stefan Jajecznyk-Kelman, *Fascism and Genocide: Russia's*

A 2021 think-tank debate, in which I became involved, is here recounted to demonstrate certain discursive challenges facing the deliberation and formulation of Western policies toward post-communist Europe in general, and U.S. policy toward Ukraine in particular. Stereotypes of a Ukraine characterized by ultra-nationalism and authoritarianism disseminated by Russian propaganda resonate not only on the far left. They are also spread by right-wing political circles, the most widely known representative of which has become notorious former Fox News host Tucker Carlson.

The below example of a less prominent conservative Washington political pundit calling, on the basis of dubious narratives, for an end to U.S. support for Ukraine is an equally extreme one. While this debate was, in contrast to Tucker Carlson's broadcasts and many reactions to them, only a relatively minor incident of 2021, it is worth a review here, as it illustrates some general issues in recent debates in Western Europe and North America. Namely, it documents the reappearance of Russian propaganda tropes in mainstream punditry based at seemingly neutral analytical institutions with otherwise good reputation. The foreign spin-offs from this US debate also illustrate the subsequent Russian re-utilization of such Western approvals of Moscow's narratives in the Kremlin's domestic propaganda effort, and its perception in other post-Soviet countries such as Ukraine. Although the below US incident remained an ephemeral one within overall Western discourses on Eastern Europe, its anti-Ukrainian contributions became for a while widely re-published and cited in Russia's government-directed electronic and social media.

The Origins of an Odd Discussion

On May 30, 2021, the web edition of the reputed American journal *The National Interest* (TNI) published a harsh critique of U.S. support

---

War Against Ukrainians (Stuttgart: *ibidem*-Verlag, 2023); Serhii Plokhy, *The Russo-Ukrainian War: The Return of History* (New York, NY: Norton & Company, 2023).

for Ukraine, by Ted Galen Carpenter.[3] Carpenter's strident text not only disarranged several facts about Ukraine. It is also an unexpected statement in view of the author's listed affiliation — Washington, D.C.'s right-libertarian Cato Institute. The attack that Carpenter presented on the (certainly imperfect) Ukrainian state is more typical of far-left writers than of conservative authors, and of Kremlin-linked rather than independent U.S. commentators.

The author alleged that Ukrainian politics is beset by deeply anti-democratic and ultra-nationalist tendencies. These putative features, Carpenter argued, make this post-Soviet state unfit for U.S. support. Why this Cato Institute fellow — with neither much interest in, nor any relevant published research on, Ukraine — came out with such a categorical judgement on this country is unclear.

Many radical left-wingers and pro-Putin observers have been disliking, at least until 2022, post-Soviet Ukraine because its recent democratic revolutions and subsequent governments have been pro-Western and pro-American. Moreover, many leftists are confused that the manifestly anti-imperial nationalism of the Orange Revolution of 2004 and Revolution of Dignity of 2013-14 was *not* rejecting U.S. or/and Western hegemony.[4] Instead, Ukraine's resistance against foreign domination was, and is, entirely focused on Russian imperialism. It sees the United States and NATO as an ally rather than a threat in defending Ukrainian independence. That Putin's Russia opposes the promotion of liberal democracy by Washington and the EU is unsurprising. Moscow sees the spread of liberal values and democratic practices in post-communist Europe as an incursion into its zone of interest and an indirect threat to its own political order.

For several years now, and especially since the large 2022 invasion, Ukraine has been fighting a multi-faceted war for survival against the world's largest nuclear-weapon country and second-

---

3   Ted Galen Carpenter, "Ukraine's Accelerating Slide into Authoritarianism."333 *The National Interest*, May 30, 2021. www.nationalinterest.org/blog/skeptics/ukraine's-accelerating-slide-authoritarianism-186368.
4   For an in-depth multiauthor investigation, see *Ukraine's Euromaidan: Analyses of a Civil Revolution*, ed. David R. Marples and Fredrik V. Mills (Stuttgart: *ibidem*-Verlag, 2015).

largest conventional military power. Already before 2022, Putin's Russia had been attempting to destroy the Ukrainian state and nation through a combination of military, paramilitary, and nonmilitary means. This aspect was largely missing from Carpenter's depiction of Ukraine — an omission also customarily found in Kremlin disinformation about Ukraine. The Cato Institute's TNI author instead made accusations against post-Soviet Ukraine that repeat arguments which had been spread by radically leftist and pro-Putinist commentators since 2014, and earlier. Namely, Carpenter painted a dark picture of allegedly rising Ukrainian authoritarianism, oppression, and ultra-nationalism. Similar caricatures have been spread through the Kremlin's massive propaganda and disinformation campaign against Ukraine for many years, and to one degree or another picked up by pro-Russian local commentators around the world.[5]

Carpenter was especially unhappy about two former U.S. ambassadors to Ukraine, Geoffrey Pyatt and William Taylor, who have supported Ukraine's assertion of national sovereignty and demonstrative turn to the West. What needs to be added to Carpenter's critique is that all other U.S. ambassadors to Ukraine over the last 30 years — from the first envoy, Roman Popadiuk, to the recent and most well-known American diplomat in Kyiv, Marie Yovanovitch — could be accused of similarly "biased" attitudes toward Ukraine. A main reason behind the U.S. ambassadors' differences with Carpenter seems to be that, by virtue of their professional specialization, they know a great deal about Central-Eastern Europe and the former USSR.[6] Carpenter, in contrast, has seemingly scant interest in the post-communist world — at least not one demonstrated by relevant publications. He reproduces distorted images that are drawn from the Kremlin's playbook of disinformation. This chapter delves into some of these distortions.

---

5   See, for the German context, for instance: Andreas Heinemann-Grüder, "Lehren aus dem Ukrainekonflikt: Das Stockholm-Syndrom der Putin-Versteher [Lessons from the Ukraine conflict: The Stockholm Syndrome of Putin Understanders]." *Osteuropa* 65, no. 4 (2015): 3-24.
6   See, for instance, Steven Pifer, *The Eagle and the Trident: U.S.-Ukraine Relations in Turbulent Times* (Washington, DC: Brookings Institution Press, 2017).

Ukraine's Imperfect Democratic State

Ukraine is—what could be called—a hybrid democracy. In Freedom House's 2021 ranking of countries according to their political and civil liberties, Ukraine received 60 out of 100 possible points. It thus lagged far behind Norway, Finland, and Sweden, the three countries assigned 100 points in this democracy ranking. Carpenter indicates, in his article, some possible reasons for Ukraine's unsatisfactory ranking.[7]

Yet within the peculiar regional context of the post-Soviet space, Ukraine is rather more democratic than one would expect in view of its geographic location and historical legacy. By comparison, nearby Belarus and the Russian Federation received, respectively, only 11 and 20 out of 100 points in the Freedom House 2021 ranking. Whereas these two countries are regarded as clearly unfree by Freedom House, Ukraine was relatively free and democratic by early 2021, according to this and other rankings.

Ukraine's mass media and political landscape were distorted by oligarchic influence, yet they were not dominated by a national autocrat, as in other post-Soviet states.[8] Ukraine's electoral campaigns suffered from distortions and manipulations.[9] Yet, Ukraine's citizens had and have a real choice; their votes are not rigged on a significant scale. Ukraine had and has several far-right parties, but they are weaker than in many other European countries and not represented with a faction, in the current national parliament (more on this below). Ukraine is infamous for its corruption, but has, in recent years, introduced several new laws and institutions designed to prevent graft. Ukraine is not a member of NATO

---

7 "Countries and Territories." *Freedom House*, 2021. https://freedomhouse.org/countries/freedom-world/scores.
8 More on this, for instance, in Andreas Umland, "Averting a Post-Orange Disaster: Constitutional Reforms and Political Stability in Ukraine." *Harvard International Review* (web edition), June 2009. https://www.researchgate.net/profile/Andreas-Umland/publication/255918342_Averting_a_Post-Orange_Disaster_Constitutional_Reforms_and_Political_Stability_in_Ukraine/.
9 Kostyantyn Fedorenko, Olena Rybiy, and Andreas Umland, "The Ukrainian Party System before and after the 2013–2014 Euromaidan." *Europe-Asia Studies* 68, no. 4 (2016): 609-630.

and the EU but wants to enter them and is working toward accession.[10]

There are good reasons to criticize various aspects of politics in Ukraine such as, for instance, its dysfunctional presidentialism,[11] underdeveloped party-system,[12] or incomplete cooperation with the International Criminal Court.[13] Yet these are neither prominent themes in Russian propaganda nor issues that Carpenter raises. The Kremlin rarely speaks about such problems as they apply even more to Russia. One suspects that Carpenter does not mention these and similar topics, perhaps, because he does not read Ukrainian. Given the contents of his articles on Ukraine, he may not have even read much of the widely available English-language scholarly literature on post-Euromaidan Ukraine.[14]

US and Russian Responses to Carpenter

Carpenter's Ukraine articles triggered, in spite of their misleading assertations, multiple reactions within the U.S. and beyond.

---

10 On the complications of Ukraine's Western integration, see Iryna Vereshchuk and Andreas Umland, "How to Make Eastern Europe's Gray Zone Less Gray." *Harvard International Review* 40, no. 1 (2019): 38-41; Pavlo Klimkin and Andreas Umland, "Geopolitical Implications and Challenges of the Coronavirus Crisis for Ukraine." *World Affairs* 183, no. 3 (2020): 256-269.

11 Kimitaka Matsusato, "Semipresidentialism in Ukraine: Institutionalist Centrism in Rampant Clan Politics." *Demokratizatsiya* 13, no. 1 (2005): 45-60.

12 Fedorenko, Rybiy, and Umland, "The Ukrainian Party System before and after the 2013-2014 Euromaidan."

13 Valentyna Polunina and Andreas Umland, "If Ukraine Wants the ICC's Help, It Must Play by the ICC's Rules." *The National Interest*, July 24, 2016. nationalinterest.org/feature/if-ukraine-wants-the-iccs-help-it-must-play-by-its-rules-17089.

14 Important recent larger English-language studies of revolutionary and wartime Ukraine published until 2021 include, in chronological order: Taras Kuzio, *Ukraine: Democratization, Corruption, and the New Russian Imperialism* (Westport, CT: Praeger, 2015); *Revolution and War in Contemporary Ukraine: The Challenge of Change*, ed. Olga Bertelsen (Stuttgart: *ibidem*-Verlag, 2016); *The Ukraine Conflict: Security, Identity and Politics in the Wider Europe*, ed. Derek Averre and Kataryna Wolczuk (Abingdon, UK: Routledge, 2019); *Three Revolutions: Mobilization and Change in Contemporary Ukraine*, 3 vols. (Stuttgart: *ibidem*-Verlag, 2019-2021); Mychailo Wynnyckyj, *Ukraine's Maidan, Russia's War: A Chronicle and Analysis of the Revolution of Dignity* (Stuttgart: *ibidem*-Verlag, 2019); Paul D'Anieri, *Ukraine and Russia: From Civilized Divorce to Uncivil War* (Cambridge, UK: Cambridge University Press, 2019).

These—partly, intense—responses rather than the odd contents of Carpenter's articles themselves make it worthwhile to engage with his arguments. Carpenter's location in Washington, D.C., appointment at one of the U.S.'s leading think tanks, and the temporary waves that his strident pamphlets generated justify the following survey and rebuttal.

The first reaction came from Moscow, although Russia was only mentioned *en passant* in Carpenter's first text. A day after his initial article appeared in the United States, on May 31, 2021, the influential Russian state-owned online resource *inoSMI* (Foreign Mass Media) published a Russian translation of Carpenter's text in the web edition of TNI. The *inoSMI* editor introduced Carpenter's article, stating:

> U.S. officials love to portray Ukraine as "a courageous democracy that reflects the threat of aggression from an authoritarian Russia." However, the idealized picture created by Washington has never really matched the darker reality, and the gap between the two, with Ukraine sliding increasingly toward authoritarianism, has now become a real chasm, the article notes.[15]

In June 2021, an interactive debate covering Carpenter's attack on Ukraine developed. A response to Carpenter's initial article was published, in TNI, by Doug Klain of the Atlantic Council.[16] A fortnight later, my rebuttal to Carpenter appeared in the Atlantic Council's *Ukraine Alert*.[17] In Ukraine, this text was translated into Russian and Ukrainian and republished by the Kyiv website *Gazeta.ua*;[18]

---

15 T. Karpenter [Carpenter], "The National Interest (SShA): Ukraina vse bystree skatyvaetsia k avtoritarizmu [Ukraine's Accelerating Slide into Authoritarianism]." *inoSMI*, May 31, 2021. https://inosmi.ru/politic/20210531/249831592.html.

16 Doug Klain, "Countering the Myth of Ukrainian Authoritarianism." *The National Interest*, June 7, 2021. https://nationalinterest.org/feature/countering-myth-ukrainian-authoritarianism-187094.

17 Andreas Umland, "The Dangers of Echoing Russian Disinformation on Ukraine." *Ukraine Alert*, June 19, 2021. www.atlanticcouncil.org/blogs/ukrainealert/the-dangers-of-echoing-russian-disinformation-on-ukraine/.

18 Andreas Umland "Zapadnye deiateli povtoriaiut rossiiskuiu dezinformatsiiu ob Ukraine [The Dangers of Echoing Russian Disinformation on Ukraine]." *Gazeta.ua*, June 2, 2021. gazeta.ua/ru/blog/55294/zahidni-diyachi-povtoryuyut-rosijsku-dezinformaciyu-pro-ukrayinu-ce-nebezpechna-gra.

further translations appeared at the Kyiv resource *Khvylia* (Wave) in Russian,[19] and on Berlin's Center for Liberal Modernity website *Ukraine verstehen* (Understanding Ukraine) in German.[20]

Jon Lerner of the Hudson Institute reviewed the debate surrounding Ukraine in broader context, on June 28, 2021, in the web edition of TNI.[21] On the same day, on June 28, 2021, Carpenter responded to Klain's and my critique of his initial text with a second article entitled "Why Ukraine Is a Dangerous and Unworthy Ally." His rebuttal was again published in the web version of TNI, and subsequently reposted on the Cato Institute's website.[22]

While none of the responses to Carpenter were re-published in Russia, his rebuttal to them was again translated by the Kremlin-controlled *inoSMI* (Foreign Mass Media) website within one day.[23] Carpenter's new article was reposted in Russian on June 29, 2021, and introduced by an *inoSMI* editor who wrote:

> In May [2021], an author of *The National Interest* took the liberty of criticizing the Zelensky regime for its authoritarian tendencies. In response, the German "Ukrainianist" Andreas Umland and similar "Maidanists" [a term referring to Kyiv's Independence Square and Euromaidan Revolution] criticized Carpenter so much that he decided to get even with them in this article "One Cannot Remain Silent: Accusations of 'Russian disinformation' are reminiscent of McCarthyism." The defenders of the Kyiv regime have a powerful lobbying organization behind them, the Atlantic Council.[24]

---

19 Andreas Umland, "'Dalekaia strana, o kotoroi my znaem malo…': o zabluzhdeniiakh amerikanskikh analitikov ob Ukraine ['A distant country, about which we know little…': On the delusions of American analysts about Ukraine]." *Khvylja*, June 26, 2021. analytics.hvylya.net/232611-dalekaya-strana-o-kotoroy-my-znaem-malo-o-zabluzhdeniyah-amerikanskih-analitikov-ob-ukraine.

20 Andreas Umland, "Die Ukraine, USA und Nichtverbreitung von Atomwaffen [Ukraine, USA and nuclear non-proliferation]." *Ukraine verstehen*, June 25, 2021. ukraineverstehen.de/umland-ukraine-usa-nichtverbreitung-von-atomwaffen/.

21 Jon Lerner, "Does Ukraine Matter to America?" *The National Interest*, June 28, 2021. nationalinterest.org/feature/does-ukraine-matter-america-188741.

22 Ted Galen Carpenter, "Why Ukraine Is a Dangerous and Unworthy Ally." *The National Interest*, June 28, 2021. nationalinterest.org/blog/skeptics/why-ukraine-dangerous-and-unworthy-ally-188742.

23 Ted Galen Carpenter, "Why Ukraine Is a Dangerous and Unworthy Ally." *Cato Institute*, June 28, 2021. www.cato.org/commentary/why-ukraine-dangerous-unworthy-ally.

24 T. Karpenter [Carpenter], "The National Interest (SShA): pochemu Ukraina — opasnyi i nedostoinyi soiuznik dlia SSh [The USA Considered Ukraine a

Also on June 29, 2021, several Russian-language outlets published sympathetic reviews of Carpenter's first article.[25] Among other Kremlin-controlled outlets, the website of the Crimean TV channel *Pervyi sevastopol'skii* ("Sevastopol's First") briefly reviewed Carpenter's June article.[26] It had already earlier introduced Carpenter's first attack.[27] Among other Russian-language video resources, the YouTube channels "Oleg Kalugin" and "Kognitive Dissonanz" (Cognitive Dissonance) published Russian audio reviews of Carpenter under the titles "On Ukraine's Lobbyists in the US" (June 29, 2021),[28] and "Senior Research Fellow of the Cato Institute [...] Ted Carpenter on Ukraine..." July 1, 2021).[29]

Carpenter's two TNI articles on Ukraine were thereafter discussed, commented on, and disseminated by, numerous Russian outlets. The Kremlin-directed propaganda instruments gleefully used Carpenter's attacks on Ukraine in their disinformation operation. They included *Yandex.ru, RIA.ru, MK.ru, Sputniknews.ru, Regnum.ru, News.ru, Tsargrad.TV, KP.ru, PolitRos.com, Life.ru, Argumenti.ru, Actualcomment.ru, RUnews24.ru, PolitExpert.net, Versia.ru, Ridus.ru, 360TV.ru, Riasev.com, Inforeactor.ru, Glas.ru, Riafan.ru,*

Dangerous and Unworthy Ally]. *inoSMI,* June 29, 2021. inosmi.ru/politic/20210629/250003969.html.

25 See for instance, the major Russian daily *Izvestiia*: "V SShA poshchitali Ukrainu opasnym i nedostoinym soiuznikom [Why Ukraine Is a Dangerous and Unworthy Ally]." *Izvestiia,* June 29, 2021, https://iz.ru/1185920/2021-06-29/v-ssha-poschitali-ukrainu-opasnym-i-nedostoinym-soiuznikom; as well as the popular internet resources *Lenta.ru*: "Ukrainu nazvali nedostoinym i nebezopasnym soiuznikom dlia SShA [Ukraine called an unworthy and unsafe ally for US]." *Lenta.ru-News,* June 29, 2021. lenta.ru/news/2021/06/29/usa_ukr/; and *Gazeta.ru:* A. Demidov, "V SShA sochli Ukrainu opasnym i nedostoinym soiuznikom [In the US, Ukraine is regarded a dangerous and unworthy ally]." *Gazeta.ru,* June 29, 2021. www.gazeta.ru/politics/news/2021/06/29/n_1617 3032.shtml.

26 "Ekspert nazval Ukrainu nebezopasnym soiuznikom dlia SShA [Expert calls Ukraine an unsafe ally of the U.S.]." *Pervyi sevastopol'skii,* June 21, 2021. sev.tv/news/46307.html.

27 "'Naikhudshii vid tsinizma': amerikanskii ekspert prizval Vashington zaniat' storonu Rossii v 'ukrainskom voprose' ['Worst kind of cynicism': An American expert called on Washington to take Russia's side regarding the 'Ukrainian question']." *Pervyi sevastopol'skii,* May 31, 2021. sev.tv/news/43821.html.

28 See https://www.youtube.com/watch?v=grnsAlb302A.

29 See https://www.youtube.com/watch?v=XBYZhM7nsK8.

Newinform.com, SMI2.ru, Iarex.ru, TopCor.ru, InfoRuss.info, Profinews.ru, Rusevik.ru, Alternatio.org, News2.ru, News22.ru, and others. The English versions of the Russian websites *TopWar.ru* (2021) and *Oreanda.ru*, published brief reviews of Carpenter's arguments under the titles "Strategically, Ukraine is a 'trap' for the United States" and "American Political Scientist Called Ukraine a Dangerous and Unworthy Ally."[30] *Oreanda.ru* remarked that, in Ukraine,

> [A] coup in 2014 was carried out with the help of ultra-nationalist and neo-Nazi groups. Carpenter noted that these organizations with their 'ugly values,' continue to influence Kiev's [sic] politics. Supporters of an alliance with Ukraine try not to notice these facts, the article says. The author of the material noted the deplorable situation with human rights and freedoms in this country.[31]

Subsequently, the already intense and multilingual debate became also noted within Ukraine, Carpenter's target. The Ukrainian news agencies *UAzmi.org* and *UAinfo.org* quoted, on July 1, 2021, the prominent Odesa blogger Oleksandr Kovalenko, who had written on June 30, 2021 about Carpenter's articles on Ukraine. Kovalenko's post noted that:

> Interestingly, he used as arguments what we have regularly heard from Russian propagandists since 2014, namely that neo-Nazism is rampant in Ukraine, rights and freedoms of citizens are trampled in Ukraine, there is no freedom of speech in Ukraine, wild monkeys and crocodiles are in Ukraine ... In fact, a full set of Kremlin fakes about Ukraine is heard from the mouth of an American expert on the pages of a respected and influential publication during the international exercise SeaBreeze-2021.[32]

---

30 "NI: Strategically, Ukraine is a 'trap' for the United States." *TopWar*, June 29, 2021. en.topwar.ru/184527-ni-ukraina-dlja-ssha-opasnyj-sojuznik.html.
31 "American Political Scientist Called Ukraine a Dangerous and Unworthy Ally." *Oreanda-News*, June 29, 2021. www.oreanda.ru/en/it_media/american-politic al-scientist-called-ukraine-a-dangerous-and-unworthy-ally/article1378860/.
32 "Rossiia cherez The National Interest pytaetsia v ocherednoi raz diskreditirovat' otnosheniia Ukrainy i SShA [Russia tries via The National Interest again to discredit the relations between Ukraine and the U.S.]." *Zloy-Odessit*, June 30, 2021. zloy-odessit.livejournal.com/3547087.html.

Ukraine's then leading English-language newspaper *Kyiv Post* declared Carpenter—with reference to his articles in TNI— Ukraine's "Foe of the Week" on July 2, 2021.[33]

The varying responses in Russia, the United States, Ukraine, and elsewhere indicate the problematic aspect Carpenter's arguments. What raised eyebrows about his claims on Ukraine was less their critical tone. Rather, Carpenter chose to remark on exactly those sensitive political topics that had been central to Russia's state-controlled anti-Ukrainian propaganda during the previous eight years, if not before. Carpenter makes far-reaching allegations about a prevalence of ultra-nationalism and putative slide to authoritarianism in today's Ukraine—claims which had been disseminated by Russian media channels and non-Russian pro-Kremlin public figures for many years. Moreover, Carpenter unapologetically called for an end to Washington's support for Kyiv. It was thus unsurprising that Carpenter's narratives were eagerly picked up and promoted by Russian state-directed media.[34]

Carpenter's Portrayal of Ukraine

Carpenter's insistence on the large role of ultra-nationalism in contemporary Ukraine runs to such a degree counter to empirical reality that it could have been only taken from the Kremlin's disinformation about the country. As shown in Table 1, the electoral results of Ukrainian far-right parties have, since the introduction of proportional representation in 1998, been largely abysmal. Unlike various other European parliaments elected by a proportional representation system, the Ukrainian *Verkhovna Rada* (Supreme Council) has not housed a far-right faction since late 2014.[35] It briefly

---

33 Ilya Ponomarenko, "Ukraine's Friend & Foe of the Week." *Kyiv Post*, July 2, 2021. www.kyivpost.com/article/opinion/op-ed/Illia-ponomarenko-ukraines-friend-foe-of-the-week.html.
34 *Russian Active Measures: Yesterday, Today, Tomorrow*, ed. Olga Bertelsen (Stuttgart: *ibidem*-Verlag, 2021).
35 Andreas Umland, "The Far Right in Pre- and Post-Euromaidan Ukraine: From Ultra-Nationalist Party Politics to Ethno-Centric Uncivil Society." *Demokratizatsiya* 28, no. 2 (2020): 247-268.

harbored the far-right *Svoboda* (Freedom) Party for two years, from 2012 to 2014.[36]

In 2019, Ukraine's far right—for the first time in its history and unlike many other nationalists around the world—took part in parliamentary elections with a united list under the *Svoboda* label. As Table 1 shows, despite such rare harmony, the joint election bloc of *Svoboda, Pravyy Sektor* (Right Sector) and *Natsionalnyy Korpus* (National Corps) received 2.15 percent of the vote. Such a result of Ukraine's far-right list was roughly equal to, or even below, what many single far-right parties in European countries receive in national elections.[37] In the 2019 presidential election, the candidate of the far right, Ruslan Koshulinskyy, gained 1.62 percent.

In post-Cold War European parliamentary elections, ultra-nationalist parties and candidates have been repeatedly elected in a number of NATO member countries, including some older democracies.[38] In Ukraine, in contrast, the far right has remained unpopular—even during long-lasting war with Russia when one could expect nationalism to be more popular. In the 2019 elections, Jewish-Ukrainian Volodymyr Zelenskyy, a Russian-speaking centrist from eastern Ukraine, won a landslide with 73.22 percent of the vote, the by far best result of any Ukrainian presidential candidate ever. Zelenskyy even prevailed, over the more patriotic Petro Poroshenko, in two out of three Galician regions, the alleged stronghold of radical Ukrainian nationalism. The election campaign was not marred by any notable anti-Semitic incidents against Zelenskyy's candidacy.

During its post-Soviet history, Ukraine has thus indeed—as Carpenter insinuates—been exceptional in terms of support for ultra-nationalism. However, Ukraine's distinction lies not in the

---

36 Viacheslav Likhachev, *Right-Wing Extremism in Ukraine: The Phenomenon of "Svoboda"* (Kyjiv: EAJC, 2013); idem, "Right-Wing Extremism on the Rise in Ukraine." *Russian Politics and Law* 51, no. 5 (2013): 59-74; idem, "Social-Nationalists in the Ukrainian Parliament: How They Got There and What We Can Expect of Them." *Russian Politics and Law* 51, no. 5 (2013): 75-85.

37 See also Alina Polyakova, "From the Provinces to the Parliament: How the Ukrainian Radical Right Mobilized in Galicia." *Communist and Post-Communist Studies* 47, no. 2 (2014): 211-225.

38 Alina Polyakova, *The Dark Side of European Integration: Social Foundations and Cultural Determinants of the Rise of Radical Right Movements in Contemporary Europe* (Stuttgart: *ibidem*-Verlag, 2015).

political *strength* of the far right but, on the contrary, in its relative electoral *weakness*. Table 1's lists the results of various far-right presidential candidates and parties since the introduction of proportional representation in 1998.[39] The only period during which the far right was able to gain notable nationwide support was during the notorious presidency of pro-Russian Viktor Yanukovych in 2010-2014.[40] Yanukovych not only triggered nationalist mobilization with his pro-Russian and mafia-like policies.[41] The Party of Regions directly promoted Ukraine's extreme right with a view to Yanukovych facing a nationalist candidate in the second round of the then regularly scheduled January 2015 elections.[42]

---

39   Andreas Umland and Anton Shekhovtsov, "Nastional-ekstremizm, shcho ne vidbuvsia? Pravoradikal'na partiyna polityka v postradyans'kiy Ukraini ta zahadka elektoral'noy marhinal'nosti ukrains'kykh ul'tranatsionalistiv u 1994-2009 rokakh," *Politychna krytyka*, no. 2 (2011): 17-34; Andreas Umland and Anton Shekhovtsov, "Pravoradikal'naya partiinaya politika v postsovetskoi Ukraine i zagadka marginal'nosti ukrainskikh ul'tranatsionalistov v 1994-2009 gg.," *Forum noveishei vostochnoevropeiskoi istorii i kul'tury* 7, no. 2 (2011): 157-180; Kirill Galushko, "Drugaia storona ukrainskogo regionalizma: kommentarii k stat'e A. Umlanda i A. Shekhovtsova," *Forum noveishei vostochnoevropeiskoi istorii i kul'tury* 7, no. 2 (2011): 181-186; Anton Shekhovtsov, "The Creeping Resurgence of the Ukrainian Radical Right? The Case of the Freedom Party," *Europe-Asia Studies* 63, no. 2 (2011): 203–28; Andreas Umland, ed., "Post-Soviet Ukrainian Right-Wing Extremism," special issue of *Russian Politics and Law* 51, no. 5 (2013): 3–95.
40   Anton Shekhovtsov, "From Para-Militarism to Radical Right-Wing Populism: The Rise of the Ukrainian Far-Right Party Svoboda," in *Right Wing Populism in Europe: Politics and Discourse*, edited by B. Mral, M. Khosravinik, R. Wodak (London: Bloomsbury Academic, 2013), 256-258; Anton Shekhovtsov, "Vseukrainskoe ob"edinenie 'Svoboda': Problema legitimnosti bor'by za vlast'," *Forum noveishei vostochnoevropeiskoiistorii i kul'tury*, vol. 10, no. 1 (2013): 22-63.
41   On the political rise of, and electoral support for, "Svoboda" in pre-Euromaidan Ukraine, see: Konstantin Fedorenko, "Protestnaia aktivnost' krainikh pravykh v Ukraine v 2010-2012 gg.: Vseukrainskoe ob"edinenie 'Svoboda' v sravnitel'noi perspektive," *Forum noveishei vostochnoevropeiskoi istorii i kul'tury* 10, no. 1 (2013): 93-110; Nataliia Belitser, "Vseukrainskoe ob"edinenie 'Svoboda' i ego elektorat, 2012-2013," *The Ideology and Politics Journal*, no. 1 (2014): 8-92; Lenka Bustikova, "Voting, Identity and Security Threats in Ukraine: Who Supports the Radical 'Freedom' Party?" *Communist and Post-Communist Studies* 48, no. 2 (2015): 239-256; Vitaliy Nakhmanovych, *Fenomen "Svobody:" Vybortsi radykal'nykh natsionalistiv u dzerkali sotsiolohii* (Kyiv: KMIS, 2016).
42   Taras Tarasiuk and Andreas Umland, "Unexpected Friendships: Cooperation of Ukrainian Ultra-Nationalists with Russian and Pro-Kremlin Actors," *Illiberalism Studies Program*, September 29, 2021. www.illiberalism.org/unexpected-friendships-cooperation-of-ukrainian-ultra-nationalists-with-russian-and-pro-kremlin-actors/.

Table 1: Vote Shares of Major Ukrainian Far-right Parties in Presidential Elections (shaded rows) and the Proportional-representation Parts of Parliamentary Elections, 1998–2019 (in percentages)

Party or alliance	Bloc "Natsionalnyy front" [National Front] (KUN, UKRP & URP) / URP / KUN	UNA / Pravyy sektor [Right Sector]	Bloc "Menshe sliv" [Fewer Words] (VPO-DSU & SNPU) / VOS
National election			
1998 (parliamentary)	2.71 (NF)	0.39 (UNA)	0.16 (MS)
1999 (presidential)			
2002 (parliamentary)		0.04 (UNA)	
2004 (presidential)	0.02 (Kozak, OUN)	0.17 (Korchyns'kyy)	
2006 (parliamentary)		0.06 (UNA)	0.36 (VOS)
2007 (parliamentary)			0.76 (VOS)
2010 (presidential)			1.43 (Tiahnybok)
2012 (parliamentary)		0.08 (UNA-UNSO)	10.44 (VOS)
2014 (presidential)		0.70 (Iarosh)*	1.16 (Tiahnybok)
2014 (parliamentary)	0.05 (KUN)	1.81 (PS)	4.71 (VOS)
2019 (presidential)			1.62 (Koshulyns'kyy)
2019 (parliamentary)			2.15 (VOS)**

Source: Umland (2020).

Notes: * In the 2014 presidential election, Dmytro Iarosh formally ran as an independent candidate but was publicly known as the leader of *Pravyy sektor* (PS). ** The 2019 *Svoboda* list was a unified bloc of the most influential Ukrainian far-right political parties, but was officially registered only as a VOS list.

Abbreviations: KUN: *Konhres ukrains'kykh natsionalistiv* (Congress of Ukrainian Nationalists); UKRP: *Ukrains'ka konservatyvna respublikans'ka partiia* (Ukrainian Conservative Republican Party); URP: *Ukrains'ka respublikans'ka partiia* (Ukrainian Republican Party); VPO-DSU: *Vseukrainske politychne ob"ednannia "Derzhavna samostiynist' Ukrainy"* (All-Ukrainian Political Union "State Independence of Ukraine"); SNPU: *Sotsial-natsionalna partiia Ukrainy* (Social-National Party of Ukraine); OUN: *Orhanizatsiia ukrainskykh natsionalistiv* (Organization of Ukrainian Nationalists); UNA: *Ukrains'ka natsionalna asambleia* (Ukrainian National Assembly); UNSO: *Ukrains'ka narodna samooborona* (Ukrainian National Self-Defense); VOS: *Vseukrains'ke ob"ednannia "Svoboda"* (All-Ukrainian Union Freedom).

Nevertheless, throughout the year 2014, there was much concern among some European anti-fascists concerning Ukraine's far right. Ukrainian ultra-nationalists still had their faction in parliament which had been elected in 2012. They had also been highly visible during the Euromaidan Revolution.[43] They had entered the first post-Euromaidan government for several months with four ministers.[44]

Above all, the Russian propaganda machine and its various Western disseminators were, on a daily basis, hammering into world public opinion the idea that former President Yanukovych had been illegally removed from power by a "fascist coup" in Kyiv. In fact, Yanukovych only left Kyiv after violence had already ended, and was impeached by the same parliament that had earlier supported him, including by former Party of Regions deputies. Of course, few Western observers bought the Kremlin's horror story in full. Nevertheless, among many Western politicians and commentators there has remained the view there can be no smoke without fire: If Russia is very concerned, ultra-nationalism must be a major problem in Ukraine.

In early 2014, a group of 41 political researchers located in or related to Ukraine published an appeal to foreign observers of the ongoing Euromaidan Revolution to not overestimate the role of Ukrainian radical nationalism in Ukraine.[45] A smaller number of scholars and experts who had researched Ukraine's far right for a

---

43   Viacheslav Likhachev, "'Pravyi sektor' i drugie: natsional-radikaly i ukrainskii krizis kontsa 2013 g. – nachala 2014 g." *Forum noveishei vostochnoevropeiskoi istorii i kul'tury* 10, no. 2 (2014): 75-116; Vyacheslav Likhachev, "The 'Right Sector' and Others: The Behavior and Role of Radical Nationalists in the Ukrainian Political Crisis of Late 2013 – Early 2014." *Communist and Post-Communist Studies* 48, no. 2 (2015): 257-27.
44   Andreas Umland, Anton Shekhovtsov, "Ukrainskie pravye radikaly, evrointegratsiia i neofashistskaia ugroza: sravnitel'nye nabliudeniia ob ukrainskom politicheskom ul'tranatsionalizme." *Forum noveishei vostochnoevropeiskoi istorii i kul'tury* 10, no. 1 (2014): 50-57; Anton Shekhovtsov, "Vseukrainkoe ob"edinenie 'Svoboda': ot uspekha na vyborakh k provalu v revoliutsii." *Forum noveishei vostochnoevropeiskoi istorii i kul'tury* 11, no. 1 (2015): 65-78.
45   "Kyiv's Euromaidan is a liberationist and not extremist mass action of civic disobedience (petition)." *Ukrainian Catholic University*, February 4, 2014 https://maidan.ucu.edu.ua/en/texts-by-other-authors/kyivs-euromaidan-is-a-liberationist-and-not-extremist-mass-action-of-civic-disobedience-petition/. See also:

while, and studied it from a cross-cultural perspective too warned as early as in 2014 that the media hype around this topic was misplaced. Among others, the Russian historian Viacheslav Likhachev (Center for Civil Liberties, Kyiv), Ukrainian political scientist Anton Shekhovtsov (Center for Democratic Integrity, Vienna), and American sociologist Alina Polyakova (Center for European Policy Analysis, Washington, D.C.) had researched pre-Euromaidan and non-Ukrainian permutations of the far right—unlike most other commentators of pre-2014, revolutionary and war-time ultra-nationalism—long before Euromaidan Revolution. From their historical and comparative points of view, i.e. as a result of diachronic and synchronic juxtaposition of Ukrainian trends during 2013-2014 with those before and elsewhere, they and others warned that alarmism is inappropriate. They spoke out against an emerging mainstream Western public opinion—principally shaped by Russian propaganda and disinformation—that ultra-nationalism is a major issue in Ukraine. Some of these researchers predicted in 2014 that the prospects of Ukraine's far right are limited which proved to be true.[46]

While many of these warnings and assessments were often first published in Ukrainian and Russian, most of them were also immediately available or became later translated in English too. They became thus quickly accessible for foreign observers not reading any Eastern Slavic languages. In the following years, the overall domestic political impact of Ukraine's far right remained relatively lower than in many democracies in Europe and elsewhere. The also highly publicized participation of radical nationalists in Ukraine's defense against Russia's hybrid war in 2014-2021 has had limited effect on their electoral fortunes, and the domestic or foreign political course of Ukraine.

The second main point in Carpenter's portrayals of Ukraine, in his two 2021 TNI essays, were also misplaced and dealt with allegedly authoritarian tendencies that disqualified Ukraine

---

46   E.g., Anton Shekhovtsov, "From Electoral Success to Revolutionary Failure: The Ukrainian Svoboda Party." *Eurozine*. March 5, 2014. http://www.eurozine.com/articles/2014-03-05-shekhovtsov-en.html/.

receiving U.S. support. This critique Carpenter was again misleading, in various ways so. First, the US has historically also provided aid to many authoritarian regimes such as Egypt's military dictatorship which was, for some time, the second largest recipient of US aid. Washington collaborates with other such regimes, including, for example, Saudi Arabia and Uzbekistan, in its war against the Taliban regime in Afghanistan.

Second, Carpenter's argument is questionable, above all, in terms of its substance. Again, Ukraine has indeed been exceptional, within the post-Soviet context—yet once more in the opposite sense in which it was presented by Carpenter. Early in its post-Soviet history, Ukraine passed, after its emergence as an independent state in 1991, one of the crucial tests that political scientists use to determine the democratic potential of a nation: Is its electorate willing and able to evict the country's sitting top official and most powerful politician via a popular vote? In 1994, Ukrainians voted out of office their incumbent leader in a presidential election. As a result, Ukraine's first president, Leonid Kravchuk (1991-1994), was replaced by its second head of state, Leonid Kuchma (1994-2005).

For comparison, the much older and wealthier Federal Republic of Germany, founded in 1949, passed this democratic test only four years *after* Ukraine. In 1998, Germans, for the first time in their history, deposed a sitting Federal Chancellor, the CDU's (Christian Democratic Party) Helmut Kohl (in office since 1982), through parliamentary elections that were won by the SPD (Social Democratic Party). The Social Democrat's then-leader Gerhard Schroeder—who later on turned into a notorious employee of the Russian state-owned companies Gazprom and Rosneft—became the new head of government until 2005 when he too was deposed by a popular vote.[47]

In the 2010 and 2019 national elections, Ukrainian voters again evicted their sitting heads of state with embarrassing results for the

---

47 In 1969, then incumbent CDU/CSU Federal Chancellor Kurt Georg Kiesinger (from 1933 until 1945 a member of Hitler's NSDAP) had been replaced by the SPD's Willi Brandt. Yet, this was the result of a change of Germany's governing coalition and not of that year's parliamentary elections that had been won by Kiesinger's CDU/CSU.

two incumbents. Outgoing Presidents Viktor Yushchenko and Petro Poroshenko manifestly wanted second terms in Ukraine's highest political office and conducted full-scale re-election campaigns. Yet they were, both with embarrassing results, defeated by opposition candidates, and duly stepped down after their crushing defeats. In fact, of Ukraine's six presidents, only one—Kuchma—served two terms, and Kuchma was able to gain reelection in the 1999 run-off round against a weak communist contender, Petro Symonenko, who was, by many voters, perceived as a representative of Russia.

In general, over the last three decades, Ukraine has conducted numerous highly competitive rounds of presidential, parliamentary, regional, and local elections, most of which fulfilled basic democratic standards. This experience is in sharp contrast to almost all other post-Soviet states that, like Ukraine, had been part of the USSR, since its foundation in 1922. What is special about Ukraine, as a successor country of the original Soviet Union, is therefore the opposite to the picture painted by Carpenter. It is not authoritarianism, alleged by the Cato Institute fellow, but the, in comparison to other founding republics of the USSR, relative *democratism* of Ukraine that is remarkable. This trait made and makes the country more worthy of Western (and not only U.S.) support than other former Soviet republics.

Carpenter's confusion about these issues became visible, in his second 2021 TNI article, where he responded to Doug Klain and my rebuttals to his first. There, replying to the specifics of our critique of his first TNI pamphlet, Carpenter compared various post-Soviet states and concluded that:

> Umland stresses that other countries emerging from the former Soviet Union are noticeably more autocratic than Ukraine, noting that [in a recent Freedom House democracy ranking in which Ukraine had received 60 out of 100 points] Russia received a rating of twenty points and Belarus received eleven points [out of 100 possible 'Global Freedom Scores']. He could have added that Kazakhstan was in the same dismal category with twenty-three points. But no one expects the United States to defend such countries

militarily or praise them as vibrant democracies. Umland, Klain, and other fans of Kiev [sic] expect Washington to do both.[48]

However, that had been exactly the point: If Russia, Belarus, and Kazakhstan achieved the same Global Freedom Scores as Ukraine in the Freedom House ranking, they should be treated like Ukraine. If they were ranked at least "Partially Free" rather than "Unfree," these three countries too would be worthy of Western and US support.

The Key Story Missing from Carpenter's Pamphlets

What is most surprising in Carpenter's articles, however, is not so much what he disseminates, but the preeminent security issue he is entirely silent about in *The National Interest* — namely, the U.S.'s national interest in Ukraine's fate as a country which underwent nuclear disarmament. As detailed elsewhere, the United States played a major role in the nuclear disarmament of Ukraine in the early 1990s.[49] Together with Moscow, Washington pressured Kyiv at the time to give up the huge atomic arsenal that Ukraine had inherited from the USSR after achieving independence in 1991. Russia and the United States made sure that Ukraine would be deprived of *all* its strategic and tactical nuclear weapons. Prior to disarmament, Ukraine possessed an atomic warheads arsenal that was significantly larger than that of the UK, France, and China combined.

The only relevant political concession that Washington made in the 1990s to Kyiv was that it agreed to supplement Ukraine's accession to the Nuclear Non-Proliferation Treaty (NPT) as a non-nuclear-weapon state with the — now infamous — 1994 Budapest Memorandum on Security Assurances signed by Ukraine, Russia, the United States, and the United Kingdom.[50] The latter country

---

48 Carpenter, "Why Ukraine Is a Dangerous and Unworthy Ally."
49 Mariana Budjeryn and Andreas Umland, "Damage Control: The Breach of the Budapest Memorandum and the Nuclear Non-Proliferation Regime." In *NATO's Enlargement and Russia: A Strategic Challenge in the Past and Future*, ed. Oxana Schmies (Stuttgart: *ibidem*-Verlag, 2021): 177-190.
50 Mariana Budjeryn, "Looking Back: Ukraine's Nuclear Predicament and the Nonproliferation Regime." *Arms Control Today* 44, no. 12 (2014). www.armscon

also underwrote this fateful document, although the UK had not taken part in the trilateral negotiations on Ukraine's nuclear disarmament with the US and Russia. London supported the agreement, however, with its official signature because the UK had, in 1968, been one of the three founding countries of the world-wide non-proliferation regime, together with United States and the USSR.[51] The UK has since been, together with Washington and Moscow, a so-called "Depositary Government" of the NPT—a specific status that, in view of the below briefly outlined 2021 episode in the Black Sea, is worth remembering about the UK. At a CSCE summit held in Budapest in December 1994, not only Washington, Moscow, and London, but also Bejing and Paris assured Kyiv, in connection with Ukraine's signing of the NPT, of their respect for Ukrainian sovereignty and borders.[52]

Moscow's and Washington's concerted efforts in the early 1990s deprived Ukraine of all of its nuclear potential in exchange for security assurances by all five official nuclear-weapon states under the NPT. These guarantees turned out to be worthless in 2014, however, when Russia's annexed Crimea and launched hybrid war and covert invasion in the Donbas region of Eastern Ukraine.[53] In April 2023, former US President Bill Clinton admitted that US pressure on Ukraine had been a mistake. Russia had apparently never intended, Clinton concluded, to honor the Budapest Memorandum.[54]

---

trol.org/act/2014-12/features/looking-back-ukraine's-nuclear-predicament-nonproliferation-regime.

51 Beate Kohler, *Der Vertrag über die Nichtverbreitung von Kernwaffen und das Problem der Sicherheitsgarantien* [The Treaty on the Non-Proliferation of Nuclear Weapons, and the Problem of Security Guarantees] (Frankfurt a. M.: Alfred Metzner Verlag, 1972).
52 Mariana Budjeryn, "The Power of the NPT: International Norms and Ukraine's Nuclear Disarmament." *The Nonproliferation Review* 22, no. 2 (2015): 203-237.
53 Mariana Budjeryn, "The Breach: Ukraine's Territorial Integrity and the Budapest Memorandum." *NPIHP Issues Brief* 3 (2014). www.wilsoncenter.org/publication/issue-brief-3-the-breach-ukraines-territorial-integrity-and-the-budapest-memorandum.
54 Graig Graziosi, "Bill Clinton reveals regret over Russia-Ukraine deal that saw Kyiv give up nuclear weapons." *The Independent*, April 5, 2023. https://www.independent.co.uk/news/world/americas/us-politics/bill-clinton-blame-ukraine-russia-nuclear-b2314999.html.

With its annexation of Crimea as well as hybrid war against Ukraine since 2014 and especially its full-scale invasion in 2022, Russia has now massively and for several years been undermining the logic of the non-proliferation regime.[55] It is no longer clear that countries that refrain from possessing, building, or acquiring nuclear weapons would be secure, and especially that they would be protected from countries that have weapons of mass destruction.[56] Russia's possession of nuclear weapons has not only given it a key military advantage and political instrument *vis-à-vis* Ukraine. It is also the main reason why the West—unlike in Yugoslavia, Iraq, or Libya—has, at least until spring 2023 when this chapter was completed, not militarily intervened in the Russian-Ukrainian War.

A June 2021 incident with a British war ship near the port of Sevastopol in the Black Sea had, against this background, a more than symbolic meaning and is a good illustration of the issue at question.[57] On a voyage from Odesa to Batumi, the UK destroyer "HMS Defender" passed by Crimea without making a detour to avoid Black Sea waters illegally claimed by Russia. The UK's behavior was a form of validation of the 1994 Budapest Memorandum and 1968 NPT. Having received Kyiv's permission to pass Ukrainian waters, the "HMS Defender" lived up to its name defending international law by way of taking the shortest path from the shores of Southern mainland Ukraine to its destination of Georgia's Black Sea coast. The British vessel also upheld the logic of the non-proliferation regime built on the premise that the borders of non-nuclear-weapon states are as respected as those of nuclear-weapon states.

With his explicit demand to end U.S. support for Ukraine, Carpenter calls not only for the US to betray Ukraine, as a beacon of

---

55 Thomas D. Grant, *International Law and the Post-Soviet Space II: Essays on Ukraine, Intervention, and Non-Proliferation* (Stuttgart: *ibidem*-Verlag, 2019).
56 Andreas Umland, "The Ukraine Example: Nuclear Disarmament Doesn't Pay." *World Affairs* 178, no. 4 (2016): 45-49.
57 For a synopsis of the incident and its implications for maritime and international law, see Andrew Serdy, "HMS Defender Incident: What the Law of the Sea Says." *The Conversation*, June 24, 2021. https://theconversation.com/hms-defender-incident-what-the-law-of-the-sea-says-163389.

democracy in the post-Soviet space.[58] He also proposes to sweep under the carpet the normative and psychological foundations of the non-proliferation regime. If, after Russia as the legal successor of the USSR, the United States, as a second founding country of the 1968 NPT, signaled to the world that Ukraine's territorial integrity and national sovereignty are of secondary importance, this could have far-reaching consequences for the international system.[59]

Conclusions

The Kremlin's manifest violation of the logic of the non-proliferation regime since 2014 can be seen as an aberration of one guarantor of the NPT from a key international norm.[60] A U. S. withdrawal from supporting Ukraine, which Carpenter proposes, would undermine the global non-proliferation regime. It would signal to political leaders around the world that international law in general, and the NPT in particular, provide no protection for non-nuclear weapons states from stronger states. A conclusion of many politicians, diplomats and experts from the Ukrainian example could be that reliable national security can only be achieved through the acquisition of weapons of mass destruction. As the ultimate instrument of deterrence, nuclear weapons can, moreover, also become useful, if a government decides — as the Kremlin did in 2014 and 2022 — to annex a neighboring country's territory and needs to threaten the neighbor's allies with nuclear escalation.

That Carpenter does not even mention these issues is both curious and disingenuous.[61] Insofar as Carpenter presents himself as

---

58 Carpenter, "Ukraine's Accelerating Slide into Authoritarianism;" idem, "Why Ukraine Is a Dangerous and Unworthy Ally."
59 Mariana Budjeryn and Andreas Umland, "Amerikanische Russlandpolitik, die Souveränität der Ukraine und der Atomwaffensperrvertrag: Ein Dreiecksverhältnis mit weitreichenden Konsequenzen [American policy towards Russia, the sovereignty of Ukraine and the Nuclear Non-Proliferation Treaty: A triangular relationship with far-reaching consequences]." Sirius: Zeitschrift für Strategische Analysen 1, no. 2 (2017): 133-142.
60 Serhiy Galaka, "Ukrainian Crisis and Budapest Memorandum: Consequences for the European and Global Security Structures." Ukraine Analytica 1, no. 1 (2015): 45-51.
61 Carpenter, "Ukraine's Accelerating Slide into Authoritarianism;" idem, "Why Ukraine Is a Dangerous and Unworthy Ally."

concerned about core U.S. national interests, one would expect that preventing nuclear proliferation is of vital concern to him. Yet he ignored this topic even after it had been explicitly mentioned in rebuttals to his first article. In fact, discussion about the grave repercussions of Russia's violation of the 1994 Budapest Memorandum and the resulting implications for U. S. foreign policy has been taking place ever since the 2014 crisis. This debate was taking place not the least among U. S. think tank experts and academics.[62]

Carpenter departs from long-standing principles of U. S. foreign and security policies when suggesting that the United States should follow Russia in ignoring international law. Former President Donald Trump's 2019 attempt to use the cancellation of U. S. military help to the non-nuclear-weapon state Ukraine as an instrument for his domestic politics and electoral campaign has already done damage to the reputation of the U. S. as a supporter of the non-proliferation regime.[63] An implementation of Carpenter's prescriptions would further spread insecurity among non-nuclear-weapon states some of whom would seek to build or acquire WMDs to protect their national sovereignty and borders. This could have a domino effect on more and more countries becoming involved in nuclear arms races with their geographic neighbors and global competitors. In the worst case, the entire NPT regime could disintegrate—hardly a scenario which is in the national interest of the United States.

---

62 E.g., Budjeryn, "The Breach;" Umland, "The Ukraine Example: Nuclear Disarmament Doesn't Pay;" Mariana Budjeryn, "Was Ukraine's Nuclear Disarmament a Blunder?" *World Affairs* 179, no. 2 (2016): 9-20; Polina Sinovets and Mariana Budjeryn, "Interpreting the Bomb: Ownership and Deterrence in Ukraine's Nuclear Discourse." *NPIHP Working Paper* 12 (2017). www.wilsoncenter.org/publication/interpreting-the-bomb-ownership-and-deterrence-ukraines-nucle ar-discourse; idem, "Denuclearization Again? Lessons from Ukraine's Decision to Disarm." *War on the Rocks*, April 19, 2018. warontherocks.com/2018/04/den uclearization-again-lessons-from-ukraines-decision-to-disarm/.

63 Mariana Budjeryn, "Impeachment Backstory: The Nuclear Dimension of US Security Assistance to Ukraine." *Bulletin of the Atomic Scientist*, November 13, 2019. https://thebulletin.org/2019/11/impeachment-backstory-the-nuclear-dimen sion-of-us-security-assistance-to-ukraine/.

SOVIET AND POST-SOVIET POLITICS AND SOCIETY
Edited by Dr. Andreas Umland | ISSN 1614-3515

1 Андреас Умланд (ред.) | Воплощение Европейской конвенции по правам человека в России. Философские, юридические и эмпирические исследования | ISBN 3-89821-387-0

2 Christian Wipperfürth | Russland – ein vertrauenswürdiger Partner? Grundlagen, Hintergründe und Praxis gegenwärtiger russischer Außenpolitik | Mit einem Vorwort von Heinz Timmermann | ISBN 3-89821-401-X

3 Manja Hussner | Die Übernahme internationalen Rechts in die russische und deutsche Rechtsordnung. Eine vergleichende Analyse zur Völkerrechtsfreundlichkeit der Verfassungen der Russländischen Föderation und der Bundesrepublik Deutschland | Mit einem Vorwort von Rainer Arnold | ISBN 3-89821-438-9

4 Matthew Tejada | Bulgaria's Democratic Consolidation and the Kozloduy Nuclear Power Plant (KNPP). The Unattainability of Closure | With a foreword by Richard J. Crampton | ISBN 3-89821-439-7

5 Марк Григорьевич Меерович | Квадратные метры, определяющие сознание. Государственная жилищная политика в СССР. 1921 – 1941 гг | ISBN 3-89821-474-5

6 Andrei P. Tsygankov, Pavel A. Tsygankov (Eds.) | New Directions in Russian International Studies | ISBN 3-89821-422-2

7 Марк Григорьевич Меерович | Как власть народ к труду приучала. Жилище в СССР – средство управления людьми. 1917 – 1941 гг. | С предисловием Елены Осокиной | ISBN 3-89821-495-8

8 David J. Galbreath | Nation-Building and Minority Politics in Post-Socialist States. Interests, Influence and Identities in Estonia and Latvia | With a foreword by David J. Smith | ISBN 3-89821-467-2

9 Алексей Юрьевич Безугольный | Народы Кавказа в Вооруженных силах СССР в годы Великой Отечественной войны 1941-1945 гг. | С предисловием Николая Бугая | ISBN 3-89821-475-3

10 Вячеслав Лихачев и Владимир Прибыловский (ред.) | Русское Национальное Единство, 1990-2000. В 2-х томах | ISBN 3-89821-523-7

11 Николай Бугай (ред.) | Народы стран Балтии в условиях сталинизма (1940-е – 1950-е годы). Документированная история | ISBN 3-89821-525-3

12 Ingmar Bredies (Hrsg.) | Zur Anatomie der Orange Revolution in der Ukraine. Wechsel des Elitenregimes oder Triumph des Parlamentarismus? | ISBN 3-89821-524-5

13 Anastasia V. Mitrofanova | The Politicization of Russian Orthodoxy. Actors and Ideas | With a foreword by William C. Gay | ISBN 3-89821-481-8

14 Nathan D. Larson | Alexander Solzhenitsyn and the Russo-Jewish Question | ISBN 3-89821-483-4

15 Guido Houben | Kulturpolitik und Ethnizität. Staatliche Kunstförderung im Russland der neunziger Jahre | Mit einem Vorwort von Gert Weisskirchen | ISBN 3-89821-542-3

16 Leonid Luks | Der russische „Sonderweg"? Aufsätze zur neuesten Geschichte Russlands im europäischen Kontext | ISBN 3-89821-496-6

17 Евгений Мороз | История «Мёртвой воды» – от страшной сказки к большой политике. Политическое неоязычество в постсоветской России | ISBN 3-89821-551-2

18 Александр Верховский и Галина Кожевникова (ред.) | Этническая и религиозная интолерантность в российских СМИ. Результаты мониторинга 2001-2004 гг. | ISBN 3-89821-569-5

19 Christian Ganzer | Sowjetisches Erbe und ukrainische Nation. Das Museum der Geschichte des Zaporoger Kosakentums auf der Insel Chortycja | Mit einem Vorwort von Frank Golczewski | ISBN 3-89821-504-0

20 Эльза-Баир Гучинова | Помнить нельзя забыть. Антропология депортационной травмы калмыков | С предисловием Кэролайн Хамфри | ISBN 3-89821-506-7

21 Юлия Лидерман | Мотивы «проверки» и «испытания» в постсоветской культуре. Советское прошлое в российском кинематографе 1990-х годов | С предисловием Евгения Марголита | ISBN 3-89821-511-3

22 Tanya Lokshina, Ray Thomas, Mary Mayer (Eds.) | The Imposition of a Fake Political Settlement in the Northern Caucasus. The 2003 Chechen Presidential Election | ISBN 3-89821-436-2

23 Timothy McCajor Hall, Rosie Read (Eds.) | Changes in the Heart of Europe. Recent Ethnographies of Czechs, Slovaks, Roma, and Sorbs | With an afterword by Zdeněk Salzmann | ISBN 3-89821-606-3

24 Christian Autengruber | Die politischen Parteien in Bulgarien und Rumänien. Eine vergleichende Analyse seit Beginn der 90er Jahre | Mit einem Vorwort von Dorothée de Nève | ISBN 3-89821-476-1

25 Annette Freyberg-Inan with Radu Cristescu | The Ghosts in Our Classrooms, or: John Dewey Meets Ceauşescu. The Promise and the Failures of Civic Education in Romania | ISBN 3-89821-416-8

26 John B. Dunlop | The 2002 Dubrovka and 2004 Beslan Hostage Crises. A Critique of Russian Counter-Terrorism | With a foreword by Donald N. Jensen | ISBN 3-89821-608-X

27 Peter Koller | Das touristische Potenzial von Kam''janec'–Podil's'kyj. Eine fremdenverkehrsgeographische Untersuchung der Zukunftsperspektiven und Maßnahmenplanung zur Destinationsentwicklung des „ukrainischen Rothenburg" | Mit einem Vorwort von Kristiane Klemm | ISBN 3-89821-640-3

28 Françoise Daucé, Elisabeth Sieca-Kozlowski (Eds.) | Dedovshchina in the Post-Soviet Military. Hazing of Russian Army Conscripts in a Comparative Perspective | With a foreword by Dale Herspring | ISBN 3-89821-616-0

29 Florian Strasser | Zivilgesellschaftliche Einflüsse auf die Orange Revolution. Die gewaltlose Massenbewegung und die ukrainische Wahlkrise 2004 | Mit einem Vorwort von Egbert Jahn | ISBN 3-89821-648-9

30 Rebecca S. Katz | The Georgian Regime Crisis of 2003-2004. A Case Study in Post-Soviet Media Representation of Politics, Crime and Corruption | ISBN 3-89821-413-3

31 Vladimir Kantor | Willkür oder Freiheit. Beiträge zur russischen Geschichtsphilosophie | Ediert von Dagmar Herrmann sowie mit einem Vorwort versehen von Leonid Luks | ISBN 3-89821-589-X

32 Laura A. Victoir | The Russian Land Estate Today. A Case Study of Cultural Politics in Post-Soviet Russia | With a foreword by Priscilla Roosevelt | ISBN 3-89821-426-5

33 Ivan Katchanovski | Cleft Countries. Regional Political Divisions and Cultures in Post-Soviet Ukraine and Moldova | With a foreword by Francis Fukuyama | ISBN 3-89821-558-X

34 Florian Mühlfried | Postsowjetische Feiern. Das Georgische Bankett im Wandel | Mit einem Vorwort von Kevin Tuite | ISBN 3-89821-601-2

35 Roger Griffin, Werner Loh, Andreas Umland (Eds.) | Fascism Past and Present, West and East. An International Debate on Concepts and Cases in the Comparative Study of the Extreme Right | With an afterword by Walter Laqueur | ISBN 3-89821-674-8

36 Sebastian Schlegel | Der „Weiße Archipel". Sowjetische Atomstädte 1945-1991 | Mit einem Geleitwort von Thomas Bohn | ISBN 3-89821-679-9

37 Vyacheslav Likhachev | Political Anti-Semitism in Post-Soviet Russia. Actors and Ideas in 1991-2003 | Edited and translated from Russian by Eugene Veklerov | ISBN 3-89821-529-6

38 Josette Baer (Ed.) | Preparing Liberty in Central Europe. Political Texts from the Spring of Nations 1848 to the Spring of Prague 1968 | With a foreword by Zdeněk V. David | ISBN 3-89821-546-6

39 Михаил Лукьянов | Российский консерватизм и реформа, 1907-1914 | С предисловием Марка Д. Стейнберга | ISBN 3-89821-503-2

40 Nicola Melloni | Market Without Economy. The 1998 Russian Financial Crisis | With a foreword by Eiji Furukawa | ISBN 3-89821-407-9

41 Dmitrij Chmelnizki | Die Architektur Stalins | Bd. 1: Studien zu Ideologie und Stil | Bd. 2: Bilddokumentation | Mit einem Vorwort von Bruno Flierl | ISBN 3-89821-515-6

42 Katja Yafimava | Post-Soviet Russian-Belarussian Relationships. The Role of Gas Transit Pipelines | With a foreword by Jonathan P. Stern | ISBN 3-89821-655-1

43 Boris Chavkin | Verflechtungen der deutschen und russischen Zeitgeschichte. Aufsätze und Archivfunde zu den Beziehungen Deutschlands und der Sowjetunion von 1917 bis 1991 | Ediert von Markus Edlinger sowie mit einem Vorwort versehen von Leonid Luks | ISBN 3-89821-756-6

44 Anastasija Grynenko in Zusammenarbeit mit Claudia Dathe | Die Terminologie des Gerichtswesens der Ukraine und Deutschlands im Vergleich. Eine übersetzungswissenschaftliche Analyse juristischer Fachbegriffe im Deutschen, Ukrainischen und Russischen | Mit einem Vorwort von Ulrich Hartmann | ISBN 3-89821-691-8

45 Anton Burkov | The Impact of the European Convention on Human Rights on Russian Law. Legislation and Application in 1996-2006 | With a foreword by Françoise Hampson | ISBN 978-3-89821-639-5

46 Stina Torjesen, Indra Overland (Eds.) | International Election Observers in Post-Soviet Azerbaijan. Geopolitical Pawns or Agents of Change? | ISBN 978-3-89821-743-9

47 Taras Kuzio | Ukraine – Crimea – Russia. Triangle of Conflict | ISBN 978-3-89821-761-3

48 Claudia Šabić | „Ich erinnere mich nicht, aber L'viv!" Zur Funktion kultureller Faktoren für die Institutionalisierung und Entwicklung einer ukrainischen Region | Mit einem Vorwort von Melanie Tatur | ISBN 978-3-89821-752-1

49 *Marlies Bilz* | Tatarstan in der Transformation. Nationaler Diskurs und Politische Praxis 1988-1994 | Mit einem Vorwort von Frank Golczewski | ISBN 978-3-89821-722-4

50 *Марлен Ларюэль (ред.)* | Современные интерпретации русского национализма | ISBN 978-3-89821-795-8

51 *Sonja Schüler* | Die ethnische Dimension der Armut. Roma im postsozialistischen Rumänien | Mit einem Vorwort von Anton Sterbling | ISBN 978-3-89821-776-7

52 *Галина Кожевникова* | Радикальный национализм в России и противодействие ему. Сборник докладов Центра «Сова» за 2004-2007 гг. | С предисловием Александра Верховского | ISBN 978-3-89821-721-7

53 *Галина Кожевникова и Владимир Прибыловский* | Российская власть в биографиях I. Высшие должностные лица РФ в 2004 г. | ISBN 978-3-89821-796-5

54 *Галина Кожевникова и Владимир Прибыловский* | Российская власть в биографиях II. Члены Правительства РФ в 2004 г. | ISBN 978-3-89821-797-2

55 *Галина Кожевникова и Владимир Прибыловский* | Российская власть в биографиях III. Руководители федеральных служб и агентств РФ в 2004 г.| ISBN 978-3-89821-798-9

56 *Ileana Petroniu* | Privatisierung in Transformationsökonomien. Determinanten der Restrukturierungs-Bereitschaft am Beispiel Polens, Rumäniens und der Ukraine | Mit einem Vorwort von Rainer W. Schäfer | ISBN 978-3-89821-790-3

57 *Christian Wipperfürth* | Russland und seine GUS-Nachbarn. Hintergründe, aktuelle Entwicklungen und Konflikte in einer ressourcenreichen Region| ISBN 978-3-89821-801-6

58 *Togzhan Kassenova* | From Antagonism to Partnership. The Uneasy Path of the U.S.-Russian Cooperative Threat Reduction | With a foreword by Christoph Bluth | ISBN 978-3-89821-707-1

59 *Alexander Höllwerth* | Das sakrale eurasische Imperium des Aleksandr Dugin. Eine Diskursanalyse zum postsowjetischen russischen Rechtsextremismus | Mit einem Vorwort von Dirk Uffelmann | ISBN 978-3-89821-813-9

60 *Олег Рябов* | «Россия-Матушка». Национализм, гендер и война в России XX века | С предисловием Елены Гощило | ISBN 978-3-89821-487-2

61 *Ivan Maistrenko* | Borot'bism. A Chapter in the History of the Ukrainian Revolution | With a new Introduction by Chris Ford | Translated by George S. N. Luckyj with the assistance of Ivan L. Rudnytsky | Second, Revised and Expanded Edition ISBN 978-3-8382-1107-7

62 *Maryna Romanets* | Anamorphosic Texts and Reconfigured Visions. Improvised Traditions in Contemporary Ukrainian and Irish Literature | ISBN 978-3-89821-576-3

63 *Paul D'Anieri and Taras Kuzio (Eds.)* | Aspects of the Orange Revolution I. Democratization and Elections in Post-Communist Ukraine | ISBN 978-3-89821-698-2

64 *Bohdan Harasymiw in collaboration with Oleh S. Ilnytzkyj (Eds.)* | Aspects of the Orange Revolution II. Information and Manipulation Strategies in the 2004 Ukrainian Presidential Elections | ISBN 978-3-89821-699-9

65 *Ingmar Bredies, Andreas Umland and Valentin Yakushik (Eds.)* | Aspects of the Orange Revolution III. The Context and Dynamics of the 2004 Ukrainian Presidential Elections | ISBN 978-3-89821-803-0

66 *Ingmar Bredies, Andreas Umland and Valentin Yakushik (Eds.)* | Aspects of the Orange Revolution IV. Foreign Assistance and Civic Action in the 2004 Ukrainian Presidential Elections | ISBN 978-3-89821-808-5

67 *Ingmar Bredies, Andreas Umland and Valentin Yakushik (Eds.)* | Aspects of the Orange Revolution V. Institutional Observation Reports on the 2004 Ukrainian Presidential Elections | ISBN 978-3-89821-809-2

68 *Taras Kuzio (Ed.)* | Aspects of the Orange Revolution VI. Post-Communist Democratic Revolutions in Comparative Perspective | ISBN 978-3-89821-820-7

69 *Tim Bohse* | Autoritarismus statt Selbstverwaltung. Die Transformation der kommunalen Politik in der Stadt Kaliningrad 1990-2005 | Mit einem Geleitwort von Stefan Troebst | ISBN 978-3-89821-782-8

70 *David Rupp* | Die Rußländische Föderation und die russischsprachige Minderheit in Lettland. Eine Fallstudie zur Anwaltspolitik Moskaus gegenüber den russophonen Minderheiten im „Nahen Ausland" von 1991 bis 2002 | Mit einem Vorwort von Helmut Wagner | ISBN 978-3-89821-778-1

71 *Taras Kuzio* | Theoretical and Comparative Perspectives on Nationalism. New Directions in Cross-Cultural and Post-Communist Studies | With a foreword by Paul Robert Magocsi | ISBN 978-3-89821-815-3

72 *Christine Teichmann* | Die Hochschultransformation im heutigen Osteuropa. Kontinuität und Wandel bei der Entwicklung des postkommunistischen Universitätswesens | Mit einem Vorwort von Oskar Anweiler | ISBN 978-3-89821-842-9

73 *Julia Kusznir* | Der politische Einfluss von Wirtschaftseliten in russischen Regionen. Eine Analyse am Beispiel der Erdöl- und Erdgasindustrie, 1992-2005 | Mit einem Vorwort von Wolfgang Eichwede | ISBN 978-3-89821-821-4

74 *Alena Vysotskaya* | Russland, Belarus und die EU-Osterweiterung. Zur Minderheitenfrage und zum Problem der Freizügigkeit des Personenverkehrs | Mit einem Vorwort von Katlijn Malfliet | ISBN 978-3-89821-822-1

75 *Heiko Pleines (Hrsg.)* | Corporate Governance in post-sozialistischen Volkswirtschaften | ISBN 978-3-89821-766-8

76 *Stefan Ihrig* | Wer sind die Moldawier? Rumänismus versus Moldowanismus in Historiographie und Schulbüchern der Republik Moldova, 1991-2006 | Mit einem Vorwort von Holm Sundhaussen | ISBN 978-3-89821-466-7

77 *Galina Kozhevnikova in collaboration with Alexander Verkhovsky and Eugene Veklerov* | Ultra-Nationalism and Hate Crimes in Contemporary Russia. The 2004-2006 Annual Reports of Moscow's SOVA Center | With a foreword by Stephen D. Shenfield | ISBN 978-3-89821-868-9

78 *Florian Küchler* | The Role of the European Union in Moldova's Transnistria Conflict | With a foreword by Christopher Hill | ISBN 978-3-89821-850-4

79 *Bernd Rechel* | The Long Way Back to Europe. Minority Protection in Bulgaria | With a foreword by Richard Crampton | ISBN 978-3-89821-863-4

80 *Peter W. Rodgers* | Nation, Region and History in Post-Communist Transitions. Identity Politics in Ukraine, 1991-2006 | With a foreword by Vera Tolz | ISBN 978-3-89821-903-7

81 *Stephanie Solywoda* | The Life and Work of Semen L. Frank. A Study of Russian Religious Philosophy | With a foreword by Philip Walters | ISBN 978-3-89821-457-5

82 *Vera Sokolova* | Cultural Politics of Ethnicity. Discourses on Roma in Communist Czechoslovakia | ISBN 978-3-89821-864-1

83 *Natalya Shevchik Ketenci* | Kazakhstani Enterprises in Transition. The Role of Historical Regional Development in Kazakhstan's Post-Soviet Economic Transformation | ISBN 978-3-89821-831-3

84 *Martin Malek, Anna Schor-Tschudnowskaja (Hgg.)* | Europa im Tschetschenienkrieg. Zwischen politischer Ohnmacht und Gleichgültigkeit | Mit einem Vorwort von Lipchan Basajewa | ISBN 978-3-89821-676-0

85 *Stefan Meister* | Das postsowjetische Universitätswesen zwischen nationalem und internationalem Wandel. Die Entwicklung der regionalen Hochschule in Russland als Gradmesser der Systemtransformation | Mit einem Vorwort von Joan DeBardeleben | ISBN 978-3-89821-891-7

86 *Konstantin Sheiko in collaboration with Stephen Brown* | Nationalist Imaginings of the Russian Past. Anatolii Fomenko and the Rise of Alternative History in Post-Communist Russia | With a foreword by Donald Ostrowski | ISBN 978-3-89821-915-0

87 *Sabine Jenni* | Wie stark ist das „Einige Russland"? Zur Parteibindung der Eliten und zum Wahlerfolg der Machtpartei im Dezember 2007 | Mit einem Vorwort von Klaus Armingeon | ISBN 978-3-89821-961-7

88 *Thomas Borén* | Meeting-Places of Transformation. Urban Identity, Spatial Representations and Local Politics in Post-Soviet St Petersburg | ISBN 978-3-89821-739-2

89 *Aygul Ashirova* | Stalinismus und Stalin-Kult in Zentralasien. Turkmenistan 1924-1953 | Mit einem Vorwort von Leonid Luks | ISBN 978-3-89821-987-7

90 *Leonid Luks* | Freiheit oder imperiale Größe? Essays zu einem russischen Dilemma | ISBN 978-3-8382-0011-8

91 *Christopher Gilley* | The 'Change of Signposts' in the Ukrainian Emigration. A Contribution to the History of Sovietophilism in the 1920s | With a foreword by Frank Golczewski | ISBN 978-3-89821-965-5

92 *Philipp Casula, Jeronim Perovic (Eds.)* | Identities and Politics During the Putin Presidency. The Discursive Foundations of Russia's Stability | With a foreword by Heiko Haumann | ISBN 978-3-8382-0015-6

93 *Marcel Viëtor* | Europa und die Frage nach seinen Grenzen im Osten. Zur Konstruktion ‚europäischer Identität' in Geschichte und Gegenwart | Mit einem Vorwort von Albrecht Lehmann | ISBN 978-3-8382-0045-3

94 *Ben Hellman, Andrei Rogachevskii* | Filming the Unfilmable. Casper Wrede's 'One Day in the Life of Ivan Denisovich' | Second, Revised and Expanded Edition | ISBN 978-3-8382-0044-6

95 *Eva Fuchslocher* | Vaterland, Sprache, Glaube. Orthodoxie und Nationenbildung am Beispiel Georgiens | Mit einem Vorwort von Christina von Braun | ISBN 978-3-89821-884-9

96 *Vladimir Kantor* | Das Westlertum und der Weg Russlands. Zur Entwicklung der russischen Literatur und Philosophie | Ediert von Dagmar Herrmann | Mit einem Beitrag von Nikolaus Lobkowicz | ISBN 978-3-8382-0102-3

97 *Kamran Musayev* | Die postsowjetische Transformation im Baltikum und Südkaukasus. Eine vergleichende Untersuchung der politischen Entwicklung Lettlands und Aserbaidschans 1985-2009 | Mit einem Vorwort von Leonid Luks | Ediert von Sandro Henschel | ISBN 978-3-8382-0103-0

98 *Tatiana Zhurzhenko* | Borderlands into Bordered Lands. Geopolitics of Identity in Post-Soviet Ukraine | With a foreword by Dieter Segert | ISBN 978-3-8382-0042-2

99 *Кирилл Галушко, Лидия Смола (ред.)* | Пределы падения – варианты украинского будущего. Аналитико-прогностические исследования | ISBN 978-3-8382-0148-1

100 *Michael Minkenberg (Ed.)* | Historical Legacies and the Radical Right in Post-Cold War Central and Eastern Europe | With an afterword by Sabrina P. Ramet | ISBN 978-3-8382-0124-5

101 *David-Emil Wickström* | Rocking St. Petersburg. Transcultural Flows and Identity Politics in the St. Petersburg Popular Music Scene | With a foreword by Yngvar B. Steinholt | Second, Revised and Expanded Edition | ISBN 978-3-8382-0100-9

102 *Eva Zabka* | Eine neue „Zeit der Wirren"? Der spät- und postsowjetische Systemwandel 1985-2000 im Spiegel russischer gesellschaftspolitischer Diskurse | Mit einem Vorwort von Margareta Mommsen | ISBN 978-3-8382-0161-0

103 *Ulrike Ziemer* | Ethnic Belonging, Gender and Cultural Practices. Youth Identitites in Contemporary Russia | With a foreword by Anoop Nayak | ISBN 978-3-8382-0152-8

104 *Ksenia Chepikova* | ‚Einiges Russland' - eine zweite KPdSU? Aspekte der Identitätskonstruktion einer postsowjetischen „Partei der Macht" | Mit einem Vorwort von Torsten Oppelland | ISBN 978-3-8382-0311-9

105 *Леонид Люкс* | Западничество или евразийство? Демократия или идеократия? Сборник статей об исторических дилеммах России | С предисловием Владимира Кантора | ISBN 978-3-8382-0211-2

106 *Anna Dost* | Das russische Verfassungsrecht auf dem Weg zum Föderalismus und zurück. Zum Konflikt von Rechtsnormen und -wirklichkeit in der Russländischen Föderation von 1991 bis 2009 | Mit einem Vorwort von Alexander Blankenagel | ISBN 978-3-8382-0292-1

107 *Philipp Herzog* | Sozialistische Völkerfreundschaft, nationaler Widerstand oder harmloser Zeitvertreib? Zur politischen Funktion der Volkskunst im sowjetischen Estland | Mit einem Vorwort von Andreas Kappeler | ISBN 978-3-8382-0216-7

108 *Marlène Laruelle (Ed.)* | Russian Nationalism, Foreign Policy, and Identity Debates in Putin's Russia. New Ideological Patterns after the Orange Revolution | ISBN 978-3-8382-0325-6

109 *Michail Logvinov* | Russlands Kampf gegen den internationalen Terrorismus. Eine kritische Bestandsaufnahme des Bekämpfungsansatzes | Mit einem Geleitwort von Hans-Henning Schröder und einem Vorwort von Eckhard Jesse | ISBN 978-3-8382-0329-4

110 *John B. Dunlop* | The Moscow Bombings of September 1999. Examinations of Russian Terrorist Attacks at the Onset of Vladimir Putin's Rule | Second, Revised and Expanded Edition | ISBN 978-3-8382-0388-1

111 *Андрей А. Ковалёв* | Свидетельство из-за кулис российской политики I. Можно ли делать добро из зла? (Воспоминания и размышления о последних советских и первых послесоветских годах) | With a foreword by Peter Reddaway | ISBN 978-3-8382-0302-7

112 *Андрей А. Ковалёв* | Свидетельство из-за кулис российской политики II. Угроза для себя и окружающих (Наблюдения и предостережения относительно происходящего после 2000 г.) | ISBN 978-3-8382-0303-4

113 *Bernd Kappenberg* | Zeichen setzen für Europa. Der Gebrauch europäischer lateinischer Sonderzeichen in der deutschen Öffentlichkeit | Mit einem Vorwort von Peter Schlobinski | ISBN 978-3-89821-749-1

114 *Ivo Mijnssen* | The Quest for an Ideal Youth in Putin's Russia I. Back to Our Future! History, Modernity, and Patriotism according to Nashi, 2005-2013 | With a foreword by Jeronim Perović | Second, Revised and Expanded Edition | ISBN 978-3-8382-0368-3

115 *Jussi Lassila* | The Quest for an Ideal Youth in Putin's Russia II. The Search for Distinctive Conformism in the Political Communication of Nashi, 2005-2009 | With a foreword by Kirill Postoutenko | Second, Revised and Expanded Edition | ISBN 978-3-8382-0415-4

116 *Valerio Trabandt* | Neue Nachbarn, gute Nachbarschaft? Die EU als internationaler Akteur am Beispiel ihrer Demokratieförderung in Belarus und der Ukraine 2004-2009 | Mit einem Vorwort von Jutta Joachim | ISBN 978-3-8382-0437-6

117 *Fabian Pfeiffer* | Estlands Außen- und Sicherheitspolitik I. Der estnische Atlantizismus nach der wiedererlangten Unabhängigkeit 1991-2004 | Mit einem Vorwort von Helmut Hubel | ISBN 978-3-8382-0127-6

118 *Jana Podßuweit* | Estlands Außen- und Sicherheitspolitik II. Handlungsoptionen eines Kleinstaates im Rahmen seiner EU-Mitgliedschaft (2004-2008) | Mit einem Vorwort von Helmut Hubel | ISBN 978-3-8382-0440-6

119 *Karin Pointner* | Estlands Außen- und Sicherheitspolitik III. Eine gedächtnispolitische Analyse estnischer Entwicklungskooperation 2006-2010 | Mit einem Vorwort von Karin Liebhart | ISBN 978-3-8382-0435-2

120 *Ruslana Vovk* | Die Offenheit der ukrainischen Verfassung für das Völkerrecht und die europäische Integration | Mit einem Vorwort von Alexander Blankenagel | ISBN 978-3-8382-0481-9

121 Mykhaylo Banakh | Die Relevanz der Zivilgesellschaft bei den postkommunistischen Transformationsprozessen in mittel- und osteuropäischen Ländern. Das Beispiel der spät- und postsowjetischen Ukraine 1986-2009 | Mit einem Vorwort von Gerhard Simon | ISBN 978-3-8382-0499-4

122 Michael Moser | Language Policy and the Discourse on Languages in Ukraine under President Viktor Yanukovych (25 February 2010–28 October 2012) | ISBN 978-3-8382-0497-0 (Paperback edition) | ISBN 978-3-8382-0507-6 (Hardcover edition)

123 Nicole Krome | Russischer Netzwerkkapitalismus Restrukturierungsprozesse in der Russischen Föderation am Beispiel des Luftfahrtunternehmens „Aviastar" | Mit einem Vorwort von Petra Stykow | ISBN 978-3-8382-0534-2

124 David R. Marples | 'Our Glorious Past'. Lukashenka's Belarus and the Great Patriotic War | ISBN 978-3-8382-0574-8 (Paperback edition) | ISBN 978-3-8382-0675-2 (Hardcover edition)

125 Ulf Walther | Russlands „neuer Adel". Die Macht des Geheimdienstes von Gorbatschow bis Putin | Mit einem Vorwort von Hans-Georg Wieck | ISBN 978-3-8382-0584-7

126 Simon Geissbühler (Hrsg.) | Kiew – Revolution 3.0. Der Euromaidan 2013/14 und die Zukunftsperspektiven der Ukraine | ISBN 978-3-8382-0581-6 (Paperback edition) | ISBN 978-3-8382-0681-3 (Hardcover edition)

127 Andrey Makarychev | Russia and the EU in a Multipolar World. Discourses, Identities, Norms | With a foreword by Klaus Segbers | ISBN 978-3-8382-0629-5

128 Roland Scharff | Kasachstan als postsowjetischer Wohlfahrtsstaat. Die Transformation des sozialen Schutzsystems | Mit einem Vorwort von Joachim Ahrens | ISBN 978-3-8382-0622-6

129 Katja Grupp | Bild Lücke Deutschland. Kaliningrader Studierende sprechen über Deutschland | Mit einem Vorwort von Martin Schulz | ISBN 978-3-8382-0552-6

130 Konstantin Sheiko, Stephen Brown | History as Therapy. Alternative History and Nationalist Imaginings in Russia, 1991-2014 | ISBN 978-3-8382-0665-3

131 Elisa Kriza | Alexander Solzhenitsyn: Cold War Icon, Gulag Author, Russian Nationalist? A Study of the Western Reception of his Literary Writings, Historical Interpretations, and Political Ideas | With a foreword by Andrei Rogatchevski | ISBN 978-3-8382-0589-2 (Paperback edition) | ISBN 978-3-8382-0690-5 (Hardcover edition)

132 Serghei Golunov | The Elephant in the Room. Corruption and Cheating in Russian Universities | ISBN 978-3-8382-0570-0

133 Manja Hussner, Rainer Arnold (Hgg.) | Verfassungsgerichtsbarkeit in Zentralasien I. Sammlung von Verfassungstexten | ISBN 978-3-8382-0595-3

134 Nikolay Mitrokhin | Die „Russische Partei". Die Bewegung der russischen Nationalisten in der UdSSR 1953-1985 | Aus dem Russischen übertragen von einem Übersetzerteam unter der Leitung von Larisa Schippel | ISBN 978-3-8382-0024-8

135 Manja Hussner, Rainer Arnold (Hgg.) | Verfassungsgerichtsbarkeit in Zentralasien II. Sammlung von Verfassungstexten | ISBN 978-3-8382-0597-7

136 Manfred Zeller | Das sowjetische Fieber. Fußballfans im poststalinistischen Vielvölkerreich | Mit einem Vorwort von Nikolaus Katzer | ISBN 978-3-8382-0757-5

137 Kristin Schreiter | Stellung und Entwicklungspotential zivilgesellschaftlicher Gruppen in Russland. Menschenrechtsorganisationen im Vergleich | ISBN 978-3-8382-0673-8

138 David R. Marples, Frederick V. Mills (Eds.) | Ukraine's Euromaidan. Analyses of a Civil Revolution | ISBN 978-3-8382-0660-8

139 Bernd Kappenberg | Setting Signs for Europe. Why Diacritics Matter for European Integration | With a foreword by Peter Schlobinski | ISBN 978-3-8382-0663-9

140 René Lenz | Internationalisierung, Kooperation und Transfer. Externe bildungspolitische Akteure in der Russischen Föderation | Mit einem Vorwort von Frank Ettrich | ISBN 978-3-8382-0751-3

141 Juri Plusnin, Yana Zausaeva, Natalia Zhidkevich, Artemy Pozanenko | Wandering Workers. Mores, Behavior, Way of Life, and Political Status of Domestic Russian Labor Migrants | Translated by Julia Kazantseva | ISBN 978-3-8382-0653-0

142 David J. Smith (Eds.) | Latvia – A Work in Progress? 100 Years of State- and Nation-Building | ISBN 978-3-8382-0648-6

143 Инна Чувычкина (ред.) | Экспортные нефте- и газопроводы на постсоветском пространстве. Анализ трубопроводной политики в свете теории международных отношений | ISBN 978-3-8382-0822-0

144 *Johann Zajaczkowski* | Russland – eine pragmatische Großmacht? Eine rollentheoretische Untersuchung russischer Außenpolitik am Beispiel der Zusammenarbeit mit den USA nach 9/11 und des Georgienkrieges von 2008 | Mit einem Vorwort von Siegfried Schieder | ISBN 978-3-8382-0837-4

145 *Boris Popivanov* | Changing Images of the Left in Bulgaria. The Challenge of Post-Communism in the Early 21st Century | ISBN 978-3-8382-0667-7

146 *Lenka Krátká* | A History of the Czechoslovak Ocean Shipping Company 1948-1989. How a Small, Landlocked Country Ran Maritime Business During the Cold War | ISBN 978-3-8382-0666-0

147 *Alexander Sergunin* | Explaining Russian Foreign Policy Behavior. Theory and Practice | ISBN 978-3-8382-0752-0

148 *Darya Malyutina* | Migrant Friendships in a Super-Diverse City. Russian-Speakers and their Social Relationships in London in the 21st Century | With a foreword by Claire Dwyer | ISBN 978-3-8382-0652-3

149 *Alexander Sergunin, Valery Konyshev* | Russia in the Arctic. Hard or Soft Power? | ISBN 978-3-8382-0753-7

150 *John J. Maresca* | Helsinki Revisited. A Key U.S. Negotiator's Memoirs on the Development of the CSCE into the OSCE | With a foreword by Hafiz Pashayev | ISBN 978-3-8382-0852-7

151 *Jardar Østbø* | The New Third Rome. Readings of a Russian Nationalist Myth | With a foreword by Pål Kolstø | ISBN 978-3-8382-0870-1

152 *Simon Kordonsky* | Socio-Economic Foundations of the Russian Post-Soviet Regime. The Resource-Based Economy and Estate-Based Social Structure of Contemporary Russia | With a foreword by Svetlana Barsukova | ISBN 978-3-8382-0775-9

153 *Duncan Leitch* | Assisting Reform in Post-Communist Ukraine 2000–2012. The Illusions of Donors and the Disillusion of Beneficiaries | With a foreword by Kataryna Wolczuk | ISBN 978-3-8382-0844-2

154 *Abel Polese* | Limits of a Post-Soviet State. How Informality Replaces, Renegotiates, and Reshapes Governance in Contemporary Ukraine | With a foreword by Colin Williams | ISBN 978-3-8382-0845-9

155 *Mikhail Suslov (Ed.)* | Digital Orthodoxy in the Post-Soviet World. The Russian Orthodox Church and Web 2.0 | With a foreword by Father Cyril Hovorun | ISBN 978-3-8382-0871-8

156 *Leonid Luks* | Zwei „Sonderwege"? Russisch-deutsche Parallelen und Kontraste (1917-2014). Vergleichende Essays | ISBN 978-3-8382-0823-7

157 *Vladimir V. Karacharovskiy, Ovsey I. Shkaratan, Gordey A. Yastrebov* | Towards a New Russian Work Culture. Can Western Companies and Expatriates Change Russian Society? | With a foreword by Elena N. Danilova | Translated by Julia Kazantseva | ISBN 978-3-8382-0902-9

158 *Edmund Griffiths* | Aleksandr Prokhanov and Post-Soviet Esotericism | ISBN 978-3-8382-0963-0

159 *Timm Beichelt, Susann Worschech (Eds.)* | Transnational Ukraine? Networks and Ties that Influence(d) Contemporary Ukraine | ISBN 978-3-8382-0944-9

160 *Mieste Hotopp-Riecke* | Die Tataren der Krim zwischen Assimilation und Selbstbehauptung. Der Aufbau des krimtatarischen Bildungswesens nach Deportation und Heimkehr (1990-2005) | Mit einem Vorwort von Swetlana Czerwonnaja | ISBN 978-3-89821-940-2

161 *Olga Bertelsen (Ed.)* | Revolution and War in Contemporary Ukraine. The Challenge of Change | ISBN 978-3-8382-1016-2

162 *Natalya Ryabinska* | Ukraine's Post-Communist Mass Media. Between Capture and Commercialization | With a foreword by Marta Dyczok | ISBN 978-3-8382-1011-7

163 *Alexandra Cotofana, James M. Nyce (Eds.)* | Religion and Magic in Socialist and Post-Socialist Contexts. Historic and Ethnographic Case Studies of Orthodoxy, Heterodoxy, and Alternative Spirituality | With a foreword by Patrick L. Michelson | ISBN 978-3-8382-0989-0

164 *Nozima Akhrarkhodjaeva* | The Instrumentalisation of Mass Media in Electoral Authoritarian Regimes. Evidence from Russia's Presidential Election Campaigns of 2000 and 2008 | ISBN 978-3-8382-1013-1

165 *Yulia Krasheninnikova* | Informal Healthcare in Contemporary Russia. Sociographic Essays on the Post-Soviet Infrastructure for Alternative Healing Practices | ISBN 978-3-8382-0970-8

166 *Peter Kaiser* | Das Schachbrett der Macht. Die Handlungsspielräume eines sowjetischen Funktionärs unter Stalin am Beispiel des Generalsekretärs des Komsomol Aleksandr Kosarev (1929-1938) | Mit einem Vorwort von Dietmar Neutatz | ISBN 978-3-8382-1052-0

167 *Oksana Kim* | The Effects and Implications of Kazakhstan's Adoption of International Financial Reporting Standards. A Resource Dependence Perspective | With a foreword by Svetlana Vlady | ISBN 978-3-8382-0987-6

168　*Anna Sanina* | Patriotic Education in Contemporary Russia. Sociological Studies in the Making of the Post-Soviet Citizen | With a foreword by Anna Oldfield | ISBN 978-3-8382-0993-7

169　*Rudolf Wolters* | Spezialist in Sibirien Faksimile der 1933 erschienenen ersten Ausgabe | Mit einem Vorwort von Dmitrij Chmelnizki | ISBN 978-3-8382-0515-1

170　*Michal Vít, Magdalena M. Baran (Eds.)* | Transregional versus National Perspectives on Contemporary Central European History. Studies on the Building of Nation-States and Their Cooperation in the 20th and 21st Century | With a foreword by Petr Vágner | ISBN 978-3-8382-1015-5

171　*Philip Gamaghelyan* | Conflict Resolution Beyond the International Relations Paradigm. Evolving Designs as a Transformative Practice in Nagorno-Karabakh and Syria | With a foreword by Susan Allen | ISBN 978-3-8382-1057-5

172　*Maria Shagina* | Joining a Prestigious Club. Cooperation with Europarties and Its Impact on Party Development in Georgia, Moldova, and Ukraine 2004–2015 | With a foreword by Kataryna Wolczuk | ISBN 978-3-8382-1084-1

173　*Alexandra Cotofana, James M. Nyce (Eds.)* | Religion and Magic in Socialist and Post-Socialist Contexts II. Baltic, Eastern European, and Post-USSR Case Studies | With a foreword by Anita Stasulane | ISBN 978-3-8382-0990-6

174　*Barbara Kunz* | Kind Words, Cruise Missiles, and Everything in Between. The Use of Power Resources in U.S. Policies towards Poland, Ukraine, and Belarus 1989–2008 | With a foreword by William Hill | ISBN 978-3-8382-1065-0

175　*Eduard Klein* | Bildungskorruption in Russland und der Ukraine. Eine komparative Analyse der Performanz staatlicher Antikorruptionsmaßnahmen im Hochschulsektor am Beispiel universitärer Aufnahmeprüfungen | Mit einem Vorwort von Heiko Pleines | ISBN 978-3-8382-0995-1

176　*Markus Soldner* | Politischer Kapitalismus im postsowjetischen Russland. Die politische, wirtschaftliche und mediale Transformation in den 1990er Jahren | Mit einem Vorwort von Wolfgang Ismayr | ISBN 978-3-8382-1222-7

177　*Anton Oleinik* | Building Ukraine from Within. A Sociological, Institutional, and Economic Analysis of a Nation-State in the Making | ISBN 978-3-8382-1150-3

178　*Peter Rollberg, Marlene Laruelle (Eds.)* | Mass Media in the Post-Soviet World. Market Forces, State Actors, and Political Manipulation in the Informational Environment after Communism | ISBN 978-3-8382-1116-9

179　*Mikhail Minakov* | Development and Dystopia. Studies in Post-Soviet Ukraine and Eastern Europe | With a foreword by Alexander Etkind | ISBN 978-3-8382-1112-1

180　*Aijan Sharshenova* | The European Union's Democracy Promotion in Central Asia. A Study of Political Interests, Influence, and Development in Kazakhstan and Kyrgyzstan in 2007–2013 | With a foreword by Gordon Crawford | ISBN 978-3-8382-1151-0

181　*Andrey Makarychev, Alexandra Yatsyk (Eds.)* | Boris Nemtsov and Russian Politics. Power and Resistance | With a foreword by Zhanna Nemtsova | ISBN 978-3-8382-1122-0

182　*Sophie Falsini* | The Euromaidan's Effect on Civil Society. Why and How Ukrainian Social Capital Increased after the Revolution of Dignity | With a foreword by Susann Worschech | ISBN 978-3-8382-1131-2

183　*Valentyna Romanova, Andreas Umland (Eds.)* | Ukraine's Decentralization. Challenges and Implications of the Local Governance Reform after the Euromaidan Revolution | ISBN 978-3-8382-1162-6

184　*Leonid Luks* | A Fateful Triangle. Essays on Contemporary Russian, German and Polish History | ISBN 978-3-8382-1143-5

185　*John B. Dunlop* | The February 2015 Assassination of Boris Nemtsov and the Flawed Trial of his Alleged Killers. An Exploration of Russia's "Crime of the 21st Century" | ISBN 978-3-8382-1188-6

186　*Vasile Rotaru* | Russia, the EU, and the Eastern Partnership. Building Bridges or Digging Trenches? | ISBN 978-3-8382-1134-3

187　*Marina Lebedeva* | Russian Studies of International Relations. From the Soviet Past to the Post-Cold-War Present | With a foreword by Andrei P. Tsygankov | ISBN 978-3-8382-0851-0

188　*Tomasz Stępniewski, George Soroka (Eds.)* | Ukraine after Maidan. Revisiting Domestic and Regional Security | ISBN 978-3-8382-1075-9

189　*Petar Cholakov* | Ethnic Entrepreneurs Unmasked. Political Institutions and Ethnic Conflicts in Contemporary Bulgaria | ISBN 978-3-8382-1189-3

190　*A. Salem, G. Hazeldine, D. Morgan (Eds.)* | Higher Education in Post-Communist States. Comparative and Sociological Perspectives | ISBN 978-3-8382-1183-1

191　*Igor Torbakov* | After Empire. Nationalist Imagination and Symbolic Politics in Russia and Eurasia in the Twentieth and Twenty-First Century | With a foreword by Serhii Plokhy | ISBN 978-3-8382-1217-3

192 *Aleksandr Burakovskiy* | Jewish-Ukrainian Relations in Late and Post-Soviet Ukraine. Articles, Lectures and Essays from 1986 to 2016 | ISBN 978-3-8382-1210-4

193 *Natalia Shapovalova, Olga Burlyuk (Eds.)* | Civil Society in Post-Euromaidan Ukraine. From Revolution to Consolidation | With a foreword by Richard Youngs | ISBN 978-3-8382-1216-6

194 *Franz Preissler* | Positionsverteidigung, Imperialismus oder Irredentismus? Russland und die „Russischsprachigen", 1991–2015 | ISBN 978-3-8382-1262-3

195 *Marian Madeła* | Der Reformprozess in der Ukraine 2014-2017. Eine Fallstudie zur Reform der öffentlichen Verwaltung | Mit einem Vorwort von Martin Malek | ISBN 978-3-8382-1266-1

196 *Anke Giesen* | „Wie kann denn der Sieger ein Verbrecher sein?" Eine diskursanalytische Untersuchung der russlandweiten Debatte über Konzept und Verstaatlichungsprozess der Lagergedenkstätte „Perm'-36" im Ural | ISBN 978-3-8382-1284-5

197 *Victoria Leukavets* | The Integration Policies of Belarus and Ukraine vis-à-vis the EU and Russia. A Comparative Analysis Through the Prism of a Two-Level Game Approach | ISBN 978-3-8382-1247-0

198 *Oksana Kim* | The Development and Challenges of Russian Corporate Governance I. The Roles and Functions of Boards of Directors | With a foreword by Sheila M. Puffer | ISBN 978-3-8382-1287-6

199 *Thomas D. Grant* | International Law and the Post-Soviet Space I. Essays on Chechnya and the Baltic States | With a foreword by Stephen M. Schwebel | ISBN 978-3-8382-1279-1

200 *Thomas D. Grant* | International Law and the Post-Soviet Space II. Essays on Ukraine, Intervention, and Non-Proliferation | ISBN 978-3-8382-1280-7

201 *Slavomír Michálek, Michal Štefansky* | The Age of Fear. The Cold War and Its Influence on Czechoslovakia 1945–1968 | ISBN 978-3-8382-1285-2

202 *Iulia-Sabina Joja* | Romania's Strategic Culture 1990–2014. Continuity and Change in a Post-Communist Country's Evolution of National Interests and Security Policies | With a foreword by Heiko Biehl | ISBN 978-3-8382-1286-9

203 *Andrei Rogatchevski, Yngvar B. Steinholt, Arve Hansen, David-Emil Wickström* | War of Songs. Popular Music and Recent Russia-Ukraine Relations | With a foreword by Artemy Troitsky | ISBN 978-3-8382-1173-2

204 *Maria Lipman (Ed.)* | Russian Voices on Post-Crimea Russia. An Almanac of Counterpoint Essays from 2015–2018 | ISBN 978-3-8382-1251-7

205 *Ksenia Maksimovtsova* | Language Conflicts in Contemporary Estonia, Latvia, and Ukraine. A Comparative Exploration of Discourses in Post-Soviet Russian-Language Digital Media | With a foreword by Ammon Cheskin | ISBN 978-3-8382-1282-1

206 *Michal Vít* | The EU's Impact on Identity Formation in East-Central Europe between 2004 and 2013. Perceptions of the Nation and Europe in Political Parties of the Czech Republic, Poland, and Slovakia | With a foreword by Andrea Petö | ISBN 978-3-8382-1275-3

207 *Per A. Rudling* | Tarnished Heroes. The Organization of Ukrainian Nationalists in the Memory Politics of Post-Soviet Ukraine | ISBN 978-3-8382-0999-9

208 *Kaja Gadowska, Peter Solomon (Eds.)* | Legal Change in Post-Communist States. Progress, Reversions, Explanations | ISBN 978-3-8382-1312-5

209 *Paweł Kowal, Georges Mink, Iwona Reichardt (Eds.)* | Three Revolutions: Mobilization and Change in Contemporary Ukraine I. Theoretical Aspects and Analyses on Religion, Memory, and Identity | ISBN 978-3-8382-1321-7

210 *Paweł Kowal, Georges Mink, Adam Reichardt, Iwona Reichardt (Eds.)* | Three Revolutions: Mobilization and Change in Contemporary Ukraine II. An Oral History of the Revolution on Granite, Orange Revolution, and Revolution of Dignity | ISBN 978-3-8382-1323-1

211 *Li Bennich-Björkman, Sergiy Kurbatov (Eds.)* | When the Future Came. The Collapse of the USSR and the Emergence of National Memory in Post-Soviet History Textbooks | ISBN 978-3-8382-1335-4

212 *Olga R. Gulina* | Migration as a (Geo-)Political Challenge in the Post-Soviet Space. Border Regimes, Policy Choices, Visa Agendas | With a foreword by Nils Muižnieks | ISBN 978-3-8382-1338-5

213 *Sanna Turoma, Kaarina Aitamurto, Slobodanka Vladiv-Glover (Eds.)* | Religion, Expression, and Patriotism in Russia. Essays on Post-Soviet Society and the State. ISBN 978-3-8382-1346-0

214 *Vasif Huseynov* | Geopolitical Rivalries in the "Common Neighborhood". Russia's Conflict with the West, Soft Power, and Neoclassical Realism | With a foreword by Nicholas Ross Smith | ISBN 978-3-8382-1277-7

215 *Mikhail Suslov* | Geopolitical Imagination. Ideology and Utopia in Post-Soviet Russia | With a foreword by Mark Bassin | ISBN 978-3-8382-1361-3

216 *Alexander Etkind, Mikhail Minakov (Eds.)* | Ideology after Union. Political Doctrines, Discourses, and Debates in Post-Soviet Societies | ISBN 978-3-8382-1388-0

217 *Jakob Mischke, Oleksandr Zabirko (Hgg.)* | Protestbewegungen im langen Schatten des Kreml. Aufbruch und Resignation in Russland und der Ukraine | ISBN 978-3-8382-0926-5

218 *Oksana Huss* | How Corruption and Anti-Corruption Policies Sustain Hybrid Regimes. Strategies of Political Domination under Ukraine's Presidents in 1994-2014 | With a foreword by Tobias Debiel and Andrea Gawrich | ISBN 978-3-8382-1430-6

219 *Dmitry Travin, Vladimir Gel'man, Otar Marganiya* | The Russian Path. Ideas, Interests, Institutions, Illusions | With a foreword by Vladimir Ryzhkov | ISBN 978-3-8382-1421-4

220 *Gergana Dimova* | Political Uncertainty. A Comparative Exploration | With a foreword by Todor Yalamov and Rumena Filipova | ISBN 978-3-8382-1385-9

221 *Torben Waschke* | Russland in Transition. Geopolitik zwischen Raum, Identität und Machtinteressen | Mit einem Vorwort von Andreas Dittmann | ISBN 978-3-8382-1480-1

222 *Steven Jobbitt, Zsolt Bottlik, Marton Berki (Eds.)* | Power and Identity in the Post-Soviet Realm. Geographies of Ethnicity and Nationality after 1991 | ISBN 978-3-8382-1399-6

223 *Daria Buteiko* | Erinnerungsort. Ort des Gedenkens, der Erholung oder der Einkehr? Kommunismus-Erinnerung am Beispiel der Gedenkstätte Berliner Mauer sowie des Soloveckij-Klosters und -Museumsparks | ISBN 978-3-8382-1367-5

224 *Olga Bertelsen (Ed.)* | Russian Active Measures. Yesterday, Today, Tomorrow | With a foreword by Jan Goldman | ISBN 978-3-8382-1529-7

225 *David Mandel* | "Optimizing" Higher Education in Russia. University Teachers and their Union "Universi-tetskaya solidarnost'" | ISBN 978-3-8382-1519-8

226 *Mikhail Minakov, Gwendolyn Sasse, Daria Isachenko (Eds.)* | Post-Soviet Secessionism. Nation-Building and State-Failure after Communism | ISBN 978-3-8382-1538-9

227 *Jakob Hauter (Ed.)* | Civil War? Interstate War? Hybrid War? Dimensions and Interpretations of the Donbas Conflict in 2014–2020 | With a foreword by Andrew Wilson | ISBN 978-3-8382-1383-5

228 *Tima T. Moldogaziev, Gene A. Brewer, J. Edward Kellough (Eds.)* | Public Policy and Politics in Georgia. Lessons from Post-Soviet Transition | With a foreword by Dan Durning | ISBN 978-3-8382-1535-8

229 *Oxana Schmies (Ed.)* | NATO's Enlargement and Russia. A Strategic Challenge in the Past and Future | With a foreword by Vladimir Kara-Murza | ISBN 978-3-8382-1478-8

230 *Christopher Ford* | Ukapisme – Une Gauche perdue. Le marxisme anti-colonial dans la révolution ukrainienne 1917-1925 | Avec une préface de Vincent Présumey | ISBN 978-3-8382-0899-2

231 *Anna Kutkina* | Between Lenin and Bandera. Decommunization and Multivocality in Post-Euromaidan Ukraine | With a foreword by Juri Mykkänen | ISBN 978-3-8382-1506-8

232 *Lincoln E. Flake* | Defending the Faith. The Russian Orthodox Church and the Demise of Religious Pluralism | With a foreword by Peter Martland | ISBN 978-3-8382-1378-1

233 *Nikoloz Samkharadze* | Russia's Recognition of the Independence of Abkhazia and South Ossetia. Analysis of a Deviant Case in Moscow's Foreign Policy | With a foreword by Neil MacFarlane | ISBN 978-3-8382-1414-6

234 *Arve Hansen* | Urban Protest. A Spatial Perspective on Kyiv, Minsk, and Moscow | With a foreword by Julie Wilhelmsen | ISBN 978-3-8382-1495-5

235 *Eleonora Narvselius, Julie Fedor (Eds.)* | Diversity in the East-Central European Borderlands. Memories, Cityscapes, People | ISBN 978-3-8382-1523-5

236 *Regina Elsner* | The Russian Orthodox Church and Modernity. A Historical and Theological Investigation into Eastern Christianity between Unity and Plurality | With a foreword by Mikhail Suslov | ISBN 978-3-8382-1568-6

237 *Bo Petersson* | The Putin Predicament. Problems of Legitimacy and Succession in Russia | With a foreword by J. Paul Goode | ISBN 978-3-8382-1050-6

238 *Jonathan Otto Pohl* | The Years of Great Silence. The Deportation, Special Settlement, and Mobilization into the Labor Army of Ethnic Germans in the USSR, 1941–1955 | ISBN 978-3-8382-1630-0

239 *Mikhail Minakov (Ed.)* | Inventing Majorities. Ideological Creativity in Post-Soviet Societies | ISBN 978-3-8382-1641-6

240 *Robert M. Cutler* | Soviet and Post-Soviet Foreign Policies I. East-South Relations and the Political Economy of the Communist Bloc, 1971–1991 | With a foreword by Roger E. Kanet | ISBN 978-3-8382-1654-6

241 *Izabella Agardi* | On the Verge of History. Life Stories of Rural Women from Serbia, Romania, and Hungary, 1920–2020 | With a foreword by Andrea Pető | ISBN 978-3-8382-1602-7

242 *Sebastian Schäffer (Ed.)* | Ukraine in Central and Eastern Europe. Kyiv's Foreign Affairs and the International Relations of the Post-Communist Region | With a foreword by Pavlo Klimkin and Andreas Umland| ISBN 978-3-8382-1615-7

243 *Volodymyr Dubrovskyi, Kalman Mizsei, Mychailo Wynnyckyj (Eds.)* | Eight Years after the Revolution of Dignity. What Has Changed in Ukraine during 2013–2021? | With a foreword by Yaroslav Hrytsak | ISBN 978-3-8382-1560-0

244 *Rumena Filipova* | Constructing the Limits of Europe Identity and Foreign Policy in Poland, Bulgaria, and Russia since 1989 | With forewords by Harald Wydra and Gergana Yankova-Dimova | ISBN 978-3-8382-1649-2

245 *Oleksandra Keudel* | How Patronal Networks Shape Opportunities for Local Citizen Participation in a Hybrid Regime A Comparative Analysis of Five Cities in Ukraine | With a foreword by Sabine Kropp | ISBN 978-3-8382-1671-3

246 *Jan Claas Behrends, Thomas Lindenberger, Pavel Kolar (Eds.)* | Violence after Stalin Institutions, Practices, and Everyday Life in the Soviet Bloc 1953–1989 | ISBN 978-3-8382-1637-9

247 *Leonid Luks* | Macht und Ohnmacht der Utopien Essays zur Geschichte Russlands im 20. und 21. Jahrhundert | ISBN 978-3-8382-1677-5

248 *Iuliia Barshadska* | Brüssel zwischen Kyjiw und Moskau Das auswärtige Handeln der Europäischen Union im ukrainisch-russischen Konflikt 2014-2019 | Mit einem Vorwort von Olaf Leiße | ISBN 978-3-8382-1667-6

249 *Valentyna Romanova* | Decentralisation and Multilevel Elections in Ukraine Reform Dynamics and Party Politics in 2010–2021 | With a foreword by Kimitaka Matsuzato | ISBN 978-3-8382-1700-0

250 *Alexander Motyl* | National Questions. Theoretical Reflections on Nations and Nationalism in Eastern Europe | ISBN 978-3-8382-1675-1

251 *Marc Dietrich* | A Cosmopolitan Model for Peacebuilding. The Ukrainian Cases of Crimea and the Donbas | With a foreword by Rémi Baudouï | ISBN 978-3-8382-1687-4

252 *Eduard Baidaus* | An Unsettled Nation. Moldova in the Geopolitics of Russia, Romania, and Ukraine | With forewords by John-Paul Himka and David R. Marples | ISBN 978-3-8382-1582-2

253 *Igor Okunev, Petr Oskolkov (Eds.)* | Transforming the Administrative Matryoshka. The Reform of Autonomous Okrugs in the Russian Federation, 2003–2008 | With a foreword by Vladimir Zorin | ISBN 978-3-8382-1721-5

254 *Winfried Schneider-Deters* | Ukraine's Fateful Years 2013–2019. Vol. I: The Popular Uprising in Winter 2013/2014 | ISBN 978-3-8382-1725-3

255 *Winfried Schneider-Deters* | Ukraine's Fateful Years 2013–2019. Vol. II: The Annexation of Crimea and the War in Donbas | ISBN 978-3-8382-1726-0

256 *Robert M. Cutler* | Soviet and Post-Soviet Russian Foreign Policies II. East-West Relations in Europe and the Political Economy of the Communist Bloc, 1971–1991 | With a foreword by Roger E. Kanet | ISBN 978-3-8382-1727-7

257 *Robert M. Cutler* | Soviet and Post-Soviet Russian Foreign Policies III. East-West Relations in Europe and Eurasia in the Post-Cold War Transition, 1991–2001 | With a foreword by Roger E. Kanet | ISBN 978-3-8382-1728-4

258 *Paweł Kowal, Iwona Reichardt, Kateryna Pryshchepa (Eds.)* | Three Revolutions: Mobilization and Change in Contemporary Ukraine III. Archival Records and Historical Sources on the 1990 Revolution on Granite | ISBN 978-3-8382-1376-7

259 *Mikhail Minakov (Ed.)* | Philosophy Unchained. Developments in Post-Soviet Philosophical Thought. | With a foreword by Christopher Donohue | ISBN 978-3-8382-1768-0

260 *David Dalton* | The Ukrainian Oligarchy After the Euromaidan. How Ukraine's Political Economy Regime Survived the Crisis | With a foreword by Andrew Wilson | ISBN 978-3-8382-1740-6

261 *Andreas Heinemann-Grüder (Ed.)* | Who are the Fighters? Irregular Armed Groups in the Russian-Ukrainian War in 2014–2015 | ISBN 978-3-8382-1777-2

262 *Taras Kuzio (Ed.)* | Russian Disinformation and Western Scholarship. Bias and Prejudice in Journalistic, Expert, and Academic Analyses of East European, Russian and Eurasian Affairs | ISBN 978-3-8382-1685-0

263 *Darius Furmonavicius* | LithuaniaTransforms the West. Lithuania's Liberation from Soviet Occupation and the Enlargement of NATO (1988–2022) | With a foreword by Vytautas Landsbergis | ISBN 978-3-8382-1779-6

264 *Dirk Dalberg* | Politisches Denken im tschechoslowakischen Dissens. Egon Bondy, Miroslav Kusý, Milan Šimečka und Petr Uhl (1968-1989) | ISBN 978-3-8382-1318-7

265 *Леонид Люкс* | К столетию «философского парохода». Мыслители «первой» русской эмиграции о русской революции и о тоталитарных соблазнах XX века | ISBN 978-3-8382-1775-8

266 *Daviti Mtchedlishvili* | The EU and the South Caucasus. European Neighborhood Policies between Eclecticism and Pragmatism, 1991-2021 | With a foreword by Nicholas Ross Smith | ISBN 978-3-8382-1735-2

267 *Bohdan Harasymiw* | Post-Euromaidan Ukraine. Domestic Power Struggles and War of National Survival in 2014–2022 | ISBN 978-3-8382-1798-7

268 *Nadiia Koval, Denys Tereshchenko (Eds.)* | Russian Cultural Diplomacy under Putin. Rossotrudnichestvo, the "Russkiy Mir" Foundation, and the Gorchakov Fund in 2007–2022 | ISBN 978-3-8382-1801-4

269 *Izabela Kazejak* | Jews in Post-War Wrocław and L'viv. Official Policies and Local Responses in Comparative Perspective, 1945-1970s | ISBN 978-3-8382-1802-1

270 *Jakob Hauter* | Russia's Overlooked Invasion. The Causes of the 2014 Outbreak of War in Ukraine's Donbas | With a foreword by Hiroaki Kuromiya | ISBN 978-3-8382-1803-8

271 *Anton Shekhovtsov* | Russian Political Warfare. Essays on Kremlin Propaganda in Europe and the Neighbourhood, 2020-2023 | With a foreword by Nathalie Loiseau | ISBN 978-3-8382-1821-2

272 *Андреа Пето* | Насилие и Молчание. Красная армия в Венгрии во Второй Мировой войне | ISBN 978-3-8382-1636-2

ibidem.eu